*Landscape, Nature, and the Body Politic*

# Landscape, Nature, and the Body Politic

## FROM BRITAIN'S RENAISSANCE TO AMERICA'S NEW WORLD

## *Kenneth Robert Olwig*

with a Foreword by Yi-Fu Tuan

THE UNIVERSITY OF WISCONSIN PRESS

The University of Wisconsin Press
1930 Monroe Street
Madison, Wisconsin 53711

www.wisc.edu/wisconsinpress/

3 Henrietta Street
London WC2E 8LU, England

1    2    3    4    5

Printed in the United States of America


Library of Congress Cataloging-in-Publication Data
Olwig, Kenneth
Landscape, nature, and the body politic : from Britain's renaissance
to America's new world / Kenneth Olwig ; foreword by Yi-Fu Tuan.
            pp.        cm.
Includes bibliographical references and index.
ISBN 0-299-17420-4 (cloth : alk. paper)
ISBN 0-299-17424-7 (pbk. : alk. paper)
1. Great Britain—Historical geography. 2. Landscape—Political aspects—
Great Britain—History. 3. Land use—Political aspects—Great Britain—History.
4. Nature—Political aspects—Great Britain—History. 5. America—
Foreign public opinion, British. 6. Landscape—Great Britain—History.
7. Landscape in literature. 8. Renaissance—England. 9. Nature in literature.
10. Place (Philosophy) I. Title.
            DA600 .O49        2002
304.2—dc21        2001006786

# Contents

# Illustrations

# *Foreword*

Among subjects of keen interest to the general public today, few are more in the air, more debated, than nature and the quality of the environment. Of course, one can think of rivals, a perennial being politics, though one might add that the debate over "nature and the environment" is itself highly politicized. When one listens to the debate, conducted not only in political forums but also in classrooms and coffee shops, one repeatedly encounters certain emotionally charged words. These include, besides nature and the environment, "scenery," "view," "landscape," "land," "countryside," "country," and—rising in scope as well as in degree of passion—"nation," "national identity," and, ultimately, "the health and genius of a people." Why does the serious discussion of one word (one concept and value) so naturally lead to another? What are the bridging ideas? What is their root commonality?

In this work of outstanding scholarship, Kenneth Olwig shows how, historically, all the above concepts and values are part of one discourse concerning the nature of people and place that began in Europe during the Renaissance and has continued there and elsewhere (preeminently in the United States) to the present day. His striking originality lies in using the key word *landscape* to refract all the others. How can that be done? For to the modern ear, *landscape* is so modest sounding. Well, it can be done, as Olwig fully demonstrates. Viewed narrowly, his book succeeds in restoring to us the richness—the lexicological heritage—of a word. But of course it does far more, for in making the restoration, Olwig opens up a whole new way of understanding who we are and how we ought to live.

A book of this scope, though deeply rewarding to read, is not easy reading. This is where I come in. A foreword written by someone (me) other than the author can provide a hint of what the book is about in simple language, using figurative or bold devices of exposition that the author himself rightly eschews. The mature scholar doesn't need a foreword. He or she should proceed straight to the body of the text. A student, however, may need help—and by student I have in mind not only the young person in the classroom but any intelligent and inquisitive citizen. So, what are the book's principal themes? A glimpse into them may be obtained through two devices: one, operating at the microscale, uses the typical American home as an analogue; the other, operating at a macroscale, strives to provide a thumbnail, historically grounded narrative.

## LANDSCAPE AT MICROSCALE: HOME AND GARDEN

A typical American suburban home is made up of three parts: house, backyard, and front lawn. An imaginary line runs through the middle, to one side of which is nature and community, to the other side splendor and society. Kitchen, located at the back of the house, caters to bodily needs. But it is also a center of communal warmth. Guests linger here, children run in and out, begging for a taste of the pie. Kitchen spills over into backyard, especially in summer. Family members, friends, and neighbors gather around the barbecue grill to chat, eat, and, after eating, perhaps sing. There pervades an air of good fellowship and informality. How can it be otherwise when one's fingers are gooey with barbecue sauce? Further out is the vegetable garden. No flowers grow there—at least, nothing fanciful. The politics on this side of the home is communal and egalitarian, its ideal one of organic wholeness and wholesomeness, of human contentment nurtured by intimate contact with people, growing things, soil and earth.

To the other side—the front side—of my imaginary line are the more formal spaces of living. Residents dress up to perform their roles. Everyone's social standing is more on display. Young children are excluded, or made to behave like adults. Low-status people (salesman, maid, and plumber) penetrate the line when their work requires it, by way of the back door. A lawn with parterres of flowers spreads before the house, its size a measure of the family's wealth and power. Life and its settings bespeak discipline, and discipline is indicative of a pretension to higher states of being. The body is disciplined by its encasement in glamorous but uncomfortable clothes. External nature is disciplined: weather is left to rage outside the house, while inside warmth rises from heat ducts, and smart conversation flows over a polished table. The lawn and its flower beds are geometrically arranged, a piece of regimented nature to be seen rather than used. From the upper floor's front window, the owner of the house commands a view—one that extends beyond his own lawn to other people's lawns.

The word "landscape" applies to the home from three points of view. The front lawn and its flower beds are a landscape: they are the works of a landscape gardener. The backyard is a type of horticultural garden—a landscape, though without a privileged perspective and less tidy. Finally, the entire complex of house and grounds, seen from a certain angle, is a landscape—an entity that an artist may want to paint. What is not landscape, as we moderns understand the word, is the social life—people's actions and behaviors in the house, front lawn, and backyard. But this exclusion did not hold in the past—far from it, as we shall see later.

The landscape or land that I have just depicted exudes personality. It is not only humanized, it is almost human. The house, for example, has a front and a back, as a human being has a front and a back. In both instances, front is social and formal, back is biological and informal. The front of the house is a human face (children's schematic drawings make that clear): the windows are eyes, the door is the nose. Windows look out to the lawn, which is the house's personal space; strangers are expected to keep their distance. At night, blinds are drawn, as eyelids would close in preparation for sleep. At night, too, garbage is taken out from the back door—a necessary practice in hygiene that keeps the house/body clean and healthy. The house is the man or woman who lives in it. House and human figure fuse—they are one. This identification of human figure with house and grounds—with landscape—is puzzling to us moderns. We see it, if at all, only in dreams and when our imagination is actively engaged.

## LANDSCAPE AT MACROSCALE: COUNTRY AND NATION

Home is made up of house and grounds. But we also use the word in an extended, figurative sense. For example, to a Californian who asks me where my home is, I am likely to say "Wisconsin." An Englishman with the same question will elicit from me "America." The first heart-warming thing I hear, upon reentering the United States, is the passport officer's "Welcome home."

Home is also homeland. Or even landscape. That sounds strange until we examine the word's meaning historically. *Land,* the first part of the word *landscape,* has ancient roots that go back to the Middle Ages and beyond. Land is a geographical unit, as in meadowland, heathland, or common land. It is, in addition, such units combined to form a larger unit. This larger unit, also called "land," may boast not only customs and mores, but codified rules of behavior derived from them that are adjudicated by responsible local people in a public place, or court. The people are proud of their land's customs and traditions, feasts and festivals, which all play an important role in their sense of identity. They are particularly proud of their land's public meeting places and courts, for these—unlike princely and ecclesiastical courts—allow for broad political participation. Partici-

pation entails shaping community and place in response to changing circumstance. To shape (that is, to modify and create) constitutes the second
part of the word *landscape—scape* being a variant spelling of *shape*.
What, then, is a landscape in its root meaning? It is a land shaped by a
people, their institutions and customs.

England is a land, and it contains smaller lands, such as Northumberland and the Midlands. England is also a country or a nation. *Land, country,* and *nation* have come to mean much the same thing. They all speak of
a place and its people, so naturally bound to each other that it is as though
the place or land has given birth to the people and their customs. Even as
the people multiply and even as the customs evolve, they—both people
and custom—continue to draw inspiration and legitimacy from native soil
or land. England has, of course, towns and cities. A country or nation has
towns and cities. Yet, in the course of time, country and land have come
to mean primarily rural places. Country is reduced or simplified to countryside. Likewise, landscape: that is, the word *landscape* increasingly
evokes images of rural scenes and wilderness rather than of village squares
and city towers.

## LANDSCAPE AS COSMIC THEATER AND SCENERY

What I have done so far is to suggest that the back spaces of a suburban
home are an analogue of the much larger spaces variously called "land,"
"country," and "nation." I now turn to the front spaces of a suburban
home. What are their analogues in the larger world? The city might be one
possible answer. But it will be a misleading answer unless we recall the ancient vocation of the city as a model of the cosmos. Scholars have shown
that many protohistorical and historical cities, far from being overgrown
market towns, began their careers as ceremonial centers that sought to
bring the regularity and splendor of the heavens down to earth. The city
itself might be a cosmic diagram, though in reality most were soon
swamped by profane activities so that in the end only the court and its cer-
emonies—centered on the priest-king or absolutist monarch—retained
the cosmic symbolism in its purity.

A difference between priest-kings of antiquity and absolutist rulers of
the Renaissance and early modern period was that the former believed
they were mediators of a vertical cosmos, with the eyes properly directed
to heaven above and earth below, whereas the latter lived and celebrated
a cosmos in which the horizontal dimension had expanded rapidly at the
expense of the vertical. In other words, from 1500 onward, European
rulers were more and more ready to discard their sacral roles to enjoy
power in purely secular terms—and that meant power over horizontal

space, or territory. But the transition took time. The earth and its inhabitants were resistant to manipulation by individuals, whatever their titles and pretensions. In one area only were premodern potentates able to savor their potency to the full, and that was the area of ritual and theater— what we moderns would call the area of make-believe. Court ritual and court theater were interchangeable: court ritual was theater—that is to say, spectacle. To produce magnificent spectacle, a great Renaissance prince had to have not only craftsmen and laborers but machines at his command. We tend to associate *machine* with the power to transform nature: machines build roads, canals, and factories. It was different in the seventeenth century. Then, machines were the lifts, cranks, and wheels that built an illusory world of theater.

One characteristic of that world is that it was observed neither at ground level nor from a vertical point infinitely above, but somewhere in between—a compromise, as it were, between the vertical and the horizontal. From the vertical axis were taken such elements as pagan gods and goddesses floating in the sky and tableaux showing the unvarying cycle of the seasons; from the horizontal axis, pastoral landscapes of Virgilian inspiration opening out to the horizon, that is, reaching deep into the recesses of an elongated stage. The potentate viewed the entire spectacle from a well-placed, elevated seat. He was the force that made it all happen and now he could see it all—an essentially harmonious universe—going through its paces before his commanding eyes.

How childish—we moderns might say—to produce a lavish world of illusion, to play and dwell in it as though it had anything to do with real life. But it isn't always easy to draw the line between make-believe and real. The potentate himself was real enough, as were his courtiers and small army of hangers-on. Architecture was real enough. The stage itself was an impressive material presence. And what lay beyond the court theater, beyond the palace? Would one be immersed in the real world of work and toil? No—not yet. For beyond lay the great landscape garden—a fantasy of geometric order or of pastoral picturesqueness stretching as far as the eyes could see, built by a master architect, with the support of hydraulic engineers, horticulturists, and hundreds of conscripted laborers. Of course, even the greatest garden must terminate somewhere, but landscape architects of the seventeenth and eighteenth centuries were able to design it so that, as viewed from the house, the estate could seem to merge seamlessly with villages and farms beyond. Steeped in ritual and surrounded by deferential courtiers, a ruler could well believe that the cosmic harmony and beauty so evident in the theater and in the design of the garden extended to his entire realm.

## COURT VERSUS COUNTRY

I have made the seventeenth-century king/potentate sound all powerful. Who could contest his power? In England, the non-noble gentry and freemen could—and did. Thus were set up rival powers that espoused different values. To the one side were the absolutist, purist, and universalist aspirations of court and monarch, to the other side the customs and traditions, the rights and obligations, of the people; to the one side, high art and artifice, to the other side, closeness to earth and organic wholesomeness. Even the senses were differently engaged. The court privileged sight: think again of the spectacles of the court theater and beyond it the splendidly landscaped gardens that stretched into the distant horizon. The country, by contrast, was multisensorial—more egalitarian and communal, in political terms. Think of the swarming sensations (some soothing, others arousing) that a man or woman living in the country could enjoy: the odor of fields and meadows baking in the sun; the hubbub of a country tavern; the sharp ringing sound of collision—ball against cricket bat— in the village green; music, laughter, and the thump of dancing feet during a festival.

Surprisingly, both sides used "nature and the natural" to back their cause. We can understand why the people of the country—the gentry and freemen or parliamentarians—would want to do so. They saw their ancient rights, privileges, and freedoms as natural, emerging (as it were) out of the soil. Their way of life had nothing willful and arbitrary about it. All the tyrannical arbitrariness lay with their opposition—the party of the court. How would the court respond? It, too, appealed to antiquity, to nature and the natural. Its antiquity, however, was not the immemorial one of soil, but rather a claim to the prestige of imperial Rome. James I, who united England and Scotland under the greater "land" (realm) of Britain, saw himself as holding an imperial scepter, continuing in some sense the pomp and might of ancient Rome: note how court spectacle and landscape also sought inspiration from classical mythology and literature.

As for nature and the natural, here the court's argument took two separate paths. One followed the medieval view that the king's body was both biological and political—an organism and a political organization, a flesh-and-blood body and the body politic. As body politic, James I embodied England and Scotland: the two parts were united in him. Moreover, as body in both senses of the word, the king was naturally generative: he stood for the principles of fertility, wholeness, and wholesomeness. This notion was essentially chthonian. The second path followed by the court was the idea, dating back to the Greeks, that nature was admirable because, like reason, it displayed lawfulness—that is to say, order, proportion, and harmony. But where was this idealized nature to be found? In human reason at its best, but where else? Certainly, not in terrestrial nature—not in the unruly weather and chaotic topography so characteristic of it; rather in heaven—in the grandeur and orderly motion of the stars. People who discerned order in heaven—in the operation of natural and universal laws—were inspired by it. Those among them who possessed great power sought to bring cosmic harmony down to earth—to impose it on earth and its denizens, if necessary. This was what seventeenth-century rulers with absolutist aspirations tried to do; and, indeed, what powerful men and women of all times, including our own, have tried to do.

## THE AMERICAN STORY

One reason why Olwig has devoted many pages to the seventeenth and eighteenth centuries is that it was then that *landscape* achieved maximum emblematic potency. Thereafter, its effectiveness in capturing political ideals and values weakened so that, in time, it became primarily an aesthetic concept—one that strongly affected how people saw nature and the countryside, and thence the artistic production of paintings and gardens. In the same two centuries, America transformed itself from colony to independent nation-state. The division between country and court that Olwig discerned in Europe has certain parallels in the New World. For example, early settlers in New England deliberately distanced themselves from the theocratic-royalist trappings of old England—trappings that they deemed pretentious and artificial. In this sense, but also in the positive sense that they yearned for a purer God-fearing community, they may be said to have belonged to the party of the country. On the other hand, the country—the countryside—of old England had no room for them. In migrating across an ocean to settle in a wilderness that constantly threatened their very existence, the settlers could not retain, even if they had wanted to, habits and customs, feasts and festivals, much of which—in any case—depended on a material base that they had lost by moving.

No matter. For what they really wanted they could have, namely, a participatory form of governing—the right to shape their own destiny. The meaning of landscape (that is, landshape) had subtly shifted: the emphasis was on the shaping of a place into something far better than the one they had left. Habitat was not just a given, as in old England, but to be carved out of a primeval forest. Even habit had to be re-created. Rules of behavior, rather than being timeless customs blindly followed, were a written covenant between God and his people, to which every responsible adult member subscribed with open eyes. Ironically, this desire to create a new, utopian community, cutting down not only trees but Indians in the process, showed more than a touch of the boldness and arrogance of the court.

The eighteenth century also had its distinctive touches in America, which gained its independence in the Age of Enlightenment—the Age of Reason. To Enlightenment thinkers—the Founding Fathers among them—reason was not at odds with nature, as the Romantics would have it; rather it was nature at its most lucid and intelligible. Reason's most transparent emblem and effective instrument—geometry—manifested its power in a variety of ways, among them surveying and mapping, the discernment of order in what could seem topographic chaos, and the imposition of order on the face of the earth. An early monument to geometric rationality was the township-and-range land survey, initiated in 1785, that eventually divided two-thirds of the country into a system of nested squares. An undertaking of this scale could only have been accomplished in a government that was centralized and efficient. So what went on in the young Republic? The United States land survey could seem a display of absolutist madness—the pushing of geometric domination over a vast territory that exceeded the wildest dreams of Old World monarchs. Yet the intent, as we know, was just the opposite. The intent was to enable the small farmer to acquire land efficiently and cheaply in the belief that, possessing such land, he could become truly independent, unbeholden to arbitrary authority.

## DOMINATION BY "COURT"

The conflict between court and country operated at various political levels. Ultimately, it was a conflict between two distinct ways of life. Over time, the court continues to gain the upper hand, although it should be obvious that in saying so, I am no longer using the word *court* in its historical and literal meanings, but rather as a shorthand for an attitude of mind that favors centralized planning and rational process, that is intolerant of messy, multiple viewpoints and, hence, is inclined to authoritarianism. Cosmic states of the past—for example, imperial China and monarchical France— were authoritarian, but they lacked both the technology and the organizational power to carry out their vision. Modern communist states commanded far greater resources, but they too were unable to realize their dreams; worse, what they did realize turned out to be the opposite of what they had hoped for—a dystopia rather than a utopia. In modern capitalist societies, great corporations enjoy almost as much power as political states, with which they are often—in varying degrees—allied. Corporations are driven by the need to make a profit, but to be successful they must be able to gauge what customers want, or can be persuaded to want. Their enterprise, therefore, is intimately tied to a people's desire for a better life. Corporations produce. Their products, individually but especially in the aggregate, are their vision. In the form of suburban homes, shopping malls, theme parks, and designer communities, the corporate vision has had an extraordinary impact on ever growing portions of the world's landscapes.

## WILDERNESS

A reader may impatiently ask, "But what about wild nature—forests, mountains, swirling clouds and the open sky? Aren't they components of landscape? Aren't they subjects for landscape painters?" The answer is yes, of course, but only since the latter half of the eighteenth century. A major contribution of this book lies in forcing us to acknowledge, through the deployment of irrefutable evidence, that the word *landscape* was, historically, a thoroughly humanized word. The "land" or "country" of landscape stood as much for a people—their customs, laws, and institutions—as for a natural unit. Through the court's eyes, landscape was again a thoroughly humanized (indeed, artifactual) world—this time, one of theater, stage scenery, and garden. Nature—wild nature—only began to draw appreciative glances when people no longer saw it as a threat. No longer a threat, wild nature could be incorporated into an aesthetic—the aesthetic of the sublime. Still, older meanings are retained, which is why deep historical accounts are so necessary. Consider America's infatuation with wilderness. The aesthetic of the sublime certainly played a role. But something else was there to fuel the passion—the belief that in wilderness lay the ultimate source of health and well-being for a nation. In the American subconscious, wilderness meant generativity. No idea was more rooted in the past. So long as there was wilderness, America, no matter how dire her mistakes in world-making, could always be restored to health, gain new energy.

## ENVOI

Kenneth Olwig is a well known and esteemed geographer throughout the Scandinavian countries and the United Kingdom for the extraordinary range and depth of his scholarship. He is also esteemed in the United States, but perhaps not so widely known as he should be, because, apart from an influential monograph, *Nature's Ideological Landscape* (1984) and three or four equally influential papers, his many works are written in Danish, or are published in collections that are not easily accessible to the English-speaking (and especially) American student. All the more welcome is the present, much awaited, book, which captures many of the ideas that Olwig has spent decades developing and articulating. I am privileged to write the foreword. A successful one should be like a road map to the country ahead, or, to change the metaphor, an hors-d'oeuvre that whips up an appetite for the main course. It remains for me to say, Enjoy!

Yi-Fu Tuan

# Acknowledgments

The complexity of my topic, and its historical and geographical range, made me very dependent on the loyal criticism and advice of others. I owe a particular debt to the anthropologist Karen Fog Olwig, the historian Carol Gold and the historical geographer Michael Jones for their careful and critical reading of the manuscript for this book at various stages along the way. I also owe thanks to Louise E. Robbins for her editorial work for the University of Wisconsin Press. She managed to combine a meticulous professional attention to detail with a sense of the book's content.

Much of the research for this book was done while I was a fellow at the Man and Nature research center, at Odense University, Denmark (1993–1996), where I benefited from the always critical mind of Søren Baggesen and the wisdom about matters Germanic of Annlise Ballegaard Petersen. I am also indebted to the sharp intellectual counterpoint of Denis Cosgrove, with whom I worked at this time on a parallel European Union research project on landscape and water together with, among other landscape cognoscente, the sage Gabriel Zanetto. During this period I spent a particularly fruitful spring 1994 semester "rethinking" nature with a group of kindred souls, under the inspired leadership of Bill Cronon, at the University of California Humanities Research Institute (Cronon 1995b). I owe a special debt to conversations and critique from Anne Spirn, Kate Hayles, Donna Haraway, Carolyn Merchant and Robert Harrison. Though the bibliography bears witness to the inspiration of a long list of scholars, the genesis of the book is probably to be found in the interstices between the otherworldly questioning of Yi-Fu Tuan and the this-worldly concerns of David Lowenthal.

# Introduction

## Nature, Country, and Landscape

This book is about the interlinked meanings of landscape and nature, and the ways they have variously been used to define the body politic. It is thus also very much about the political landscape and the relationship of that landscape to our ideas of country, its nature and preservation. The book draws upon a myriad of texts to construct a narrative moving from continental Europe to Britain and thence to America. It moves, in particular, from the tale of England and Scotland's Renaissance "rebirth" as Britain, sundered from the European continent, to the "birth" of America as a brave New World, sundered from the Old World. The book is also, finally, about the role of these text-born narratives as subtexts in a larger metadiscourse concerning the relationships between place, space, and body in the making of the political landscape.

It seems so natural to see nature in terms of landscape scenery that it feels almost pedantic to ask what the two actually have to do with one another. It seems, likewise, natural to associate a country with images of its landscape scenery and nature, such as America's "purple mountain majesties above the fruited plain."[1] But is "my country 'tis of thee, sweet land of liberty," as praised in the American national hymn, the country of the Pilgrims, or is it the American soil upon which the people live?[2] Is the country a polity, defined by political, legal, or ethnic criteria, or is it a landscape, defined by the scenery of a geographical body? How do the two meanings relate one to the other? It is not easy to answer these questions, and this can make one wonder why it seems so natural to take for granted the links between ideas of nature, landscape, and country.

In one sense, a country is a political community, or commonwealth, founded on law and united by compact or tacit agreement of the people for the common good. England is a country in this sense because it is the domain of the English polity as represented in Parliament. The land in the word Eng*land*, thus defined, is the land or place of the English polity. It is the area of the English polity's activity, their political landscape (MWC10: landscape). Country, however, can also be defined in terms of the landscape scenery of the countryside of a geographical body. The landscape scenery of the British and American countryside is thus spatially delimited by the physical bounds of the British Isles and the American continent. The body politic of the British nation takes its name from the geographical body of Britain, which encompasses a number of countries with differing historical and cultural backgrounds. Americans likewise take their collective name from the name of the geographical body of a continent that, at the same time, embodies political communities with varying historical backgrounds and culture, including those of Canada and Mexico. There is thus an underlying conflict between the physical bounds of the continent and the more fluid bounds of these political communities.

The apparent unity created by the identification of a political community with the physical bounds of a geographical body and its scenic surface can mask a contested terrain—as in Britain, where territorial unity has helped conceal rifts between differing polities. In the United States the tension between local, state, and regional political cultures, on the one hand, and identification with an American national unity stretching from sea to shining sea, on the other, is an abiding feature of national life. In Germany the identification between the blood of the German body politic and the soil of Germany also provided a means of uniting a politically and culturally divided state, but here, unfortunately for Germany's neighbors, the physical boundaries of Germany are rather poorly defined.

## THE LANDSCAPE OF POLITY

The present-day association between country, body politic, and the landscape scenery of a particular natural geographical body cannot be regarded as a given. It must be seen as the outcome of a long historical process, spanning continents and centuries, through which the Renaissance architects of Britain defined Britain as a world apart vis-à-vis continental Europe, and America's founders defined America as a new world vis-à-vis Britain and Europe. To understand this process it is useful to counterpose the discourses of landscape, country, and nature in order to bring out the ways they have interacted in various narrations and colored each other. My story begins at the time of Shakespeare's Britain, when the fabled Elizabethan Tudor era was drawing to a close, and the Stuarts' ill-fated reign was just getting under way. The word *landscape* had apparently become moribund in English, but it was now reintroduced from the discourse of other Germanic languages and began morphing into its modern form.

"It is well known," a modern British writer on landscape contends, "that in Europe the concept of landscape and the words for it in both Romance and Germanic languages emerged around the turn of the sixteenth century to denote a painting whose primary subject matter was natural scenery" (Cosgrove 1993, 9). Much contemporary writing on landscape is informed by such assumptions, but they are misleading for a number of reasons.[3] One is that they tend to focus attention upon a newly born pictorial signifying system and to divert attention from that which was being signified.[4] The artistic genre of "landscape" painting did emerge at this time, but its conceptual subject matter, "the concept of landscape and the words for it in both Romance and Germanic languages," did not "emerge" around the turn of the sixteenth century. The concept of landscape had been present in European discourse for a long time at this politically critical juncture in its history. The assertion that landscape painting's "primary subject matter" was "natural scenery" diverts attention from the politically charged connotations of landscape in the artistic and political discourse of the sixteenth century (Sullivan 1998).[5] As will be seen in chapters 1 and 2, the word *landscape* in the various Germanic languages, as well as in older forms of English, designated an area, or region, and meant much the same as country—Drenthe, one of the Low Countries, was termed a *landschap*. It therefore makes sense that paintings of scenes from such a landschap/country, be it Drenthe or "Constable country," were called "landschap" or, in English, "landscape" (or, in French, *paysage*).[6] Yet somehow the idea of natural scenery has become so firmly attached to landscape that many apparently assume that landscape is inherently pictorial and that its primary subject, from the beginning, has been natural scenery. A glance at a standard history of European art (for example, Clark 1949) would show that from the time of its emergence in the sixteenth century the primary subject matter of landscape paintings was not predominantly "natural scenery." These paintings usually depicted life in countries filled with culture. Rather than nature, they were concerned with the regional habitation, or habitus, of a polity, to borrow a term from the sociologist-anthropologist Pierre Bourdieu (Bourdieu 1977; see also Bender 1993; Ingold 1993; Spirn 1998, 13–81). The subject matter of such paintings is thus closer to the meaning of landscape as a polity's area of activity, as in the term "political landscape".

## REPRESENTING LANDSCAPE'S CONTESTED TERRAIN

To understand the full meaning of landscape as pictorial scenery it is necessary to take a closer look at the evolving relation between the form of representation and what is being represented. The meaning of landscape is closely tied, I argue, to questions concerning representation, both artistic and political. These questions have deep roots in the era before our language and culture were walled up by the armies and navies of the nation-state, when cosmopolitan Renaissance men and women introduced the word *landscape* into Modern English discourse.

At the time when *landscape* resurfaced in the English language, the notion of land, in the sense of *country,* lay at the heart of a Europe-wide struggle concerning the legitimate representation of the polity. The Austrian historian Otto Brunner tells us that though "the *Land*" comprised its lord and people, an opposition between them was forming in which the people took on the mantle of "the land" and organized themselves as a "corporate community" called "the *Landscahft*" (landscape in modern English). This led to a struggle between lord and *Landschaft* over the land's representation ([1965] 1992, 341). The equivalent struggle in England, as will be seen, was between the court of the king and country as represented by Parliament.

The ascendancy of James VI of Scotland to the throne of England as James I in 1603 brought latent conflicts of a similar sort to a head in England. This was particularly due to James's belief that it was his destiny, as the inheritor of both crowns, to amalgamate his two separate kingdoms of Scotland and England into one British state. This amalgamation would transcend the polity of England as customarily represented by Parliament. The struggle between defenders of the prerogatives of the court and those of Parliament, as the representative of the country, would have implications for the thinking of the American republic's founders. The parallels between the struggle of court versus country (as the conflict eventually came to be known) and the struggle of lord versus Landschaft would not have been lost on the Renaissance English court.[7] The court even included a Danish queen who had been brought up in the domain of such a Landschaft. This was a cosmopolitan court that not only helped introduce the word *landscape* into Modern English, but did so in the context of an ongoing European discourse concerning the nature of the body politic.

In retrospect it is tempting to represent the Renaissance conflicts tied to the meaning of landscape and country as if people were battling over the definitions listed in a modern dictionary. It is likewise tempting to define such conflicts in terms of agglomerations of power defined geographically or politically or both, as suggested by the phrases "lord versus landscape" or "court versus country." Such abstractions and dichotomous generalizations, tied to well-defined modern ideologies, are not very useful, however, if one is to understand what was actually happening at the time when such meanings and ideologies were still emergent. I believe that it is more useful to describe the process by which these abstract meanings and ideological conflicts emerged in terms of a struggle within the polity to come to grips with the idea of representation itself. James's dream of uniting Scotland and England as Britain thus provoked, in the Parliament, an intensified interest in Parliament's legitimacy as the customary representative of the English polity. The Stuart court countered by using landscape scenery to represent the state of Britain as a country naturally defined by the British geographical body under the headship of the monarch. It is in the context of such conflicting approaches to the representation of country and landscape, I will argue, that these concepts took on their modern meanings and became linked with ideas of nature and the natural.

## THE METHOD

"Subtext" refers to implicit or metaphorical meaning and can apply to a literary text or even a landscape. Landscape is often conceived, today, in scenic, pictorial terms. The meaning of such visual images is, however, notoriously labile unless these images are supplied with a clarifying written text (Barthes [1957] 1972; Berger 1972). As legends under a picture, such texts might literally be described as subtexts. This book attempts to supply the subtexts for landscape, understood as scenery, through a study of the evolution of the larger meaning of landscape as a concept. These subtexts are concerned with the interlinked meanings of landscape and nature and with the ways they have variously been used to define country and the place of the body politic. I approach these meanings through the analysis of texts, both written and pictorial, especially as they were used to construct particular geographical narratives of national identity. These texts, however, must be understood within the woof and warp of their historical contexts. Thus, this is a historical geography of ideas, mentalities, and narrations, not a history per se, even if history is constantly in the background. In this sense, it is about history's "subtexts."

The technique used is primarily that of the close reading of selected texts to illuminate their explicit and implicit narrative content.[8] The book is thus full of bits and pieces of written text as well as graphics and pictures. These are not simply illustrations to an argument that is buried in my text; they are the actual stuff from which the argument is woven. So, it is wise to pore over the tidbits of text and illustrations rather than to skip over them. I have sought to consider issues relevant to several fields of interest, including geography, environmental studies, literature, art, and landscape architecture. This broad orientation, in turn, means that I have attempted to avoid the specialized terminology of semiotics or iconography and the rarefied terrain of postmodern discursive and narrative analysis, which might distract the uninitiated. Readers may, nevertheless, initially find the book difficult because I think it is important to treat words like codes whose established meanings need to be broken to allow for new understanding to emerge. I also avoid paraphrases in favor of direct quotations out of respect for the integrity of these words and texts, and the multiple meanings they can generate for different readers.

This book, of course, has its own narrative. I have thought of it as something of a detective story, inspired perhaps by Umberto Eco's *The Name of the Rose* (1983). The "body" in the library in this case is that of the body politic, but it is an open question whether or not it is a dead body. The underlying reason for the parallel with a mystery tale, however, is that this book is actually concerned with unearthing the secrets of what once were known as the "mysteries of state." The state, which was already seen as mysterious, was deliberately mystified further to make its power seem all the more secret. Thus, it required some sleuthing to uncover the mysterious means, such as optical illusion, that the architects of the state used to transform landscape from a form of polity to a visual scene. This approach is not so much a narrative device as the outcome of a research process that required the skills of a detective because the clues were well hidden and the logical connections between them relatively unexplored. Much of the book takes place in times long past, but in the end it is about today. Though the foreword and introduction provide clues, the challenge for the reader lies in digging out the traces of meaning buried deep in the discursive layers of landscape's textual sites. Step by step the answers to the questions posed at the outset will, I hope, become clearer and more "elementary," as Holmes would say to Watson. Each circuitous step along the way is a bit of a mystery play—this is a pilgrim's progress. What on earth, for example, do obscure rural Landschaften territories on the marshy western coast of Jutland have to do with landscape's "dramatic" entrance into the Modern English language at an exclusive Renaissance court masque? The prosaic mind will no doubt be inclined to dismiss the whole question, and the Anglo-American chauvinist may not want to be bothered with such foreign arcana, but it can take *outlandish* questions to challenge entrenched native narratives. Once the answers to this book's mysteries are solved, however, I would hope that the reader would never think about the meaning of landscape in quite the same way. Those who can't stand the suspense are welcome, however, to jump to the conclusion to find out "whodunit" (metaphorically speaking).

## LANDSCAPE'S "THEATRICAL" ENTRANCE INTO MODERN ENGLISH AND THE "INVENTION" OF BRITAIN

*The Masque of Blackness* (1605), with a text by Ben Jonson and scenography by Inigo Jones, begins with Jonson's description of the staging: "First, for the Scene was drawn a Landtschap." This is an early use of the word landscape in modern English and it comes, as shall be seen, in the context both of a dramatic breakthrough in English dramaturgy and British political life. I have elected to take as my point of departure the text of a theatrical masque by Shakespeare's friend and colleague Ben Jonson and the architect and scenographer Inigo Jones. Just as all roads in Anglo-American literature often seem to lead back to Shakespeare, all clues in this book lead back to this Renaissance masque, because, I believe, this era was a time when much that we have subsequently come to take for granted was in utero, and this masque encapsulates much of that which was then busy being born.

On Twelfth Night, 1605, the London court of the newly crowned King James I staged *The Masque of Blackness*. This was an auspicious occasion. It was on this evening that Ben Jonson and Inigo Jones marked the beginning of their stormy collaboration with a command performance of this innovative masque at Whitehall. Jonson, whose reputation as an author was at the time second only to Shakespeare's, wrote the text, and Jones, a founding figure in British architecture and planning, did the costumes and scenography. A masque is a form of combined opera and ballet that has been judged the supreme artistic expression of the Stuart court. The masque was commissioned by James's queen, Anne of Denmark—a blond who gave herself the leading role as a "negroe" princess. This first masque marked an early entry of the word *landscape* into the modern English language, and it did so on the occasion of what is thought to be the first use in England of stage scenery with central-point perspective, which creates a three dimensional spatial illusion on the stage (Kernodle 1944, 212).

The scenery for *The Masque of Blackness* was not that of England, but of "Britain." Britain was then a recently revived figment of the court's imagination. The idea of Britain provided a means, first conceived by the Tudors, of unifying England, Scotland, and Wales by linking them to a mythic Roman heritage (OED: Britain). Scenes of this imagined British landscape were created to provide the setting for a sequence of narratives legitimating the British hegemony of the new century's new Scottish-English Stuart dynasty. Britain was not, as Linda Colley suggests, first invented as "a would-be nation" in 1707, when the Parliament of Westminster passed the Act of Union linking Scotland to England and Wales (Colley 1992, 11). It had already been invented at least a century earlier, when James I had himself proclaimed King of Great Britain, but it took one hundred years to make it work.

The country depicted in the masques was presented by the court as a revived ancient Britain that was comparable to Rome in its ancestry. This Britain came to be envisioned, via the medium of perspective illusion and theatrical "inventions," as the staged landscape scenery upon which a unified national narrative was performed. The theatrical landscape conflated the nation, as a people, with the landscape identity of a geographic body, thereby facilitating this envisioning of the nation as a unity of physical nature and people. The stage scenery masked the differences between the separate lands under James by unifying them within the natural landscape scene of Britain under the equally "natural" laws of the monarch. Landscape scenery, I argue, was later to play a similar role in helping to fuse divergent territories into the modern German nation-state. As I show in the last chapter, it also played a role in uniting the states of America as a nation within the bounds of the American continent.

*The Masque of Blackness* forms the book's leitmotif because it provides a prismatic artwork through which to approach the various facets of the evolving meanings of nature, landscape, country, and the body politic. The brilliant partnership of Jonson and Jones produced a masque in which the use of landscape scenery remarkably foreshadows the subsequent history of British and American ideals concerning the natural landscape scenery of the countryside. It also provides a link, backward in time, to classical precedent concerning the ties between environment and nation.

## MASKING THE NATION-STATE

This book does not just revolve about the story of (and in) a masque; it is also about the process of masking. While the masque involved the wearing of masks, as at a masquerade costume ball, it was also a form of total court theater which engaged the personae of both spectators and players in a fable that masked the new British Stuart state. As Thomas Hobbes pointed out in *Leviathan,* his seminal work on the state:

> *Persona* in latine signifies the *disguise,* or *outward appearance* of a man, counterfeited on the Stage; and sometimes more particularly that part of it, which disguiseth the face, as a Mask or Visard: And from the Stage, hath been translated to any Representer of speech and action, as well in Tribunalls, as Theaters. (Hobbes [1651] 1991, 112, emphasis in original)

The idea of the masque is deeply implicated in the way the authority to speak on behalf of the state was constituted in the Renaissance. The world of the court masque was a microcosm of the larger theater of the state itself, and those who spoke upon its stage received their personae, and their "authority," from the state as represented in the symbolic form of the theater and its scenery.[9] The landscape of the masque thereby became a means of making visible, and audible, the abstract power of the state. The stage designer Inigo Jones was, as Ben Jonson ironically put it, the "wise surveyor! Wiser architect," who would "survey a state" ("An Expostulation with Inigo Jones" [1631], in Jonson 1985, 462–65).

The envisioning of the "ancient" nation, Britain, in terms of landscape scenery had a built-in duplicitous quality because it was based upon a visual deception.[10] The landscape illusion of an idyllic British countryside represented on the stage was very convincing, but it masked the reality of a territory divided between countries constituted on the basis of differing custom and law. The problem with this duplicity is that there is an easy transition from "landscaping" to "mindscaping" (my term), or, in other words, from the deception of the eye to the deception of the mind. This is the sort of mindscaping that facilitates the construction of imagined nation-state communities (Anderson 1991). Such a duplicity has become the hallmark of modern nationalism. In the words of the British anthropologist Ernest Gellner:

> Generally speaking, nationalist ideology suffers from pervasive false consciousness. Its myths invert reality: it claims to defend folk culture while in fact it is forging a high culture; it claims to protect an old folk society while in fact it is helping to build up an anonymous mass society. (Pre-nationalist Germany was made up of a multiplicity of genuine communities, many of them rural. Post-nationalist united Germany was mainly industrial and a mass society.) (Gellner 1983, 124–25)

Gellner does not explain how nationalism accomplished this "false consciousness." To understand how such consciousness comes into being, I argue, one should look behind the scenes at the stage machinery which was used to induce audiences to envision the "nation" of Britain as landscape scenery. This occurred, it will be seen, at a time when the modern idea of the nation was still on the historical horizon.

## LANDSCAPE SCENERY AND COMMUNITY

Landscape as natural scenery provided a means of embodying an image of the country, as the place of community, within the hierarchically organized space of an emerging state. The techniques applied in the court masque were also later applied to the countryside itself through the practice of landscape architecture. This culminated, a century after Jones, in the vast landscape gardens of a landed gentry which legitimated its power in terms of country values. Landscaping provides a means of training the mind to envision the country in particular scenic, spatial terms. It can mindscape a people, or at least some of the people, so that they think of their homeland as Britain, rather than England, Scotland, Ireland, or Wales. It can mindscape a people, or at least some of the people, to identify with a united German state and forget their identification with particular ancient homelands. It can help a people forget bitter sectional divi-

*I don't*
*(bus)*

sions and learn to identify with a country that is united by the continent of America. A consequence of this mindscaping is that landscape and country have come to be perceived largely in scenic terms. The identification of country as a polity characterized by a socially constituted political landscape has become subordinated, in many ways, to the idea of country as scenic physical landscape.

The complex of meanings identified with country, nature, and landscape that emerged in the Renaissance provide the framework for an examination of the coevolution of these ideas in the context of the developing nation-state. This study moves in time and place from Renaissance England and northern Europe to the Great Britain of the Enlightenment and thence to nineteenth- and twentieth-century Germany and the United States, where the idea of nature and country as landscape scenery developed much of its present-day meaning. Though the focus moves in place and time, the book is ultimately about the often hidden agendas concerning polity and place which we broach when we are ostensibly engaged in discourses concerning nature, landscape, and the state of our environment. Our environment, conceived as landscape scenery, is fundamentally linked to our political landscape.

*Landscape, Nature, and the Body Politic*

# One

# The Political Landscape
# as Polity and Place

First, for the Scene was drawn a Landtachaap . . .
Ben Jonson, *the Masque of Blackness*, 1605

*Landscape* made its dramatic entrance onto the English stage, and into influential realms of Modern English discourse, through the vehicle of a fabulously expensive and prestigious court masque, *The Masque of Blackness,* written by Ben Jonson and staged by Inigo Jones.[1] The masque was called "The Queen's Masque" because it was James I's queen, Anne of Denmark, who conceived the idea for the masque and arranged to have it produced with herself in a leading role. She took over the services of Inigo Jones from her renowned brother, King Christian IV of Denmark, and had Jones do the stage design and scenography.[2] She made Ben Jonson her protégé at court when she asked him to do the text (Jonson 1969, 48). This international mix suggests that the renewed interest in the concept of landscape at this juncture in English history must be seen in the light of ongoing discourses and practices within Europe more generally.

The Renaissance was a cosmopolitan era, and the English court was a cosmopolitan place. Anne had lived in Denmark, Mecklenburg, and Scotland; Jones had explored Italy and worked for a Danish King; and Jonson had been in the Netherlands. This was an era before nationalism had narrowed the language and minds of Europeans. To understand the developing meaning of landscape, it is thus wise to look at the larger international Renaissance context within which English discourse on landscape and country took place. Discourses reflect an era, but they are the product of concrete individuals expressing themselves within the personal contexts of their lives. For this reason, this chapter traces the steps of Queen Anne and King James back to Anne's Danish home, where they began what became an often tempestuous marriage, augured by storm.

Fig. 1.1. Sketch by Inigo Jones showing a woman, most likely Queen Anne of Denmark, in masque headdress. Photo: Photographic Survey, Courtauld Institute of Art. Reproduced by permission of the Devonshire Collection, Chatsworth; the Duke of Devonshire; and the Chatsworth Settlement Trustees.

Retracing the trail of the royal couple's progress provides a narrative means to uncover clues to the continental background of the word *Landtschap,* before it turns up in the introductory scene of the British *Masque of Blackness.* The point of this tale is to facilitate the understanding of the differing meanings of landscape, nature, and country. The tale of James's Danish connection helps reveal how differing meanings of these concepts were linked in a context that informed the lives of people who were to play lead roles in the English court's "invention" of Britain.

## KING JAMES'S TEMPESTUOUS DANISH CONNECTION

James VI of Scotland was opposed on principle to allowing his queen "to meddle with the Politick gouvernemente of the commonn-weale" (James I [1599] 1969, 98). Anne, however, would have learned from her own shrewd mother, the Danish Queen Sophie of Mecklenburg, that much of the power at court lay in the manipulation of the symbolic face which it presented to the body politic (Bech 1963, 510–21). Anne literally cast herself in the role of "the glorious patroness of this mighty Monarchy."[3] If James lent his support to his wife's theatrical interests it might have been because the reclusive king understood what the role of the masque could be in furthering his political goals (Parry 1981; Goldberg 1983; Marcus 1986, 25–26).

With the notable exception of a female biographer (Williams 1970), historians of Britain have largely disparaged or ignored Queen Anne of Denmark. Her relationship with James was tempestuous, and historians have a tendency to side with the native British monarch—even though Anne's marriage to a man who is reputed to have been a neurotic and a misogynist can hardly have been easy. "Alas! James had married a stupid wife," one of James's biographers gallantly exclaims (Willson 1956, 95). "Her love for gaiety and dancing, for games, masques and pageants," we are told, "was childish rather than courtly. The [Scottish] ministers quickly condemned her 'want of godly and virtuous exercise among her maids', her absence from the Kirk, her 'night-waking and balling'" (Willson 1956, 94; see also Akrigg 1962, 21–22). Modern custodians of British heritage similarly feel obliged to inform visitors to the Queen's House in Greenwich that Anne was "extravagant and pleasure-loving," even though the building she commissioned Jones to design and build was revolutionary in its time as a model of classical restraint (National Maritime Museum n.d., 4). The historian George Macaulay Trevelyan, author of the classic *England Under the Stuarts,* snubs Anne, not even bothering to have her indexed (Trevelyan [1904] 1960). This dim view of the queen, and the women of the court with her, gives grounds for one modern authority on the Stuart court to warn: "In considering the Jacobean Court culture, it would be unwise to underestimate the intelligence of the female participants" (Parry 1981, 49).[4] As both a woman and a foreigner, Anne was at a double disadvantage. A nineteenth-century historian of British pomp and circumstance thus notes, condescendingly, how he imagines Anne must have reacted to the presentation of an entertainment created by Ben Jonson at the time of her procession from Scotland to London in 1603 to become queen: "It is easy, or rather, it is not easy, to conceive the surprise and delight with which Queen Anne, who had a natural taste for these elegant and splendid exhibitions, must have witnessed the present; she who in Denmark had seen perhaps no Royal amusement but drinking-bouts . . ." (Nichols 1828, 176). Actually, nothing could have been further from the truth.

The Danish monarchs might have been accomplished drinkers, capable of teaching Scottish kings the Nordic royal art of imbibing, but this did not hinder the court of Anne's father, King Frederik II, and her brother, King Christian IV, from becoming a mecca of Renaissance culture in northwestern European (Strong 1986, 187). Prominent members of Shakespeare's troupe had played for the Danish court, and Anne's brother-in-law, Duke Heinrich Julius of Braunschweig-Wülfenbüttel (Brunswick), wrote English-style plays for his court's troupe of English actors (Neiien-

Fig. 1.2. The Queen's House, Greenwich. Designed in 1616, it was commissioned from Inigo Jones by his early mentor, Queen Anne of Denmark. Photo: author.

dam 1988, 94–95).⁵ In England, by contrast, it is likely that these same players would have performed in theaters which had largely been banished beyond the bounds of the city, and respectability, by London's city fathers (Marcus 1986, 41). After Anne's husband was crowned James I of England and the couple moved to London, Anne followed her Danish and German families' examples by helping to bring the theater under the protection of the court. She became the protectress of her own troupe (members of which gave guest performances at her sister and brother-in-law's court in Wülfenbüttel, Braunschweig-Wülfenbüttel), and she is believed to have helped convince her husband to remake Shakespeare's troupe into the King's Players (Harrison 1948, 35–36; Williams 1970, 88; Neiiendam 1988, 112–13).⁶ Anne was the mentor at court for intellectuals and artists including the poets Ben Jonson and Samuel Daniel, the translator and lexicographer John Florio (under whose tutelage she became fluent in Italian), and the scenographer and architect Inigo Jones (Yates 1934, 54, 246–48). For Jones's rising authority at court we must "thank the good Queen Anne," as Ben Jonson (ruefully) noted ("An Expostulation with Inigo Jones" [1631] in Jonson 1985, 462–65). Jones eventually was appointed as court surveyor, with a portfolio typical of the Renaissance and worthy of a "Renaissance man" like Jones. The position involved everything from surveying and designing fortifications and their environs to designing theaters and stage scenery, and, hence, also required the ability to draw and paint. Jones advanced from designing stage buildings to becoming the architect of actual theaters, royal palaces, and their grounds.

Anne's passion for the theater and for masques is largely responsible for her unpopularity with posterity. The Scottish Presbyterians and the English Puritans of the civil war era despised the theater for political as well as religious and moral reasons. Their puritanical disdain for the theatrical face of the Stuart court complemented their repugnance at the astronomical sums spent by Renaissance courts on pageantry and masques (Orgel 1975, esp. 40–42; Parry 1981, 40–63; Strong 1984). Nationalistic historians have, in turn, canonized the Puritans' judgment. Trevelyan thus dismissed the supreme artistic expression of the Jacobean court by tut-tutting that "the more self-respecting of the Lords preferred the retirement of their mansions . . . to Court masques in which ladies were too drunk to perform their parts" (Trevelyan [1904] 1960, 103). Anne brought a taste for continental Renaissance spectacle to the London court, but she would never have had a virtual carte blanche to drain the royal treasury if James I had not allowed her to do so. James would have learned the value of the arts as a means for strengthening the image of the monarchy during the long period in which he assiduously prepared himself for his hoped-for ascension to the English throne. One of the places where this lesson would have been most impressed upon him was Denmark. King James VI of Scotland had never been to London before he was crowned King James I of England in 1603, but over a decade earlier, he had been to Copenhagen.

James's visit to Copenhagen resulted from a hitch in the plans for his wedding with Anne. In 1589, while still a young teenager, Anne, the daughter and sister of powerful Danish kings, sailed from Denmark, with a Danish navy flotilla, to wed the Scottish king, James VI. Anne's mother, Queen Sophie of Mecklenburg, had arranged for the marriage after the death in 1588 of her husband, King Frederik II of Denmark, who had opposed the marriage. Frederik was worried, for one thing, about the question of Danish sovereignty over the Orkney Islands. In 1468–1469 the islands had been "temporarily" transferred to Scotland as a form of security for the dowry of King Christian I of Denmark's daughter Margrethe, who was to wed James III of Scotland (Bech 1963, 516; Donaldson 1984, 13). The marriage of Anne to James VI of Scotland would mean that Denmark's claims to the Orkneys, for a time at least, would be forgotten (Donaldson 1984, 18, 40). Frederik's widow, however, was more worried about the fate of her children than about that of the Orkneys, and she was quick to apply her wiles to negotiating the betrothal of her daughter to James VI—who, himself, was quite concerned about the Orkneys.

The peaceful diplomatic climate that ensued upon the betrothal of Anne to James was broken by a violent tempest of a meteorological kind. While Anne's flotilla was en route to Scotland, storms drove the ships to seek shelter in Oslo, Norway. Enflamed, perhaps, by the portrait of the light blond, nubile princess sent to him by Queen Sophie, the young king made an uncharacteristic display of romantic gallantry and set sail for Oslo himself. He was braving not only wind and waves, but the witchcraft that he believed had caused the supernaturally tempestuous weather—a belief that later cost the lives of numerous "witches" on both sides of the North Sea.[7] The couple were married in Oslo and spent Christmas there, after which they were sledded down the coast to Denmark, where the marriage ceremony was performed again at the magnificent new Renaissance castle in Elsinore—the location of Shakespeare's *Hamlet*. James then stayed on in Denmark for the April 1590 festivities in connection with the wedding of Anne's sister Elizabeth to Duke Heinrich Julius of Braunschweig-Wülfenbüttel (Neiiendam 1988, 94–95). What James saw in Denmark is likely to have outshone anything he knew from Scotland.

James's new Danish brother-in-law was yet too young to be crowned, but he had already begun preparing himself for the glories of his coming reign as King Christian IV. The grand edifices and planned cities which were to become Christian's legacy to Denmark and Norway still only existed in his mind, but they would have made for good conversation with the young James, who was making plans of his own (Gamrath 1993). James met with much in Denmark that must have strengthened his belief that governmental ideals based on science and the principles of "natural law" should provide the foundation of government. One of the people he was most anxious to meet in Denmark was thus the theologian Niels Hemmingsen, who was one of the first modern thinkers to apply the rationale of science to the study of the premises of law and justice (Petersen 1929, 373–74; Hemmingsen 1991). Denmark had only recently emerged from a period of political turmoil which ultimately revolved around many of the same issues that bedeviled James at home in Britain. James wished to rule over the geographical territory of Britain, within the bounds of which England and Scotland would be unified under the divine right of his law. In Denmark he found a Dano-Norwegian state that had succeeded in uniting a diversity of lands and was well on the path to the absolute rule of the monarchy's law. The Danish court was in the ascendancy, and young Christian did not have to contend with anything resembling the power of the English Parliament that James was later to face.

The Danish kings had triumphed in a situation in which civil war had threatened the very existence of the Danish state. These internal struggles basically turned on conflicting conceptions of what was the most legitimate representative of the polity. Was it the monarch in his person, or was it the members of a representative body? It is in this context that James would have met with the contested concept of Landschaft—to use the German spelling of Landtschap (German would have been a lingua franca at the cosmopolitan Danish court).

LANDSCAPE AS THE MIRROR OF POLITY AND PLACE

*The Contested Terrain of Landschaft*

One of Anne's father's first acts after becoming King Frederik II in 1559 had been to play heroic knight in shining armor. He did this by conquering a little Saxon country—and nearly getting himself captured in the process. The unfortunate victim of this manifestation of royal power was a wealthy little farming republic on the west coast of Jutland, the Landschaft of Dithmarschen. Frederik attacked it because he claimed it belonged to his neighboring duchy of Holstein. Against the Dithmarschers' army of six to seven thousand farmer-infantrymen, the brave new Danish king marched at the head of an army of twenty thousand infantrymen and three thousand cavalrymen who pillaged and burned everything from farms to churches on their path through the country. Though a divided Dithmarschen was eventually allowed to retain a degree of local rule, it became firmly subordinated to Frederik's duchies of Schleswig-Holstein. Seen from within, Dithmarschen still maintained some independence as a political land-scape—continuing to think of itself as a Landschaft—but to the Danish king it had become a royal province. The coat of arms of Dithmarschen was duly incorporated into the royal Danish coat of arms, where it re-mained until 1972 (Molbech 1813, 223–27; Bech 1963, 314–15; Sante 1964, 437–38; Rying 1974, 16–21; Gregersen 1981, 256–60).

What sort of a place was Dithmarschen, and why was it anathema to the king? Several centuries later, in 1813, when the political climate of Eu-rope was moving away from absolutism, the respected Danish lexicogra-pher, librarian, and historian Christian Molbech felt prompted to answer this question. In reading his history of the wars with Dithmarschen it be-comes clear why this Landschaft was a thorn in the side of a consolidating monarchical state. The tone of Molbech's language also makes clear how the precedent set by Dithmarschen could have inspired dreams of a repre-sentative form of government at a time when such a system was rare:

> It could hardly be said of the people of any of the other German states and *landskaber* [modern Danish spelling of Landschaft] united under the [Holy Roman] Empire that though they were supposed to be the subjects of a prince, they nevertheless were not the subject of any dominion, ex-cept that of the gathered people, nor that they recognized any other au-thority than that which the ordinary commoners' will gave to the power of the courts. It is true that the Frisians and most of the other dwellers in Germany's northwestern marshland coast had a more or less democratic constitution, but no others had understood how, under the appearance of dependency [to the bishop of Bremen], to preserve complete freedom so safely and for so long. (Molbech 1813, 87–88)[8]

Molbech uses the term "*landskab*" to refer to Dithmarschen as a par-ticular kind of polity. The Dithmarschers themselves also applied this term to their representative assembly and to the inn where the assembly met, the *Landschops-huus* (Mensing 1931, 401–2: Land-dag). A Landschaft was more than a place; it expressed the very idea of political representa-tion as manifested in the representative body that stood for a political community. The Landschaft as place was thus defined not physically, but socially, as the place of a polity. The physical manifestation of that place was a reflection of the common laws that defined the polity as a political landscape.

## Frisian Landschaften

Historically, Dithmarschen was by no means the only Landschaft in Schleswig-Holstein. The Landschaft of Angeln, on the southern side of the

Flensborg Fjord, was the legendary home of the Angles, who gave their name to England. They, along with Saxons and people from the Frisian Landschaften (north of Dithmarschen, on the southwest coast of Jutland), were, according to legend, the settlers who pushed the Britons into the mountain fringes of the British Isles and founded Anglo-Saxon England in the fifth century.[9] By the time of James's visit, however, the most viable Landschaften remaining were the Saxon and Frisian communities that had managed to survive in the difficult marshy terrain of the western coast of Jutland and along the rivers of the region. The Frisian Landschaften maintained their special status until as recently as 1864, so they make particularly accessible examples of the historical reality of the Landschaft.

Schleswig (Slesvig in Danish) is a territory with a long history as a contested marshland between the Danish kingdom and the German states of the former Holy Roman Empire. Because it formed a narrow neck in the Jutland peninsula, it provided an important transshipment region for trade between the Baltic Sea and the North Sea—the sea route around the northern tip of Jutland was long and dangerous. Both Schleswig and Holstein (Holsten in Danish), to its south, were made up of a complex amalgam of territories whose governance, by various German and Danish noblemen and by the Danish king, was determined according to an endless series of compromises between factions. This lack of unity created the free space which allowed relatively independent areas like the different Landschaften of North Friesland to maintain their ancient bodies of law and, hence, an independent legal identity as political landscapes.

One of the most detailed and methodical sources on the Schleswig Landschaften is a volume published in 1864 (the last year of Danish rule) in the now standard multivolume Danish topographical reference work, *Traps Danmark.* According to the author, Jens Peter Trap, there was historically a difference between a landskab and an *amt. Amt* is the term for a German administrative district which was applied in Schleswig-Holstein by the end of the fifteenth century and subsequently became, until this day, the standard regional administrative subunit of the Danish state administration (Gregersen 1981, 222). Amt means office or bureau, and the leading state officer in the amt, the *amtmand,* was thus literally a bureaucrat. Amt is usually translated into English as "county," though the amter in question here were smaller than English counties (Vinterberg and Bodelsen 1966: amt). The Schleswig landskaber were quite different from the amter because they "have had a more independent development, both in relation to the other districts and internally, and they therefore have territorial constitutions which give the population a greater right to self-determination and participation in the judicial process and in government" (Trap 1864, 67). These Landschaften were therefore able to preserve their Frisian heritage as "free farmer estates."[10]

One Landschaft, Eidersted, is particularly notable. Trap emphasizes that "no other district in the duchy of Slesvig is equipped with a district constitution which expresses such a high degree of freedom and independence."[11] "It has gradually," he continues, "developed into its present state and it rests just as much upon rules which have developed through autonomy and custom as through law and privilege" (1864, 81). Trap's explanation for the peculiar depth of local rule in Eidersted, which was unusual even in Schleswig, was that the Landschaft constituted an amalgamation of three formerly autonomous lands. Eidersted originally consisted of three polities, Eyderstett, Euerschop, and Uthholm, which, as the name Uthholm ("Out Isle") suggests, were united through diking and draining the shallow marshy area at the mouth of the Eider. Each of these districts had its own representative council or assembly with judicial functions, which Trap terms a *"Thing"* and which he elsewhere identifies with a *landret* (provincial common-law court) (1864, 601). Euerschop and Uthholm were united in 1370, and all three joined together in 1456. Each retained, however, its own assembly. According to Trap, the customary law of the district had been transmitted orally from generation to generation through the institution of the assembly. This law, when written down in 1426, was prefaced with these words: "Hir schaltu hören und sehn de Krone der Rechten warheit Alsse ist ein Recht willkorts Recht ist in Eyderstett, Euerschop und Uthholm" (Trap 1864, 267). The sentence includes a play on words involving the various meanings of the German words for right and rights, ranging from court to law to justice and rights, but it might be translated: "Here shall you hear and see the crowning glory of true justice, which is a law that is the law (rights) of Eyderstett, Euerschop, and Uthholm."[12]

The Landschaften described in Trap's topography were contested territory, though they managed to maintain their legal identities.[13] Trap recounts that in 1251–1252 the "violent" Danish King Abel, in order to force the Frisians to pay an extraordinary tax, attacked the Frisian landscape of Eidersted and made camp at the village of Oldenswort. Since the Frisian Landschaften had no central government, it took them some time to organize a counterattack. First the chosen leaders from the various territories met at the site of their ancient *Thing* at Buermannsweg ("Farmer's Way"). Then the united Frisian army, making good use of their knowledge of the marshy terrain, met, pursued, and destroyed the Danish army on St. Peter and Paul's day, June 29, 1252. The Danish king tried to escape, but his head was split by the ax of a wagoner named Wessel Hummer, who was from the Frisian island Landschaft of Pelvorm (Trap 1864,

124–25). One reason that it took the Frisians time to organize their resistance was that this area was culturally and politically fragmented, and relations between the differing landscapes, as well as between families within landscapes, could be contentious. Partly because they were not above fighting amongst themselves or with the Saxons, the Frisians were fierce warriors. This fractiousness, however, explains why the fiercely independent Landschaften might nevertheless accept the stabilizing and unifying effect of a superior authority. The people of Dithmarschen thus accepted the nominal external authority of the bishop of Bremen.

The Danish kings had nominal sovereignty over North Friesland, but time and time again the Frisians and the populace of other Landschaften fought to defend their special rights and independence. By exploiting the factional strife between the kings and the nobility, the Landschaften sought to maintain their special legal and political identities.[14] It was in such a situation that the people of Eiderstedt elected to write down their ancient law and thereby help formalize their political status. The Schleswig Landschaften, however, did not always pick the winning side. This could have disastrous consequences, as in the case of an unsuccessful revolt against King Christian I, in 1472, in which the Schleswig Landschaften played an important role. Many members of these communities lost their farms and privileges, and some lost their lives. A Frisian leader, Edlef Knudsen, was strapped to a plank in Husum's town square in full view of the king and many noblemen and presented with the sight of his own still beating "traitorous heart" by the royal executioner, who then cut the body into four pieces for public display (Trap 1864; Poulsen 1988, 19–33). Another leader, Henneke Wulfe, who came from Elbe Marshes, was captured and killed while fleeing through Dithmarschen. The local perception of the man's heroism during an earlier revolt is reflected in a portrait of him in the Wevelfleth church. It shows him shooting an apple from the head of his son at the demand of the king. Just as in the famous Swiss version of the story identified with William Tell, he has a spare arrow in his mouth which was designated for the king should he have missed the apple (Poulsen 1988, 30–31).[15]

### Lost Schleswig Landschaften

Military force was not the only threat to the Landschaften of Schleswig. Eighteenth-century topographical reference works list a number of "landskaber" on the dry, fertile soils of eastern Schleswig which are no longer recorded in Trap's nineteenth-century topography, or which are recorded as having an uncertain status. Angeln and the peninsula Svansø (Schwansen in German), for example, which were recorded as landskaber in the eighteenth century (Pontoppidan 1781, 5, 6), are not identified as

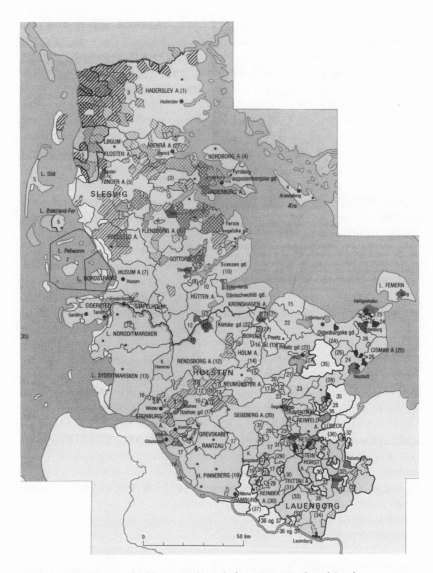

Fig. 1.3. Political map of Schleswig-Holstein before 1864. North and South Dithmarschen (Ditmarsken) are in the southwest. These and the other Frisian *landskab* polities, which stretch northward along the western coast and islands, are prefixed with an "L." Districts under the state bureaucracy, or *amt*, are followed by an "A." From Jette Kjærulff Hellesen and Ole Tuxen, *Historisk Atlas Danmark* (Copenhagen: Gad, 1988), 249. Reproduced by permission of Gad Publishers.

14

such in Trap's topography. The nearby island of Femern (which was settled successively by Slavs, Danes, and Saxons from Dithmarschen and the Elbe marshlands), on the other hand, is listed as both an amt and a landskab (Trap 1864, 67, 670–71), whereas earlier sources defined it exclusively as a landskab (Pontoppidan 1781, 816–65).[16]

The explanation for why some Landschaften were "lost" or disappearing appears to be that they were located on the eastern side of the peninsula. This region was subject to considerable manorialization because of the suitability of its soil for agriculture and because its thriving cities on excellent Baltic harbors provided a good market for the products of intensive manorial agriculture (Hellesen and Tuxen 1988, 249; Poulsen 1988). The Landschaften on the western coast, on the other hand, did not present an attractive environment for manorial investment because of the danger of flooding and the need for specialized local knowledge and complex systems of organization to maintain the intricate system of dikes. The shallow waters off the western coast also made for poor harbors that did not favor the development of urban ports. The marshland farmers of the coast and islands were nevertheless skilled navigators of the treacherous Wadden Sea (Waddenzee), and they maintained ancient coastal trading links with other Frisian societies along the North Sea. All these factors mitigated against both a manorial takeover and the penetration of urban political and economic centers (Poulsen 1988; Knottnerus 1996).

There may have been cultural as well as geographical factors that worked to preserve the Frisian Landschaften. The historian Marc Bloch has noted that "in the area of Western civilization the map of feudalism reveals some large blank spaces—the Scandinavian Peninsula, Frisia, Ireland" ([1940] 1961, 445). Alongside these blank spaces were places like Saxony which "by the number of its free peasants—free both as to their lands and as to their persons—seemed to represent a transitional stage from that of Frisia, which had no manorial system and consequently no serfs" (ibid., 267). In the areas without manors there was no vassalage. This is, according to Bloch, because "Where men of all ranks were able to rely for support on other forms of strength and solidarity than personal protection—kindred groups especially among the Frisians, the people of Dithmarschen and the Celts, kindred groups again among the Scandinavians, but also institutions of public law [such as the *Thing*] of the type common to the Germanic peoples—neither the relationships of dependence peculiar to territorial lordship, nor vassalage and the fief invade the whole of social life" (ibid., 247–48).

Bloch's analysis suggests that it was the strength of kinship ties and community organization that helped the Landschaften of Dithmarschen and Friesland survive.[17] Ferdinand Tönnies, who coined the terms *Gemeinschaft* and *Gesellschaft* (community and association), in his classic sociological study of that name, was born in 1855 in Eiderstedt on a farm just outside Oldenswort (Tönnies [1887] 1974, [1887] 1979). He is believed to have been motivated to develop this bipartite division of society by his experience, in 1864, of the incorporation of the duchies of Schleswig and Holstein into Prussia, which changed "a political community into a mere administrative district" (Loomis 1955, xxv; Knottnerus 1992, 334, 341–42, 345–46).

Though such Gemeinschaft communities might be seen as being traditional, isolated, and backward by those who equate modernity with a centralized state, the Schleswig-Holstein Landschaften were progressive and well connected, and their livestock, agricultural products, and salt were well known along the coastland of the North Sea. They were part and parcel of a range of such territorial communities, or peasant republics, which stretched along the coast of the Wadden Sea from Denmark down through the Netherlands, forming a rural counterpart to the free Hanseatic cities. This area, as a whole, provided an important hearthland for the origins of modern society in terms of trade, manufacturing, private ownership, egalitarian ideals, and civil freedoms, yet it has been characterized by a vigorous defense of local autonomy based upon ancient rights. Going against the centralizing grain of inland state formation, this area succeeded because its economic and social systems provided a flexible alternative to the centralized state (Rokkan 1975, 576; Schama 1987b; Knottnerus 1996).[18]

### Land, Law, and -Schaft in Landschaft

The concept of Landschaft as used in Renaissance Europe referred to a particular notion of polity rather than to a territory of a particular size. It could be extrapolated to polities of varying dimensions, ranging from tiny Uthholm to the whole of Northern Jutland. In this way, as will be seen in the following chapter, it is comparable to the English concept of country, which ranged from polities the size of the county to those the size of Scotland and beyond. The mindset fostered by a standard map tempts one to use the term *scale* when referring to landscape polities (or countries) of different sizes. The process of extrapolation which allows such a variety of polities to bear the name of Landschaft or country is not, I would argue, the quantitative geometric, spatial, rationality of the map. It is rather a qualitative logic based on an analogic "platial" imagination, in which place, as will be seen, is conceivable at differing levels of abstraction.[19]

The root of the word *Landschaft* is *Land,* and the two terms were sometimes used interchangeably. To appreciate this broader meaning of Landschaft it is necessary to look more closely at the relation between Land and Landschaft. Translators and dictionaries invariably translate the German word *Land* as "country" (Langenscheidt 1967: Land), and in

English the words *land* and *country* can have the same meaning. The country of England is, thus, also a land—the land of the English. The etymologically primary Germanic meaning of *Land* was an area, such as the various lands constituting a farm or manor (e.g., cultivated land, meadow land, common land) (Grimm and Grimm 1855: Land; Jackson 1984, 6). In the feudal era, these lands were not generally separate properties owned by individuals. Rather they formed a complex of use rights that were determined by custom and by personal feudal obligations. These lands, taken together, could constitute larger lands under a given body of law and with ancient origins predating feudalism (Gurevich 1985, 153–209; Hastrup 1985, 220, 236; Hedeager 1993).[20]

The link between ideas of customary law, the institutions that embody that law, and the people enfranchised to participate in the making and administration of law is of fundamental importance to the meaning of the root *Land* in Landschaft. Jutland (Jylland in Danish) is thus defined as a land because it "has its own particular legal system and its own *(lands)ting*," or representative council (ODS: Land).[21] It is this law which constituted the Jutes as a people. The institution of the *ting* (*Ding* in German) was also found in England, where it was known as a *thing* (or *moot*—"meeting"). The Danish land was divided into *herreder*, each with its own ting, much as the English shire or county (which could also be a "land," e.g., Northumberland) was divided into hundreds. The Scandinavian *ting*, which may date back to prehistoric times, had evolved by the Renaissance into a representative body that functioned from the level of the village, to that of the *herred* (roughly equivalent to the Norwegian *bygd'*, up to that of the land. It had a dual nature, partly as a body for internal self-rule and partly as a means of cooperation, conflict, and communication between local communities and central authorities. All important decisions binding the community were made at the *ting*. It also acted as a court, particularly in Denmark and Sweden (Imsen and Vogler 1997, 10).

Custom and culture defined a *Land*, not physical geographical characteristics—it was a social entity that found physical expression in the area under its law. The identification between the meaning of *Land* as a political community and *Land* as dry land, terra firma, was strengthened by the fact that *Land* was often translated into Latin as *terra* or *territorium*. This meant an area of the surface of the earth that formed a territorial jurisdiction, such as that under a territorial lord. The *Land* was initially defined by a given body of customary law that would have developed historically from within through the workings of the judicial bodies of a given legally defined community. It was not, first and foremost, an area of the earth's surface defined and ruled according to administrative regional boundaries such as we know from the Roman system of hierarchical, top-down, territorial rule, though many lands were eventually formalized as units within larger state systems. The translation of *Land* as terra or territorium was not unreasonable, since many *Länder* were often coequal with the territory under the jurisdiction of a lord, but this was not always the case. A lord might have jurisdiction over several *Länder,* and a *Land* need not have a lord.[22]

The importance of law to the identity of a land is suggested by the proverb that prefaces a number of ancient Scandinavian bodies of law, including the first written version of the Jutland Law from 1241. This proverb reads "Mæth logh scal land byggæs," which translates literally as "With law shall land be built" (Jansen and Mitchell 1971, 3–7).[23] The word *build* is related to *bower,* meaning dwelling, and *abode,* the place one abides, the place generated through *being* home (WC7: be, bower, abide, abode). A more correct translation might thus be "The abode of the land is created by abiding by the law." The bonds holding the landscape together were thus bonds of law, not bonds of blood. One of the most important functions of this law, in fact, was to mediate disputes between families or clans and thus prevent destructive blood feuds and preserve the peace of the land (Fenger 1992, 1993).

The law, according to the preface to the Jutland Law, shall be "ærlic oc ræt, thollich, æftær landæns wanæ," ("honorable, just, and tolerable, in accordance with the customs of the land") (Jansen and Mitchell 1971, 4–5). Another way of putting this might be to say that the law of the land must be in accordance with the Landschaft, or, to use the Danish spelling, the landskab. Landskab in this context would have meant (1) conditions in a land, its character (*beskaffenhed*), its traditions or customs; (2) the organization of things in a land; and (3) the landskab district (Fritzner 1886–96: landskapr; Kalkar [1881–1918] 1976: landskab).[24] Even when a land, for example, Jutland, became incorporated into a larger land such as Denmark, it still retained the character of a landskab if it retained its law and customs. The Jutland law thus eventually became known as a *landskabslov,* or "landscape law."[25] A landskab was not so much a region as it was a nexus of law and cultural identity. The meaning of landskab, in this sense, was thus quite similar to that of the term "political landscape," a polity's area of activity or place of action (MWC10: landscape). It was, to use Pierre Bourdieu's term, a habitus (Bourdieu 1977; see also MWC10: habit), in which habit, custom, and law are inextricably linked through the practice of habitation and accustomation. This is why a Frisian Landschaft could not accept the Jutland law, or even the law of another Frisian Landschaft. The various Landschaften of Frisia maintained separate identities, although they shared a similar language and ethnicity.

The various usages of the term *Landschaft* may seem confusing, but they are not all that different from those of related terms in English. The suffix *-schaft* and the English *-ship* are cognate, meaning essentially "creation, creature, constitution, condition" (OED: -ship). *-Schaft* is related to the verb *schaffen*, to create or shape, so *ship* and *shape* are also etymologically linked (OED: shape). The citizens in good standing of a New England town shape the polity of the town*ship* as constituted under a body of law. A township is at the same time a body of citizens, the representatives who make decisions on behalf of those citizens (as in "the township voted to raise taxes"), and the place of a polity shaped by those citizens. The condition of being in good standing as a town citizen is expressive of the more abstract notions of community values identified with citizen*ship*. The use of the suffix *-ship* in this way is actually common in English. The word *fellowship* thus refers not just to a body of fellows, but also to a higher community ideal shaped or created by fellows. *Friendship*, likewise, refers to more than just the ties between friends. It also refers to an abstract ideal form of human relations shaped by friends.

The suffix *-ship*, or *-scape*, does not indicate scale, as in cartography, but rather an analogic process of symbolic abstraction and extrapolation. Friendship, thus, is not a large-scale version of what transpires between two friends. The word *fellow* appears to derive from a Nordic expression referring to an association of fellows (*fellagi*) who graze animals together (MWC10: fellow), as under the bylaws of a collectivity.[26] Fellowship as a community of interest is, however, hardly a large-scale version of community sheep grazing, even if members of a church fellowship may have a pastor, and Oxford fellows share a common lawn—a word with the same etymological origins as land (Klein 1967: land, lawn). Contemporary expressions such as "grassroots democracy" recall the symbolic importance of common grazing land for the generation of community fellowship.[27]

This cluster of abstract symbolic meanings tied to concrete social phenomena illustrates how such social relations can act as the symbolic referent for more general ideas. These ideas might then be applied to social relations that are expressed at a larger spatial scale that they transcend in concrete daily experience. In this way, sheep grazing can provide the referent for national fellowship or international religious fellowship. The use of *-scape* or *-ship* to generate such abstract meanings was more common in the past, however, than today. English once included many words which encompass a range of meanings similar to that of Land*schaft*, such as country*ship*, burg*scipe* (municipality), folc*scipe* (nation) (OED: -ship) and *burgess-ship* (citizen of a town) (Underdown 1985, 16).

The primary meaning of Landschaft appears to have been a judicially defined polity, not a spatially defined area. It referred to the estates represented in a land's parliament (*Landtag* in German) or to the representative body itself. The Landschaft could also be defined to exclude the *Ritter-*

*schaft* (nobility) and the clergy, making it comparable to the English estate of the commoners who were represented in the House of Commons.[28] The *Landstandschaft*, the estates (*ständen*) of a land, were the equivalent of the law-abiding and tax-paying citizens who, by virtue of their good *standing*, have the right to representation. In this sense, the Germanic word *Landschaft* was parallel to the Latin-derived word *estate*, or *state*. Both Landschaft and various versions of estate (e.g., the German word *ständen*) were thus used somewhat interchangeably to refer to "one of the great classes, as the nobility, the clergy, and the commons, formerly vested with distinct political powers" (WC7: estate). These estates made up the polity of a state.[29] At a time when the medieval ascetic ideal was being replaced by the humanist ideal of the active, engaged citizen, the legitimacy of the right to represent this body became an important ideological issue (Pirenne 1958, 221–69).

Queen Anne of Denmark would have encountered in family conversation the use of Landschaft to refer to the representative body of the estates. Her beloved grandfather, Duke Ulrik of Mecklenburg (with whom she spent part of her childhood), ruled a country south of Denmark, across a narrow stretch of the Baltic, in which the representatives of the Landschaft had unified in opposition to the possibility of dynastic division in 1484. They formed a union in 1523, which enabled them to remain one corporation until 1918, despite a partitioning of the duchy in the early seventeenth century (Carsten 1959, 427; Sante 1964, 540–43). Here, as in many other areas, particularly in the Alps and in northwestern Europe, people were beginning to see the Landschaft as the legitimate representative of the interests of the political community.

*Political Landscape Ecology*

To comprehend the idea of the *Land* or the Landschaft as a community in law requires the ability to think abstractly. Since such an abstraction is intangible, this is difficult. The abstract idea of the political community becomes clearer when manifested through its concrete representation by particular people in the legal body (also called Landschaft) that defined and interpreted the law of the land. The polity of the land, furthermore, found concrete expression in the physical place of the polity and its physical environment, shaped under the governance of its laws. The shape of the material environment of the land reflected the condition of the polity that formed it. The laws of the landscape polities can therefore be used as a means to study the physical landscapes of places built on law (Hoff 1998). The land was not just "built" as a polity through law, it was also materially built through customary practices regulated by the law. "Eyderstett, Euerschop, and Uthholm" thus not only became united as a single polity, but also were physically united through the process of diking and reclamation by which the Frisian Landschaft polities created dry land from the shifting sands under the shallow waters of the Wadden Sea. The complex social process, regulated by custom, by which the Frisian Landschaften maintained an equally complex system of dikes is a study in what might be called "political landscape ecology."

It would be a mistake, however, to reduce these societies to mere expressions of an ecological adaptation to a particular physical environment. It would be more correct to state that Landschaft communities adapted specific environments to their needs. Such communities were comparatively well equipped to manage the challenging, and sometimes highly destructive, environment of the Wadden Sea, and this explains their continued survival in the face of competing political systems. The material face of the land reflected the social face of the landscape polity both when things went well and when dikes failed and disaster struck. The physical environment was a reflection of the political landscape. This reflection suggests the metaphor of the mirror as a means of representing the idea of political community under law.

## Mirroring the Law of the Land

The most famous written body of Germanic customary law is the *Sachsenspiegel,* or Saxon Mirror, from the period 1220–1235. The *Sachsenspiegel* provided the model for similar collections of law both in other parts of Germany (e.g., the Deutschenspiegel and the Schwabenspiegel) and outside Germany, as in Livonia, Poland, and in Holland. Some have argued that the *Sachsenspiegel* also influenced the written formulation of the Jutland law, the Jyskelov (Ancher 1809). Much as the Jyskelov effectively became the central law for Denmark, the *Sachsenspiegel* provided the constitutional basis of law for much of northern Germany and functioned, up until this century, as a subsidiary body of law in this area.

*Spiegel* is the Germanic word for mirror, but its full meaning is more easily grasped if it is also seen in the light of the related English (and German) word *spectacle*—which in Renaissance English could be used to mean mirror. The words *Spiegel* and *spectacle* derive from common Latin roots carrying meanings such as "to look" or "to observe" and are related to words like *spectator* and *speculate.* The *Sachsenspiegel* was compiled by the knight and judge Eike von Repkow and was written down first in Latin and then in the vernacular. It is based primarily upon the unwritten, memorized, customary law of the author's home district of Reppichau near Dessau, just down river from Wittenberg.[30]

Law had once been a personal issue in which individuals were governed by the law of their own tribe, even in cases where people of different backgrounds resided in the same area. After the ninth century law gradually became place bound, so that it applied to the area under the jurisdiction of a particular representative legal body. It was upon the basis of such a body of local place-bound law that the *Sachsenspiegel* was developed. Eike appended three prefaces to his work, one in verse and the other two in prose, in which he made it clear that his written text was a true reflection, or representation, of the Saxon law. It includes these famous words:

> spigel der Saxen
> sal diz buch genant.
> wende Saxen recht ist hir an bekant,
> als an einem spiegele de vrouwen
> ire antlize beschouwen.
> (cited in Grimm and Grimm 1855:
> Sachsenspiegel; see also Eckhardt
> 1955, 43)

Roughly translated, it reads, "This book shall be named the mirror of the Saxons. The Saxons can turn to this book and become acquainted with their law, much as women turn to a mirror and gaze upon their countenance."

The introduction of the *Sachsenspiegel,* we must remember, marks a momentous occasion with considerable implications for the conception of law. Because customary law was not written down, it could not encompass more than that which could be memorized by someone with a good memory. The early practice of holding the *Ding, ting,* or *Thing* out-of-doors in a public place, and the emphasis upon the role of voiced speech, meant that the law was a public possession. The word for "vote" in most Germanic languages is some version of *stimmen,* meaning "to voice," just as the word for speech forms the root of the word *Parl*iament. The law could not become the private domain of those who owned, and could read and interpret, abstruse books of law—as was the case with Latin Roman law. It was for this reason that the decision of the Icelandic Alting, the central council for all Iceland, to allow the law to be written down in 1117–1118 also had momentous social implications (Hastrup 1985, 123). The change required not only the ability to write, but also the adoption of a new, Roman-like way of thinking about law as permanent written text.[31] To this day, the writing down of legal rights derived from custom is a contentious issue because it can reduce a flexible set of principles to a more dogmatic and inflexible set of statutes. Eike's introductory verse provides, however, an ingenious argument for writing down the customary law.

By representing the law in written words, the text became, according to Eike's metaphor, a mirror image upon which one could reflect and speculate. More than this, however, it could also be seen as providing an ideal upon which one could model one's behavior; this is where the image of the person gazing into the mirror becomes pertinent. The metaphor is simple, and thus especially ingenious. A mirror can be seen to function as a model because when people see themselves in one they inevitably begin to straighten their clothes and hair. The mirror image, however, includes not just you, but also that which surrounds you. The mirror provides a literal image as well as the basis for a process of *reflection* (or *speculation*) in which one's ideal self-image, also in relation to one's surroundings, and the mirror image of the moment are compared.

It is important to remember that Eike's text (like the text of the Jyskelov) is significant because it combines cultural meaning and expression with legal and moral ideas. This is what makes it a literary monument. It also, furthermore, inspired pictorial representations mirroring the principles of law expressed in the text (Koschorreck 1970). These have subsequently become an invaluable source of information on daily life in medieval Germany. The full cultural significance of these works made them worthy alternatives to the models of law and society deriving from Rome. As early as the fourteenth century the *Sachsenspiegel* was being viewed as a Germanic counterweight to Roman law, much to the consternation of the Pope. The importance attributed to the *Sachsenspiegel* is suggested by Martin Luther's statement that the Law of Moses is "the *Sachsenspiegel* of the Judaic people" (quoted in Grimm and Grimm 1855: *Sachsenspiegel*) (the Pentateuch, particularly as reflected in Talmudic tradition, might be interpreted to be a formalization of the customary law of Israel's people). The fact that the *Sachsenspiegel* was written in German, and helped set the written standard for the German language, also recommended it in the era of the Reformation, which placed great store in the importance of translating the Bible into the vernacular. The *Sachsenspiegel* thus came to play an important cultural role in the development of a new spirit of non-Roman based place identity and pride in the sixteenth century.

*note Anderson*

### Landscape Painting's Origins North of the Alps

Today, landscape is often identified with painting, and some scholars, as noted in the introduction, even see it as deriving from painting. Landscape painting, I would argue, derives from the ideas of custom, law, and community expressed in *Sachsenspiegel* and Scandinavian bodies of "landscape" law. There is thus an intimate relation between the origins of the pictorial idea of landscape and the political landscape. Though they do not necessarily depict actual places, the works of early Landschaft painters such as Pieter Brueghel (c. 1525–1569) are fascinating sources on the customs of the time, both rural and urban. Brueghel's illustrations of traditional proverbs (an artistic genre at the time) are, to my mind, strikingly similar in appearance and intent to those used to illustrate the *Sachsenspiegel;* to quote the German art historian Max Friedländer, they are "as final and comprehensive as a lexicon. . . . Popular imagination had made itself vivid precepts, and out of these precepts Brueghel made vivid pictures" (1949, 161–62). Brueghel, as Friedländer has pointed out, combined landscape painting with the form of painting known as "genre" or *Sittenbild* (*Sitten* = custom, *Bild* = picture) (ibid., 76–77). This style of painting is concerned with the "common" world of the people. "In the genre-picture," Friedländer tells us, "the particular case points to other cases, so that a certain happening or state is illustrated as an example or, to put it philosophically, as 'an idea'" (ibid., 154–55). The customs or *mores* of a people give rise to both law and *morality.* Custom has moral authority, and the general moralizing tendency of Dutch Renaissance art, including landscape art, is well known (Wheelock 1977, 7).

The landscape paintings of the Netherlands remind us that customary

Fig. 1.4. Sketch based on Pieter Brueghel's *Haymaking* (ca. 1565).

law was not just the preserve of the courts. This law was also inscribed and memorized in the material world of the Landschaft. Customary obligations were responsible for the maintenance of bridges and roads, the maintenance and use of the fields, and the demarcation of areas (Milsom 1981, 12). Brueghel's painting, as the art historian Michael Rosenthal writes, "emphasizes not only the logic of the terrain," but also "the logic of the activity" shown in the paintings. It contains "an element of explanation, sometimes to the near-diagrammatic" (Rosenthal 1982, 12; see also Alpers 1983, 144–45). The writing of Henry Peacham, a roughly contemporary English landscape painter who admired the artistic and political culture of the Netherlands, suggests that this didactic artistic emphasis on the local customs and qualities of a country was intentional. Art, according to Peacham, was a medium of preserving and transmitting geographical and social knowledge because it "bringth home with us from the farthest part of the world in our bosoms whatsoever is rare and worth of observance, as the general map of the country, the rivers, harbors, havens, promontories, etc., within the landscape; of fair hills, fruitful valleys. . . . It shows us the rites of their religion, their houses, their weapons, and manner of war" (1962, 127–28). Landscape painting was thus a way of representing, and making concrete, the more abstract, social idea of landscape expressed by representative legal bodies and the law they generated.

## Landschaft and the Space of the State

The contradictions between the interests of the lord and those of the Landschaft, such as Anne would have known from Mecklenburg, were not unlike the emerging opposition between court and country which she and her husband were later to experience in England (as will be seen).[32] The historian Otto Brunner's description of these contradictions, noted in the introduction, bears quoting in full:

> The *Land* comprised its lord and people, working together in the military and judicial spheres. But in other matters we see the two as opposing parties and negotiating with each other. Here the Estates appear as the "Land" in a new sense, counterposed to the prince, and through this opposition they eventually formed the corporate community of the territorial Estates, the *Landschaft*. At this point the old unity of the *Land* threatened to break down into a duality, posing the key question that became crucial beginning in the sixteenth century: who represented the *Land*, the prince or the Estates? If the prince, then the *Landschaft* would become a privileged corporation; if the *Landschaft*, then it would become lord of the *Land*. (Brunner [1965] 1992, 341)

Brunner's text helps explain why the Danish monarch and the local lords of Schleswig-Holstein were so bent on subduing Dithmarschen. It also helps explain why the resistance of the Dithmarschen people was so fierce. Brunner's text gives the impression of a civil struggle. Actually, the struggle between lord and Landschaft could be violent and uncompromising. In 1500, for example, the Danish King Hans tried to conquer Dithmarschen at the head of a large feudal army of knights in armor. In the battle of Hemmingstedt, on February 17, the people of Dithmarschen took advantage of the marshy terrain by using staves to vault across the complex network of ditches that drained their farms. The knights, on the other hand, were restricted to the space of a narrow road, and once knocked into the mire by a blow from a stave they were weighted down by their armor and helplessly drowned in the mud. The king's army was wiped out in what was perhaps the greatest disaster in Denmark's long history of military disasters. It cost the life of someone in virtually every Danish noble house, and even the Danish standard, the legendary flag Dannebrog, was lost, ignobly put on display in a church in Heide town. Several decades later, Frederik II, Anne's father, burned the church to the ground; there was no better way to mark the beginning of his reign than by recouping the honor of the monarchy by sacking this Landschaft (Bech 1963, 307–15).

## LANDSCAPE SCENERY AS THE MIRROR OF NATURAL LAW AND THE STATE

### *Appropriating the Landschaft of Community with Maps and Scenery*

One way of countering the power of the Landschaft as a community shaped by a representative legal body was to represent the Landschaft by means that are more suited to the top down power of the Lord—the map and the prospect drawing. This can be illustrated by what transpired in Jutland after the Dithmarschen conquest. The commander of Frederik II's Dithmarschen expedition was Field Marshal Johan Rantzau, from the German-speaking duchy of Holstein. Rantzau was a proven military tactician who had brutally suppressed a series of popular Jutland revolts that had threatened the Danish crown. The campaign against Dithmarschen was both an expression of the hegemonic territorial designs of the lords and nobility of Schleswig-Holstein, as well as the imperial designs of the Danish king (Bech 1979, 11:627–31; Gregersen 1981, 220–24, 229–32). The result was that the different lands under the authority of the Danish king now included the entire landmass of Jutland down to the Elbe River. Unlike Johan, who used military means, his son Henrik, who succeeded him as power broker, was a Renaissance scholar and admirer of Italian

Fig. 1.5. Henrik Rantzau (1526–1598), age 63, at the height of his powers as Royal Statholder in Schleswig-Holstein (Jørgensen 1981, 11).

27

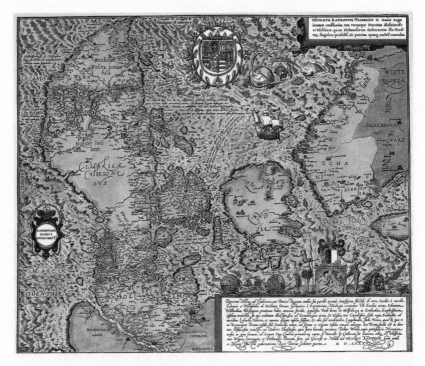

Fig. 1.6. Marcus Jordan's 1585 map of Denmark, made at the behest of Henrik Rantzau (Jørgensen 1981, 17).

statecraft. Henrik brought the humanism and science of his time to bear upon the task of appropriating the independent-minded Landschaften under the authority of the state.

After receiving his education in Luther's Wittenberg, Count Henrik Rantzau served the Danish state in a number of bureaucratic positions before being appointed the royal *statholder* (viceregent) in Schleswig-Holstein in 1556. After the conquest of Dithmarschen, Henrik Rantzau represented the royal interests and supervised the legal aspects of its subjugation; he followed this up in 1570 with a historical treatise on the military campaign. Rantzau's power lay in his command of written and graphic representation. He possessed an invaluable 6,300-volume library based, in part, upon the collections of a Roman Catholic monastery (made defunct by the Protestant Reformation, which his father had helped foster), and he corresponded with scholars throughout Europe about both scholarly and occult, astrological matters. He was particularly close to the astronomer and astrologer Tycho Brahe, whose cartographic theories he helped put into practice. The earliest extant printed map of Denmark of

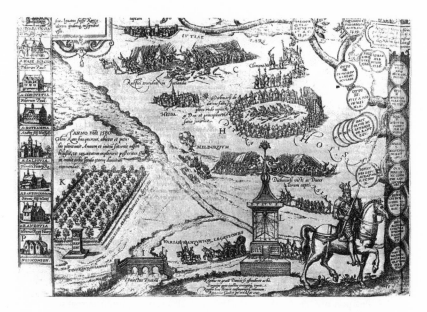

Fig. 1.7. Detail from the Rantzau family tree (rooted in the map of Jutland), commissioned by Henrik Rantzau. The kneeling, encircled figures are the people of Dithmarschen begging for mercy after their defeat at the hands of Johan Rantzau and King Frederik II (Jørgensen 1981, 16)

Danish origin was executed under commission to Henrik Rantzau in 1585 by the Holstein-born Marcus Jordan, a mathematics professor and lecturer on Ptolemaic geography at the University of Copenhagen. Abraham Ortelius and Gerhard Mercator both drew upon it for their cartographic works (Jørgensen 1981, 15–18).

This map was a monument to Rantzau's conception of the estate of the Danish king as encompassing the lands of Schleswig-Holstein and Denmark. It includes textual inserts memorializing the military victories of Henrik Rantzau's father over the enemies of the Danish state, as well as a pictorial insert in the lower right-hand corner in which the leader of a popular regional insurrection in Jutland, a privateer named Skipper Clement, is shown imprisoned while awaiting his execution in 1536. The text, originally in Latin, reads, "here Johan Rantzau crushed the rebellious peasant army of 25,000 men and took Skipper Clement prisoner" (Bramsen 1965, 51–55). This map, and other supplementary maps, were accompanied by illustrated regional geographic (chorographic) works depicting scenes from the peninsula and the peoples defined by its boundaries.[33] One of the pioneering graphic techniques developed under

Fig. 1.8. Prospect of Odense, Denmark. The original was made, using cartographic techniques, at the behest of Henrik Rantzau in 1593. It was printed in Georg Braun and Frans Hogenberg's *Civitates orbis terrarum* (Cologne, 1597), 5:30. This version is from *La galerie agréable du monde* (Leyden, 1729; Jørgensen 1981, 93).

Rantzau was the use of cartographic methods, which had been developed by Tycho Brahe, to create perspective drawings of landscape scenes. In this way Landschaften such as Dithmarschen, which had hitherto been defined by their representative bodies, were now represented as provinces of the state within the mapped and pictorialized space of the peninsula's land boundaries. Using armies at first, and then text, maps, and graphics, the Rantzaus helped create the idea that Schleswig-Holstein and the Danish state together constituted a unity of people and territory, tied together by geography.[34]

Henrik Rantzau's use of graphic techniques deriving from cartography to construct a new mode of visualizing the Landschaft polities under his control both contributed to, and exemplified, a larger movement within the Renaissance courts of Europe. If the political landscape of the Landschaft as place mirrored custom and practice as it shaped the land from the bottom up, the courts of Europe sought to mirror their authority in the celestial rationality mapped by the heavenly bodies of the cosmos.

*Landscape Scenery as the Mirror of Celestial Nature's Law*

The preferred Renaissance words for mirror derived from the Latin *spectaculum*, from *spectare*, to watch (MWC10: spectacle). In the *Sachsen-*

*spiegel,* as has been seen, the mirror (Spiegel) was seen to function as a model or standard which ought to be reflected in people's behavior (OED: mirror II: 5; spectacle II: 5). The *Sachsenspiegel* reflected the common, customary laws of the land. A spectacle, however, need not reflect. It can also be a lens, as in a pair of spectacles, which shapes our perception. The *Oxford English Dictionary* illustrates this double sense with a quotation from Polydore Vergil's 1575 *English History* which refers to the old saw that "preestes were the spectacles and looking glasses of the whole worlde" (OED: spectacle II: 5, 6). Painting could use optical means to reflect the world shaped by custom, as in the Netherlands, but it could also be used to shape an ideal perception of the world, as in Italy. Netherlands's art is characterized by fascination with optics and with the use of optical devices to mirror multiperspective representations of the places around them. This contrasted with the emphasis in Italy upon geometry as a means of structuring an ideal unified perspective space like that of the heavens (Wheelock 1977; Alpers 1983). The idea of the mirror/spectacle is present in both approaches, but its perspective is different. The optical device that faced upward, to the heavens, was used in Italian art as a means of reflecting the unvarying geometrical laws of the heavenly bodies. This differed from the *Sachsenspiegel*'s mirror, which faced earthbound landscape communities.

## Customary versus "Natural" Justice

The difference between the customary laws of the land and the laws of the heavens is important because it can be related to a fundamental legal distinction between customary, or conventional, and "natural" justice. This distinction can be traced back at least as far as a passage in Aristotle's *Ethics* which reads: "There are two kinds of political justice: the natural and the conventional. Natural justice has the same force everywhere and it does not depend upon its being agreed upon or not. Conventional justice is justice whose provisions are originally indifferent, but once these have been established they are important" (1934, 295–98). The eternal, timeless veracities of geometry provided inspiration for the conception of "natural" law. This is a notion of justice which probably can be traced back to ancient mathematician priest-kings, and which is reflected in mathematical/geometrical terms such as *right, rule* (of law), *straight,* and *just,* which still infuse the language of statutory justice. Words like *rule, ruler, regulate, regent,* and *region* (the territory ruled) are etymologically related (Benveniste 1973, 311–12).

The distinction between the two forms of justice was important in the context of empire (Aristotle himself was the teacher of Alexander the

Great) and the contact empire building brought with differing bodies of customary law (Nisbet 1969, 141). The Romans thus distinguished between Roman law, which governed equally throughout the empire, and the customary law that, by grace of the empire, was allowed to continue in effect in specific places.

Henrik Rantzau, as has been seen, placed great store in maps, prospect drawing, and chorographic description as means of representing the landscape polities of Jutland as part of a larger territorial whole defined by the natural boundary of the sea. Rantzau was concerned with more than the science of astronomy and its practical applications in map and prospect making, however; he also saw the stars as a source of occult power. Monuments suggesting a connection between the cosmos and particular loci in the territory under the rule of the Rantzaus thus mark the landscape scenes on his maps. The ultimate source of Rantzau's ideas on the interrelation between astronomy, astrology, and cartography would have been Ptolemy, the second-century A.D. Greek astronomer, astrologer, and geographer who had framed the cosmology within which Rantzau and his Renaissance cohorts worked.

The early fifteenth-century Italian rediscovery of Ptolemy's *Guide to Geography* provided the basis for the methodological development of modern cartography. As the author of the *Almagest*, Ptolemy had become established as the leading ancient astrological and astronomical authority of the Middle Ages.[35] Now this revered authority on the heavens suddenly gave posthumous birth to a book on the relation between the heavens and the earth.[36] Joan Gadol, in her study of Leon Battista Alberti, a quintessential fifteenth-century Renaissance man (cartographer, architect, artist, theoretician, and so on), places this discovery at the heart of the Italian Renaissance:

> The systematic origins of Renaissance art and of the Copernican astronomy can be found in a movement of thought which may be properly called a "Ptolemaic renaissance" even though Ptolemy was to be deprived of his authority because of it. We have seen how Alberti established the rules of artistic representation by modifying Ptolemy's principles of projection. When scientific "pictures" of the world came to be constructed according to these same principles, modern astronomy and geography began their rise. (Gadol 1969, 157)[37]

For Ptolemy, geography proper was essentially equivalent to the graphics of mapping and thus to the use of mathematical and astronomical science and the methods of projection. These methods were based upon a coordinate system derived from celestial measures. It is little wonder that Ptolemy's *Guide* was translated into Latin under the title of *Cosmo-*

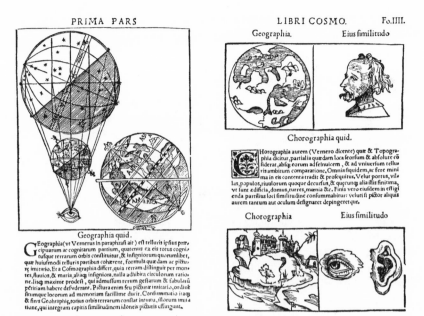

Fig. 1.9. Ptolemy's division of geography into geography proper, chorography, and topography, from Peter Apianus, *Cosmographia* (Antwerp, 1540). The globe of the earth represents geography proper, the regions of the earth, top right, are analogous to the face, and represent the geographic subdiscipline of chorography whereas, topography is a subset of chorography concerned with particular locations, analogous to the eye and ear.

*graphia.* Ptolemy's map provided a means of representing the universe in terms of universal natural laws, not unlike the principles of law seen to govern Roman justice. Under the overall heading of geography, Ptolemy designated two subdisciplines. The first was topography, which was concerned with providing graphic depictions of the *topoi*, or locations, which could be coordinated within the grid of the map. As an astronomer and astrologer, Ptolemy felt that he could predict a great deal about the physical and social climate (originally an astronomical term) of a topos if he knew its spatial coordinates. The second subdiscipline was chorography, which Ptolemy felt belonged more to the realm of the descriptive artist than to that of the mathematician and scientist. As he put it:

Geography looks at the position rather than the quality, noting the relation of distances everywhere, and emulating the art of painting only in some of its major descriptions. Chorography needs an artist, and no one presents it rightly unless he is an artist. Geography does not call for the same requirements, as any one, by means of lines and plain notations,

can fix positions and draw general outlines. Moreover Chorography
does not have need of mathematics, which is an important part of Geography. (1991, 26)

*Choros,* the root of chorography, meant both land/country and place in
Greek (Olwig 2001). Chorography was thus a discipline that was concerned
with the graphic depiction of such lands. The shape of a choros was that of
an enclosed, room-like area such as the agricultural lands that emerge
through clearing.[38] It constituted an organic space like that of the body, and
Plato used a variant of the term (spelled *chora*) to refer to a kind of primor-
dial, feminine, bodily receptacle through which the world is generated.[39]

Chorography may have required an artistic sensibility, but the geometrical skills of the geographer and surveyor provided the spatial framework
within which this sensibility could unfold. These surveyor-geographers
were initially people like Marcus Jordan, who, as noted, worked for
Rantzau in helping to delineate and depict the chorography of Jutland.
Their skills were also critical for building the roads, bridges, and fortifications which initially secured the military power of the court, but which
subsequently served civil purposes. Eventually, as fortresses were transformed into palaces, the surveyor transformed into an architect and artist,
shaping the image of power exercised by the court. It was the application
of Ptolemy's principles of projection to drawing, largely by court-affiliated
Renaissance "surveyors" (architects) and artists, which facilitated the development of single-point perspective in art, and hence the representation
of landscape as scenery (Edgerton 1975, 91–123; Ptolemy 1991).

*Doing It with Mirrors*

The techniques of perspective drawing were first developed in approxi-
mately 1410 to 1415 in Florence by the Renaissance architect Fillippo
Brunelleschi (Edgerton 1975). Brunelleschi's technique was mathemati-
cally formalized and written down in a 1435 treatise on art by his friend
Leon Battista Alberti. For Alberti, a painting was ideally like the mirrored
image Narcissus saw when he bent over a pool of water and spied his reflection against the background of the sky (Alberti [1435–36] 1956, 64;
Damisch [1987] 1994, 384). Alberti's technique depended upon the use of
a "window" frame, within which the lines of perspective were constructed
(Alberti [1435–36] 1956, 56; Gadol 1969, 29). A mirror, like a window,
can be framed, and the word *spectacle* could refer to either (OED: spectacle II: 5). The reflection of nature was created by using techniques of surveying that involved projecting coordinates, derived from the geometries
of the cosmos, upon the surface of the earth. As Gadol put it: "Perspecti-

val art restored and expressed the theoretical outlook in which objectivity is attributed, not to perceptual experience, but to the abstract, general rules which reason discovers in it, those 'first principles' which man discerns 'in nature'" (1969, 69; see also 55).

The connection between art as the mirror of nature and the regular geometrical laws of the infinite universe helps explain why Brunelleschi used a mirror to demonstrate the veracity of the technique of perspective drawing. As with the stereo illusion in the reproduction of music, there is only one point where the illusion of depth is perfect in the Brunelleschi system. Brunelleschi used mirrors to create a perfect illusion of "natural" spatial depth while at the same time showing that the vanishing point and the point at which the lines of perspective converged upon the eye were mirror images of each other.[40] The mirror was placed in front of a building and used to reflect the image of a perspective drawing of that building back toward a person looking from behind the picture, through a hole bored through the picture, at the vanishing point. The viewer would see the mirrored image of the painting as it blended miraculously into the space of the sky and the actual Florentine architecture that was the subject of the picture. Brunelleschi located the eye of the viewer at the central point where the lines of perspective both disappear into the geometrical infinity represented in the picture and converge upon the eye of the viewer, thereby creating a perfect pictorial illusion of spatial depth.

There was a distinctive difference in the approach to art as a mirror between artists working in the tradition of Brunelleschi and Alberti and the northern European Landschaft artists discussed above. The latter mirrored, from multiple perspectives, the myriad customary laws of the land, whereas the former, in effect, mirrored what were seen to be the natural and regular geometrical laws of the heavenly regions, as surveyed from a single, central point.

## FROM CHOROGRAPHY TO LANDSCAPE SCENERY

Ptolemy saw chorography as belonging to the realm of art. Renaissance artistic theorists, as noted, discovered that his techniques of cartographic projection could also be used to create perspective drawings. These were used, for example, to illustrate the great sixteenth-century cosmographic atlases, complete with maps and sketches of Landschaft territories. The Holy Roman Emperors sponsored the production of these atlases because they created an impression of chorographic unity that, it was hoped, would help in the political process of consolidating the empire. The image of the mirror was common in these cosmographies, which included both pictures and maps. The Protestant reformer and cosmographer Sebastian

Franck thus titled his 1534 cosmography *World Book: The Mirror and Portrait of the Earth*. In the introduction, he told the reader: "I myself want to spread out before your eyes the characteristics, beliefs and laws of the earth" (quoted in Gibson 1989, 54).

This was the era during which artists produced the earliest "Landschaft" paintings; the techniques they used to mirror both imagined and actual Landschaft areas were similar to those used by makers of the cosmographies. These paintings, particularly those of Joachim Patiner, often placed the viewer in a position high above the land, like a map reader, thus making it possible for the painting to encompass whole districts. One contemporary described the paintings as "pregnant with whole provinces" (Gibson 1989, 6). Since the Greek root *choros* in chorography means "land" (in the sense of country), and since these (choro)graphic depictions were representations of lands, or landscapes, it was natural for such paintings to be termed "landscape" pictures in the Germanic languages. Albrecht Dürer thus termed Patiner (in 1521) "der gut landschafft mahler" (the good landscape painter) (quoted in Mander [1603–4] 1994, 3:87).[41] Though these cosmographies may have been intended to mirror the provinces of a Rome-inspired universal empire, they inadvertently also helped stimulate a countervailing local awareness of the historical particularity of the provinces' place identity as countries. The Swiss, who battled to maintain their independent confederation, were naturally in the forefront in developing this place identity (Strauss 1959, 60–64, 86–92; Pearson 1976; Schmithüsen 1976, 91–93; Gibson 1989, 53–54). The term "landscape" as used in painting thus could be used both to refer to scenic images in the tradition of Italian single-point perspective and to styles, identified with northern Europe, that sought to reflect the laws of custom that shaped the land. This was true not only of the Germanic term but also of the French and Italian equivalents, *paysage* and *paesàggio*.[42]

Artistic traditions originating both north and south of the Alps influenced each other and drew upon similar techniques of perspective drawing (Wheelock 1977). Nevertheless, Italian painting, as an idealized window on an elevated nature, differed from the Alpine and northwestern Landschaft tradition in much the same way that the principles of Roman and natural law differed from those of customary law.[43] Both traditions may have been concerned to "mirror" nature, but the question is, which nature is of primary interest? Is it the nature that mirrors the geometrical laws ruling the universe? Or is it the organic nature of the earth, a nature that is constantly growing and changing like the laws of custom? Art, in the Italian tradition, is constructed architecturally upon the basis of a rational, lawful framework that is not unlike the principles of Roman and natural statutory law. Customary law, on the other hand, is built up through a process of development based upon the precedence, detail by detail, of particular concrete cases. The layered development of customary law is not unlike the principles used to create landscape art north of the Alps, as elucidated by the art historian E. H. Gombrich using the example of the early-fifteenth-century artist Jan van Eyck:

> The southern artists of his generation, the Florentine masters of Brunelleschi's circle, had developed a method by which nature could be represented in a picture with almost scientific accuracy. They began with the framework of perspective lines, and they built up the human body through their knowledge of anatomy and the laws of foreshortening. Van Eyck took the opposite way. He achieved the illusion of nature by patiently adding detail upon detail till his whole picture became like a mirror of the visible world. (1972, 178–79)

The art historian Arthur Wheelock describes a similar shaping process at work in seventeenth-century Dutch paintings such as those of Johannes (or Jan) Vermeer: "His space is determined empirically by overlapping forms rather than by orthogonal projections. Similar compositional devices are evident in paintings by the Utrecht *Caravaggisti,* in some church interiors by Saenredam, and to a certain extent in those by Houckgeest and de Witte." Vermeer developed this mode of representation as part of his "continual search for a means of expressing the interaction of a figure and his environment." The end result was that "in the subtle balance and internal logic of his best compositions, [Vermeer] managed to create a sense of space for his figures without forcing the observer to view them from a single vantage point or at a single instant" (Wheelock 1977, 274, 282, 327). Thus, though the painters of the Low Countries had been exposed to the geometrical theories of perspective developed by the Italians, many opted, in the end, to develop new techniques that were better suited to the landscape depiction of their homelands.

A distinction between artists north and south of the Alps is also drawn by Svetlana Alpers, an art historian who notes how, by the seventeenth century, the Dutch concern with landscape was tied to descriptive regional geography, or chorography. "Pictures in the north," she argues, "were related to graphic description rather than to rhetorical persuasion, as was the case with pictures in Italy" (1983, 136; see also Edgerton 1975, 86). The Italians were inspired by the ideal visions of the natural, pastoral *locus amoenus,* or beautiful location, of classical literature, just as they were inspired by the ideal forms of classical architecture (Turner 1966, 39, 212). "Northern mapmakers and artists," Alpers contends, "persisted in conceiving of a picture as

Fig. 1.10. Illustration from Albrecht Dürer, *Underweyssung der Messung* (Nuremberg, 1538). The male draughtsman is using the techniques of surveying to create an illusion of three dimensional, bodily space, as represented by a woman.

a surface on which to set forth or inscribe the world rather than as a stage for significant human action" (1983, 137). This would also appear to be the way landscape painting was conceptualized by contemporary English practitioners of the art, such as Peacham. He wrote: "Lantskip is a Dutch [i.e., Germanic] word, & it is as much as wee shoulde say in English landship, or expressing of the land by hills, woodes, Castles, seas, valleys, ruines, hanging rocks, Citties, Townes, &c." (quoted in Ogden and Ogden 1955, 5).[44] The difference between the approaches of the artists of the Netherlands and those of Italy, according to Alpers, is a result of the difference between the Albertian perspective, which "posits a viewer at a certain distance looking through a framed window to a putative substitute world," and the Dutch distance-point perspective, which "conceived of the picture as a flat working surface, unframed, on which the world is inscribed" (1983, 138).

The difference between art north and south of the Alps was apparent to contemporaries, as this disparaging comment on "landscape" art from the Low Countries, attributed to Michelangelo, illustrates: "It will appeal to [those] who have no sense of true harmony. In Flanders they paint with a view to external exactness. . . . They paint stuffs and masonry, the green grass of the fields, the shadow of trees, and rivers and bridges, which they call landscapes, with many figures on this side and many figures on that. And all this, though it pleases some persons, is done without reason or art, without symmetry or proportion" (quoted Alpers 1983, xxiii). This "landscape" art represented Landschaft as place and polity, rather than as ideal scenes structured by a geometrically harmonious space.

Fig. 1.11. The Italianate penchant for idealized scenes inspired by classical sources reached a climax in the work of the French artist Claude Lorrain, as exemplified by this sketch for a painting titled *Landscape with Mercury and Argus* (ca. 1660). Courtesy of the Trustees of the British Museum.

Landschaft painting was imbued with meanings, inscribed by custom in the land, which were at the heart of the major political, legal, and cultural issues of the time. The emergence at this time of a genre of "landscape" painting can thus be seen as part of a process by which the members of the non-noble estates of emerging states sought to establish a cultural identity as an active, politically engaged, and patriotic citizenry. The importance of community and law was particularly critical for the people of the European lowlands who, in the seventeenth century, had to battle both the sea and jealous feudal overlords (Clark 1946, 195–97). This helps explain the popularity of paintings of familiar home environments amongst the burghers and farmers who are pictured recreating together—skating, for example, on a common pond (Alpers 1983, 148–51; Schama 1987a, 71–72; Schama 1987b). Such scenes may have been informed by classical and Renaissance Italian idealizations of the rural pastoral, but they generally expressed the workaday life and customs of a northern European Landschaft (Olwig [1983] 1987; Cafritz 1988; Newman 1990).

CONCLUSION: KING JAMES AND THE NEW AGE

We have now seen that idea of landscape as a representation of the country was at the heart of a complex European conflict concerning the relative strength of the lord or monarch and representative legal bodies such as Parliament. The way one represented landscape was related to one's situation with relation to those conflicting legal, governmental, and social ideals. James's visit to Denmark brought him to an area where these conflicts were manifest, and it is clear that his visit informed his conception of his ideal role as a monarch in the new age of a reborn Britain. The tensions between lord and Landschaft, like those between court and country, tended to separate the two and thereby create an awareness of their differences and separate identities as representatives of the land or country. This awareness in turn created an awareness of the very idea of representation, in which something stands for something else. The representation of the Landschaft could take place in a representative legal body, in a written "mirror" of the law like the *Sachsenspiegel,* or it could take place through cartography and the arts. The nature of the Landschaft was open to contestation. Queen Anne's theater-minded brother-in-law, Duke Heinrich Julius of Braunschweig-Wülfenbüttel, thus ruled over an area in which the dukes appear to have actively sought to cultivate the idea of the Landschaft, or country, as an abstract commonwealth of interests under their overall guardianship. They did this in order to avoid a situation in which the Landtag, the representative body of the estates, could establish itself as the legitimate representative of the entire Landschaft as a political community (Benecke 1974, 109–23).[45]

The principles according to which Landschaft was represented in the arts clearly had implications for the way in which the political community of the Landschaft was conceptualized. When James VI went to the duke's Danish wedding, he would have been exposed to both the duke's and the king's use of theater and spectacle to promote an image of themselves as the legitimate representatives of the interests of their lands. James and Anne's wedding, as well as that of the Duke, were lavish affairs where various international forms of theater and spectacle would have been presented, including, in all likelihood, performances by James's new brother-in-law's English theater troupe.[46] Such theatrical presentations made it possible for a lord to present himself as the representative of the larger interests of the land over which he ruled. When James returned to Britain, he brought with him a queen whose family was skilled in the art of representing the lord or king as the embodiment of his land. When the resources of the English crown became available to her, Anne knew how to use them. Anne brought with her to England a cosmopolitan royal concept of Landschaft as the scenic setting of the state; the Stuart court then mobilized this concept in its increasing confrontations with the "country."

## Science and Natural Law

One of the people James most wanted to visit while in Denmark was the astronomer, cartographer, and astrologer Tycho Brahe, an irascible silver-nosed nobleman (he lost his nose in a duel) who was perhaps the most prestigious scientist in Europe at the time. Brahe inhabited a Renaissance fantasy palace, Uranienborg, with a professionally staffed and well-equipped underground observatory, Stjerneborg, located on a small island off the Danish coast. James arrived, according to Brahe's notes, at eight o'-clock in the morning on March 20, 1590, and stayed until three (Thoren 1990, 334). Brahe's breakthrough as a scientist had come with his discovery in 1572 of what he convincingly pronounced to be a new star (which, after a blaze of glory, subsequently faded from the skies). This was a momentous event because the heavens were then thought to be the immutable realm of celestial law, and stars were not supposed to come and go. The previous recorded sighting of such a star was by Hipparchus, some 125 years before the Christian era; it was generally seen in the Renaissance to have been a sign of the spiritual and political decline of the Jews and the transfer of Mediterranean hegemony from Greece to Rome. Brahe predicted that equally momentous political, legal, and religious changes would follow the appearance of the new star. These millenarian ideas were further strengthened by Brahe's 1577 discovery of a new comet, which led him to believe that the renaissance of the golden age of classical and biblical myth might soon be at hand (Thoren 1990, 40–73, 123, 131).

Brahe's work fostered millenarian speculation not only because the new star raised questions about the immutability of the heavens, but also because the comet smashed through the crystalline spheres which, according to Aristotelian tradition, were supposed to support the planets in their orbits. The demolition of the imagined barrier between the supposedly immutable realm of heavenly law and the changing temporal realm of the earth had revolutionary theoretical implications comparable in scope to those of Copernicus's theory of heliocentrism (which Brahe did not believe in) (Spitzer 1948, 246; Kuhn 1957, 201, 205–6). This breakthrough turned the scientific world on end by implying that the same timeless laws that governed the heavens might also govern the earth.

## James's Revelation

In Copenhagen, there was much to open James VI's mind concerning the potential power and glory of a modern monarch. His own great dream was to be king not only of Scotland, but also of England and all of Britain. This would mean a new British age under the law of a new Stuart dynasty born at the turn of a new century. The astronomy and astrology of Tycho Brahe would have given him every reason to believe that such a new age was at hand. He had seen the outlines of this new age, furthermore, in Denmark itself. Here it was not the old law of custom that governed, but statutory law based on rational principle. In a 1616 speech to the assembled judges of England in the Star Chamber, James held up Denmark as a shining example for them to behold:

> But in Countreys where the formalitie of Law hath no place, as in Denmarke, which I may trewly report, as hauing my selfe beene an eyewitnesse thereof; all their State is gourned onely by a written Law; there is no Aduocate or Proctour admitted to plead, onley the parties themselues plead their owne cause, and then a man stands vp and reads the Law, and there is an end, for the very Law-booke it selfe is their onely Iudge. Happy were all Kingdomes if they could be so: But heere [in England], curious wits, various conceits, different actions, and varietie of examples breed question in Law. (James I [1616] 1918b, 332, emphasis in original)[47]

James eventually realized his dream of becoming the monarch of both Scotland and England. He met with resistance, however, and he never became the monarch of a united British kingdom. Parliament saw itself as representing the "country" of England, much as representative bodies in Germanic countries saw themselves as representing the Landschaften. It was in this context that James and Anne sought to mobilize the power of theater to represent their vision of Stuart Britain. Later in the century this came to be known as a conflict between the court and the country. It is tempting to reify this conflict as one between an urban court and the rural countryside, but the heart of the conflict was ultimately between differing ideals of polity. The future meaning of landscape was shaped by this contention.

# Two

# Country and Landscape

*Representation* can refer to an image or likeness (as in art) or to political representation. The foregoing chapter explored the overlapping of these two meanings in the context of continental conflicts between proponents of the autocratic power of the prince or king, on the one hand, and those of representational forms of government, on the other. The key issue was the legitimate representation of the Landschaft as a polity. This chapter provides the basis for comprehending similar forms of contestation as they apply to England and America by examining the parallels between the Anglo-American understanding of *country* and the continental understanding of *Landschaft*.

## ENGLISH AND "NEW ENGLISH" IDEAS OF COUNTRY

One of the "crimes" of the British king enumerated in the Declaration of Independence of the Thirteen United States of America is the forcing of "our fellow Citizens . . . to bear Arms against their *Country,* to become the executioners of their friends and Brethren" (emphasis in original). Prior to its independence, the United States was thus already a "country." The idea that country had precedence over duty to the British king came, ironically, from the English against whom the colonists were revolting.[1] In England, a century earlier, the same idea had been used by the English to help justify revolution against their monarch. Clearly, there is more to the meaning of country than simply a rural scene, with amber waves of grain framed by purple mountains' majesties (Bates [1895] 1974). The country of "my country 'tis of thee" was not simply a *land*scape scene, but "a sweet *land* of liberty" (Smith [1831] 1974, emphasis added).

The immediate reason why *country* was part of the vocabulary of the American revolutionaries was that they were inspired by the ideas and rhetoric of the Englishmen who had revolted, in the name of Parliament, against the Stuart kings in the mid-seventeenth century (Zagorin 1969, 5–7). During the period of seventeenth-century political turmoil, the notion of country provided the basis for a polarization between what later in the century became known as the "party of the court" and the "party of the country" (ibid., 19–39). According to the historian Perez Zagorin, "the Country" was "the label most commonly applied to the opposition to the crown before the civil war." Other terms, such as *patriots* and *parliamentarians,* were occasionally employed, but by the 1620s, *country* was current, and it was in wide use at the commencement of Charles I's reign (ibid., 33). By the mid-eighteenth century, when the American Revolution had begun to brew, it had become possible to speak, with Lord Bolingbroke, of "the voice of the country," a voice which "must be formed on principles of common interest. It cannot be united and maintained on the particular prejudices . . . or . . . particular interest of any set of men whatsoever. It is the nation, speaking and acting in the discourse and conduct of particular men . . . " (quoted in ibid., 38). It was this idea of country that the American revolutionaries were defending against the autocratic rule of their British overlords.

## ENGLAND—THE COUNTRY OF THE ENGLISH

King James fulfilled his dream of becoming the king of both Scotland and England in 1603, but this did not make him, as he had hoped, the monarch of a politically united "Britain." The English parliament steadfastly refused to go along with James on this, and a century went by before the union of kingdoms as "Great Britain" became a Parliament-sanctioned reality. The country of England, in the eyes of Parliament, was manifested as a polity through its representation by Parliament, as legitimated by age-old rights of custom. Parliament would not have this same legitimacy with regard to the amalgamated body politic of Britain since there was no precedent by which the English parliament could claim a customary right to represent a country such as Scotland. The legal prerogative of the monarch to rule according to his statutory law would be correspondingly greater, however, in a united Britain, because the monarch was legally entitled to rule in both countries. This conflict between James and Parliament concerning the legitimate right to represent the country thus resembled the conflict between lord and Landschaft explored in the previous chapter.

Country occupied a semantic space in the English language similar to that of *Landschaft* and its root *Land* in the languages of Alpine and northwestern Europe.[2] *Land* is commonly translated directly as country (Langenscheidt 1967: land). The words can be used synonymously in English, as in: "England is the land/country of the English." The terms *land* and *country* were also applied to English counties, as in Westmorland. The word *Landschaft* is likewise often translated as country, as well as region or province (Langenscheidt 1967: Landschaft; Benecke 1974, 109–23). As was seen in chapter 1, the perception of a Landschaft such as Dithmarschen as a distinct *Land* or country was, in great measure, a question of perspective. The Danish king saw this Landschaft as a province, or region, which should be under his rule, whereas the Dithmarschers tended to see their homeland more as their particular land or country. It will be seen that James adopted a similar attitude toward Scotland, seeing it as a province of Britain, whereas the English parliament tended to oppose it to England as a separate country. Chapter 3 is concerned with how the Stuart court mobilized the use of the idea of landscape as scenery in order to help counter the ideological power of the Parliament as the customary representative of the country. The present chapter paves the way by focusing upon the meaning which the concept of country attained in the political landscape of England and, by extension, in that of England's American colonies.

## COUNTRY, COMMUNITY, AND COMMONWEALTH

As early as the time of the Tudors, as a result of the growth of Parliament, the concept of country had become fused with the general idea of representation of the public interest. An expression of this feeling is found in the words of John Poynet, the bishop of Winchester in the early sixteenth century, who wrote: "Men ought to have more respect to their country than to their prince, to the commonwealth than to any one person. For the country and the commonwealth is a degree above the king" (quoted in Kohn 1940, 71).

The words *country* and *county* had long been used interchangeably at the time when country became identified with the rights of Parliament (Zagorin 1969, 33; OED: country 2).[3] Members of the House of Commons talked, in this spirit, of their duty to the "Countries" or "Country," meaning the county which they represented (Zagorin 1969, 33). They meant representation in the abstract because, unlike the members of the upper house, not every commoner with right to representation in the House of Commons had an individual right to be present. When parliamentary representation ceases to be direct, it gives rise to a more abstract conception of representation. The House of Commons, as James I explained, is "composed of Knights for the Shire; and Gentry, and Burgesses for the Townes. But because the number would be infinite for all the Gentlemen and Burgesses to bee present at euery Parliament, Therefore a certaine number is selected and chosen out of that great Body, seruing onely for that Parliament, where their persons are the representation of the Body. Now the matters whereof they are to treate ought therefore to be generall . . ." (James I [1616] 1918a, 287–88).[4]

In a time of crisis this legal principle of general representation could take on an even more abstract character. When it was discovered in 1604 that Guy Fawkes had placed a large store of gunpowder under the House of Parliament, for example, an agitated King James I exclaimed to the as-sembled MPs (members of Parliament): "these wretches thought to haue blowen vp in a manner the whole world of this Island, euery man being now commen vp here" (James I [1616] 1918a, 286). Thus, the parlia-mentarians represented not just their particular "countries" but also the sum of the countries that made up the more abstract "community of the English realm" (*communitas regni Angliae*). It was the parliamentarians who (together with the king) constituted this commonwealth, and with it, the country of England (Brunner [1965] 1992, 349). The word *country,* like the words *land* and *Landschaft* explored in the previous chapter, could thus be used at a variety of levels. At one level it could be identified with the county, and at another with the entire English "commonwealth": a country founded on law and united by compact or tacit agreement of the people for the common good (commonweal) (WC7: commonwealth). The ability of Englishmen to identify with the notion of country/landscape at a variety of nested levels is illustrated by the words of an MP who, in 1628, proclaimed: "I speak . . . not for myself, that's too narrow. . . . It is not for the country for which I serve. It is not for us all and the country which we represent, but for the ancient glory of the ancient laws of England" (quoted in Holmes 1979–80, 70).

The English used *landscape* as well as *country* in an abstract represen-tational sense. Ben Jonson's Scottish friend William Drummond of Hawthornden, a poet and jurist, used landscape in this way, I believe, when he condemned the parliamentarian executors of Charles I for hav-ing created "new Magistracies, offices of State, imaginarie and fantasticall counsilles, landskippes of Common Wealthes" (Drummond [1638] 1976, 181).[5] Landscape still held this encompassing meaning a half century later when the author John Hacket named London the quintessential "Land-skip" of England: "*London,* which, as you know, is . . . our *England* of *England,* and our Landskip and Representation of the whole Island. For here strangers no sooner arrive but they first take unto themselves, and then vent abroad unto others, a Scantling and Platform of the *British* Gov-ernment, as well in Matters concerning the Church, as in those that touch upon the State, and Commonwealth" (Hacket 1693, pt. 2, 59, emphasis in original).

In principle, it was the king in Parliament who represented the country, not the Parliament minus the king. The problem lay in determining the balance of power between king and Parliament. James I was careful to give the impression that he respected the basic principle of parliamentary representation—which he struggled to comprehend (see, for example James I [1599] 1969, 33). James, however, made sure to let the parliamentarians know that he held the ultimate authority. In a "discourse" on "the trew nature and definition of a Parliament," given after three years of on-the-job experience, the king pointed out to the assembled MPs that even though the parliamentary body represented the body of the people, he was the head of that body, and his head gave expression to the laws of God and Nature (James I [1616] 1918a, 286–87). He went on to exhort the parliamentarians to "remember that they are there [in Parliament] as sworne Councellours to their King, to giue their best aduise for the furtherance of his Seruice, and the florishing Weale of his Estate" (ibid., 288).

As James well knew, contemporary opinion about the constitution of English political society was divided. There were those who argued that the foundation of English law was not the statutes of the king, but the customary laws of the country as it was represented in Parliament. For them, the office of the king was constituted through Parliament, and not vice versa (McIlwain 1918, xxxiii–xlv). The king, of course, held the opposite view. It was through the developing conflicts between court and Parliament that modern abstract constitutional principles of representative government, in which the office of the executive body is distinguished from the body of the person executing that office, began to emerge. It then became possible for the continuity of the position of king, or the office of president, to be retained even when a new leader of the executive branch of government was elected.

## COUNTRY AND THE PLACE OF LOCAL COMMUNITY

When a frightened King James I, after the discovery of the Gunpowder Plot, exhorted the MPs to hasten home to their "charges" in "your Countreys," he did not mean that they should return to the rural countryside (James I [1616] 1918a, 289). These MPs also included "Burgesses for the Townes." James did not define the country as the opposite of the city, as we commonly do today. Instead, he contrasted the country as the place represented in Parliament with the capital, London, as the setting where this representation was periodically constituted under his headship. Thus, he urged the MPs to return home because when the MPs were in London "the Countrey by the foresaid occassions is in a manner left desolate, and waste vnto them," and this meant that the "rebels" would be free to "wander through the Countrey" (Ibid., 286). This notion of country, however, did incorporate a latent contradiction between the city of London as the seat of court power and the country as the body politic governed by the capital (head city) of London.[6]

From the twelfth to the fourteenth centuries, the term *country* was applied in England to a jury summoned from the neighborhood (or "hundred") to decide some question debated between litigants who had formally agreed to be bound by their decision. The issue was then said to be tried by the neighborhood or the "country" (OED: country). The phrase "trial by country" is still used in England. *Country* could thus be used for a body of jurors or for the neighborhood community to which they belonged, as well as to the territory in which they dwelled. In this respect, it  resembled *Landschaft,* which could be applied to a deliberative representative body with legal court functions, such as the *thing* (to use the English spelling). These smaller English country communities were part of the larger unit of the shire or county to which, as has been seen, the name *country* could also be applied. This usage is again comparable to the Germanic Landschaft or -land, which shows up in shire names such as Westmoreland. Both before and after the Norman Conquest, the shire and its legal subunit, the hundred, were, to quote a legal historian, the "primary government of England" (Milsom 1981, 13). At the time of the Stuarts the role of the county/country (shire) as a locus of legal and community identity was well developed, though this did not necessarily exclude a broader identification with the larger country of Eng*land,* or a more exclusive identification with smaller country communities (see Butlin 1978; Everitt 1979; Holmes 1979–80). This was also a time, however, when the growing power of propertied yeoman farmers and squires was creating a more hierarchical form of rural society which, together with the growth of rural manufacturing industry, threatened established ideals of community solidarity (Underdown 1985, 9–43).

Like *country,* the earliest English meaning of *county* was not territorial, but judicial. It was used to refer to "the periodical meeting, convention, or court held under the sheriff for the transaction of the business of the shire, the shire-moot, shire-court, county-court" (OED: county 4).[7] Thus it was the community constituted by the operation of the court that defined the area thereafter known as the shire or county/country, much as the jurisdiction of the Landschaft as one with its *thing* defined the area of the Landschaft as place. The term *county,* then, could be used to refer to one's local community as well as to a larger political unit which, though it might be subordinated to a central monarch, nevertheless possessed a certain amount of autonomy and had its own political identity. The customary law generated by the courts of the county was, in the words of a legal historian, the expression of "communities whose geographic boundaries had in some cases divided peoples and cultures, and not just areas of governmental authority. But within each body of custom, what we think of as the law was not marked off from other aspects of society. Courts were the governing bodies of their communities, dealing with all their public business; and to us they would look more like public meetings than courts of law" (Milsom 1981, 12). Here again, the parallels to the Germanic institution of the *thing* are noteworthy.

The fact that some shires were also known as "land" (e.g., Westmorland) or "folk" (e.g., Suffolk) suggests their past autonomy (OED: county 2).[8] Such terms call forth memories of counties which were once separate countries, in the sense of country as "a region once independent and still distinct in race, language, institutions or historical memories, as England, Scotland and Ireland in the United Kingdom" (OED: country 7). King James I saw the amalgamation of once-independent countries or lands into subunits of progressively larger states as an ongoing process that would soon lead to the creation of the unified state of Britain. The subjection of Scotland to England, according to a 1607 speech by James to Parliament, would thus mean that Scotland would "with time become but as Cumberland and Northumberland, and those other remote and Northerne Shires." Scotland and the "other Northerne Countreys" would be "seldome seene and saluted by their King, and that as it were but in a posting or hunting ioruney" (James I [1616] 1918c, 294).

The decentralized framework of legal communities identified with the idea of country and countyprovided, according to Marc Bloch, a basis for the development of a central parliamentary institution: "[it was] within the framework of the county, mainly, but also in the more restricted sphere of the hundred, that the most vital elements in the nation preserved the habit of meeting to determine the customary law of the territorial group. . . . And so it continued till the time when, summoned to meet as one body, the representatives of the shire courts formed the earliest nucleus of what was later to be the House of Commons" (Bloch [1940] 1961, 371).

The opposition between the urban London court and the country was not, thus, a simple spatial opposition, but an opposition between different conceptions of legitimate government (Zagorin 1969, 41).[9] This idea of the country as the ultimate source of representative government is preserved today in the phrase "going to the country," which is used in connection with the calling of a British national election (Williams 1976: country).

The idea of country signified a legally defined political community, or polity. This community, however, was not homogeneous, but included different social groups or "estates." The transformations in the idea of country that are traced in this book are thus paralleled by similar transformations in the meaning of *estate*.

COUNTRY AND ESTATE

Representation in the parliaments of Europe was based on one's estate or status. The *Oxford English Dictionary* defines *estate* as "An order or class regarded as part of the body politic, and as such participating in the government either directly or through its representatives." The term is also applied to the assembly of these estates. England had three estates represented in Parliament: the Lords Spiritual, the Lords Temporal, and the Commons (which represented the communities of the shires and the towns) (OED: estate). One's estate, or status, was not a consequence of land ownership. One could not become a lord simply by acquiring property in land. It was not until the late eighteenth century that it became common to use the word *estate* in its predominant modern meaning of a landed property (OED: estate 13). Inheritable rights in the land, as guaranteed by customary and common law, were, however, of importance to the rising power of a rural gentry, who saw themselves as the representatives of the rights of "the country" in the House of Commons (Pocock 1957, 124–47; 1972, 211–13).

The rise of the institution of Parliament was related to the increasing economic importance of those who had established rights in the land. By the end of the sixteenth century, the society of the country, which encompassed both towns and their rural surroundings, was characterized by a social mobility which had placed increasing amounts of land in the hands of country squires and yeoman farmers. By 1640 the middle and lesser gentry are believed to have held about half of the land in England and Wales (Zagorin 1969, 21; Bunce 1994, 6–8). When the monarchs of sixteenth- and seventeenth-century England, like those elsewhere in Europe, needed money to fund the ever more expensive machinery of war, they knew where to find the it—in the hands of the burgesses and the landed gentry. To legitimize the taxation of this money they called national parliaments, and this, in turn, strengthened the bargaining position and status of Parliament. In Britain, this eventually led to a power struggle between court and Parliament that ended in the revolt against Charles I. When Americans later argued that they had a right to refuse taxation without representation, they were following good English precedent. The idea of country upon which Parliament legitimated its position was fundamentally legal and institutional. It takes more than legal and institutional principle, however, to motivate a revolution in which people risk their lives for a cause. The power of the idea of country lay in the way it embodied the memory of the rights that constituted people's place and community identity.

CUSTOM, COMMUNITY, AND MEMORY

The American Declaration of Independence argued that it was not acceptable that Americans were being forced "to bear Arms against their *Country*," that is, against their "friends and Brethren." The Declaration gives an indication of the kinds of subjective factors that can motivate a populace to take arms. The power of the idea of country was linked in great measure to its ability to call forth images of a community of friends and brethren. The defense of country was the defense of this community and the memories and customs binding it. The idea of country as a legal community has long antecedents rooted in the principles of customary law.

According to Sir Edward Coke, who became a chief justice in 1606, and who was the great ideologue of the parliamentarian countrymen, there are "two pillars" for customs: common usage and "time out of mind."[10] Customs, for Coke, "are defined to be a law or right not written; which, being established by long use and the consent of our ancestors, hath been and is daily practiced" (quoted in Thompson 1993, 97, 128–129). Customary law thus involves a form of collective memory formed by daily usage but then projected back to a quasi-mythical time out of mind.

Sir John Davies, then attorney general for Ireland, explicated the role of memory in the generation of customary law in 1612:

> For the *Common Law* of *England* is nothing else but the *Common Custome* of the Realm; and a Custome which hath obtained the force of a Law is always said to be *Jus non scriptum*: for it cannot be made or created either by Charter, or by Parliament, which are Acts reduced to writing, and are alwaies matter of Record; but being onely matter of fact, and consisting in use and practice, it can be recorded and registered no-where but in the memory of the people.

This memory is based upon a principle of continued repetition by which the law becomes one with the people, as Davies puts it: "For a Custome taketh beginning and groweth to perfection in this manner: When a reasonable act once done is found to be good and beneficiall to the people, and agreeable to their nature and disposition, then do they use it and practise it again and again, and so by often iteration and multiplication of the act it becometh a *Custome;* and being continued without interruption time out of mind, it obtaineth the force of a *Law.*" Customary law, for Davies, is peculiarly English because of the way it is generated. It contrasts, therefore, with bodies of law derived from classical tradition. Such custom-based law, according to Davies, "doth demonstrate the strength of wit and reason and self-sufficiency which has been always in the People of this land, which have made their own Laws out of their wisedome and experience, . . . not begging or borrowing a form of a Commonweal, either from *Rome* or from *Greece*, as all other Nations of *Europe* have done; but having sufficient provision of law and justice within the Land" (quoted in Pocock 1957, 32–33, emphasis in original).[11] It is these "ancient and excellent laws of England," according to Coke (whose use of "country" is synonymous with Davies' use of "land"), which "are the birthright and the most ancient and best inheritance that the subjects of this realm have; for by them he enjoyeth not only his inheritance and goods in peace and quietness, but his liberty and his most dear country in safety" (quoted in Hill 1958, 65).

It is a paradox of customary law that, though it is ostensibly rooted in ancient precedent, it is also constantly being updated.[12] Eric Hobsbawm has explained the logic of this mode of thought by comparing it to a motor and flywheel: "'Custom' in traditional societies has the double function of motor and fly-wheel. It does not preclude innovation and change up to a point, though evidently the requirement that it must appear compatible or even identical with precedent imposes substantial limitations on it. What it does is to give any desired change (or resistance to innovation) the sanction of precedent, social continuity and natural law as expressed in history" (1983, 2). The remembrance of custom is fundamentally flexible. "The human memory," according to historian Marc Bloch, "is a marvelous instrument of elimination and transformation—especially what we call collective memory" (Bloch [1940] 1961, 114; see also Lowenthal 1985, 206–10).

The force of law generated by memory through time provided the basis by which it was possible to defend the prerogatives of the country and its customary law against the edicts of the royal court. One of those prerogatives, it was thought, was the right of the country to parliamentary representation in situations where, for example, the king wished to impose taxes upon the people of the country. Taxation should not be undertaken without representation. The belief in these customary privileges formed what was known as "the ancient constitution," a body of legal principles which were thought to have largely predated the Norman invasion and which had been reaffirmed in documents like the Magna Charta. When Americans placed great store upon the role of a constitution in constituting a country, they were using an idea that was thoroughly rooted in English ideas of country.

ROMAN LAW VERSUS CUSTOMARY LAW

Davies and Coke did their legal philosophizing on custom at a time of intense interest in "the ancient constitutions" of the northern Europeans

(Pocock 1957). "Constitution" did not mean a written document, but rather the legal principles embodied in customary northwestern European law. This was an era that sought alternatives not only to the universalism of the Roman Catholic Church but also to the universalism of the written, codified, Roman law that the church had reintroduced to European society. Brilliant jurists, such as the sixteenth-century Huguenot François Hotman, argued that customary law, though rooted in the ancient precedent of time out of mind, was in fact always up-to-date because custom was constantly being reinterpreted in the light of present circumstances. Roman law, on the other hand, though it pretended to be universal in scope, was in fact an expression of the time and society which had created it (Hotman [1573] 1972; Pocock 1957, 14–29; Giesey and Salmon 1972).

The study of customary law did not only help to create an interest in historical change; it also legitimated those representative local and national institutions, such as Parliament, which were believed to have helped generate that law (Hotman [1573] 1972).[13] The search during Hotman's day for the ancient constitution led to the search for the roots of the north European ancient past as preserved in the *Germania* by the Roman historian Tacitus, a work that had been rediscovered in 1425 and published in 1470 (Tacitus 1948; Strauss 1959, 10, 31; Schama 1995, 75–100). This search also led to the politically peripheral regions of feudal Europe, such as the Netherlands and Switzerland, where these ancient institutions appeared to have been best preserved. One such institution was that of common land, in which customary law governed use rights. The feudal lord did not possess the land as property, as was the case under the Roman law concept of *possessio* (Tacitus 1942, 721, sect. 26; Bloch [1940] 1961, 116; Gurevich 1977, 6; Milsom 1981, 119–51). Feudal ties to the lands under the lord's domain were through interpersonal relations of fealty (Gurevich 1985, 91), whereas the customary law, which guaranteed access to the commons, was the expression of particular local and national communities.

The linking of the origins of the "ancient constitution" to the peoples north of Italy described by Tacitus provided the basis for contrasting a supposedly despotic Roman South with a supposedly free Germanic North. Tacitus counterposed the ideal qualities of the northern peoples to the corruption of his Roman countrymen as a means of criticizing Roman society. This polarized portrait of Europe was welcomed by the Renaissance descendants of Tacitus's northern peoples. This was a time when the peoples of the north felt culturally inferior to the Italians, supposed to be descendants of the Romans. The northerners were, as the Italians liked to remind them, descendants of the barbarians who had destroyed classical civilization. Tacitus provided an antidote to this accusation by making the northerners out to be the sort of people who could rescue the world from southern corruption. Tacitus's rhetorical counterposition of North and South then became mythologized as "fact" (Kliger 1947, 1952; Strauss 1959, 10, 31). This tendency to mythologize the role of custom in counterposing northern and southern Europe was strengthened by the way in which defenders of customary law legitimated it in terms of a principle of precedent that could be traced back to an ancient time out of mind. In practice, time out of mind may not, in fact, involve the memory of more than a generation, but its moral authority is premised upon its seeming to be of ancient origin. In times of conflict this mode of thought has a tendency to legitimize and make absolute the principles of custom by making a myth of their origin (Pocock 1957, 19, 22, 42–55, 64).[14] This mythologizing tendency focused interest upon the links between the origins of parliamentarianism and the peoples of northwestern Europe. As will be seen, the idea of the Anglo-Saxon origins of the ancient English constitution attained, as a result, a particular political (as opposed to racial) potency. This idea, in turn, was eventually to play a role in constituting the American identification with Anglo-Saxon values.

The American revolutionaries were quite taken by the notion of the ancient Saxon origins of representative government and law that were promoted by the parliamentarians. Thomas Jefferson even sought to learn the language of the Anglo-Saxons in order to get a better grasp of their judicial and political principles (Gossett 1963, 87). Modern scholarship owes a great deal to the seventeenth-century English scholars who, motivated by their political and religious beliefs, helped found modern historical scholarship in the area of law during the Anglo-Saxon era (Holdsworth 1928; Douglas 1939; Pocock 1957; Parry 1995). The leaders of the new American republic, like their revolutionary English forebears, took a scholarly interest in law and history.

Though the idea that English legal institutions rooted in custom had descended from the Anglo-Saxons and Vikings played an important part in both English and American political thinking, one should be wary, however, of overemphasizing the polarity between northern and southern Europe. *England* may have meant land of the Angles, but before the arrival of the Anglo-Saxons, *Britain* had a long history that included the Britons and the Romans and a legal tradition influenced by Roman legal ideas. In classical Greece and Rome, as well as in Renaissance Italy, the distinction between empires built on natural law and countries founded on custom was long recognized. The Renaissance tendency to oppose and contrast these forms of law also had classical roots. The legal distinction can be traced, as seen in the previous chapter, at least back to Aristotle and the

Greek word *choros,* which expressed much the same meaning as *Land, Landschaft,* and *country.* It should also be noted that Renaissance Italy contained polities, such as Sienna and Venice, which were noted for their representative forms of government. The conflict between this form of government and the authority of a prince inspired pioneering reflections, such as those of Machiavelli, on the character of the state. Thus, alongside the English interest in Anglo-Saxon customary precedence for representative English legal bodies, there was also interest in both classical and Italian examples of such forms of government, particularly as represented by Venice (Pocock 1975).

The supposed Anglo-Saxon heritage of freedom, as usurped by the Norman "bastard" William, probably struck closer to the heart of the average seventeenth century Englishman than Greek or Italian precedent. For the landless as well as the landed, the idea of a past golden age prior to the "Norman yoke" exerted considerable appeal, and this myth helped cement an uneasy early-seventeenth-century alliance between social groupings with highly divergent visions of the ideal society. During this period the idea of throwing off the Norman yoke and returning to a state of preconquest political freedom went hand in hand with ideas deriving from an odd mixture of folklore, classical cosmology, and Christian eschatology (Hill 1958, 50–57; Ladner 1959, 30; Jacob and Lockwood 1972; Jacob 1976).

NATURE AND CUSTOMARY LAW

Both Parliament and the common law, according to Coke and other spokesmen for the country, had their origins in a pre-Norman era, prior to the introduction of a strong, centralized, hereditary monarchy (Pocock 1957, 19, 22, 42–69, 148–81; Hill 1958, 50–57). The work of Coke, however, was much more rooted in the history of actual English legal practice than it was in myths of a pre-Norman golden age. Customary law, as Coke was wont to say, was a "birthright" rooted in custom (quoted in Hill 1965, 257) This right was associated with a particular idea of nature (Hill 1958, 78–79) that had a well-established legal history and that was diametrically opposed to the idea of nature enshrined in the concept of natural law (see chapter 1). As Hotman wrote: "Just as our bodies, when dislocated by some external blow, cannot be repaired unless each member be restored to its natural seat and place, so we may trust that our commonwealth will return to health when it is restored by some act of divine beneficence into its ancient and, so to speak, its natural state" ([1573] 1972, 143).

This idea of nature is related to the concept of birth. The word *nature* has the same root as *nativity, native,* and *nation.* As the philosopher John Passmore explains it: "The word 'nature' derives, it should be remembered, from the Latin *nascere,* with such meanings as 'to be born,' to 'come into being.' Its etymology suggests, that is, the embryonic, the potential rather than the actual" (Passmore 1974, 32). Customary law is "natural" in this sense because, though it has its origins generations back in time, it is nevertheless in a constant state of renewal and growth. The attorney general for Ireland, Sir John Davies, illustrated this mode of thought when, in 1612, he praised English customary law as being "so framed and fitted to the nature and disposition of this people, as we may properly say it is connatural to the Nation, so as it cannot possibly be ruled by any other Law" (quoted in Pocock 1957, 33–34). This concept of nature does not dichotomize between nature and society, but rather sees them in terms of community relations that change through time.[15]

## COUNTRY AS THE PLACE OF COMMUNITY IDENTITY

The English opposition to Charles I and the American support for revolution against George III both had bases that extended well beyond the educated and landed classes. For the lower orders, the rule of customary law was of much more immediate importance than Parliament and its workings. The memory of custom embedded in the land was, for them, a living reality, and it continued to provide a limited bulwark against the power of both the old feudal nobility and the rising gentry.

"Custom," as Edward Coke put it in 1641, "lies upon the land"; that is, the customary law of the land binds the land (quoted in Thompson 1993, 97–98; see also Gurevich 1985, 157–59).[16] The land is bound by custom, but the land also binds the memory, which in turn is the bearer of custom. Land and custom thus bind each other through memory. Memory, as any schoolchild knows, can be reinforced through repetition. It also can be reinforced through attachment to objects, which then become mnemonic devices. This mode of thinking is regarded as particularly characteristic of children and the illiterate (Piaget 1973; Goody 1975; Goody 1977). Thus, when the members of an English parish have, since time immemorial, "beat the bounds" during Rogation week in May, and when this perambulation process involves standing children on their heads, or even striking them, at the site of a boundary marker so that they will remember the spot, we are dealing with a proven method of binding memory to place (Bushaway 1982, 25, 36, 81–86, 92, 99–100, 149; Thompson 1993, 98–100).[17]

Repeated, ritualized activities like beating the bounds formed the elements of what the historian E. Le Roy Ladurie has called a "symbolic gram-

Fig. 2.1. Anonymous illustration showing Reverend Thomas Wakefield and his parishioners breaking into Richmond Park. It shows villagers using the customary practice of beating the bounds to break down a barrier to their access to a commons which has been emparked. Frontispiece to *Two Historical Accounts of the Making of the New Forest and Richmond Park* (London, 1751). I am indebted to Stephen Daniels for this print.

mar" that was suited to a people who were, in his words, "spontaneous nominalists, better adapted to handling objects (maypole, sheep) as it saw fit than dealing with abstract concepts such as class struggle, reforms etc." (1980, 318). For the time out of mind of an adult who has had his head dunked as a child during Rogation week, the bounds of the village, and the social values attached to those bounds, will be fixed. In such rituals, "the medium," to use the words of the anthropologist Victor Turner (paraphrasing Marshall McLuhan), "is the message, and the medium is nonverbal, though often meticulously structured." It is "a way of inscribing in the mentalities of neophytes generative values, codes, and media" (Turner 1974, 240).[18] According to Marc Bloch, "Whether it was a question of particular transactions or of the general rules of customary law, memory was almost the sole guardian of tradition" (Bloch [1940] 1961, 114).

If a given area is a commons belonging to the people of the village, and if someone should claim that it is his private property, then the memory of a person who had been head-bumped during Rogation week might play an important legal role for the entire community. This form of memory is evident in the following disposition, which is from eighteenth-century England but is reminiscent of similar statements made in other time periods:

Gervas Knight . . . aged sixty seven yeares and upwards Maketh Oath
that ever since he can remember . . . he has known Farming Woods Walk
within the Forest of Rockingham . . . and says that ever since he was big
enough . . . viz. from about the yeare 1664 until about the yeare 1720 he
yearly or every two yeares . . . went with the Vicar and Parishioners of
Brigstock to perambulate publickly for the same Parish and thereby
make clayme of the Lands thereto belonging and to set forth their
bounds. (quoted in Thompson 1993, 98)

The custom of binding remembrance to the landscape is at the root of
the idea of justice upon which customary and, ultimately, common law is
founded. It is a long way, however, from the customs of a small community to ideologies that bind the imaginations of a people to the land of vast
states. In the end, however, these two dimensions of social existence must
necessarily link if a state is to function. At some point the abstract legal
and political principles that govern at the level of the state must touch
down at the local level and mesh with local practice. Custom, according
to the historian E. P. Thompson, is the interface between law and practice,
since it may be considered both "as praxis and as law" (ibid., 97). This, in
turn, means that there is an important link between customary law and the
habitude of culture, a link which creates a common identity (Thompson
1975, 102; Bourdieu 1977, 72–95). Custom is a formalization and ritualization of the habits that form the practice of human habitation. It is this
continuum between local custom and formalized law that makes possible
the successful development of a legal system based on common law. If law
does not express a reasonably shared system of values, it ultimately comes
to be viewed as unjust and becomes ineffective (Thompson 1975,
258–69). One of the factors which plays a role in linking this shared system of values is the idea that the system is based on fair play—if not, it is
just not cricket.

### JUSTICE AND THE GAMES PEOPLE PLAY

Customary law depends upon repetition. Rogation week rituals are effective because they are repeated every year. Games and play provide the
framework and the enticement for this repetition. "Fair play" is also basic to the shared sense of justice. Litigants must feel that they have had an
equal and fair chance if justice is to be done and reprisal is to be avoided.
The loser must be a good sport.

The Dutch historian Johan Huizinga, shortly before he was murdered
by the Nazis, managed to complete a provocative book called *Homo Ludens* on the play element in culture. One of his theses was that our concept
of law and justice originated in play. The court, to begin with, thus had

much in common with a cricket pitch or a tennis court. That is, it was a bounded space in which special rules, governed by respected judges, were held to apply (Huizinga 1955, 76–104). Huizinga's idea also brings to mind the fact that the ancient law courts of northwestern Europe were demarcated as places and times of hallowed peace. Weapons were forbidden, and accused criminals were allowed free entrance and egress. It was the peace of the court that guaranteed the peace and social harmony of the district under its jurisdiction—an idea which lingers in the title "justice of the peace" (Fenger 1993). This principle (and terminology) still functions with regard to the "safe" places where one can find refuge when playing tag, baseball, or cricket. It is the same principle that likewise applies to the corners of the ring, which guarantee that boxing matches do not degenerate into fights to the death.[19] The space of the court was expected to guarantee a justice that was right and just to all. In this respect, then, the court of justice, like a cricket court, creates a situation in which all are ostensibly equal before the rules of law. According to Huizinga, the court expressed another element of play besides competition according to rules—special costumes and special roles. Even today, the roles of the judge, jury, witnesses, and adversaries are defined by a set of rules, and the courtroom drama resembles theater.

Rituals like those of Rogation week were not only accompanied by games but also by pageants and plays, which also helped to maintain the memory of customary law (Malcolmson 1973, 112, chap. 4). A popular English sixteenth-century play, performed on the green adjacent to the church, was *Robin Hood*. Though Robin was an outlaw, the play, in which the youths of the village dressed up as Robin, Maid Marian, Little John, and so on, was sponsored by the community as a whole (including the priest) (Wiles 1981, 19, 56; Holt 1982, 159). Just as the law court turned an unegalitarian world on end by creating an ostensible situation of equal justice for all, so did the games and plays, which reinforced the practice of customary law. Plays like Robin Hood, in which an "outlaw" is the hero, turn the normal social world on end. All, even the corrupt sheriff who abuses the law, are subject to Robin's justice (see Malcolmson 1973, 81, 86; Hill 1975, 43, 47, 77; Wiles 1981, 51–58; Bushaway 1982, 135, 149). Ultimately, the repetition of these ritual games and plays had the effect of creating a place in which a feeling of community equality could develop within a world which was otherwise rent by social divisions and hierarchy (Turner 1974, 201; Thompson 1993, 182).

The development of a sense of community through carnivalistic rituals, games, and sports did not mean that community life was all idyllic fun and games. These activities were rooted, rather, in real legal conflicts related to the control of scarce resources. The games and sports could be as brutal as the conflicts. This brutality was recognized during the reign of the Tudors, when the representatives of a consolidating Protestant state sought to forbid such activities because they saw them as inherently subversive, and dour prelates denounced them as relics of heathen practices countenanced by the Catholics. Coke built his conception of English common law upon the precedent of legal custom as written in the land, but his Puritan allies in the fight for the rights of Parliament had little use for the associated customs identified with country sports. The Puritans identified such sports with paganism, Catholicism, and licentiousness (Marcus 1986, 214). James's court, however, took a different tack; it sought both to neutralize the force of these activities and to cultivate the favor of the broad mass of the population through its support of a courtly conception of Britain's traditional sports and pastimes. As Lea Marcus writes: "In his *Basilikon Doron,* even before he was anointed King of England, James had published his views as to the utility of the traditional customs in governing the lower orders." In order to allure them "to a common amitie among themselues," James declared that "certain dayes in the yeere would be appointed, for delighting the people with publicke spectacles" (quoted in Marcus 1986, 3). The Stuart court thus helped begin the process by which the vision of villagers dancing 'round a maypole has been reduced to a sentimentalized and harmless "traditional" country heritage.

## MASQUING CUSTOM AS HERITAGE

The rule of customary law was based on a notion of precedent rooted in a continuity with the past; the approach of the Stuart court to community and custom, however, made it possible, in effect, to reinvent custom in terms of what we now call "tradition" and "heritage." Custom is based upon the idea of "time out of mind" which, in practice, means that the past can be forgotten and reinterpreted according to the contemporary situation; as a result, custom gives a community possession of its past. Heritage, by contrast, creates a situation in which people become, as it were, possessed by a past which has been transformed into tradition (see Lowenthal 1985; 1996). The historian Eric Hobsbawm argues that tradition "must be distinguished clearly from 'custom' which dominates so-called 'traditional' societies":

> The object and characteristic of "traditions," including invented ones, is invariance. . . . "Custom" cannot afford to be invariant, because even in "traditional" societies life is not so. Customary or common law still shows this combination of flexibility in substance and formal adherence

to precedent. The difference between "tradition" and "custom" in our sense is indeed well illustrated here. "Custom" is what judges do; "tradition" (in this instance invented tradition) is the wig, robe and other formal paraphernalia and ritualized practices surrounding their substantial action. . . . Inventing traditions, it is assumed here, is essentially a process of formalization and ritualization, characterized by reference to the past, if only by imposing repetition. (Hobsbawm 1983, 2–3)

The Stuart court, it might be argued, helped initiate the transformation of custom into fixed tradition, much as, under Francis Bacon, it sought to fix the laws of Britain according to Roman-inspired principles of justice. It is in this context that one must approach the political and social power of the masque and its representation of landscape as scenery. The masque was a play and festivity held on customary holidays, not unlike the festivities that marked Rogation. The masque used the same sort of means to create a sense of community solidarity amongst the elite as did customary festivities amongst the commoners. In the masque, however, custom was replaced with costume, a matter of design and style, just as, through the representation of landscape as perspective scenery, unchanging geometrical principles replaced the evolving laws of custom. In the masque the landscape ceased to be the "habitus" of a people, an environment shaped through customary practices and bodily activity; instead, it became the scene upon which the personages of the state performed their roles under the authorial gaze of the ruler.

# Three

# "Masquing" the Body Politic of Britain

The first two chapters have explored the meaning of landscape as an area of human activity, a political landscape. This meaning was tied, it was argued, to the meaning of land as country, and thereby to historically constituted places with particular cultural practices, customs, legal traditions, and forms of political representation. Landscape, however, also formed the subject matter of artistic genres: landscape painting and the painting of stage scenery. The meaning of landscape thus began to merge with that of scene: "a real or imaginary prospect suggesting a stage setting" (MWC10: landscape, scene). This chapter and the following are concerned with the relationship between these ways of representing landscape and the development of the idea that the body politic is not the historical outcome of custom, but rather an expression of the natural geographical body within which it grows.

Discourses are the products of particular speakers and writers living in particular historical contexts. Discourses are also framed within narratives, such as the narrative of *The Masque of Blackness* that serves as the focus of this book. *The Masque of Blackness* contains a narrative that helps shed light on the relationship between two different notions of landscape: as polity and place, or as natural geographical scenery. The previous chapters focused on landscape as place. The present chapter focuses on landscape as scenery, by carefully unpacking the narrative of the masque. This narrative is concerned with the symbolic (re)discovery of England's identity as a subunit of a larger British "nation." The body politic of Britain, it will be seen, was defined as a country not in terms of its historical customs, but in terms of the landscape scenery of its geographical body.

## SEIZING A CENTENARY MOMENT

*The Masque of Blackness* was staged in early 1605, twelve nights after Christmas, in conjunction with the celebration of Epiphany, a feast day that commemorates the manifestation of God as Christ. This was an auspicious time, as it marked the beginning of a new year's cycle of fertility and, by extension, the manifestation of new beginnings more generally (Barber 1959, 3–15; Eliade 1971; Frye 1971, 158–86). The masque was performed less than a year after the festive official entry of the new king into London, which had been delayed by plague until March 1604. This official entry was a lavish theatrical affair, staged by the playwrights Ben Jonson and Thomas Dekker, complete with seven vast triumphal arches (the largest ninety feet high and fifty feet wide) which, at long last, marked the ceremonial beginning of James's reign (Parry 1981, 4). Plague had dampened the July 1603 coronation, and now it was time to celebrate properly the beginning of the new reign at Whitehall, in London. The 1605 *Masque of Blackness* was thus part of the elaborate process by which the new century's new British Stuart dynasty was staged for the English.[1]

When James became king of England, he not only unified the crowns of the greatest British Isle but also was put in the position of being able to unite the isles of Britain through the definitive 1603 defeat of the Irish. The new Stuart monarch could thus complete the work of union begun by Henry VIII, who had taken the title king of Ireland in 1541 and who had effectively brought Wales within the English realm by 1543 (Smith 1984, 37, 57, 246–49). The Scottish king had long dreamed of uniting the countries of Britain under the rule of his law, just as he had fought to unite a divided Scotland under the single body of his prerogative justice (James I [1599] 1969, 58–59; Anderson 1974, 135–37; Donaldson 1984, 33–34). James's ascendancy to the English throne had been carefully planned by Queen Elizabeth's influential chief minister Robert Cecil, who, as had his learned father, William Cecil, long used his influence to develop the ideological foundations for a unified Britain. The great project of James's reign was to finalize the renaissance of Britain as a unified imperial state (James I [1599] 1969, 43, 59, 65, 99, 154; Trevelyan [1904] 1960, 100; Smith 1984, 255; Cormack 1994).[2] This project, I will argue, was made manifest in *The Masque of Blackness*.

## JONSON AND CAMDEN'S NEW WORLD OF BRITAIN

Of critical importance to the idea of a born-again Britain was its status as a "blessèd isle," a geographical body which, together with Ireland and adjacent islands, formed Great Britain. The name "Great Britain," as Francis Bacon wrote in 1603, was an expression of the "perfect union of bodies, politic as well as natural" (quoted in Kantorowicz 1957, 24). What made Britain a separate bodily entity was the fact that it was, as Jonson wrote in the masque, *"A world divided from the world"* (Jonson 1969, 56, lines 216–18, emphasis in original). This was an idea that Jonson had already used in the iconography for an arch made for the official royal entry into London. The central statue in the arch was the figure a woman representing the British monarchy, underneath the crowns of England and Scotland, who carried in her lap a globe upon which was written "Orbis Britannicus. Divisus ab Orbe," to show, as Jonson explained, "that this empire is a world divided from the world" (quoted in Parry 1981, 4).

The geographical body of Britain was defined by a bounding sea which gave it a special identity vis-à-vis the remainder of the world. This is why the scenery of the masque, from the very outset, is defined by the meeting of the land, in the sense of both country and soil, with the rush of sea. Britain as a geographical body originated, according to ancient myth, as Albion, a body of land personified as a king, that lifted its white cliffs from the sea, its father:

> This land that lifts into the temperate air,
> His snowy cliff is Albion the fair,
> So called of Neptune's son, who ruleth here;
> (Jonson 1969, 54, lines 179–81)

Jonson's theatrical construction of Britain as a world apart, bounded and defined by the sea, was not a simple flight of fantasy. It was based upon the best geographical scholarship of the time.

There can be little doubt that Jonson derived his conception of Britain from his mentor and teacher William Camden. Jonson felt that he owed to Camden "All that I am in arts, all that I know" (Jonson 1985, 226).[3] Camden was a founding figure in British regional geography (chorography), antiquarian studies, and civil history more generally (Taylor 1934, 9–13; Trevor-Roper 1971; Cormack 1997). His scholarly fame was based upon his chorographical study *Britannia,* which was first published in Latin in 1586; later editions were printed with a frontispiece consisting of a map of the blessèd British isle flanked by Neptune and an Albion-like figure (Camden [1607] 1806). The idea that terra firma was made up of organically shaped parts was built into the chorographic approach to geography. This approach, as noted in chapter 1, derived ultimately from Ptolemy—an authority named at the very outset of *The Masque of Blackness.* Chorography was concerned with describing self-contained bodies, analogous to the head, whereas topography was concerned with parts of the whole, such as the ear or eye. The chorographic approach thus lent itself to a perception of Britain as the geographical embodiment of the British body politic.

According to a modern British archaeologist, *Britannia* is "one of the most formative books on our country's past ever written" which "still fundamentally colours the way in which we . . . look at our country" (Boon 1987, 1). In the preface to the book, Camden writes that he "entered the theatre of this learned age" at the instigation of "that excellent reviver of antient geography [Abraham Ortelius]" in order to illustrate "the antient state of my native *country* of Britain" (Camden [1607] 1806, 1:xxxv, emphasis added).[4] His goal was "to restore antiquity to Britain, and Britain to her own antiquity" (from the 1586 edition of *Britannia;* translated by Boon 1987, 3). Jonson felt that it was principally to Camden that "my country owes the great renown and name wherewith she goes." In the 1607 edition of *Britannia,* however, Camden modestly (and wisely) gave the credit for the revival of Britain to James I. That edition is dedicated to "James, King of Great Britain, France, and Ireland; Defender of the Faith; born for the eternity of the British name and Empire" (Camden [1607] 1806).

Britain, in Camden's *Britannia,* consisted of England (with Wales), Scotland, Ireland, and the adjacent islands. Camden recognized that Scotland was a "country," but that due to the ascendancy of the Stuarts to the English throne Britain had become one "state" and "nation":

> Britain, for so many ages divided and disunited, now forms as it were one large *state,* united under one august monarch, the founder of perpetual peace, who, ordained by the favour of Heaven, born and preserved for the good of both nations, endowed with consummate prudence and fatherly affection to all his subjects, has so completely removed all causes of fear, expectation, revenge, and complaint, that the fatal discord which so long engaged against each other these *nations,* invincible by all arms but their own, is now extinguished and stifled, while concord exults and triumphs. And according to the Poet's song:

> Jam cuncti gens una sumus.
> We are one people now,
> we can answer,
> Et simus in ævum.
> And be we ever so.
>     (Camden [1607] 1806,
>     4:17, emphasis added)

This is an interesting statement, because modern authorities tend to view the nation-state and nationalism as phenomena belonging to a later era. Yet, Camden is clearly referring to Britain as a nation, a state, and a people. If this is not an expression of nationalist feeling for a nation-state, it certainly must foreshadow the process by which printed media were used to create an "imagined" national community (Anderson 1991, 5).[5] Jonson and Jones continued the process by envisioning this community in their masques through the vehicle of theater landscape scenery. They not only used scenic illusion to imagine a born-again Britain, however; they also used it to mask and obliterate the memory of country as a polity based upon custom.

### THE LORD OF THE RING

Camden devoted several pages of *Britannia* to the classical literary sources that he believed had identified the British Isles as "the Fortunate Islands." As a geographer, Camden was, furthermore, able to ascertain that there was scientific evidence for the idea that Britain was specially blessed (Camden [1607] 1806, 1:xlix–li). Camden knew that Britain had a milder climate than one would expect given its latitude, though he could not have known that the Gulf Stream is responsible for this anomalous situation (Bennett 1956, 118–19). Great Britain, however, was more than an island that was both separated from and more "fortunate" than the remainder of the world; it also formed an organic bodily union encircled and bounded by coastline. The British Isles clustered around, and belonged to, this larger geographic body. In his companion compendium to the *Britannia,* called *Remains Concerning Britain,* Camden thus claimed that Britain was "well known to be the most flourishing and excellent, most renowned and famous isle of the whole world. So rich in commodities, so beautiful in situation, so resplendent in all glory that if the most Omnipotent had fashioned the world round like a ring, as he did like a globe, it might have been most worthily the only gemme therein" (Camden [1605] 1674, 1). Camden's geographical science lent "sciential" substance to the idea that the geographical body of Britain was a natural unity. The symbol of the ring, however, belongs to a realm of discourse which was anything but scientific.

The ring motif in Camden's description of an idyllic Britain might have been inspired by an epigram by his protégé, Ben Jonson, from his 1604 work *On the Union:*

> When was there contract better driven by fate?
> Or celebrated with more truth of state?
> The world the temple was, the priest a king,
> The spouse'd pair two realms, the sea the ring.
> 　　　　　　　　　　(Jonson 1985, 223)[6]

The most prestigious source of this ring motif, however, was probably King James's 1603 statement to his first English Parliament:

Do we not yet remember, that this Kingdome was diuided into seuen little Kingdomes, besides Wales? And is it not now the stronger by their vnion? . . . But what should we sticke vpon any naturall appearance, when it is manifest that God by his Almightie prouidence hath preordained it so to be? Hath not God first vnited these two Kingdomes both in Language, Religion, and similitude of maners? Yea, hath hee not made vs all in one Island, compassed with one Sea, and of it selfe by nature so indiuisible. . . . These two Countries being separated neither by Sea, nor great Riuer, Mountaine, nor other strength of nature. . . . And now in the end and fulness of time vnited, the right and title of both in my Person, alike lineally descended of both the Crownes, whereby it is now become like a little World within it selfe, being intrenched and fortified round about with a naturall, and yet admirable strong pond or ditch. . . . What God hath conjoined then, let no man separate. I am the Husband, and all the whole Isle is my lawfull Wife; I am the Head, and it is my Body. . . . When this Kingdome of *England* was diuided into so many little Kingdoms as I told you before; one of them behooued to eat vp another, til they were all vunited in one. . . . And since the successe was happie of the *Saxons* kingdomes being conquered by the speare of *Bellona* [Mars/war]; How much greater reason haue wee to expect a happie issue of this greater Vnion, which is only fasted and bound vp by the wedding Ring of *Astrea* [the stellar goddess of love, peace and justice] (James I [1616] 1918e, 271–73, emphasis in original).[7]

James presents the body of Britain as a female figure that is united through marriage to the king.[8] James, as he himself points out, brought Scotland and England (and Wales) together by virtue of his blood, which enabled him to become the hereditary king of both countries. The unification of the British Isles through marriage was not, furthermore, simply a question of metaphor. James had strengthened the union with the Orkneys through his marriage to Anne of Denmark (Donaldson 1984, 23–24, 33–34).[9]

When, in 1603, the ambitious courtier Francis Bacon termed Britain the "perfect union of bodies, politic as well as natural," this had metaphoric as well as literal meaning, much as the union of bodies which occurs in a wedding involves both a social/spiritual union and a physical union. Bacon's "natural" body might fittingly be termed the "body geographical," since he was referring to the geographical area of Britain. Bacon, here, is implying that the body politic forms a unity with the body geographical of Britain. There is but a short step from this idea to the idea that the body politic of Britain, an abstraction, has the physical form of the body geographical and this, in turn, can lead to the idea that the character of the body politic reflects, to some degree, its body geographical. This body geographical could be represented by a human body, as in the frontispiece to Michael Drayton's *Poly-Olbion: Or A Chorographicall Description of*

*Tracts, Rivers, Mountains, Forests, and other Parts of this renowned Isle of Great Britaine* (1612). Here the female iconographic figure of Britain, with the right breast of her fruitful young body exposed, is shown draped in a map of the territory of Britain (Helgerson 1986, 62–65, 73). The *Poly-Olbion* is based on Camden's *Britannia* (Drayton [1612–22] 1961, vi) and is illustrated with maps which are crammed full of bodies. It includes a large number of lightly clad (or naked) nymphs and various mythological figures which recall the figures in Jonson and Jones's masques (Ewell 1978).

King James I's use of the body metaphor for the state in his political writings and speeches to Parliament helps explain the means by which the geographical body of Britain gained its political importance. In his inaugural speech to Parliament, James begins by referring to the parliamentarians as "you who are here presently assembled to represent the Body of this whole Kingdome." The language changes slightly in his second speech to Parliament. Here he begins by recounting how, in his inaugural speech, he had congratulated "this House, and in you, all the whole Commonwealth (as being the representatiue body of the State)" for "so willing, and louing receiuing and embracing of mee in that place." His place in Parliament, he hastens to point out, was given to him by "God and Nature by descent of blood" (James I [1616] 1918a, 281). His physical body is thus literally connatural with the state in that his head directs the action of the larger body politic that he embodies in his person. This embodiment is particularly important because it is via James's role as head of state that the lands of Scotland and England are united within the geographical body of Britain. Parliament may have *represented* the body politic of the state, but James saw himself as its bodily "head."

## THE "SCIENTIAL" STATE

*The Masque of Blackness* makes use of a blend of ancient myth and science that may seem peculiar to the modern mind. Britain thus is said to make up the "happy isles" not only because ancient literary sources apparently identified it as such, but also because contemporary geographical science showed that its climate was atypically warm for a place with Britain's location on the globe. In this masque the mild British sun/king is presented as a "sciential" (endowed with the powers of science) source of the peculiarly mild British climate that can, among other things, make Ethiopians white and revive dead bodies:

> Ruled by a sun [James] that to this height doth grace it,
> Whose beams shine day and night, and are of force
> To blanch an Ethiop, and revive a corse [corpse]

His light sciential is, and, past mere nature,
Can salve the rude defects of every creature.
(Jonson 1969, 56, lines 223–27)

Science is used here to bolster the mytho-poetic image of the Apollonian, godlike powers of the monarch. The sun, however, is not simply a symbol; it was actually considered, following a tradition deriving in part from Pythagoras, as being the driving physical force in the cyclical hydrological process which brought moisture and fertility to Britain (Tillyard 1960, 58). As Jonson explains in a note to *The Masque of Blackness:* "All rivers are said to be the sons of Ocean, for, as the ancients thought, out of the vapors exhaled by the heat of the sun, rivers and fountains were begotten. And both by Orpheus in the *Hymns* and Homer, *Iliad* XIV, Oceanus is celebrated *as father and source of gods and things, because nothing is born or decays without moisture"* (Jonson 1969, 510, line 79, emphasis in original).

This notion of the cyclical flow of vital fluid was important to the idea of the body geographical because the flow of water through the land was paralleled to the flow of blood through a human body (Tuan 1968, 21–85). The ideological importance of the parallel was not lost on James I, who lectured his first English Parliament on how the union of Scotland and England was "made in my blood, being a matter that most properly belongeth to me to speake of, as the head wherin that great Body is vnited" (James I [1616] 1918e, 271). He also describes his beneficence to particular members of that body politic in terms of his regulation of the flow of life-giving fluid: "That being so farre beholding to the body of the whole State, I thought I could not refuse to let runne some small brookes out of the fountaine of my thankefulnesse to the whole" (ibid., 279).

In the masque, Albion and the sun are both symbols of the king/emperor, James. The waters give birth to Albion and its ruling sun, which, in turn, circulate the waters of the earth in a hydrologic cycle which brings life-giving and -tempering vapors into the atmosphere. Thus, Neptune's waves give birth to a son, Albion of Britannia, but Britannia's sun rules the waves.[10] As the masque figure Oceanus proclaims:

This land . . .
. . . is Albion the fair,
So called of Neptune's son, who ruleth here;
For whose dear guard, myself four thousand year,
. . . have walked the round
About his empire, proud to see him crowned
Above my waves.
(Jonson 1969, 54, lines 179–85)

## THE LAW OF THE LAND

The Albion represented in *The Masque of Blackness* is a physical land that is unified by natural laws. These laws are not the customary/common laws of the Parliament but eternal laws given by God, promulgated by Nature, and made manifest by the sciential king and his court. As James put it in the *Basilicon Doron,* written for his son, the crown prince:

> If then ye would enjoy a happie raigne,
> Observe the Statutes of your Heavenly King;
> And from his Lawe make all your Lawes to spring . . . .
> And so ye shall in princely vertues shine.
> Resembling right your mighty King divine.
> (James I [1599] 1969, 4)[11]

To James, the king was "a speaking law, and the Law a dumbe king" who was "countable to God" for his administration of the law (James I [1616] 1918f, 63). The difference between the two concepts of law is well illustrated by a famous exchange between James and Sir Edward Coke, as reported here by Coke:

> Then the king said, that he thought the law was founded upon reason, and that he and others had reason as well as the judges: to which it was answered by me, that true it was, that God had endowed his Majesty with excellent science, and great endowments of nature; but his Majesty was not learned in the laws of his realm of England, and causes which concern the life, or inheritance, or goods, or fortunes of his subjects are not to be decided by natural reason, but by the artificial reason and judgement of law, which law is an act which requires long study and ex-perience before that a man can attain to the knowledge of it. (quoted in Pocock 1972, 214)

This was a time when the judicial concept of natural law, which was fa-vored by monarchists, and the scientific laws of physical nature were not clearly distinguished.[12] Thus, King James's lord chancellor, Sir Francis Ba-con, was the leading jurist of the court and a bitter personal rival of Coke, and he was also the author of a scientific vision of another happy isle, the *New Atlantis* (Hill 1965, 85–130). This fictional island state is ruled by a benevolent despot who is the lineal descendant of Solamona, "the Law-giuer of our nation"—James saw himself as a modern Solomon. The monarch in the story rules with the aid of a team of scientists like Bacon. They study the natural law of God and hence "the Knowledge of Causes, and the Secrett Motion of Things" (Bacon [1627] 1915, 21, 35).[13]

In their masques, Jonson and Jones promoted the ideal of the Baconian, sciential philosopher-king, who brings enlightenment to his realm (Mebane 1989, 156–73). According to Stephen Orgel, a leading authority on the Jonsonian masque, this conception of the sciential state included "among the promised benefits of the new learning the most fabulous wonders of masques: dominion over the seasons, the raising of storms at will, the acceleration of germination and harvest. Every masque is a celebration of this concept of science, a ritual in which the society affirms its wisdom and asserts its control over its world and its destiny" (Orgel 1975, 55). If the idea of Landschaft and country as expressions of custom tended to spawn utopian visions of a return to an edenic egalitarian age, the Stuart court ideal tended to spawn utopian visions of an approaching renaissance of a mythical golden age under a god king. In this vision, the king becomes a creature which God created, as James told his son, "first, for that he made you a man; and next, for that he made you a little God to sit on his Throne, & rule over other men" (James I [1599] 1969, 4).[14] The masque was the product of an ideology which was determined, in the words of Orgel, to "purify, reorder, reform, reconceive a whole culture" (Orgel 1975, 87). It is in this context that the idea of Britain as the Elysian fields gains importance, because these mythical fields were the place where the past of English custom could be forgotten in order that the brave new sciential world of Britain could be begotten.

## LETHIAN SCENERY

In *The Masque of Blackness,* Jonson weds the theme of the unity of Britain to revived ancient myths of the British Isles as happy, paradisiacal islands, the "isles of the blest" where the Elysian fields were located (Bennett 1956). This theme plays an important role in *The Masque of Blackness* and its sequel from 1608, *The Masque of Beauty,* and forms the basis of an entire masque, *The Fortunate Isles, and Their Union,* which was performed on Twelfth Night, 1624 (Jonson 1969, 433–53). *The Masque of Beauty* concludes with these lines:

> May youth and pleasure ever flow;
> But let your state, the while,
> Be fixèd as the isle.
> *Chorus* So all that see your beauty's sphere
> May know th' Elysian fields are here.
> *Echo* Th' Elysian fields are here.
> *Echo* Elysian fields are here.
>             (Jonson 1969, 74, lines 340–46)[15]

The Elysian fields would have been familiar to the courtiers from their reading of the classics, particularly Virgil's *Aeneid.* There are important parallels between the role of the Elysian fields in the *Aeneid* and their celebration of the new "British" dynasty in the masques of *Blackness* and *Beauty.*

In Virgil's epic the Trojan hero Aeneas is forced to flee from Troy, which had been, as recounted in Homer's *Illiad*, defeated and sacked by the Greeks. Aeneas and his followers, under the guidance of the sun god, Apollo, sail from place to place across the Mediterranean in search of Italy, where they believe they are destined to settle. Finally, after landing on Italian shores, Aeneas makes a journey to the underworld, accompanied by the seer Sibyl, where he enters the Elysian fields in order to visit his father. These fields are ruled by Apollo, under whose reign worthy men are restored to the state of life that had once existed in the ancient golden age when human society originated. Here the ancient heroes drink the Lethian waters of the Elysian fields, causing them to forget their previous existence (Grimal 1990: Lethe). The Trojan heroes are then able to return to earth, as Aeneas's father had prophesized, not as Greek Trojans, but as the Italian heroes who would found the Roman empire (Virgil 1990, 132–61).

Much as Virgil's Elysium naturalized the Trojans as the native Romans of Italy and obliterated the memory of the Etruscans, so did the masques' Elysium provide a theatrical means of naturalizing the different peoples of Britain as a single British nation, while simultaneously obliterating the memory of the Anglo-Saxons, Scots, Irish, and so on. James, at this time, was vainly imploring the English Parliament to "naturalize" Scots born after his accession to the English throne, thus paving the way for the establishment of British nationhood and citizenship (James I [1616] 1918c, 299; Trevelyan [1904] 1960, 100). A solution to this problem would be to create a new, overarching British national identity which encompassed all native-born British people. This people, however, also had to have a pedigree suitable to an era that was witnessing the renaissance of classical culture. The solution was to trace that pedigree back to the same Trojan origins to which the Romans had traced theirs. Albion was thus the mythic place born of the sea and then settled by Trojans. Trojan ancestry provided, as will be argued, a vehicle by which the Stuart court was able to smuggle a new Roman/British state identity into the country of England.

## TROJAN BRITONS

James attempted to give credence to the idea of a common British national identity by following the example of the Tudors in tracing his regal line back to a Trojan great-grandson of Aeneas named Brutus (Smith 1986, 109, 250 n. 49). In this way everything from the British monarchy to the Anglican Church could be given classical origins which were separate but equal to those of Rome (Kunst 1994, 85–88). James was also thereby able to avoid tracing the heritage of his government and church back to the Germanic "Goths" (as they were then known) who had, according to Tacitus, a proclivity for representative political institutions (Kliger 1945, 1947, 1952; MacDougall 1982, 31–70).

The principal source of the idea of Britain's Trojan origins was the twelfth-century *History of the Kings of Britain* by the Welsh bishop Geoffrey of Monmouth (Monmouth [ca. 1136] 1966). According to Geoffrey, Brute, a great-grandson of Aeneas, followed in Aeneas's footsteps by making an odyssey through the Mediterranean, after which he wound up conquering Britain (rather than Italy) and making it his domain. The mythical figure of Arthur, who supposedly established an empire ranging from the Orkneys to Norway, is the most famous king in this Wales-based British/Trojan royal line.[16] By following the Tudor practice of naming the crown prince the Prince of Wales, James was underlining his claim to this heritage of conquest (Boon 1987, 3; Kunst 1994, 72–85). In *The Trew Law of Free Monarchies* James made clear that the right of the king as "ouer-Lord of the whole land" and "Master ouer euery person that inhabiteth the same" derives from the right of conquest (James I [1616] 1918f, 62–63; MacDougall 1982, 54).[17]

The Tudors, followed by the Stuarts, traced their lineage back to the British/Trojan conquerors (MacDougall 1982, 7–27; Boon 1987, 3). This implied, by extension, that they were not just the kings of the Anglo-Saxon kingdom of England, but the rightful emperors of the whole of the sea empire of Britain (Parry 1981, 8–9, 16). This empire was, in principle, their personal domain according to the Renaissance conception of the natural right of conquest. This right abrogated native claims to sovereignty based upon customary domain and gave the conqueror the absolute right to impose his own rule of law (Sutherland 1972, 45). The right of conquest, in this way, made the conquered territory analogous to the conqueror's private property, which, in turn, was inheritable by his descendants. In this way, the Stuarts sought to define the state of Britain as a property in the possession of a monarchy of quasi-Roman origin (McIlwain 1918, xxxiii–xxxviii).

Camden felt that Monmouth's Trojan British heritage lacked historical documentation, and, to his credit, he paid only lip service to the idea (MacDougall 1982, 46; Boon 1987, 3).[18] He was, however, able to document the presence of classical Roman civilization in Britain prior to the decline represented by the "middle ages" (a term he may have coined) (Piggot 1976, 38). Classical Roman imperial ideology and British imperial ideology sprang, of course, from the same mythical Trojan heritage. Camden's *Britannia* was essentially Roman Britain as seen in relation to its later growth (Copley 1977, xv; Boon 1987, 3; Parry 1995, 23).[19] As the historian of antiquarianism Stuart Piggot writes:

> I do not think we can escape from the conclusion that the *Britannia* was
> originally planned to elucidate the topography of Roman Britain, and to
> present a picture of the Province, with reference to its development
> through Saxon and medieval times, which would enable Britain to take
> her rightful place at once within the world of antiquity and that of inter-
> national Renaissance scholarship. (Piggot 1976, 42–43)

The British court's identification with things Roman helps explain why
Camden's *Britannia* was first written in Latin, why Jonson mined the classics for his literary construction of Britain, and why Jones found such inspiration in the architectural heritage of ancient Rome. Much as Jones's
model, the sixteenth-century Italian architect Andrea Palladio, had sought
to revive the ancient Vitruvian "Roman" architectural heritage of Venetian Italy, Jones was reinventing what he saw to be the ancient "Trojan"
British architectural heritage of his country. In principle he was not, therefore, bringing a foreign architecture to England, but restoring the native
classical architecture of Britain. This is why Jones was sometimes called
"Vitruvius Britannicus," after the first-century B.C.E. Roman architect Vitruvius (Yates 1969, 169–85; Parry 1981, 75–76).[20]

Jones went to great lengths to trace the British origins of his architectural
style. He even undertook a study of Stonehenge, at the behest of King James,
in order to prove that it had originated as a classical temple/theater dedicated
to Coelus, the god of the heavens. Like Geoffrey of Monmouth, Jones argued
that the buildings of the ancient inhabitants of Britannia were "a match for
Rome" (quoted in Yates 1969, 175; see also ibid., 169–85; Gotch 1968,
13–21; Parry 1981, 155–58; Kunst 1994, 186–90). The confluence of the
myth of Trojan origins with an actual Roman presence provided a basis for
treating Jones's Palladianism as an expression of the native British culture of
Albion (Gotch 1968, 1–27; Woodbridge 1970, 18; Parry 1981, 146–64).

The attempt to substitute a British absolute monarchy for English parliamentarianism was tantamount to proclaiming a revolution. It meant
overturning established ideas of justice, government, country, and community. It is an irony of history that the concept of revolution was first applied to the later revolt of the countrymen against the Stuarts. It was actually the Stuart court that initiated a revolution. The countrymen's revolt
was thus, in reality, a counterrevolution.

## THE REVOLUTIONARY "TRANSLATION" OF EMPIRE
## TO BRITAIN

The idea of revolution is ever present in the masques and their scenery. A
speech addressed to James in the masque *The Fortunate Isles, and Their
Union* states that the "point of revolution being come" the union of the

Fig. 3.1. Atrium from a 1632 masque entitled *Albion's Triumph*. This stage scene suggests the Roman influence upon Inigo Jones's vision of Albion, which was traditionally taken to be England. Photo: Photographic Survey, Courtauld Institute of Art. Reproduced with the permission of The Devonshire Collection, Chatsworth. Reproduced by permission of the Duke of Devonshire and the Chatsworth Settlement Trustees.

isles as Britannia will then occur (Jonson 1969, 447, line 297). This union creates a golden age in which:

> There is no sickness nor no old age known
> To man, nor any grief that he dares own.
> There is no hunger there, nor envy of state,
> Nor least ambition in the magistrate.
> (Ibid.,449, lines 344–47)

In 1624, when this masque was first performed, the term *revolution* primarily referred to the motions of the heavenly bodies. Jonson and Jones's masques are also full of revolving cosmic forces (Wiles 1993, 43).[21] This was a time when, due to the influence of the sister "sciences" of astronomy, astrology, and geography, the revolution of the heavenly bodies was seen to have great significance for the affairs of men (Hatto 1949, 510–11; Thomas 1971, 283–357; Cohen 1976, 261; Rachum 1995). In *The Fortunate Isles, and Their Union* the "union" is thus seen to be revolutionary, a British geoterritorial marriage made in heaven and signified by ring-like motion.

The idea of the golden age was itself linked to ancient ideas of a revolutionary movement of time according to which the ages perpetually roll and thereby return to their point of origin. In his *Statesman,* Plato presented a cosmology—well known in Stuart England—in which the revolution of the universe periodically reverses in a process that causes time to repeat itself and results in both a return to the golden age and a forgetting of the past age.[22] Virgil's famous eschatological fourth Eclogue builds on such a cosmology and includes a prophetic passage on the revolutionary turning of the ages which, as will be seen, helps explain the importance of the myth of the blessèd isles for the generation of the new British identity. It reads:

> The last age told by Cumæ's seer [the Sibyl] is come,
> A might roll of generations new
> Is now arising. Justice [Astraea] now returns
> And Saturn's realm, and from high heaven descends
> A worthier race of men. Only do thou
> Smile, chaste Lucin, on the infant boy,
> With whom the iron age will pass away.
> The golden age in all the earth be born;
> For thin Apollo [identified with the sun] reigns.
> (Virgil 1946, 24 [*Eclogues* 4.4–12])

The importance of this poem lies in the fact that it was seen to predict not only the cyclical coming of a new golden age in time, but also the cyclical movement of this golden age to a new location in space, Britain. Virgil had portrayed the decline of Rome as causing the good shepherds, whose forefathers had founded Rome, to flee to "Britain," a world "wholly sundered from all the world" (Et penitus toto divisos orbe Britannos) (Virgil 1946, 10 [*Eclogues* 1.77]; see also Bennett 1956, 114–17). Since Virgil had also stated that the last traces of the goddess of Justice (Astraea) were seen in the midst of these shepherds, it was also reasonable to assume that she would return to them in Britain (Virgil 1946, 114 [*Georgics* 2.564–66]; Yates 1975, 6). This is why James I was able to claim, as seen earlier, that it was the "wedding Ring of *Astrea*" which unified Scotland and England (James I [1616] 1918e, 269). The work of Plutarch, who was widely read in translation at the English court, further encouraged this association by recounting Roman stories of how Saturn, the god of the golden age, was imprisoned by Jupiter on an island off the British coast (Yates 1934, 239; Bennett 1956, 120–21).

The belief in a cyclical renaissance of the golden empires of the past was linked, during the Renaissance, to the idea of a parallel cyclical movement in space. The rebirth, or renovation (*renovatio*), of the Roman Empire thus also involved the "translation of empire" (*translatio imperii*) to a point farther west (Yates 1975, 38–39). This spatial movement followed the cycle of the sun. The Romans had argued that their empire had been translated west from the empire of Greece, and the new British empire involved another westward translation (Glacken 1967, 276–85). The idea of the "renovation" and "translation" of empire was employed by Charlemagne in 800 (Yates 1975, 2–12), and it was revived under the continental empire of Charles V before being picked up by Elizabethan promoters of Britain as the future island seat of a western world empire. It was natural, in this context, to identify Elizabeth with the figure of Astraea, the goddess of justice and natural law, because of both her feminine sex and her reputed virginity (Yates 1975, 29–87; Strong 1977, 46–54; Mebane 1989, 83; Kunst 1994, 164).[23] Just as the Stuarts inherited Elizabeth's throne, so did they inherit the identification with Astraea (Parry 1981, 15–18, 52–53, 73–74).

The revolutionary roll of the ages was the temporal equivalent to the circular movement in geographical space that the progress of empire takes, following the revolving movement of the earth. Thus each new golden age of empire was translated farther west, and the site of the next golden age ought to be those British happy isles, divorced from the rest of the world. The Virgilian origin of these ideas is important because Virgil had the position "as the prophet of the imperial mission of Rome" (Yates 1975, 33). Virgil's Romans were thus the mythological descendants of the Trojans and the Arcadians, and Arcadia was thought to be the home of Pan and the locus of the first golden age (Snell 1953). Just as Virgil by means of this mythology relocated the hearth of Greek civilization westward in Rome, so did the ideology of England as "Britain" relocate the new golden age of empire within the damp shores of the British Isles. This reinvented Britain, however, was easier to represent on the court stage than to accomplish in the representative body of Parliament.

Time and time again, despite James's almost pathetic pleading to the Parliament, his will was frustrated by the recalcitrant MPs (Camden [1607] 1806, 4:1–5; James I [1616] 1918a, 286; [1616] 1918c, 293–305; [1616] 1918e, 271–73). James considered it to be "a foolish Querke of some Iudges, who held that the Parliament of *England,* could not vnite *Scotland* and *England* by the name of *Great Britaine,* but that it would

Fig. 3.2. Inigo Jones's final design for the emperor Albanactus of Albion, for the masque *Albion's Triumph*, showing Roman-inspired garb. The emperor is described as being of Scottish origin, and the queen, Alba, is described as having "native beauties" with a "great affinity with all purity and whiteness." Photo: Photographic Survey, Courtauld Institute of Art. Reproduced with the permission of The Devonshire Collection, Chatsworth. Reproduced by permission of the Duke of Devonshire and the Chatsworth Settlement Trustees.

make an alteration of the Lawes" (James I [1616] 1918b, 329, emphasis in original). The judges and Parliament, however, stood by their quirks, and they had "good reasons" for doing so, because "such a fusion of the laws and Governments of the two nations," to use G. M. Trevelyan's words, would have "rendered the King independent alike of Scottish nobles and of English Parliaments" (Trevelyan [1904] 1960, 100–101). The idea of Britain, though popular with the court, was apparently broadly unpopular with the masses, as is suggested by an anonymous popular writer who asserted, in a message directed to James, that the people, "make a mock of your word 'Great Britain,' and offter to prove that it is a great deal less than little England was wont to be, less in reputation, less in strength, less in riches, less in all manner of virtue" (quoted in Trevelyan [1904] 1960, 123).

What James could not achieve in the political arena he was able to envision on the theater stage of his court, where he helped give the concept of landscape a new, and politically charged, meaning. It is in this context that landscape scenery entered the theater of modern English discourse.

# Four

# Landscaping the Body Politic
# of the British State

First, for the Scene was drawn a Landtschap . . . which falling, an artificial
sea was seen to shoot forth, as if it flowed to the land raised with waves
which seemed to move, and in some places the billow to break, as imitating
that orderly disorder which is common in nature. . . . [T]he scene behind
seemed a vast sea, and united with this that flowed forth, from the
termination or horizon of which (being on the level of the state, which was
placed in the upper end of the hall) was drawn, by the lines of perspective,
the whole work shooting downwards from the eye. . . . So much for the
bodily part, which was of Master Inigo Jones his design and act.

Ben Jonson, *The Masque of Blackness,* 1605

When Jonson stated that Jones's perspective scenery for *The Masque of
Blackness* "imitat[ed] that orderly disorder which is common in nature,"
he was describing a scene which was something other than a view of natural scenery (Jonson 1969, 48). In fact, the earliest citation listed in the
*Oxford English Dictionary* for a meaning of nature that readily calls to
mind scenery dates from a half century later (OED: nature 13). A more
precise description than Jonson's would be to say that the landscape
scenery of the theater was used to present a scene shaped in imitation of
natural law. This scene represented a fragment of a cosmos whose natural
laws were thought to govern the realms of nature and humanity.

Jonson's description of Jones's scenery for the masque contains important clues to how such a theater scene could be made to embody the body
politic of Britain as governed by natural law. The theater was so constructed that (to use Jonson's words) the "termination or horizon" of the
scene was at "the level of the state, which was placed in the upper end of
the hall." This horizon is so "drawn by the lines of perspective" that "the
whole work" appears to be "shooting downwards from the eye" (Jonson
1969, 48–50). The focal point for the lines of perspective was the seat of

Fig. 4.1. Portrait of Benjamin Jonson by Abraham van Blyenberch (ca. 1617). By courtesy of the National Portrait Gallery, London.

"state," or royal throne.[1] This throne of state was elevated above the public upon a palisade so that the king's eye was at the focal point of the lines of perspective, giving the scenery the illusion of three-dimensional depth.[2] At one end of the hall we have the royal spectator, the "head" of state, commanding the scene from his seat of power, and at the other end we have the spectacle of the lightly clothed bodies of the queen and her consort, forming a living and moving dimension of the stage scenery—the "bodily part," as Jonson called it. This was a form of total theater, running for hours, in which the spectators were overwhelmed by music, dance, song, and spectacle. The players were chosen by the court from amongst the leading ladies and men of the realm, supplemented by professionals. At certain set times the invisible line between audience and spectators was broken, and all participated in a ritualized unifying dance (Strong 1984, 42–62). The line between theater and "reality" was blurred in the masque. One reflected the other, but it was also possible, at certain privileged moments, to go through this looking glass and enter the staged illusion of an imagined world.

### THE MIRRORED MASQUE OF BRITAIN

The miraculous medium that allowed the monarch his encompassing perspective on the scenery was rooted in the symbolism of the mirror. The lawful relationship between the "bodily part" of the theater, the stage with its perspective scenery and players, and the gaze of the head of state, who commanded the scene, was that of a mirror image. This relationship parallels that between the sphere of the higher celestial law of God and the sphere of monarchical law. As James I admonished his son Henry, the crown prince, in his *Basilicon Doron,* also titled *Princes Looking Glass,* "Remember also, that by the right knowledge, and fear of God (which is the beginning of wisedome (as SALOMON saith)) ye shall know all the things necessarie for the discharge of your duety, both as a Christian & as a King, seeing in him (as in a mirrour) the course of al earthlie things, whereof he is the spring & onely moouer" (James I [1599] 1969, 6).[3]

The mirror plays a central and explicit role in *The Masque of Blackness.* The masque begins with a story similar to that of the biblical Magi: a group of black African princesses receive a sign from the heavens telling them to set sail for a reborn "Britain." This sign comes in the form of a mirror reflection in a lake of the moon goddess Aetheopia, who declaims:

> . . . I was that bright face
> Reflected by the lake, in which thy race
> Read mystic lines; which skill Pythagoras
> First taught to men by a reverberate [reflecting] glass.

The mystical ciphers in the mirror of Pythagoras (580–ca. 500 B.C.E.), a Greek geometer, astronomer, and mystic, are the reflection of a three-tiered message linking heaven, earth, and underworld, which proclaims the rebirth of "Britannia":[4]

> This blessèd isle doth with that -tania end,
> Which there they saw inscribed, . . .
>
> .  .  .  .  .  .  .  .  .  .  .  .  .

Fig. 4.2. Portrait of Inigo Jones by Anthony van Dyck. The inscription reads: "Vandyke's original drawing, from which the Print by Van. Voerst was taken, in the Book of Vandyke's Heads. Given me by The Duke of Devonshire." It is signed "Burlington," who, as noted in the text, was an influential Whig architect who worked together with the pioneer of British landscape gardening, William Kent. Photo: Photographic Survey, Courtauld Institute of Art. Reproduced with the permission of The Devonshire Collection, Chatsworth. Reproduced by permission of the Duke of Devonshire and the Chatsworth Settlement Trustees.

Britannia, which the triple world [heaven, earth, and underworld] admires,

. . . . . . . . . . . . . . . . . . . . . . . .

With that great name Britannia, this blessèd isle
Hath won her ancient dignity and style.
                 (Jonson 1969, 55, lines 204–17)

The idea of the mirror provides an important key to the role of landscape scenery in the theatrical construction of the Stuart British state. The "King's Actions (euen in the secretest places)," as James told the English Parliament, "are as the actions of those that are set vpon the Stages" (James I [1616] 1918d, 310). The word *theater* derives from the Greek word *theasthai,* meaning to view, with the root *thea,* or the act of seeing; *thea,* in turn, is akin to the word *thauma,* or miracle, a word which was closely associated in the Renaissance mind with the magic of the mirror and other optical devices identified with the mirror (Wheelock 1977, 143–45; MWC10: theater, mirror). At this time, to play upon a stage was "to hold as 'twere the mirror up to Nature" (Shakespeare 1948, 628 [*Hamlet* 3.2.24]). The symbols decorating Shakespeare's theater, the Globe, thus mirrored the cosmic order (Yates 1969).

The perspective stage created by Jones accomplished this mirroring not so much by the use of symbols as through the very structure of the theater. The king's eye is positioned at the point where the lines of perspective converge, seeming, in Jonson's words, to "shoot downwards from the eye" toward the vanishing point, where they penetrate through the bodily part of the stage scene and disappear into "the termination or horizon." The two convergence points are mirror images of each other, as discussed in chapter 1 in the context of Brunelleschi's path-breaking demonstration of the use of perspective.

The relation between the head of state and the staged body politic, represented in the theater, resembled the structure of "just symmetrie and proportion" described by James to his oldest son as representing "the height of your honourable place," in contrast to "the heavie weight of your great charge; and consequentlie in case of failzie (which God forbid) of the sadnes of your fall, according to the proportion of that height" (James I [1599] 1969, epistle).

Jonson labeled Jones the "spectacles of state" ("An Expostulation with Inigo Jones" [1631] in Jonson 1985, 462–65). Jonson, who loved plays on words, seems to be referring here both to the function of Jones's scenic entertainment as spectacle and to the role which these spectacles played as lenses, or mirrors, creating an illusory image of the state. At this time, as discussed in chapter 1, the mirror was seen as not simply reflecting passively, but also functioning as a model or archetypal standard which ought to be reflected in people's behavior (OED: mirror II: 5; spectacle II: 5).

Mirrors were thought to have *mir*aculous properties, particularly when used to reflect the elevated nature of the celestial heavens. It had long been conventional for European theatrical settings to include symbols of heavenly figures, or a monarch in an elevated position, or both (Kernodle 1944, 29, 71, 81–82, 95, 218). Now, however, this symbolic position of a monarch controlling space from above was supplemented by that of a monarch controlling the illusory horizontal space of landscape scenery (Tuan 1974b, 129).

The staged perspective illusion of Britain's landscape provided an ingenious means of mirroring the estate of the monarch as the state of a unified Britain. This was because the natural, mathematical laws of its absolute, homogenous space transcended the legal bounds, established through custom, of the individual countries, and hence their parliaments. Parliament represented each separate country/county during the time period when it met; the surveyed map of the British state, like the landscape scene of that state surveyed in the theater by the head of state, represented these countries/counties synchronically, as a unified spatial totality. This idea was implicit in the project of Ptolemaic geography, which, as seen in chapter 1, helped give rise to perspective representations of landscape scenery.[5] Ptolemy, as noted, saw the depiction of the chorographic regions delineated by the geographer as being the stuff of art, with the delineated regions having a decidedly bodily quality. According to a modern authority on the history of geographical concepts, "Choros technically means the boundary of the extension of some thing or things. It is the container or receptacle of a body" (Lukermann [1961] 1967, 64; see also Olwig 2001). The cartographic creation of such a uniform, bodily, national space was the goal of such English cartographers as William Lambarde. Writing in 1576, he expressed the wish that someone in each shire would do a chorography "for his own country to the end that by joining our pens and conferring our labors . . . we might at the last by the union of many parts and papers compact one whole and perfect body and book of our English topography" ("A Perambulation of Kent," quoted in Helgerson 1986, 75). The theater of the Stuart state applied the same cartographic logic to the scenic representation of Britain.

The unified geometric space of the map, as well as the landscape scene, facilitated the ability to imagine that these historically and geographically diverse "countries" made up a single country at the grand scale of Britain—masking the divergences between them by reducing qualitative differences to a question of quantitative scale. Distinctive places, each with its own history and customs, were thereby reduced to locations within the spatial coordinates of the map (Olwig 2001). Within this uniform space, each distinctive country was reduced to a province suitable for governance, under the provenance of an emerging bureaucracy, according to the methods of rational, statistical compartmentalization then being developed by a centralizing monarchy, in England as well as elsewhere in Europe.

## THE STATE OF THE BODY POLITIC

The idea that the bodies on stage represented the body politic might seem a bit literal-minded to a modern sensibility, for which the idea of a *corporate* body has become just another abstraction. At that time, however, the idea of the state as a corpus or body was more than a metaphor; this is why the iconographic symbolism used to express this idea was so graphic. The tendency to think of the state in literal bodily terms was not novel. The idea had a long history that is traceable back to the Christian doctrine, espoused most notably by St. Paul, that the church, with its *members,* represented the mystical body of Christ. Paul, in turn, was influenced by Greek ideas concerning the idea of the cosmos and microcosmos as a body. Christ thus had "two natures," one godly and one human. Christian monarchs and emperors saw their government as being a secular parallel to the rule of the church, in which they acted as the head of state in much the same way that the Pope, as the representative of Christ, acted as head of the church. Precedence for this conception of the sacred quality of the monarch's person was also found in Roman emperor worship. This idea of a secular body politic, as embodied in the monarchy, perpetuated the aura of the religious concept of a mystical body united as a community under a leader who represented higher heavenly powers (Kantorowicz 1957, 7–23, 193–232; Barkan 1975, 61–115). The Protestant state church of England, much to the chagrin of the Puritans, built on this tradition by placing great emphasis on a theatrical ritual of the communion service in which the bread and wine is transubstantiated into the body and blood of Christ, which is then consumed by the members of the body of the church.

The monarch, according to the Elizabethans, was incorporated with the subjects of the body politic, just as they were incorporated with the monarch. Sir Francis Bacon, James's lord chancellor, defined the king as "a body corporate in a body natural, and a body natural in a body corporate" (corpus corporatum in corpore naturali, et corpus naturale in corpore corporato) (quoted in Kantorowicz 1955, 80). According to this idea, as English judges were wont to point out:

> [T]he King has two Bodies, the one whereof is a Body natural . . . and in this he is subject to Passions and Death as other Men are; and the other is a Body politic and the Members thereof are the subjects, and he and they together compose the corporation, and he is incorporated with them and they with him, and he is the Head, and they are the Members; and

this Body is *not* subject to Passions and Death, for as to this Body the King never dies. (quoted in Kantorowicz 1955, 91, emphasis in original)

The frontispiece to Thomas Hobbes's *Leviathan,* roughly contemporaneous with the quotation above, is a particularly famous example of the depiction of the body politic as an assemblage of bodies within the larger body of a figure representing the state. It shows the figure of a man wearing a crown and holding a sword and scepter who surveys a landscape scene. The body of this figure is entirely made up of the bodies of countless individuated *personae* (Latin for mask), which are held together and given form by the larger body of this "artificiall man," to use Hobbes's terminology. The crowned head on a body of bodies represents the subject of the book, which is "the Matter, Forme, & Power of a Commonwealth" or, in other words, the "state," which Hobbes named "Leviathan," or "*Mortall God*" (Hobbes [1651] 1991, lxxiv, 9–11, 120, emphasis in original). Above the figure is a Latin quote from the book of Job in which God proclaims, of Leviathan: "Non est potestas Super Terram quæ Comparetur" (There is no power on earth that compares with him/it). Those who chose to look in their new King James Bible would have found that the full passage read: "Upon earth there is not his like, who is made without fear. He beholdeth all high *things:* he *is* a king over all the children of pride" (Job 41.33–34 AV).[6] Here again, the notion of God and king are linked, and their power is signified by their ability to behold an elevated world.

Hobbes believed that, without the infinite rationality of natural laws backed by state power, human beings' "natural" self-interest in self-preservation would lead them to destroy each other in a condition of perpetual "Warre." Without the state, life would be, in Hobbes's famous words, "solitary, poore, nasty, brutish and short" (Hobbes [1651] 1991, 28–37, 73–74, 86–90, 91–115). In the frontispiece to *Leviathan,* the terrifying, awesome, masked embodiment of the commonwealth towers over and surveys a landscape scene of the country and capital viewed as on a stage.[7] Jones's scenic representation of the landscape of the British body politic sometimes included a similar figure of a monarch hovering over the scenery. When James, in *The Trew Law of Free Monarchies,* wrote that "the King is ouer-Lord of the whole land: so is he Master ouer euery person that inhabiteth the same, hauing power ouer the life and death of euery one of them," one can imagine that he saw himself in something of the same position as the sword-wielding monarch of the frontispiece (James I [1616] 1918f, 63). It is this figure, according to Hobbes, who is the "author" that "owneth" the "words and actions" of the "Actor" who "acteth" under the "*Auth*ority" of the monarch and thereby "represents" the state (Hobbes [1651] 1991, 112, emphasis added).[8]

Fig. 4.3. Engraved title page for the 1651 edition of Thomas Hobbes's *Leviathan*. Reproduced by permission of Cornell University Library, Division of Rare and Manuscript Collections.

The representation of the body politic by actual bodies cavorting on a stage under the (super)vision of the monarch provided a means of symbolizing the embodiment of the state in a new and abstract way as a relationship in geographic space. This freed the monarch from having to be bodily present at manifestations of the state. The state was becoming an abstraction embodied in what I have called "the body geographical." This change is illustrated by the family life of monarchs. Anne and her brother Christian spent their early childhoods not in Denmark but in Mecklenburg, with their grandfather the duke, because their father was required by his status as king to be constantly on the move through the different lands of his realm in order to manifest his physical presence as the embodiment of the law of the state. Since this was a difficult situation in which to raise children, their mother, Queen Sophie, who traveled with the king, sent the children to be raised in her homeland of Mecklenburg. The childless Queen Elizabeth was likewise required to make her "royal progress" through the counties/countries of her realm in order to manifest her unifying bodily presence as the centerpiece of what approached a cult (Strong 1977; Smith 1984, 121–22; Helgerson 1986, 80). Though infinitely more pompous, the circuitous structure of the royal progress was much the same as that of the villagers who perambulated during Rogation week in order to lay bodily claim to their customary domain (Olwig 2002).[9] It is little wonder that the Danish king, Christian IV, wished to centralize the administration of law under his domain in his Copenhagen *hovedstad* (literally "head place" or *cap*ital city), or that the Stuarts would see the advantage of focusing authority at a British court in London. The localization of state power over a body politic in geographical space made it possible for the monarch to sever his role as head of state from his personal bodily movements. The physical role of the monarch's persona as the embodiment of the state was being taken over by the "body geographic." The state was becoming a geographical entity

It was a problem for King James, who was shy and fearful of public exposure, that he was constantly expected to expose the progress of his "body natural" to the public. He had been unable to avoid doing this because his body natural was inextricably incorporated into his being as the head of the body politic. If people were to believe in the power of the state, they needed to see the body of the king who gave it authority. The masque, however, provided a means for envisioning the body politic in abstract spatial terms. It provided a symbolic way to separate the king's role as the surveilling head of state from his physical corpus as the symbol of the body politic. In the theater of the masque, the "members" of the state who make up the king's symbolic body are incorporated into the "bodily part" of the stage landscape scenery. The head of state, however, is not a member of this bodily part, but rather is placed upon a scaffold in a position where the invisible lines of perspective structuring the scene converge upon his eye. It is he, as head, whose gaze symbolically gives an abstract order and structure to his body politic as represented in the landscape scenery.

The masque provided a means of representing a state that no longer needed to manifest itself to its leading members via the monarch's bodily progress through the commonwealth. In the masque the authority of the state is represented in terms of a spatial structure, or "body geographical," in which the body of the state becomes one with the landscape. The authority of the monarch now transcends his physical body and is made tangible in the landscape scene that he surveys and controls.[10] The power of the state is made manifest by the servants of the state, under the authority of the surveilling monarch, to control the scene, from behind the scenes, via the mysterious, invisible, geometrical laws of visual perspective.[11] The monarch on his elevated throne is no longer the primary object of the public's gaze; the focus of attention is now upon the actors and scenery on the stage. The monarch, however, is also visible, elevated above the public on his throne of state. This placement was in keeping with James's view of the position of the monarch. He wrote, for example, that "a King is as one set on a skaffold, whose smallest actions & gestures al the people gazingly do behold" (James I [1599] 1969, 121). The amateur actors on the stage of the masque were an elite, chosen by the court, who represented the state's landscape embodiment as the body geographical. The spectators were also the elite of the realm. It was this elite who were being induced to envision this conception of the state.

THE STATE OF PROGRESS

The centralization of state power at the court of the capital city allowed for a form of progress which was very different from the circuitous progress that monarchs had been forced to make in order to manifest their estate to the members of the body politic (Olwig 2002). Jones's representation of the theater of this estate created a basis for conceptualizing this very different kind of royal progress. Now it was the monarchical head on the throne of state who, via his servants, controlled the scene. The monarch occupied a fixed position while the scenery changed and moved in a progression through the uniform space of the stage. The masque thus manifested the symbolic power of the monarch to make progress by moving the world.

Jones had learned stage design in Italy, where the theater adhered to the ancient classical rule of the three unities of time, place, and action; hence, changes of scenery were unimportant. England, however, preserved a medieval drama tradition (including the street theater, associated with processions and state progresses of various kinds) in which changes of locality and scene were an important aspect of the plot (Kernodle 1944; Chambers 1951, 18–19). In this tradition the movement from conflict to resolution often involved a movement in space from court/town to the forest, a utopian "green world" where the conflict was resolved, and then back to the point of origin (Frye 1971, 182; see also Frye 1965, 142; 1967, 85). This movement, in turn, has roots in the folk ritual of the carnival and the spring festivities which mark the yearly epiphany of new life on earth (Frye 1965, 54, 72, 104–6, 119; Bakhtin 1984, 11; Wiles 1993, 86–99). The use of theater scenery in Jonson and Jones's masques involved progressive changes of scene that tended to follow the older ritual pattern. This type of masque is "always about the resolution of discord; antithesis, paradoxes, and the movement from disorder to order are central to its nature" (Orgel 1969, 3). Thus, the masque provided a means for spectators to envision a form of state progress through time, scene by scene, stage by stage, which involved movement through space as well as the revolutionary transformation of scenery through time.[12] The state of human society was shown as changing in accordance with the progressive changes of the scenery. The perspectives provided by the scenic landscape prospects pointed forward to a future ideal state. In staging masques rather than traveling around the country, the monarch shifted the focus from the progress of his body to the reflection of himself in the landscape, itself perceived as a body.

The masques used landscape scenery to make visible a message of social and political "revolution." They portrayed a revolutionary turning of the cycles of the ages that would return through the golden age renaissance of an earlier imagined Britain and, simultaneously, obliterate the memory of contemporary disunity. It was by means of such a revolution that the British monarch would be made heir to the imperial glories of the classical era (Gordon 1949, 163), the era of *Pax Romana*. Such a transformation is represented in Inigo Jones and Aurelian Townshend's masque *Albion's Triumph*, which was performed on Twelfth Night, 1632, for the court of James and Anne's son Charles I. The stage entrance of the monarch is the signal for a change of scenery: "The scene is varied into a landscip in which was a prospect of the King's palace of Whitehall and part of the city of London seen afar off, and presently the whole heaven opened, and in a bright cloud were seen sitting persons representing Innocency, Justice, Religion, Affection to the Country, and Concord, being all companions of Peace" (quoted in Orgel and Strong 1973, 457, lines 337–45).

The landscape made manifest here is that of a country, united within

Fig. 4.4. "A Peaceful Country." This scene by Inigo Jones from the 1640 masque *Salmacida Spolia* captures the ideal of the landscape of "Innocency" under the enlightened monarch's reign, as described in *Albion's Triumph*. The allegorical figures seem to float in the clouds (they are suspended in "flying machines"). Photo: Photographic Survey, Courtauld Institute of Art. Reproduced with the permission of The Devonshire Collection, Chatsworth. Reproduced by permission of the Duke of Devonshire and the Chatsworth Settlement Trustees.

the space of the landscape scene, making progress under an enlightened monarch (Olwig 2002). It would naturally have included an image of the physical progress made in British architecture through Jones's introduction of Renaissance principles of design. The landscape represented on the stage might thereby be seen to upstage the monarch in the back of the room.

THE DISEMBODIED HEAD OF STATE

A curious thing about the invisible, all-surveilling structure of the state represented by the theater of the masque is that the importance of the physical person of the monarch was actually reduced. James's "head" held a symbolic position that could in practice be occupied by a figurehead (as in modern constitutional monarchies), without affecting the behind-the-scenes structuring power of the theater of state. James was the symbol of

the centralized state that the state servants were then working to construct
(Smith 1984, 116–17). As a physical being ("the body natural"), however,
he was not vital to the functioning of this state because his body was no
longer represented as being entirely connatural with the estate of the
monarch ("the body corporate"). The monarch's body natural had now,
in effect, been reduced to the role of an eye in a disembodied head located
in an abstract system of coordinate lines that had the power to frame and
shape the body politic as represented on stage.[13]

The real holders of power in the theater of state were the invisible state
servants, the architects of the state who framed its power structures, not
the person who happened to sit in the symbolic seat of power. Theatrical
illusion, in this context, served to mask the work of the state, then known
as the "mysteries of state." This idea of the state as mystery goes back to
the roots of the idea of the body politic as a secular version of the church,
with its members representing the "mystical" body of Christ. The word
*mysteries* means secrets, and the term "mysteries of state" plays on the
technical, theological, and political senses of the word (OED: mystery 1,
5c; Jonson 1985, 722). The wonders worked by Jones belonged, in this respect, to an established tradition going back in England to the scenography of John Dee, the mathematician, scientist, surveyor/architect, magus,
astrologer, and Neoplatonic mystic who served Elizabeth's court (Yates
1969, 52–88; Mebane 1989, 84–87). The secretive, mystifying character
of the Stuart state is evidenced by its fondness for closed bodies like the
Privy (private) Council.

The symbolic, and practical, dematerialization of the monarch's physical role as head of the body politic no doubt suited the shy James, who
feared attack upon his body natural and shunned the limelight. It will be
seen, however, that there were others, among them Ben Jonson, who began to have second thoughts about the official architect of the Stuart state,
Inigo Jones, and his role in creating the symbolic edifice of that state.

THE ARCHITECT OF THE BRITISH STATE

The theatrical space in which the masque was performed gave an elevated
place of honor to the monarch, from which he surveyed the landscape scene
before him. The term *surveyor* was synonymous with architect, and the
"supreme architect" was God (Gordon 1949). The leading surveyor-
architect of the Stuart court was Inigo Jones, the "Surveyor of the King's
Works." It was Jones who designed the theatrical "machinery" by which the
spectral image of the Stuart British body politic was made manifest to the
leading figures of the realm. It was by Jones's "omnipotent design," as Jonson later put it, that the "wise surveyor! Wiser architect," would "survey a

Fig. 4.5. Background scenery for a scene by Inigo Jones for a 1632 masque, *Tempe Restored*, illustrating a long-standing theatrical tradition, predating the introduction of perspective scenery, of representing the king as a god-like figure (Jove in this case) looking down upon his people from the sky. Photo: Photographic Survey, Courtauld Institute of Art. Reproduced with the permission of The Devonshire Collection, Chatsworth. Reproduced by permission of the Duke of Devonshire and the Chatsworth Settlement Trustees.

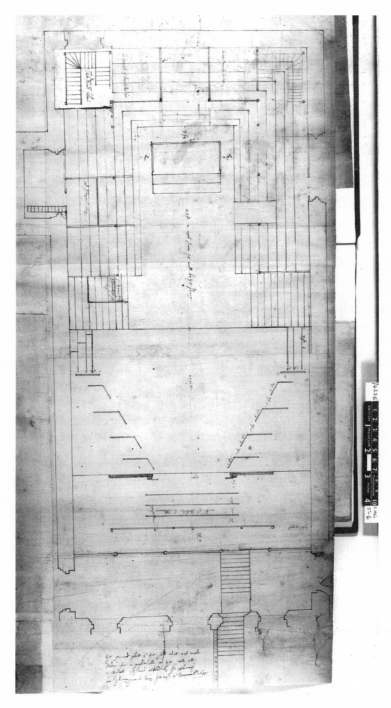

Fig. 4.6. Plan of the stage and auditorium in Whitehall for the play *Florimène* in 1635. The "state" or throne was located in the area marked by a box in the center of the hall, opposite the stage, at an ideal spot for experiencing the illusion of three-dimensional scenic space. It was not, however, an ideal spot for hearing the text of the play or masque. By permission of the British Library: Lansdowne Ms 1171 ff. 5b-6.

state" ("An Expostulation with Inigo Jones" [1631] in Jonson 1985, 462–65).[14]

The lines of perspective that converged upon the head of state from the horizon of the scene were constructed with techniques derived, as noted in chapter 1, from surveying. Like the figure of the state in Hobbes's frontispiece, the king "oversaw" the space of the state as it was embodied in the landscape scenery of Britain. In practice, men like Jones were the actual architects of the theater of state, both literally and metaphorically. Jones believed that the idea or conception precedes the invention or form of a construction. Design, to him, meant "the expression of the idea, or conception, or invention" (Gordon 1949, 169–70). Jones characterized himself as a "designer" and demanded to be known as the co-inventor with Jonson of the masques, much to Jonson's anger (ibid., 168–71).[15] It might thus be said that Jones used his art to "invent" and "design" the renaissance of the British state.

Nobody was more disturbed by Jones's inventions and designs than Jonson, who watched with growing horror as the upstart designer of the stage sets upstaged his own texts and turned the poet's *audience* into Jones's *spectators* (Orgel and Strong 1973, 7). The author's authority was being subverted by the designs of the scenographer.[16] Jonson's unease increased after Jones was made surveyor of works in 1615 and his designs were no longer limited to the stage. Now in his masques he was able to create models of buildings that he built out of real wood and stone for the people of the court. A masque scene might thus include a representation of the palace he had built for Queen Anne in Greenwich, the first classical-style villa in England. The masque theater really became a hall of mirrors when the scenery included the image of the theater within which it was being performed—the Banqueting House at Whitehall, which Jones designed and built after a fire in 1619 (ibid., 40–41, 354–57). The power of the architect is infinitely mirrored in a situation in which the spectator gazes upon the three-dimensional scenic illusion of a building (designed according to the same perspectival principles as the scenery) that represents the building within which the spectator is standing and gazing at a three-dimensional scenic illusion of the building—and so on ad infinitum.

From court masques to military defense works, royal palaces, and town plans for the capital, Jones now set the stage for the state. To Jonson, Inigo became "Iniquo," which meant, as a reader of John Florio's contemporaneous Italian-English dictionary would have known, "impious, wicked, unrighteous" (Florio 1611: iniquo). Johnson and Jones's partnership ended in 1631 with a vituperative quarrel that led Jonson to portray Jones in a sketch as an arrogant "Coronel Iniquo Vitruvius" who proclaims: "Do you know what a Surveyor is now? I tell you, a supervisor! A hard

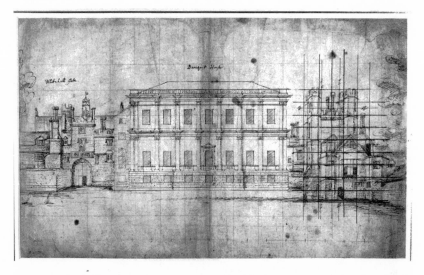

Fig. 4.7. Whitehall Banqueting House, a stage scene by Inigo Jones including the architect's drawings for the actual Banqueting House, from the 1623 masque *Time Vindicated to Himself and to His Honours.* The Banqueting House was fitted in 1636 with ceiling paintings by Peter Paul Reubens showing, among other things, the union of Scotland's and England's crowns under the Stuarts and over the dead bodies of the allegorical female figures of Envy and Ignorance. Photo: Photographic Survey, Courtauld Institute of Art. Reproduced by permission of the Conway Library, Courtauld Institute of Art.

word, that; but it may be softened, and brought in to signify something. An overseer! One that overseeth you. A busy man!" (Jonson [1634] 1873, 664; see also Yates 1969, 88).[17] Jonson's term "spectacles of state" for Jones could call forth associations to the idea of surveillance, since the word *spectacle* is related to the Latin *specere,* to look at, which is akin to the word *spy* (MWC10: spectacle, spy).[18] If the Banqueting House should burn again, Jonson now hoped "thy architect [it would] to ashes turn!" ("An Expostulation with Inigo Jones" [1631] in Jonson 1985, 462–65).[19]

## THE BEHEADING OF BRITAIN'S STATE

There was no more than a fine line between stage scenery and the designs that Jones sought to impose upon the buildings and plan of the capital, as in the Banqueting House at Whitehall. "All the world" was indeed becoming "a stage," a "wide and universal theater," as Shakespeare put it in *As You Like It.*[20] This world was a stage which the king viewed from a seat of state placed on a pedestal like the one James described, as has been seen, to his first son: "a King is as one set on a skaffold, whose smallest actions

& gestures al the people gazingly do behold" (James I [1599] 1969, 121). This pedestal proved to be a dangerous place for James's surviving son, Charles I. It was upon a scaffold just outside Jones's Banqueting House where the head of the head of the state was momentously severed from Charles's body in full view of the body politic.[21]

The revolt against the court of James I and Charles I was also a revolt against its theater and its landscape image of the Stuart British body politic. The great upwelling of support for the "country" and English Parliament against the British court, and for customary and common law against the statutory law of Bacon and the Stuarts, bespeaks a counter-revolution against the court's landscaped vision of the country. The revolution proclaimed on the Jacobean court stage bred the contrary idea that the state could also be overthrown by revolution.[22] It was the countrymen who overthrew the power of the Stuart court, but according to a latter-day countryman, Robert Molesworth, it was the Stuart court that set the wheel of revolution turning:

> And because some of our *Princes* in this last Age, did their utmost Endeavour to destroy this Union and Harmony of the *Three Estates,* and to be *arbitrary or independent, they* ought to be looked upon as the *Aggressors* upon our Constitution. This drove the other Two Estates (for the Sake of the publick Preservation) into the fatal Necessity of providing for themselves; and once the Wheel was set a running, 'twas not in the Power of Man to stop it just where it ought to have stopp'd. This is so ordinary in all violent Motion, whether mechanick or political, that no body can wonder at it. . . . When Subjects take Arms against their *Prince,* if their Attempts succeeds, 'tis a *Revolution;* if not, 'tis call'd a *Rebellion:* 'tis seldom consider'd, whether the first Motives be just or unjust. (Molesworth 1738, viii–ix, emphasis in original)[23]

The Stuarts' theatrically landscaped dreams of founding a new state of Britain under the rule of their absolute law definitively melted into thin air when the Glorious Revolution of 1688 put an end to their dynasty. The country defeated the court at this time, but the dream of a unified British state did not die. Inigo Jones's landscape visions did not perish with the Stuarts; instead, the parliamentarians who inherited the Stuart state gave them new form. Jones masqued the power of the state as landscape stage scenery. His successors went one step further and literally landscaped the country itself, transforming it, in the process, into what came to be perceived as the natural countryside of Britain.

# Five

# Landscaping Britain's Country and Nature

Roughly a century after landscape made a dramatic entry into Modern English discourse at an urban court masque in 1605, it became a focus of interest as the scenery surrounding the countryseats of an oligarchy of great estate owners. This landed gentry controlled the Parliament that consummated James I's dream of wedding the countries of Britain together into a single state within the naturally defined geographical body of the British Isles. The rediscovery at this time of Inigo Jones's scenic vision of Britain as landscape helped inspire the redesigning of the countryside in the style of the "natural" or "landscape" garden. This process not only transformed the physical landscape scene; it also "landscaped" the meaning of both nature and country so that each came to be identified with scenery.

Landscape, conceived as scenery, now provided a template for the transformation of great swaths of the country. Because the landscaped estates were fashioned from the physical substance of the countryside itself, it could be difficult for the inexperienced eye to distinguish the designed representation of the country from the actual country environment upon which the design was imposed. This difficulty facilitated and masked the merging of the ideas of landscape, country, and nature to produce a potent ideational cocktail that still influences the modern perception of the environment. The concept of country thereby gradually ceased to be understood primarily in terms of customary law and justice and instead came to be seen in terms of the landscape scenery of the countryside. This countryside scenery became valued for its aesthetic qualities and for the cultural status which it conveyed upon those who possessed an elevated countryseat with a commanding view, or who had the standing to be allowed to perambulate within its circumambient space.

## THE LANDSCAPE GARDEN AS THE THEATER OF BRITAIN

A century prior to the vogue for Palladian-style country estates, Inigo Jones, the founder of British Palladianism, had created visions of similar country landscape scenes on the stage. This was a form of total theater where the illusive world of masque and theater scenery merged with the political world of actual courtiers and monarchs. Now, it was as if this "masqued," designed world had been moved out of the theater and court into the very countryside itself. The elevated countryseat from which the gentry surveyed the landscape scene took the place of the elevated throne of state as the seat of power. As in the masque, the scenery framed the actions of the members of the body politic who were permitted to share the scene. Such a transferal of scenic ideas from the theater to the garden was a common theme in the discourse of the time, as when Horace Walpole wrote of garden design: "Prospect, animated prospect, is the theatre that will always be the most frequented" (Walpole [1782] 1943, 34).

Gardens had long been used, both in Britain and on the Continent, as sites for masques and other theatrical presentations, and it was natural for theater scenery to inspire developments in garden design (Strong 1979, 11, 200–203; Hunt 1992, 49–73). Queen Anne of Denmark thus made her first acquaintance with the theater of Ben Jonson in a formal garden. On her procession from Scotland to London, to be recrowned as James's English queen, she visited Althorp, the Spencer family seat. Here she was met by an actor playing Mab, queen of the fairies, who emerged out of the shrubbery to present her with a jewel and thereby introduce the play (Akrigg 1962, 23). When Jones later teamed up with Jonson to make the court masques for Queen Anne, he used such verdant settings indoors. These settings included landscape backdrops that framed representations of his British Palladian architectural visions. The open arcadian vistas which characterized this scenery, however, represented a distinct break from the closed geometric rigidity of the formal garden of Jones's day. In the course of the eighteenth century the conception of the garden would change in favor of such open landscape vistas. This occurred concurrently with the spread of what Lord Shaftesbury called a "new national taste" for architecture in "the stile of *Inigo Jones*" (quoted in Woodbridge 1970, 18, emphasis in original).

Whereas the formal Renaissance gardens of the Stuart era appeared to be an extension of the architecture of the mansion (Strong 1979, 169), the arcadian landscape gardens of the following century were oriented toward the surrounding countryside and were consciously blended with it as "natural" landscape scenery. The boundary between garden and countryside was deliberately blurred by erecting the fence in a ditch, below eye level, so that there seemed to be no barrier between the garden and the outside world. The subterfuge was called a "ha-ha" because this is what a stroller in the garden would exclaim on the verge of falling into the hidden ditch. The obliteration of boundaries helped create the illusion of a pastoral, Arcadian golden age when, as Virgil put it, there was "no fence or boundary-stone to mark the fields" (Virgil 1946, 69 [*Georgics* 1.151–52]). The device of the ha-ha made it possible for the Jones-inspired garden architect William Kent to "leap the fence" surrounding the garden, as Horace Walpole put it, and thereby to show "that all nature was a garden" (Walpole [1782] 1943, 25). The corollary was that all the garden was also nature, and Kent's gardens were duly described by contemporaries as a "triumph of nature" (e.g., Boyse [1742] 1990).

"Delusive comparison," according to Walpole, facilitated the "leap of imagination" across the hidden fence ([1782] 1943, 26). This delusion, in turn, made it easy to forget that these idyllic landscaped images of classical pastoral scenes were often created upon parcels of land that, until their recent enclosure, had been the common pastures of English villagers. By this time the country had become "but a canvass on which a landscape might be designed" (ibid., 37). The function of the park, according to another contemporary, was "to extend the idea of a seat and appropriate a whole country to a mansion" (quoted in Daniels 1988, 45). This delusive comparison, however, also seemed to embody a paradox: the Whigs, who were the political descendants of the countrymen opponents of the court, were in the forefront of the revival of the British Palladian designs of Inigo Jones, the architect of court iconography (Clarke 1973, 569).

WHIG COUNTRY

The Glorious Revolution of 1688 was a triumph for the Parliament and hence, one would suppose, the triumph of the country over the court. Yet, this triumph was to be monumentalized by country estates in the British Palladian style of Inigo Jones, the Stuart court's premier architect. The explanation for this apparent paradox lies in the changes that occurred in English/British society between the Commonwealth and the Glorious Revolution. The Glorious Revolution, an essentially bourgeois "revolution," was virtually bloodless, which is indeed glorious, but it was hardly a revolution. It did not, as did the American Revolution a century later, overthrow the monarchy and create a republic. It overthrew James II and installed monarchs who were willing to accept parliamentary power, thus paving the way for an alliance between the court and powerful members of the Whig-dominated Parliament. Sir Robert Walpole, the father of Horace Walpole and a member of parliament, thus became a powerful de facto secretary of state for the court (though he did not bear the title). Much of the state's power came to lie in the hands of Sir Robert. His political career began in 1701 when he became an MP and he became leader of the House of Commons—effectively Britain's first prime minister—in 1721.

The Glorious Revolution resulted in a weakening of the personal authority of the monarch vis-à-vis Parliament, representing a further step in the reduction in power of the head of state over the body politic to that of figure head. This, in turn, had the effect of drawing attention to the scene of power, the landscape "body geographical." A countryseat, not London courtly pomp, legitimated political authority in postrevolutionary England. The Whig gentry might have disagreed amongst themselves over Walpole's politics, and disagreed, more generally, with the ancient landed nobility and conservative Tories, but all tended to identify with the country as the natural source of political legitimacy. The landscape of the country provided the site for a social and political discourse concerned with the naturalization of power. The idea of country played an important role in establishing the framework of this discourse (Williams 1973; Mennell 1985, 62–101; Bunce 1994). Was "country," as Old Whig countrymen maintained, the bastion of the customary rights and obligations upon which the ancient constitution had been founded, or was it a form of genteel landscape scene? The power to define the meaning of country gave the power to define the social and political legitimacy of political and economic power.

The Old Whig ideology of country contradicted the interests of men whose vast wealth did not stem so much from the country of little England as from the large-scale worldwide agricultural, industrial, and trading interests of imperial Britain. What the powerful Whig oligarchy needed was a means of preserving the image of legitimacy identified with the English country ideal while transcending the country ways of life, regulated by custom, that hindered agricultural "improvement" and commerce. This sense of country would be English in aspect, but British in its ability to embrace a world imperium ruled from a countryseat in a united Britain. If this new image was to be effective, the aura of country legitimacy would have to be transferred from the England of custom to the Britain of empire.

## British Country

Parliamentary opposition to the political unification within a British state changed considerably after the Glorious Revolution. During the course of the seventeenth century, English hegemony over the British Isles became virtually complete. Ireland was ruthlessly subdued, and British settlers colonized large areas of Northern Ireland. The expediency of a unified kingdom became apparent to the English Parliament when Catholic Jacobite pretenders to the English and Scottish thrones threatened, with the aid of France, to gain a foothold in Scotland. The union of parliaments led to the establishment of Great Britain as a single entity in 1707.

England was now incorporated within the unified Britain that had once been the stuff of Stuart dreams, but it was controlled by the political successors to the countrymen who had spoiled those dreams. The historian G. M. Trevelyan offers a sympathetic interpretation of the Whigs' motives. In his opinion the central power of the royal court ceased to be a problem once the danger to parliamentary rights posed by Stuart absolutism had passed and the "central power" thereby "became representative." Thus, "in the reigns of William III and Anne, the Whig Ministers carried out the schemes of James I—united, taxed, and armed Great Britain, and so enabled her in the eighteenth century to take a place in the world's politics." This change of circumstance explains why "the members of the House of Commons, fearing for British freedom, refused in 1607 to countenance a Union, which in 1707 their successors passed under changed conditions, as the surest guarantee of those very liberties" (Trevelyan [1904] 1960, 100). Trevelyan's "Whiggish" interpretation of the historical progress of parliamentary Britain overlooks, however, the autocratic abuse of power by the Whig oligarchs, most notably by Robert Walpole himself (Butterfield [1931] 1973; Thompson 1975).

By 1707, the term *British* was applied to a great deal more than the territory encompassed by the British Isles. Like the Britain envisioned in the masques by Ben Jonson and Inigo Jones, this Britain ruled the waves and hence knew no land boundary. It was a Britain that might, in principle, be extended to any location that was connected by water to the British Isles. This British Empire was in the process of redefining its identity. The overseas colonies established under Elizabeth I and James I tended to reproduce English society abroad and thus also reproduced a shared heritage of belief in the political rights of free English countrymen (Robbins 1961). This kind of settler colonialism replanted the ideological seeds of the contradictions between court and country in the colonies, and these contradictions then grew to encompass the relations between the British court and the country of the colony. It can be argued that these contradictions eventually led to the American Revolution (Bailyn 1967, 66–67). By the eighteenth century, however, the pattern of colonization had changed. The small-scale tobacco and indigo farms that had been settled by English farmers in the West Indies and the southern American colonies were now being replaced by huge, highly capitalized, slave-based plantation and factory complexes producing sugar and cotton. Plantation society thus did not, of course, foster the same sort of countryman ideal that had developed in England, that of the free yeoman farmer. In many cases these plantations were not owned by local gentry, but were rather the overseas extensions of the large-scale operations of absentee owners based on landed estates in Britain (Bridenbaugh and Bridenbaugh 1972; Hilliard 1990; K. F. Olwig 1993, 19–38). These landscaped estates thus became the seat of a world empire, constituting a global commonwealth of British power dotted with similar estates (Seymour et al. 1998). Ideas concerning the power of country changed radically from the earlier ideal of country as the place of a polity constituted through indigenous custom. Through the landscaping of the countryside, however, it became possible to create a new image of an ideal British country.

## British Landscape

The eighteenth century saw the revival of the "Britain" that had been identified with the court a century earlier, and it likewise saw the revival of British Palladian architecture in Jones's style. The Jonesian revival owed much to the efforts of Richard Boyle, third earl of Burlington (1694–1753), the great Whig patron of the arts. With the aid of the architect and painter William Kent, Burlington made an extensive collection of the works of Jones and Palladio, and together they developed the neo–Palladian style which set the standard for the typical British country estate (Clarke 1973, 569; Cosgrove 1984, 206–10; 1993, 21). Jones's Palladianism helped create the framework by which people like Burlington and Kent could situate Italianate aesthetics within a British national context. This helps explain the vogue for Italianate art which spread across Britain at this time (Manwaring [1925] 1965). The revival of Jones's Palladianism was part of a larger revival of the conceptualization of Britain that once had been identified with the Stuart court. Camden's *Britannia* now received renewed attention as a new generation of scholars worked to bring this definitive and defining British chorography up to date. An expanded English translation was published in 1695 and a revised edition in 1722 (Douglas 1939, 334–36; Piggot 1976, 44–52; Parry 1981, 331–57). An examination of a couple of the most important landscape gardens of the time illustrates how British ideals, originally identified with the court, became wedded to the lands of the country.

### A "WHIGSCAPE"

One of the earliest landscape gardens, dating from the 1720s, was on the estate of the Whig politician Robert Walpole (Everett 1994, 41). Walpole's landscape, however, was upstaged by the lavish scenes staged by one of his Whig opponents, Sir Richard Temple, who had become Viscount Cobham in 1719. After his falling out with Robert Walpole, in part over defense issues, Cobham had become a representative of the "patriot" Whig opposition. Cobham thereafter symbolically withdrew to Stowe, his country

Fig. 5.1. The Temple of Apollo. Design by Inigo Jones from the period 1630 to 1640. Photo: Photographic Survey, Courtauld Institute of Art. Reproduced with the permission of The Devonshire Collection, Chatsworth. Reproduced by permission of the Duke of Devonshire and the Chatsworth Settlement Trustees.

estate in Buckinghamshire, where he created a symbolic Whig landscape garden (Woodbridge 1970, 7–10; Hunt 1992, 75–102).

The garden iconography from this period at Stowe reflects an eclectic blend of pro-war British imperialism (Cobham was a distinguished military officer) and old-guard countryman Whig paeans to ancient liberties (Clarke 1990, 7–8). The complex symbolism of temples and statues at Stowe was the result of a collective effort by a large circle of Cobham's highly literate friends, including the poet Alexander Pope. Continuity was maintained, despite the many contributors, because Cobham personally directed the effort. A succession of Britain's foremost landscape gardeners served Cobham, beginning with Charles Bridgeman (?–1738) and continuing on to William Kent (ca. 1685–1784) and Lancelot "Capability" Brown (1715–1783); they all, along with Humphry Repton (1752–1818) (see Daniels 1999), would reshape large areas of Britain in the new English/British country style.

From 1724, when Cobham's gardening activities first gained a national reputation for Stowe (he had inherited the estate in 1697), these gardens became the most frequently visited and no doubt most influential gardens in Britain. "The gardens here," as the learned Jeremiah Milles put it in 1735, "are accounted the finest in England" ([1735] 1990, 61). The gardens contain many references to Rome and the Roman poet Virgil. They

Fig. 5.2. Temple of Ancient Virtue overlooking the Elysian fields, Stowe. Photo: author.

include a structure called Dido's Cave (named for Aeneas's lover in the *Aeneid*) as well as a Temple of Ancient Virtue modeled on a famous Roman temple near the gardens at Tivoli outside Rome (Whistler et al. 1968, 17–26; Woodbridge 1974, 136 n. 10). The references to Virgil would have provided an educated visitor to this eighteenth-century "heritage" park with a clue to its deeper meaning. A central element of the park was the "Elysian fields," which were developed in 1733–1739 and are usually identified as the work of Kent, who was responsible for the architecture of the buildings. The Elysian fields, which the novelist Samuel Richardson called "the most charming Place that ever Eyes beheld" (Defoe and Richardson [1742] 1990, 88), came complete with grazing horses. This was interpreted by contemporaries as being an iconographic reference to Virgil's depiction of the resting heroes as being accompanied by their beloved equestrian companions to the Elysian fields (Virgil 1990, 153, lines 650–60; Anonymous [1738] 1990, 69).

In the sixth book of the *Aeneid,* as noted in chapter 3, the Trojan hero Aeneas makes a journey with the Sibylline prophetess into the underworld to meet his dead father. After crossing the River Styx, they enter the idyllic pastoral environment of the Elysian fields, where Aeneas's father resides. Here they meet the ancient heroes who are worthy of being admit-

Fig. 5.3. View across the Elysian fields (sans horses) and the River Styx toward the Temple of British Worthies at Stowe. Photo: author.

ted and it is here that these ancient Trojan heroes lose their memories of their prior identities before returning to the world of the living, reborn as the Italian heroes who founded the Roman Empire (Virgil 1990, 132–70). Stowe's Elysian fields included a River Styx, pools of water, and both a Temple of Ancient Virtue and a Temple of British Worthies, complete with a head of Mercury, the messenger god who led the souls of heroes to the Elysian fields (Whistler et al. 1968, 22). Here, however, ancient heroes would have been transformed not into Roman founders of the Roman Empire, but into British founders of the British Empire.

The temple for the worthy British at Stowe was dominated by the busts of figures who personified the principles of the Glorious Revolution, but it also included a bust of Inigo Jones.[1] Jones's style of architecture was now identified with William Kent and Kent's mentor, the earl of Burlington, in whose minds this style was an expression of Whig ideals (Clarke 1973, 569). The inscription on Jones's bust reads: "Who, to adorn his Country, introduced and rivaled the *Greek* and *Roman* Architecture" (quoted in Defoe and Richardson [1742] 1990, 89, emphasis in original). Kent had a detailed knowledge of the work of Jones, and the Elysian fields bear resemblance to many of Jones's scenic designs with their open vistas scattered with Palladian temples.[2] Jones's bust must have looked at home in the landscape scenery of the Elysian fields at Stowe because the design and iconography of the gardens was so similar to the complex iconography of the masque landscapes he had created to celebrate the rebirth of Britain. The designers of the gardens consciously drew parallels with the stage by applying the name "theater" to particular locations. One of the first garden architects to work at Stowe was Charles Bridgeman, and one of his "signatures" was the garden theater (Hunt 1992, 6–61).

It was no accident that the Temple of British Worthies at Stowe included monuments to Locke, Bacon, and Newton. Newton is memorialized with the inscription "Whom the GOD of Nature made to comprehend all his Works; and from simple Principles to discover the Laws never known, and to explain the Appearances never understood, of this stupendous Universe" (quoted in Defoe and Richardson [1742] 1990, 89). Nature at this time, according to Basil Willey, was seen to conform to "the laws of reason; they are always and everywhere the same, and like the axioms of mathematics they have only to be presented in order to be acknowledged as just and right by all men." The vision of an ideal state of nature governed by natural laws provided the "means whereby the new ruling classes could vindicate, against the surviving restraints of the old feudal and ecclesiastical order, their cherished rights of individual freedom and of property" (Willey 1940, 14–18, quotation on 17). This mindset is well illustrated by the architect Christopher Wren's statement that,

Fig. 5.4. Bust of Inigo Jones at the Temple of British Worthies, Stowe. Photo: author.

There are two causes of Beauty—natural and customary. Natural is from Geometry, consisting in Uniformity (that is Equality) and Proportion. Customary Beauty is begotten by the Use of the four Senses to those Objects which are usually pleasing to us for other causes, as Familiarity or particular Inclination breeds a Love to Things [such as "Gothic Cathedrals"] not in themselves lovely. . . . Geometrical Figures are naturally more beautiful than any other irregular; in this all consent, as to a Law of Nature. (quoted in Bennett 1982, 120–21)

The landscape garden at Stowe was informed by the "Natural" ideal of beauty. Though it was not rigidly geometrical, like the Renaissance garden, it expressed uniformity and proportion in its carefully balanced harmonious scenes. Arbiters of classical Augustan taste, like the painter Sir Joshua Reynolds, praised art in the Italianate tradition and denigrated Dutch landscape painting (Alpers 1983, xvii–xxvii). Dutch painting was marred by its concern with the "particularity" of place and time; Reynolds preferred paintings which expressed an "eternal invariable idea of nature." He felt that art should represent that which was characteristic of "all ages and all times," not the particularities of local custom (quoted in Barrell 1986, 138, 141).

The landscape garden provided a stage upon which to impose a scenic vision of a country governed by the higher laws of nature, as reflected in Newtonian science. It is characteristic that one of the earliest uses of the word *nature* to refer to scenery that is recorded in the *Oxford English Dictionary* is from John Dryden's translation of Virgil's *Georgics* (OED: nature 13). The passage reads:

> But time is lost, which never will renew,
> While we too far the pleasing path pursue,
> Surveying nature with too nice a view.
>         (Dryden [1697] 1806, 175
>         [*Georgics* 3.448–50])[3]

Dryden's nature, surveyed as view, was identified by contemporaries with a didactic mode of transmitting useful practical knowledge, as exemplified by the *Georgics* (Aubin 1936; Wilkinson 1969). Dryden had been the poet laureate of the Restoration, but the introduction to his translation was written by the budding Whig literary figure and arbiter of taste Joseph Addison (Smithers 1968, 35), who is thought to have later helped inspire the design of Stowe's Elysian fields.[4] In a passage that brings to mind the inscription on Newton's bust at Stowe, Addison wrote in the introductory essay to Dryden's translation:

> Natural philosophy has indeed sensible objects to work upon; but then it often puzzles the reader with the intricacy of its notions, and perplexes

him with the multitude of its disputes. But this kind of poetry I am now speaking of [didactic Georgic poetry], addresses itself wholly to the imagination: it is altogether conversant among the fields and woods and has the most delightful part of *nature* for its province. It raises in our minds a pleasing variety of scenes and *landscapes* [*landskips* in original], whilst it teaches us; and makes the driest of its precepts look like a description. (Addison [1697] 1806, 85, emphasis added; OED: landscape 2)

Nature became virtually synonymous with landscape scenery in the thinking of the time. It was in the landscape scene that the laws of nature became manifest, and it was the poet who gave aesthetic expression to these laws. Dryden saw himself as a "kind of lawgiver" writing in a "legislative style" that instructed by showing its objects in "their true proportions" and thus "shewing them what they naturally are" (quoted in Aubin 1936, 85). "Happy the man," Dryden's Virgil thus tells us, "who through known effects can trace the secret cause" by "studying Nature's laws" (Dryden [1697] 1806, 152 [*Georgics* 3.698–99]).[5] Stowe included statues of men of science because it was not just the site of a pastoral landscape garden, as idealized in Virgil's *Eclogues;* it was also the core of a working agricultural landscape, as idealized in Virgil's *Georgics.* The didactic transmission of agricultural science, as exemplified by the *Georgics,* was seen to be the key to agricultural improvement (Fussel 1972, 138–74). "A Georgic," as Addison put it, "therefore is some part of the science of husbandry put into a pleasing dress, and set off with all the beauties and embellishments of poetry" (Addison [1697] 1806, 85). To be able to gaze into the space of the landscape scene and comprehend its scientific and aesthetic didactical meaning became the mark of education (Barrell 1972; 1992, 41–62). This would explain why Addison pronounced Virgil's poem to be "the most complete, elaborate, and finished piece of all antiquity" (Addison [1697] 1806, 95) and Dryden saw it as "the best poem of the best poet" (Dryden [1697] 1806, 66). There was no perceived contradiction between the aesthetics of landscape design and the ethos of improvement—quite the opposite (Daniels and Seymour 1978).

Virgil's works described the temporal course of empire from the pastoral golden age of shepherds, to the age of the hardworking farmers described in the *Georgics,* and, finally, to the age of empire traced in the *Aeneid* (Olwig 1984, 1–10). From the typical landscaped estate house, one's gaze followed a similar path through pastoral scenes and over agricultural fields before disappearing into the distant space occupied by the British Empire, upon which the sun eventually was never to set. The landscape garden may have looked like a site of pastoral leisure under scattered shade trees, but it was penetrated by pathways, and the visitor was expected to rise up and move along them from one edifying monument to the next, reading the didactic text of the landscape inscribed at each site.

## Landscape under Command

Cobham and his circle of friends, such as the statesman and gardening enthusiast William Pitt and James Thomson, author of *The Seasons* and *Rule Britannia,* were militant British patriots (Woodbridge 1970, 9–10). The link between a military command and a commanding view is suggested by a question put to Cobham in a poem by William Congreve: "tell how thy pleasing Stowe employs thy Time, . . . what amuses thy Retreat, Schemes of War, or Stratagems of State?" ([1728] 1990). Cobham's nephew, and contributor to the garden's iconography, Gilbert West, supplies something of an answer to this question in another poem describing the military cast of the Stowe landscape:

> Far o'er the level Green, in just array,
> Long Rows of Trees their adverse Fronts display.
> So when two Nations, fierce in Arms, prepare
> At one decisive Stroke to end the War
> In seemly Order, e'er the Battle joins,
> The marshal'd Hosts extend their threat'ning Lines,
> And Files to Files oppos'd await the Word,
> That gives a Loose to the destroying Sword.
>                       (West [1732] 1990, 49–50)[6]

The perspective of the commanding view is that of the conqueror who attains, by right of conquest, absolute sovereignty over the "uncivilized" territory under his control (Barrell 1972, 24–25, 94). There was a long-standing relation between surveying and the military mindset. Surveying was a technique of great military importance. A royal surveyor, such as Inigo Jones, also had responsibility for overseeing the building of defense works. The aiming of artillery also required techniques affiliated with those of surveying, and this helped generate a conception of the terrain as a stage for plotting military action, a theater of war. The landed nobility had traditionally used their military obligations to justify their privileged position, and many of the estates that, like Stowe, were enclosed, emparked, and improved in the eighteenth century, were owned by families with a strong base of power in the military. The pastoral landscapes of the garden seem peaceful, just as the word "defense" in a modern government's Defense Department exudes peace, but they veiled a countryside that was often marked by violent conflict.

## Masking the Country

Stowe was fitted with the sunken fences, or ha-has, which concealed the border between garden and countryside. From the beginning, visitors commented on this feature: "What adds to the bewty of this garden is, that it is not bounded by Walls, but by a Ha-hah, which leaves you the sight of a bewtifull woody Country, and makes you ignorant how far the high planted walks extend" (Perceval [1724] 1990, 16). Others noted how the garden framed "agreeable Prospects into the Country" (Defoe and Richardson [1742] 1990, 81; see also ibid., 84). The arbiter of picturesque taste William Gilpin, in his 1748 *Dialogue Upon the Gardens at Stow*, expounds upon how the view from Stowe is so framed that "the Garden is extended beyond its Limits, and takes in every thing entertaining that is to be met with in the range of half a County." In this way the entire country around the park comes to be *improved* by being viewed aesthetically as *picturesque* scenic *landskip* (Gilpin [1748] 1976, 52; see also ibid. iii, 5).

The country might have been absorbed into the landscape scene, but the idea of country had not entirely lost its older social meaning. This is clear from the inscriptions on the monuments at Stowe that were intended to help the viewer interpret the scene. One inscription thus read: "Maintain Justice, and thy relative Duty; which, as it is great, when exercised to-

Fig. 5.5. "Ha-ha," or sunken boundary line, at Stowe. Photo: author.

ward our Parents and Kindred, so is greatest toward our Country." According to another inscription, "To be dear to our Country, to deserve well of the State, to be praised, honoured, and beloved, is glorious" (quoted in Defoe and Richardson [1742] 1990, 87). To serve the country, however, appears to have meant to serve the state, not a polity rooted in local community and custom. The Stowe gardens, in fact, effectively obliterated the memory of three country villages, a road, and a mill. It is little wonder that Oliver Goldsmith called such parks "a garden and a grave" in his poem *The Deserted Village* ([1773] n.d., 35–36). William Wordsworth similarly compared such mansions to the fabled Upas trees that "breathe out death and desolation" ([1810] 1968, 37–38). A medieval church at Stowe, however, was carefully hidden behind trees and allowed to remain standing—though its disrepair, vis-à-vis the newly constructed classical pagan temples, dismayed some contemporary commentators (Whistler et al. 1968, 18; Anonymous [1743] 1990).

The spreading lawns of the Elysian fields, where Stowe Village is thought to have lain (the "River Styx" might have been the village pond), erased not only the features of the original village lands but also the memory of customary country rights, which they had preserved in their material fabric (Turner 1976, 163–64; Bermingham 1987, 9–54; Bevington 1997). Just in case a commoner remembered the villagers' rights to the resources of their former commons and dared to take game on the land, the Whigs were ready with the dreaded Black Acts, which imposed vicious penalties on trespassers (Thompson 1975; Munsche 1981). This helps explain the following lines in Goldsmith's poem:

> The man of wealth and pride
> Takes up a space that many poor supplied;
> Space for his lake, his park's extended bounds,
> . . . . . . . . . . . . . . . . .
> His seat, where solitary sports are seen,
> Indignant spurns the cottage from the green.
> ([1773] n.d., 33)

The rural community sports that had once helped establish customary rights and mutual obligations had now become the symbols of individual privilege for the country gentry.

Cobham himself is remembered locally for his brutal punishment of commoners who trespassed upon his estate (Trench 1967, 123–24; Everett 1994, 41). The landscaping of Stowe may have erased the memory of the area as an actual country community, but it did provide, in its stead, a gothic-style Temple of Liberty dedicated to the ancient "liberty" of Great

Fig. 5.6. The church is all that is left of the ancient village at Stowe. Photo: author.

Britain as founded by Alfred the Great (Whistler et al. 1968, 18, 23; Wood-bridge 1970, 55; Everett 1994, 41).

Not all landscape gardens, however, were as politically motivated as the "Whigscape" created at Stowe. The mantle of the country was of social as well as political value. A good example of this is the estate of Stourhead, which was acquired by the Hoares, a newly rich family of London financiers.

### The Banks of the Stour

The Hoare family, who started out as horse dealers, rose to prominence in the course of the seventeenth century. By 1672, they were active on the London gold market. Gold trading led to money lending and banking, and it was through banking that the Hoare financial dynasty, which still exists, was founded. Although money was made in London, social legitimacy was ultimately rooted in the country. It was not enough to be lord mayor of London, as was Sir Richard Hoare, the founder of the bank. The Hoares needed to be "landed," and so Richard's son Henry bought the Stourtons' Stourhead estate in Wiltshire in 1717. The Stourtons were Catholic earls who had held lands along the banks of the Stour since before the conquest

(Woodbridge 1970, 1, 11–12). Henry then proceeded, like so many others in this situation, to tear down the ancient baronial mansion and build a new one in the British Palladian style. Henry Hoare the younger inherited the estate in 1725 and began work on the garden in the early 1740s, building a dam to create the lake in the 1750s. Though he was no Whig, Henry included Burlington and his circle among his friends. Hoare knew his Pope, and he knew the work of Jones. One of Henry's earliest commissions for Stourhead was "a bust of Inigo Jones in statuary marble" and "two figures of Inigo Jones and Palladio in plaster" (ibid., 21).

Henry Hoare created a veritable theme park for his garden in which the rise of Britain, as well as the Hoare family, was inscribed in its landscape scenery. The story of Trojan/Roman Britain that Ben Jonson had once used to fabricate the lineage of the Stuarts was now reformulated so that it became the heritage of the Hoare family. The path through the garden thus moves us deftly from classical architecture symbolic of the world of Aeneas and his great-grandson Brutus to the British Palladian architecture of the new estate house (ibid., 36).

The theme for Hoare's garden was taken from Virgil's *Aeneid*, the scenic setting was that of the arcadian pastoral lawn strewn with groves and monuments (ibid., 24). The garden, however, did not simply memorialize the Hoare's personal rise to fortune. Britain, now undergoing a rebirth concomitant with the rise of Hoare's own family's social and economic situation. Stourhead's landscape scenery was, in effect, the image of the restored nature of Britain; it both obliterated the country of the Stourtons while naturalizing the power of the new empire's financiers. If the country had been the expression of custom, this new landscape scene was the creation of a nature that both encompassed and transcended that country.

Stourhead appropriated England within the space of its British scenic frame. Stourhead encompassed, rather than destroyed (as at Stowe), a village that provided convenient housing for the estate workers. Henry Hoare's grandson, Richard Colt Hoare (known as "Colt"), inherited Stourhead in 1783 and proceeded to construct old English "follies" (as the various decorative temples and other structures were called) alongside the classical originals (ibid., 145–53). By Colt's (and Horace Walpole's) time, the landscape garden gloried in its ability to encompass "gothic" ruins (both real and constructed) and ersatz old English structures.

THE CHANGING LAND IN LANDSCAPE

The aesthetic experience of Jones's landscapes derived from theatrical illusion. The landscape park went one step further and applied these scenic

Fig. 5.7. Scene from Stourhead. The photo is taken from the vantage point of the English village, looking out toward the classical architecture inspired by Virgil's *Aneid*. Photo: author.

principles to the construction of "natural" scenes out of the living fabric of the countryside. It was in this landscaped environment that the educated classes learned to see all the world as a scenic resource. The meaning of the prefix *land-* in landscape thereby underwent a subtle but important shift. It ceased to be equivalent to *country*, an area, like England, defined by culture and custom, and came instead to have the sense of *terra firma*, a stage surface with infinite spatial perspectives, shaped by the surveyor and architect.[7] Social values no longer emanated from the customary law of the community; they came rather from the natural laws embodied in the scenery of the physical landscape and in its improvement. This was a new and naturalized vision of land and country that by its very striking beauty has since caused many to forget the older meanings. The transition in the meaning of country, which legitimated the power of the British elite, was made to seem natural through the medium of landscape scenery which, in effect, masked the original meaning of country.

## The Proprietary Space of Empire

The eighteenth-century estate owner, astride his countryseat, was in a situation analogous to that of James I astride his throne of state a century earlier. Both represented their power vis-à-vis the legal community of the commonwealth in terms of a unified geometric maplike space.[8] The right to individual domains, for both the Stuart court and the Whig oligarchy, was based upon propriety over a bounded territory. This territory was defined in terms of a quantity of geometric space that could not, by definition, overlap the territory of another domain. Each square foot could be valued in qualitatively comparable terms of size and monetary cost. By contrast, customary law, as it "lies upon" the land, defines place in terms of a community of overlapping, inherited, qualitatively different rights of usage. The goal of the Stuart court, in effect, was to establish the absolute authority of the royal estate over a British body politic enclosed by the boundaries of Britain. The scenic landscape of the masques provided a means of picturing this state and the progress that the body politic would achieve under state rule. The possessor of a countryseat likewise sought to consolidate power through the establishment of absolute rights of property over his enclosed estate. The landscape scenery surrounding his estate similarly provided a means of picturing the "improvement" which his enlightened overview would bring to the country (Barrell 1972, 64–97).

Surveying and mapping provided the techniques for the design and painting of landscape scenery (Daniels 1993b). The idea of the surveyed view and that of landscape had become nearly synonymous by the seventeenth century. Landscape might thus be defined as "A bird's-eye view; A plan, sketch, map," and it would be natural for an author, writing in 1642, to describe how "Some have used to get on the top of the highest Steeple, where one may view . . . all the Countrey circumjacent . . . and so take a Landskip of it" (OED: landscape 4f). The mapping of an estate brought much the same kind of status to the proprietor as landscaping. According to historians of cartography Roger J. P. Kain and Elizabeth Baigent, "The ownership of a landed estate with its fields, woods, mansion, farms, and cottages was the entrée to landed society, an estate was 'a little commonwealth' in its own right. A map pictured this cosmology and was a touchstone to the rights and privileges which possession of land brought in train" (Kain and Baigent 1992, 7).

Surveying and mapping provided a means of getting down to business. It was by surveying the land that it became possible to divide it into measured parcels which could then become the object of private ownership and investment (Edgerton 1975; Cosgrove 1985; 1988). All the resources within the bounded space of the property could then, in principle, be the possession of the owner. Surveying created a plottable space by making parcels of divisible and salable property out of lands which had previously been defined according to rights of custom and demarcated by landmarks such as topographical features, merestones, and balks (Kain and

Baigent 1992, 5). The landscape created by the laws of custom did not provide a suitable stage surface upon which to project one's improvements (Bushaway 1982, 22). The solution was to survey and enclose the land and eliminate, with or without compensation, local customary rights (Malcolmson 1973, 40, 107–8; Williamson and Bellamy 1987; Neeson 1993).

## Old Whigs versus New Whigs

Enclosure provided the means by which customary restrictions upon the rights of property could be removed, thereby creating the uniform space of an estate property (Butlin 1982; Neeson 1993; Thompson 1993, 97–351). To engage in enclosure, however, was morally problematic for anyone seeking to clothe himself in the countryman mantle because it meant dissolving the ancient customary rights upon which common law and country ideology had been built (Robbins 1961, 3–133; Pocock 1975, 423–61).[9] The so-called Commonwealthmen, or Old Whigs, perpetuated the "country" ideals of the early parliamentarians and countrymen (Robbins 1961). Robert Molesworth, a leading Old Whig who translated Hotman's *Francogallia* into English (Molesworth 1738; Giesey and Salmon 1972, 123–25), opposed the idea of Britain as a united body politic, favoring instead a federal structure in which the customs of each land would be respected. Molesworth saw the ancient rights of the English as a heritage of the Anglo-Saxons and Danes and, as might be expected, had no use for Roman political ideals:

> 'Tis said of the *Romans*, that those Provinces which they Conquer'd were amply recompensed, for the loss of their Liberty, by being reduced from their Barbarity to Civility; by the Introduction of Arts, Learning, Commerce and Politeness. I know not whether this manner of Arguing hath not more Pomp than Truth in it; but with much greater reason may it be said that all *Europe* was beholden to these [northwestern European] People for introducing and restoring a Constitution of Government far excelling all others that we know of in the World. 'Tis to the ancient Inhabitants of these Countries, with other neighbouring Provinces, that we owe the Original of Parliaments. (Molesworth 1694, 38–39, emphasis in original)

The new-guard Whigs, however, had an alternative, Italian ideal to oppose to the Roman imperium: Palladian Venice.

Venice provided, for the new-guard Whigs, the perfect source of parliamentary ideals to counter the Old Whigs who would root those ideals in ancient English custom. Venice, like Britain under Walpole, was led by an oligarchy that controlled a representative form of government. Venice, again like Britain, was an island state that had built its strength upon sea power and trade. It was also, in Palladio's day, a territory in which urban merchant capitalists were seeking to legitimate and ground their power by becoming landowners on the Veneto hinterland. Here they competed with the local landed aristocracy by creating vast estates on lands appropriated from the native peasantry. These estates centered upon country villas in an architectural style, pioneered by Palladio, that found inspiration in the architecture of ancient Greece and Rome and the pastoral scenery of ancient Arcadia, as idealized in Roman poetry. It is little wonder, given the similarities between the Whig oligarchs and the Venetian estate builders, that the Whigs were drawn to the ideals identified with Palladian Venice. Palladianism, however, also was identified with a compatible ideology that became known as "civic humanism," which traced its progress from the representative governments of the classical Mediterranean, starting with that of Arcadia in ancient Greece (Hunt 1991; Cosgrove 1993).[10]

The British political ideal of the new-guard Whigs was not republican, as was the Venetian, since it retained a monarchy. The British ideal was rather a generalized conception of a classical "Augustan" era, inspired by the peaceful reign of the Roman emperor identified by Virgil with the birth of a new golden age, and by Christians with the birth of Christ. The leading poet ideologue of "Augustan" Britain was Alexander Pope. According to Pope, the landscape garden created a copy of nature in the ancient Arcadian golden age. To imitate "nature," in Pope's view, was to imitate the way in which Virgil imitated Homer, for as Virgil discovered: "*Nature* and *Homer* were . . . the *same*." Pope thus concluded: " Learn hence for Ancient *Rules* a just Esteem; to copy *Nature* is to copy *Them* [the ancient rules]" (Pope [1711] 1963, 148, emphasis in original). The new garden style was "natural" because it involved adapting the natural, classical principles of design to the particular character of the British countryside. The point was that one should not slavishly copy the work of Jones and Le Nôtre, but rather adapt classical principles to the British scene. Pope gave succinct expression to these ideas in his 1731 manifesto for a "natural" style, *An Epistle to Lord Burlington*—inspired in great measure by his frequent visits to Stowe. Pope's natural garden is a veritable theater scene floodlit by the light of personal taste:

> A Light, which in *yourself* you must perceive;
> *Jones* and *Le Nôtre* have it not to give.
> To build, to plant, whatever you intend,
> To rear the Column or the Arch to bend,
> To swell the Terras, or to sink the Grot;
> In all, let *Nature* never be forgot.
> Consult the *Genius* of the *Place* in all,

> That tells the Waters or to rise, or fall,
> Or helps th' ambitous Hill the Heav'ns to scale,
> Or scoops in circling Theatres the Vale,
> Calls in the Country, catches opening Glades,
> Joins willing Woods, and varies Shades from Shades,
> Now breaks, or now directs, th' intending Lines;
> *Paints* as you plant, and as you work, *Designs.*
>
> .  .  .  .  .  .  .  .  .  .  .  .  .  .  .
>
> In you, my *Lord,* Taste sanctifies Expense,
> For Splendor borrows all her Rays from Sense.
> You show us, *Rome* was glorious, not profuse,
> And pompous Buildings once were things of use.
> (Pope [1731] 1988, 212–13)

Pope's ideal garden was not nature conceived as a material thing but an imitation of natural aesthetic laws as manifested in the classics. This emphasis on the natural eventually caused the British landscape garden to be thought of as romantically "natural" and organic, in contrast to the rational geometries of the formal garden (Neumeyer 1947). This perception was the result, in no small measure, of the influence of Robert Walpole's son, Horace, in his late-eighteenth-century reinterpretation of garden history, *The History of the Modern Taste in Gardening.* Here, Horace Walpole portrays Kent's "natural" style as being something of a glorious English "revolution" against the unnatural, despotic geometries of French gardening (Walpole [1782] 1943, 23–26, 37; Woodbridge 1974, 126).[11] This was not Pope's conception of the nature of the garden, however.

Pope began his literary career with a translation of Virgil's arcadian *Eclogues* in which he was careful to remind his readers that the shepherds depicted there should not be confused with contemporary herdsmen: "If we would copy Nature, it may be useful to take this Idea along with us, that pastoral is an image of what they call the Golden Age. So that we are not to describe our shepherds as shepherds of this day really are, but as they may be conceiv'd then to have been, when the best of men follow'd the employment" (Pope [1704] 1963, 120). It was the "best of men" who were permitted to perambulate in arcadian idylls that surrounded the Palladian country estate houses. The actual shepherds, such as the poet John Clare, obviously had no "natural" place in these legally, if not visually, enclosed landscape scenes of an Augustan golden age (Barrell 1972; see also Bermingham 1987; Williamson and Bellamy 1987; Everett 1994). Seen in this golden Augustan light, the enclosure of such symbols of ancient English custom as the commons in order to create a landscape park was not an *unnatural* blow to country values. It was rather an attempt to create a more elevated symbol of such values, appropriate to the glorious *natural* golden age of the future envisioned by the poets for Britain (Burd 1915). This was a place reserved for the best of men, who, by engaging in the economic and aesthetic improvement of the land, brought forth its latent potential. It was not the place of a traditional peasantry bound by the "unnatural" and "unaesthetic" vagaries of custom.

*Place Making*

The force of the Old Whig ideology weakened because the political balance of power changed radically between the time of the civil wars and that of the Glorious Revolution. Unlike the revolt against Charles I, the Glorious Revolution against James II did not depend on the support of dissident religious and social elements from the lower orders of society. Quite the opposite—post-1688 parliaments restricted the freedoms of religious dissidents and solidified the alliance between Anglican parson and rural squire which was subsequently to characterize country life. Whereas support for Cromwell had often been spurred by the opposition of the poor to an enclosure identified with the Stuarts, the post–Glorious Revolution country gentry became major instigators of parliamentary enclosure (Hill 1975, 50–56; Neeson 1993). In the past, the member of Parliament had represented his social estate as a member of a local "country"

Fig. 5.8. Pastoral idyll at Stowe. Photo: author.

community; now, however, the meaning of estate was changing such that one's social and political position in the nation was more closely related to the ownership of a country estate. One did not belong to a country defined as the place of a polity; one owned a place in the country. The landscaping of this country estate thus provided a means of veiling the revolution in the ideas of country and estate that had occurred in relation to the place of polity. Places generated by custom were thereby reduced to a position in the scenic space of a social landscape controlled by the landlord. The genius of a landscape gardener such as "Capability" Brown thus lay in his ability to perceive that an estate could be transformed through a process of architectural design that he called "place making" (quoted in Barrell 1972, 49–50).

An individual's "estate," be it that of a noble, commoner, or king, had traditionally been a function of the social standing of the person with respect to inherited rights and obligations. The estate, standing, or position of a person was thus intimately related to a web of interpersonal relations that were governed by both feudal obligation and custom. The lord had "seigneurial rights" over the land but did not own the land in the modern sense that a "landlord" lords over his private property. The Roman idea of *possessio* as applied to land was foreign to the customary conceptions of estate and land, and thus it could not determine a person's estate, or standing (Boserup 1965, 87). The problem for the gentry was solved by redefining *estate* in terms of a bounded parcel of land, "a country property" (OED: estate 13). This countryseat was landscaped so that each social group was carefully located in scenic space. The workers were situated in cottages nestled in the dale, and the proprietor overlooked the property from the mansion on the hill (Aubin 1936; Barkan 1975, 4–151; West [1732] 1990). "'Land' and 'place' became equivalent to 'propriety'— meaning in seventeenth-century English both *property* and *knowing one's place*" (Turner 1976, 5, emphasis in original). Property became the source of "all human liberty and all human excellence" for the oligarchs who took on the mantle of the country (Pocock 1972, 124–25). One's landed property became coequal with one's estate, the seat of one's status in the country and nation.

## NATION AND COUNTRY

The conception of landscape as natural scenery was the product of centuries of contention over the representation of the legal and political values identified with the country (and Landschaft). Gradually, as we have seen, the idea developed that the landscape is nature, and that it embodies the nation. Virgil is a recurrent figure in British discourse on landscape, nature, and nation. From the era of Inigo Jones to that of William Kent, his work continually reappeared as a source of inspiration. At Stowe, one crossed the Styx into Virgil's pastoral Elysian fields, and at Stourhead, the paths of the park traced the narrative of the *Aeneid*. Virgil's poetry was concerned with the essential *nat*ure, or character, of the Roman *nat*ion. *Nature* shares a common root with *nativity, native,* and *nation,* and it is also related conceptually to *kin* and *kindred* and to the Latin concept of the *genus,* from which words like *gene, genetic,* and *generate* derive (Lewis 1967, 26–33). There is thus a link between this sense of nature and the etymologically primary meaning of *nation* as "an extensive aggregate of persons, so closely associated with each other by common descent, language, or history, as to form a distinct race or people usually organized as a separate political state and occupying a definite territory" (OED: nation I: 1). Whereas *country* was seen to be constituted as a legal community united by customary law, the *nation* was an expression of the bonds of blood and territory. In Britain, these bonds came to be constituted by the landscape of the "body geographical" as the embodiment of the body politic. Part of the power of this identification lies, I will argue, in the fact that the body is gendered, as is the generative force of nature. When landscape becomes the embodiment of this generative, natural power, it takes on the added dimension of a sexual force. The relationship between landscape, nature, sexuality, and power is the subject of the next chapter.

# Six

# Gendering the Nation's Natural Landscape

Some of the high points of the 1605 *Masque of Blackness* were the scenes in which a bevy of revealingly clad nymphs, some of whom were virtually topless, were displayed before the king upon a stage. In casting a masque a premium was placed upon physical beauty, and the casts included the most beautiful people in the realm. The most important figure in this landscape was the king's queen and mate, Anne of Denmark, whose bare arms scandalized some puritanical members of the audience.[1] The whole space of the theater, which is located at Whitehall, the royal seat of power, expressed a cosmology in which a celestial male potentate brings order and fertility to the landscape of his natural realm as it is spread out before him.

The landscape scenery of the masque combined images of the natural with symbols of procreation and sexuality, and hence the concept of love in both the physical and social sense. Love, like the natural, is a concept that is both abstract and concrete. As an abstraction love, like the natural, is imbued with normative social values, and as with nature, these values are identified with the physical. Both terms blend when one speaks of "natural" or "unnatural" or abnormal ("deviant") love and sexuality. It is particularly this identification between nature/procreation/love which, I will argue, causes the meaning of nature in the objective physical sense to be conflated with ideas of the normal and natural. This combination of meaning makes nature, as Raymond Williams has written, "perhaps the most complex word in the language," much to the bedevilment of those who would cleanse nature of its hidden, value-laden connotations (Williams 1972, 184; Evernden 1992). This same identification of nature with love leads to a gendering of the nature of landscape scenery—with all its ramifications for the politics of social and national power (Olwig 1993b; Rose 1993, 86–112).

Landscape, conceived as natural scenery, owes its power in large measure to the way this confluence of ideas drew upon, and gave form to, centuries of thought and belief that identified nature with procreation and fertility, and hence gender. By "gender" I mean a sexual identity as male or female. Nature has been termed "the chief and most pregnant word in the terminology of normative provinces of thought in the West" (Lovejoy 1927, 444). It is first and foremost this identification with fertility and gender, I would argue, that gives the concept of nature its all-powerful normative content as the signifier of the natural. This normative power long predates the origin of the idea of nature as landscape scenery (Lovejoy and Boas 1935, 103–16; Olwig 1984, 1–9; Evernden 1992, 18–35). It is this power that is appropriated and expressed by *natural* landscape scenery.

The masques of Ben Jonson and Inigo Jones provide a key to understanding how the construction of nature as landscape scenery both incorporated a long history of gendered ideas of nature and gave them a new scenic form which is still influential. This chapter pivots on these masques, looking back, through the eyes of Jonson and Jones, into the ancient past, and looking forward toward our own time, in order to suggest the implications of this gendered landscape scene for the present.

## GENDERING THE BODY LANDSCAPE

The English subjects of the popular Queen Elizabeth were dismayed and preoccupied by the fact that she would not marry and produce an heir for the realm. By dying childless, she paved the way for the Stuart dynasty's entrance upon the scene. This new male dynasty was fittingly ushered in by a series of masques that played upon the symbolism of regal male potency. The representation of the monarch as the potent master of a fruitful national landscape harmonized with the vision of the monarch's "marital" relationship to his British state that James had presented, as noted, to his first parliament a year before the presentation of *The Masque of Blackness:* "What God hath conjoined then, let no man separate. I am the Husband, and all the whole Isle is my lawfull Wife; I am the Head, and it is my Body" (James I [1616] 1918e, 272).

This was a time, as we saw, when the idea of the body politic was taken quite literally. It was also a time when geographical areas were commonly represented with organic human shapes and considered to function much as a human body. This perception of Britain is illustrated by Michael Drayton's chorographic poem *Poly-Olbion*. Britain is represented in the frontispiece by a nubile blond, bare breasted goddess dressed in the map of Britain and surrounded by the figures of a Trojan/Briton (Brut), a Roman (Laureate Caesar), a Saxon (Hengist), and a Norman (William). After the Norman Conquest, according to Drayton: "She change'd hir Love to Him, whose Line yet rules" (Drayton [1612–22] 1961, ii; on Drayton's Trojans see MacDougall 1982, 22).

William Camden's *Britannia* provided the primary source for the geography of *Poly-Olbion,* just as it had done for the masques of Jonson and Jones (Drayton [1612–22] 1961, vi). In the *Poly-Olbion* Britain is described as if it were a living body with organs and limbs, "brancht with rivery veines." "In an amazing conceit," a modern British archaeologist comments, "Drayton turned the whole land into one vast court-masque, or a series of them, personifying the rivers and other natural features as one sees in the maps by Saxton which decorate each of the songs [poems]" (Boon 1987, 17–18). The relationship between maps and theater scenery was familiar to Renaissance cartographers, as indicated by titles of atlases and maps such as John Speed's *Theater of the Empire of Great Britain* (1611) and Abraham Ortelius's *Theatrum Orbis Terrarum* (Theater of the lands of the globe, 1570). Drayton himself explains that the maps that illustrate his poem are "lively" delineations of "every Mountaine, Forrest, River and Valley; expressing in their sundry postures; their loves, delights, and naturall situations" (Drayton [1612–22] 1961, vi). When Drayton writes of "love," he uses the word in a corporeal sense. The male wind thus comes sweeping down on the female Cluyd Vale, "survaying every part, from foote up to thy head," duly notes her "full and youthfull breasts," and comments seductively upon how sweets "from thy bosome flowe." The sight naturally pleases the "amorous eye" of this fertile wind, and he praises the valley's "plumpe and swelling wombe." Her "most precious lap" is described as smelling of "odoriferous flowers" in whose "velvit leaves" the airy suitor "en wraps" himself (ibid., 203).

In the maps in the *Poly-Olbion,* nearly every river and island is represented by a naked female. The towns and valleys also appear to be female, but are, as befits their civilized state, primly clothed.[2] The elevated hills, on the other hand, are men. The map-landscapes of Drayton's Albion thus worked to facilitate the perception of Britain as a single body politic, with a single personal history. "All of the conflicting variety of nature—and art—and politics—becomes harmonized," according to a literary analysis, "into a single whole: Arthur and Merlin, the Saxons and the Normans, become part of a single history—the history of Drayton's Albion—just as their divergent aesthetic traditions combine in the single poem which celebrates it" (Ewell 1978, 315). The point of the poem, it has been argued, was to portray Britain as an ideal organic and aesthetic unity, a body in which the various discordant parts were physically united by love, thereby illustrating the Renaissance principle of *discordia concors*—unity in diversity (Ewell 1978). This was also the intention of Inigo Jones's landscape scenery, the "bodily part" of the masque "imitating," according to

Jonson, that "orderly disorder which is common in nature" (Jonson 1969, 48). Drayton's attempt to represent the land in bodily terms is awkward and unintentionally comical when compared to the elegance of Jonson and Jones's scenic visualization, but they were all engaged in the same basic project—the visualization of Britain as a landscape "body geographical," the natural place of the British body politic.

## NATURAL NATURE

There is a connection between the ideological importance of the concept of nature and its complexity of meaning. This complexity derives from the inextricable link between the idea of *nature* and that of the *natural,* or normal. That which is natural is taken for granted as being normal—but therein lies the rub. What, for example, could be more natural than that James I should be king of Great Britain? After all, he *nat*urally inherited the throne of Scotland as well as England and Wales by virtue of his *nat*al background, which made him the "natural successovr." These realms, furthermore, were naturally united within the bounds of an island that was separated from the rest of the world by a "moat" of water (quotations from James I [1599] 1969, 1). Thus, Britain must naturally constitute a single realm under a British king, forming what Francis Bacon termed "the perfect union of bodies, politic as well as natural" (quoted in Kantorowicz 1957). But was Britain necessarily a more natural unity than was England, as represented by Parliament and defined by custom?

The marital metaphor deployed by the ideologues of the Stuart court provides a clue to understanding the relation between the idea of nature and that of the natural, which is expressed by natural landscape scenery. We saw in chapter 2 that the word *nature* is related to the concept of birth. The birth of children is, of course, the natural outcome of a fertile marriage. By the same token, the outcome of James's royal marriage with Britain should "naturally" be the rebirth of a fertile nation. This idea, as we have seen, was the persistent theme of Jonson and Jones's masques. Jones's landscape scenes were a means of representing this "natural" state resulting from James's marriage with Britain—the "happie issue," to use James's own words, "of this greater Vnion" (James I [1616] 1918e, 271–73). James believed that this union was an expression of the "love" that his people should feel for him as the head of state; for example, he spoke of the Parliament, the "representatiue body of the State," as "so willing, and louing receiuing and embracing of mee in that place [Parliament]" (James I [1616] 1918a, 281). Love was the key to the creation of a naturally happy, just, and fertile state. The concept of love is the key to understanding the complex double character of nature as being, on the

Fig. 6.1. A Daughter of the Morn, probably from the 1611 masque *Love Freed from Ignorance and Folly* by Jonson and Jones, in which Queen Anne of Denmark played a lead role. The "bodily part" of the masques included players dressed in revealing clothing. Photo: Photographic Survey, Courtauld Institute of Art. Reproduced with the permission of The Devonshire Collection, Chatsworth. Reproduced by permission of the Duke of Devonshire and the Chatsworth Settlement Trustees.

one hand, an abstract ideal norm (the *natural*), and, on the other, a physical presence (*nature*). The abstract and ideal dimension of love coexists uneasily with the concrete and physical dimension, just as in the case of nature. The call to "make love not war" is provocative precisely because it plays upon the tension between these two meanings of love. When Jesus, the prince of peace, speaks of loving thy neighbor as thyself, we assume that Christian love is an abstraction. He is not calling for us to make physical love to our neighbor or to engage in autoerotic behavior. Yet, there is also a distinctly physical dimension to Christian love. Christ was God made flesh, and Christian nuns see themselves as brides wedded to a Christ whose body and blood are present at the celebration of the Eucharist (Bataille [1957] 1987, 117–28).

The Christian Church has long been seriously divided, particularly since the Protestant Reformation, over the issue of whether or not the sacrament in the celebration of the Eucharist *is* actually the body and blood of Christ, or whether it is symbolic of that body and blood. This illustrates the problem of distinguishing between abstract symbolic meanings and the physical vehicle of that symbolic meaning. The same problem manifests itself when making the distinction between making bodily love and loving in a more abstract sense. This same uneasy tension between the abstract and the physical characterizes the relation between the concept of nature and that of love. James's contemporary, the poet and jurist John Davies, captures this relation in a poem: "What makes the vine about the elm to dance, With turnings windings and embracements round? . . . Kind nature first doth cause all things to love; Love makes them dance and in just order move" (quoted in Tillyard 1960, 97).

The ideas of love and nature have long been inextricably bound to one another, yet somehow the mind has difficulty grasping the connection. It is this mind-boggling quality which, I would argue, is the driving force which makes both concepts enormously powerful and enormously complex. The problem, however, becomes significantly easier to grasp if one unravels the intertwined meanings of love and nature step by step, thus revealing a logic that turns out to be quite familiar, and not at all mysterious. Because of Ben Jonson's enormous ability to synthesize a complex body of ideas, and Inigo Jones's ability to express them as landscape scenery, their masques provide an excellent place to start this process of unraveling.

The continuing theme of Jonson and Jones's masques is the idea of return, under the rule of the Stuarts, to the golden age. The golden age is the natal, and hence natural, original state of human society.[3] Jonson and Jones drew upon a rich panoply of sources in creating their image of the golden age. One source, of course, was the Judeo-Christian story of the paradisiacal Garden of Eden.[4] This story provides a particularly concrete means of elucidating the relation between the ideas of love and nature.

The word *paradise* made its way from Persian to Greek and from thence to Latin and the languages of Europe. The primary derivation is "enclosed park," and the first paradises were hunting grounds (WC7: paradise). Paradise also came to mean enclosed orchard or pleasure ground. In this context, it was natural to describe the Garden of Eden as a paradise. According to the Bible, humankind was born in this fertile orchard, which was watered by a river and grazed by various creatures. The Germanic word *Garden,* which is related to the Modern English word *yard,* also means enclosed area. The garden is a potent idea because it has long been a vital symbol of a "natural," moral society living in social harmony and in harmony with its environment.

Historically, counterposing the paradise, or garden park, to the wilderness was a means of making a symbolic statement about the nature of natural social existence. The delightful and garden park is a fertile blend of the four elements: earth, wind, fire, and water. In contrast, a wild wasteland is characterized by infertility resulting from the dominance of one element. Wastelands could range from dry desert (a plethora of fire and earth) to sea (a plethora of water) to steamy jungle (a plethora of water and earth) in which there is an overabundance of fertility (Auden 1967). When an environment is infertile it is "deserted" by life and becomes a desert. This concept is central to the biblical representation of Eden, where members of the nation of Israel are told that if they behave according to God's command, "the Lord will comfort you; he will comfort all her waste places, And make her wilderness like Eden, her desert like the garden of the Lord." The Lord transforms the desert into a garden by rectifying the balance of the elements with water: "I will make the wilderness a pool of water, and the dry land springs of water. I will put in the wilderness the cedar, the acacia, the myrtle, and the olive; I will set in the desert the cypress, the plane and the pine together." When the Israelites did not love and obey the Lord, however, "Their lands became a wilderness because of the glow of Yahweh's wrath" (Isaiah 51.3, Isaiah 41.18–19, and Jeremiah 25.38, as quoted in Williams 1962, 9, 12).

The same counterposing of a garden to the desert wilderness that is found in the Bible can also be seen in the cultural traditions of classical Greece and Rome, as exemplified in the influential poetry of Virgil. In Virgil's poetry, the importance of love and community is an important theme. In the *Eclogues* a ruler of the Roman Empire is thus depicted as behaving unnaturally when he expropriates Arcadia's common garden pastures in order to divide the area into properties for outsiders. This unnatural behavior is symbolized by the native shepherds being sent into exile to "thirsty Afri," to Scythia, "turbulent with mud," and to Britain, "sundered far off from the whole world" (Virgil, *Eclogues* 1.64–68, as quoted in Putnam 1970, 56). The home they leave becomes a wilderness: the oak under which they sang is struck by lightning, and the land they cross becomes dry, formless, barren, and plagued by wolves. The reverse situation, however, is also possible; in the *Georgics,* Virgil describes the peace that results in swords being hammered into plowshares and gives birth to the fertile rural idyll of a community of farmers and shepherds.

The physical "nature" of both the biblical and the classical stories reflects the spiritual "nature" of the human community. The moral is that if people act naturally and love both their god(s) and one another, they will be able to live in fertile and comfortable environments; if they act unnaturally, they will struggle in the rugged, infertile wilderness. There is thus a clear relation between the character of physical nature and the idea of the natural as related to the behavior of the human community.

The physical environment of Eden is usually depicted as a womblike, well-watered, and fertile grassy grove. This is also the characteristic environment of the Arcadian golden age in classical pastoral poetry such as Virgil's *Eclogues*. There is a practical reason for why the environment is described in this way. Grazing animals tend to remove the lower branches of trees and bushes, leaving a carpet of grasses. This effect becomes even more pronounced when pastoralists prune trees and burn the underbrush to encourage the grazing of wild or tame animals. Virgil would have depicted the golden age as pastoral because the ancient Greeks and Romans believed that the earliest human societies were based on herding. The sharing of common grazing resources was also thought to stimulate feelings of love for the commonweal. The birth of society, however, called for more sensual forms of love, and pastoral existence, at least as conceived by Virgil, was highly conducive to amorous pursuits such as singing lyric love songs to the accompaniment of appropriately rustic instruments. Shepherding was supposed to give ample leisure time for making use of the shady and comfortable grassy environment. The bucolic scenery of the ideal Britain that Jones depicted in his landscapes thus built upon a whole complex of Judeo-Christian and classical Mediterranean ideas about natural forms of individual and social love. This symbolic landscape of personal and civic virtue, as embodied in the landscape gardens, was inscribed into the material environment of Britain in the eighteenth century.

The bucolic environments depicted in Jones's scenery, and in the British landscape garden, are infused with classical references to the arcadian realm of love. There is, nevertheless, an important difference between ancient ideals of nature and the idea of nature as landscape scenery that emerged in the Renaissance. The classical shepherds in pastoral poetry do not refer to their environment in terms of scenic landscape. We hear the babbling brook where the shepherd waters his flocks, and we experience the cooling shade under the broad crown of the tree where the shepherd sits, "oaten" flute in hand; we do not, however, find anything resembling sustained descriptions of landscape scenery, and we hardly ever find classical authors referring to this scenery as being, in and of itself, nature (Parry 1957). The scenery is at most an expression of the generative, creative power of nature.

Examination of a passage from Virgil's *Georgics* illustrates the difference between the classical conception of nature and that of the Renaissance and Enlightenment. John Dryden's translation of the passage reads:

> But time is lost, which never will renew,
> While we too far the pleasing path pursue,
> Surveying nature with too nice a view.
>     (Dryden [1697] 1806, 175 [*Georgics*
>     3.448–50]; see OED: nature 13)

A more literal translation of the same passage reveals that Virgil was describing not a view, but a manifestation of love:

> But time flies on, irrevocable time,
> While we with love-lit eyes divert our course
> To gaze on each delight.
>     (Virgil 1946, 135 [*Georgics* 3.353–54])

The "nature" Virgil is describing in this passage is the powerful physical force of sexual love that drives man and beast to mate. It is the power of this force, described in graphic terms, which diverts Virgil from the more mundane subject of animal breeding—not a pleasing view of natural landscape scenery (ibid., 135 [*Georgics* 3.303–51).

For the classical writers, nature was not scenery, but a generative force that involved love in both the physical and spiritual senses (Olwig 1993b, 1995b). This force was symbolically manifested in Virgil's poetry through the "natural" process of the development of human society from a wild, asocial state to a pastoral communality expressive of fruitful physical love in a context of reciprocal social love (the lyric *Eclogues*), thence to the agricultural stage where people no longer simply graze their environment, but engage in a reciprocal relationship with their environment involving cultivation and fertilization by which nutrients are returned to the soil (the didactic *Georgics*), and finally to the urban imperium (the epic *Aeneid*) (Olwig 1984, 1–10). It is the generative force of love which the poets and painters of the Renaissance transformed into a gendered, largely female, landscape scene. The male principle, on the other hand, was expressed by the invisible celestial geometries of the lines of perspective, which penetrated the scene and gave it spatial form.

When Britain's bridegroom, King James I, sat upon his elevated throne of state and watched topless nymphs cavort in a landscape scene spread out before him, the intended perspective on nature was, we can be sure, deeply gendered. The landscape "body geographical" in the masques is the feminine bride of the male Stuart Sun King. This scene reflects a cosmology in which a rational male principle, identified with the sun, is counterposed to a passive, "natural" female form upon which the sun's light and gaze fall. In this way, the idea of nature as a creative birthing principle is wedded to ancient ideas concerning the fruitful relationship between a celestial father and a mother earth.

### THE MARRIAGE OF EARTH AND SKY

The idea that life is created by the union between a celestial king/father and a terrestrial queen/mother is found in much ancient mythology (Duerr 1985; Olwig 1993b). The literary scholar Northrop Frye has argued that this notion derives from the simple act of looking down and looking up. Hunter and gatherers, or farmers, would have been aware, when looking downward, of how the richness of game or plant growth depended upon a complex range of organic factors relating to the availability of water, the character of the soil, the climate of the area, and so on. Looking up, however, they would have become aware that the fruitfulness of the earth and of female beings was cyclical and seemed to correlate with the cyclical movement of the heavenly bodies. It is this looking down and up which explains, in Frye's view, the distinction Roman writers made between *natura naturans* and *natura naturata:*

> In the sexual creation myth with its earth-mother, the earth-mother is the early stages of the symbol of *natura naturans,* nature as a bursting forth of life and energy, its divine personalities the animating spirits of trees, mountains, rivers, and stones. This is the basis of what is called paganism, the instinctive faith of the *paganus* or peasant who is closest to the natural environment and furthest from the centre of the insulating envelope of culture. In the later stages of such "paganism," the preoccupation with cyclical movement climbs up into the sky and annexes the sense of *natura naturata,* nature as a structure or system which also manifests itself in cycles. (Frye 1980, 38–39)

The sort of myth which comes from looking downward at the earth is characterized by a cyclical pattern marked by rupture. The earth is both womb and tomb: "newborn animals are not the reborn forms of their parents; the flowers that bloom in the spring are not the same as those that bloomed last spring" (ibid., 30–31). Looking up, however, one sees a cycle of the sun and the moon which suggests "a cycle of the same," for "it seems to be unmistakably the same sun that comes up the next morning, the same moon that waxes and wanes" (ibid., 32). This regularity, according to Frye, suggests the work of an intelligent being who has created a perfect world in which "becoming" is subordinated to "being," of ruptured cyclical change subordinated to a stabilizing power that controls and plans cyclical change but is not subject to it (ibid., 321).

The idea of nature as natura naturans, a principle of becoming, is related to the Latin root *nascere,* to be born, or to come into being (Passmore 1974, 32). This concept also has forerunners in Greek thought. In Plato's dualistic philosophy, for example, an idea impresses itself upon the material receptacle of the chora. A look at the original text shows that this "receptacle" has decidedly feminine characteristics. We may, as Plato puts it, "liken the receiving principle [chora] to a mother, and the source or spring to a father" (Plato 1961b, 1177–79). Chora thus resembles nature in the sense of being a source of birth. The spelling *chora* is a variant of *choros,* the root of chorography, which, as we have seen, is the study of the enclosed, bodily shapes of the earth.[5]

The tendency to identify the celestial godhead as a male and the earth as a female who is made fruitful by him has been traced to early folklore and religion. In classical mythology, it is probably best known from the *Theogony* by Hesiod, a Greek poet of the eighth century B.C.E. In Hesiod's version the story of the golden age begins when Cronus (Saturn in Latin) murders his father, Uranus, thereby separating the realm of the cosmos from that of earth, Gaia (Hesiod 1987). The word for time in Greek was *chronos* and, as a play on words, the God and time ideas appear to have been linked in ancient Greek antiquity. It was with the separation of earth and sky, and the resultant possibility of intercourse between them, that time, and hence mutability and change, began. Time is measured by the pendular motion between two poles, back and forth, like the tide which waits for no man (Leach 1966, 124–36). The Roman version of this myth, as retold by Virgil in the *Georgics,* would have been familiar to Ben Jonson and to the poets of the British "Augustan" age, a century later. Dryden gives the following translation of Virgil's rendition of this myth:

> The spring adorns the woods, renews the leaves;
> The womb of earth the genial seed receives;

For then almighty Jove descends, and pours
Into his buxom bride his fruitful show'rs;
And, mixing his large limbs with hers, he feeds
Her births with kindly juice, and fosters teeming seeds.
                    (Dryden [1697] 1806, 142, lines 438–43)

The difference between the classical version of the idea of a celestial male god bringing fertility to a female earth and that represented in the landscapes of the masque lies in the relative position of the male and female deities. In the classical stories, we are dealing with a "vertical" cosmos in which the celestial male godhead is positioned over the female earth. In this cosmology, the nature of the celestial realm is fundamentally different from the nature of the earth, from which it is rigidly separated by spatial barriers. The complete union of the two natures can only be achieved in the eons of time's revolutionary cycle, which restores the golden age harmony of the elements. Renaissance landscape scenery, by contrast, presents a "horizontal" cosmos in which cosmic laws of nature, *natura naturata*, are represented by the shooting "rays" of perspective that infuse a timeless, harmonious structure into the terrestrial scene, *natura naturans*.[6] In this vision of nature, the celestial and the terrestrial are not divided into separate temporal and spatial realms. The celestial principle penetrates and gives form to the terrestrial, thereby giving rise to a pictorial representation of nature in which both principles are simultaneously present. One is an abstract and elevated masculine nature, the other is a supine and bodily feminine nature. In the idealized landscape scenes of the masques, the two conceptions of nature are locked together in a harmonious totality that presents a vision of a new golden age under the sciential Stuart court. This golden age represents a fundamental revolution in the character of society and its relation to nature.

## The Revolutionary Nature of the Golden Age

There is a long history to the idea that a revolution brings about the transition from a harmonious golden age to a contemporary era of strife and that another revolution could restore this golden age. The pre-Socratic philosopher Empedocles (ca. 490–430 B.C.E.) developed a cosmology which gives this idea a logic expressed in myth. In Empedocles' theory, the universe is made up of four elements: earth, air, fire, and water. When the cosmos is under the control of "love," or Aphrodite, the elements combine in a gigantic "harmonious" sphere. When the cosmos is ruled by strife, however, the elements are gradually separated from each other (Empedocles 1981; see also Glacken 1967, 9–11). The cosmic era in which Empedocles lived was seen to lie midway between the extremes of love and strife.

Plato gave Empedocles' ideas new form in his *Statesman.* Instead of the metaphor of a pendulum swinging from love to strife and back again, Plato used that of a turning ball (as on a string) revolving first in one direction and then the other.[7] When the ball stops and changes direction, a revolutionary change takes place in the nature of the universe. As Plato put it: "There is an era in which God himself assists the universe on its way and guides it by imparting its rotation to it. There is also an era in which he releases his control. He does this when its circuits under his guidance have completed the due limit of the time thereto appointed. Thereafter it begins to revolve in the contrary sense under its own impulse. . . . The age in which God controls the rotation is the golden era of Cronus (or Saturn)." "In that era," according to Plato:

> God was supreme governor in charge of the actual rotation of the universe as a whole, but divine also, and in like manner was the government of its several regions, for these were all portioned out to be provinces under the surveillance of tutelary deities. . . . When God was shepherd there were no political constitutions. . . . [All] men rose up anew into life out of the earth, having no memory of the former things. Instead they had fruits without sting from trees and bushes; these needed no cultivation but sprang up of themselves out of the ground without man's toil. For the most part they disported themselves in the open needing neither clothing nor couch, for the seasons were blended evenly so as to work them no hurt, and the grass which sprang up out of the earth in abundance made a soft bed for them. This is the story, Socrates, of the life of men under the government of Cronus.

A reversal in the movement of the cosmos brings this golden age to a revolutionary end:

> And now the pilot of the ship of the universe—for so we may speak of it—let go the handle of its rudder and retired to his conning tower in a place apart. Then destiny and its own inborn urge took control of the world again and reversed the revolution of it. The gods of the provinces, who had ruled under the greatest god, knew at once what was happening and relinquished the oversight of their regions. A shudder passed through the world at the reversing of its rotation, checked as it was between the old control and the new impulse which had turned end into beginning for it and beginning into end. . . . Thus likened to the universe and following its destiny through all time, our life and our begetting are now on this wise now on that. (Plato 1961a, 1033–40, lines 250–70)

James envisioned, as the sign of the renaissance of the golden age, that the birth of the new British Stuart dynasty would take place at the outset of a new century. He, as the subvicar of God, would regain godly oversight and control of his British region. Jonson and Jones gave form to this vision in the texts and scenery of the masques. The landscapes that Jones created were visions of an ideal, golden age, a *natural* realm. *Nature* is a key concept here because, according to the cosmology which the Renaissance inherited from the Middle Ages, the goddess of nature played an active role, via her love, in shaping the terrestrial world according to God's celestial principles. In the Renaissance cosmology represented in Jones's landscape scenes, the male monarch takes over this role, and nature begins to be reduced to the passive position of terrestrial scenery. To understand the implications of this transformation it is useful to take a closer look at the comparatively more active role of nature in the Middle Ages.

## *Natura, the Goddess of Nature*

In the course of the Middle Ages nature was personified as the goddess Natura, the *"mater generationis,* the intermediary, subordinate, or vicar of God *[vicaria Dei]* in the universe, which humankind imitated via the arts" (Economou 1972, 2). This is exemplified in the works of medieval writers of allegory, in which Natura performs "a critical function between the worlds of being and becoming, for she joins the soul, the image of the divine image of man, to the body; she connects the earthly with the heavenly, the divine with the material" (ibid., 66). As the goddess of a birthing creation, Natura naturally became identified with Venus, the goddess of love. Among those who made this association were Alan of Lille, who, in his twelfth-century allegories, made an important contribution to the establishment of Natura as "the most heroic figure in the medieval personification allegory" (ibid., 72).

Natura performs many of the same functions as love, or Aphrodite (Venus in Latin), in the Empedoclean myth, or the subordinate gods in Plato's. She thus brings the warring elements into harmony by reestablishing their natural bonds of union. Plurality thereby becomes unity, diversity identity, dissonance consonance, and discord concord (Economou 1972, 83). According to Alan of Lille, Natura prefers to inhabit the pleasant, changeless palace of the ethereal celestial realm, and for this reason she makes Venus (with Venus's husband Hymen, the Greek god of marriage, and son Cupid) her subvicar in the sublunar realm of the four elements (ibid., 8–9, 82–124). She does this because she has been "ordained by God to give to the world of mutability its continuity through procreation" (ibid., 72). She becomes very unhappy with this arrangement, however, because "of all her creatures man alone does not act in accordance with her laws. Whereas all other terrestrial creatures propagate themselves in obedience to her, man performs acts of fruitless and vicious perversion" (ibid., 73). The problem of explaining this human propensity is solved through the common medieval device of positing a duality. One Venus, or aspect of Venus, is the Venus impudica, the goddess of lechery and fornication, whereas the other, Venus legitima, is the goddess of chaste, legitimate love. Venus legitima is sometimes identified with Astraea, or natural justice (ibid., 85). In some cases the idea of harmony and justice identified with Astraea/Natura is identified with both procreation and social justice and peace. This occurs, for example, in Geoffrey Chaucer's *The Parlement of Foules* (ibid., 125–50). Here she works to unite the elements:

> Nature, the vicire of the almyghty Lord,
> That hot, cold, hevy, lyght, moyst, and dreye
> Hath knyt by evene noumbres of acord.
> (quoted in ibid., 141–42)

She also, however, works to unite the birds in pairs on St. Valentine's day. Finally, nature works for social harmony and "commune profyt." In the parliament of the birds the different species symbolize the various estates of human society, and when disharmony threatens their community, it is nature, as ideal love, which restores harmony and leads to a happy conclusion to the poem (ibid., 141–44).

## LANDSCAPING LOVE AND NATURE

Many of the ideas concerning the relation of nature and love that were developed in the Middle Ages are readily apparent in the masques of Jonson and Jones. There is, however, the major difference that in the masques, nature is also given a visual form through the vehicle of landscape scenery. In these scenes, the male figure of the Stuart monarch, as head of state, takes over the role of Astraea/Natura (with whom Elizabeth had been identified) as the vicar of God. It is his male head that surveys and controls a feminine landscape. The implications of this gendering of nature's landscape become more apparent if one takes a closer look at its role in the masques in which Jonson and Jones presented their vision of Stuart Britain.

## MASQUING NATURE

*The Masque of Blackness* is incomplete without its sequel, *The Masque of Beauty*. *The Masque of Beauty* presents an intricately worked out symbolic representation of the heritage of ideas concerning love and nature. Jonson based his symbolism upon his own erudite command of the classics and upon Neoplatonic Renaissance thinking (Gordon 1943).

In the first masque, the African princesses have reached Britain's shores, but they are called back from the land to the water for a year's respite before the grand finale, where they are supposed to be presented to the court in *The Masque of Beauty*. Since the sequel had to be postponed, it became necessary to begin the second masque with an explanation for the delay in the plot. The reason provided is that the princesses had been imprisoned (along with four new sisters) on a floating island by the malicious, black figure of the Night, who was mad with jealousy at the prospect of the black princesses being made light (Jonson 1969, 64 [*Beauty* line 67]). The princesses were finally liberated by the moon after which they were reborn of the sea, like Venus, under the sign of love.

The return of the princesses to Britain in *The Masque of Beauty* is marked by the full panoply of golden age symbolism discussed above. The island is equipped with a "seat of state, called the Throne of Beauty," upon which the nymphs are arranged (Jonson 1969, 67 [*Beauty* line 147]). This island doesn't just float, it revolves, according to the motions and countermotions of the celestial cosmic celestial bodies, which turn

> . . . unto the motion of the world [*motum mundi*]
> Wherein they sit, and are, like heaven, whirled
> About the earth; whilst to them contrary [*motum planetarum*],
> Following those nobler torches of the sky,
> A word of little loves and chaste desires
> Do light their beauties with still moving fires.
> (ibid., 65 [*Beauty* lines 111–17])

This island, which moves as it turns, is intended, according to the chorus, to recall the birth of the world out of chaos:

> When Love at first did move
> From out of chaos, brightened
> So was the world, and lightened
> As now!
> As now!
> As now!

It is a birth which echoes the biblical command "Let there be light":

> Yield, night, then, to the light,
> As blackness hath to beauty,
> Which is but the same duty.
> It was for beauty that the world was made,
> And where she reigns Love's lights admit no shade.
> Love's lights admit no shade.
> Admit no shade.
> (ibid., 70–71 [*Beauty* lines 235–46])

The first golden age is again suggested when the girls dance onto the shore of James I's British landscape scene:

> So beauty on the waters stood
> When Love had severed earth from flood!
> So when he parted air from fire,
> He did with concord all inspire
> And then a motion he them taught
> That elder than himself was thought,
> Which thought was, yet, the child of earth,
> For Love is elder than his birth.
>                    (ibid., 72 [*Beauty* lines 265–72])

Though Jonson makes much of the fact that his nymphs and cupids represent chaste love and are intended to call forth chaste desires, this whirling, brightly lit island must have been quite a sight. It included nymphs like Splendor, who was dressed "in a robe of flame color, naked-breasted, her bright hair loose-flowing." Splendor, and eight other ladies of the court (including such personages as Queen Anne and James's cousin the beautiful Lady Arabella Stuart), escorted by their lightly clad male partners, were accompanied by an escort, revolving in the "contrary" direction, of torch-bearing cupids armed with "bows, quivers, wings and other ensigns of love." These had been "chosen out of the best and most ingenuous youth of the kingdom, noble and others" (ibid., 67–69 [*Beauty* lines 159–204]). It is little wonder, then, that James, after watching the party dance ashore to his Britain, "incited first by his own liking" wished a repeat performance "after some time of dancing with the lords" (ibid., 72 [*Beauty* lines 273–76]).

*The Masque of Beauty*'s "contrary"-whirling spheres of the earth and the sky, moving in opposite directions, not only reproduce the golden age birth of the world, but also replicate the cosmic structure of a universe. In this universe, Natura acts as the creative force mediating between the ethereal realm of the heavens and the temporal realm of the earth. This is why the throne of beauty is occupied both by Serenitas, dressed in symbols of the sky, and by the green and earthy Germinatio.[8] Germinatio is clothed in the color of spring and represents the fertility which ethereal Natura brings to the earth (Gordon 1943, 134). Germinatio, like the landscape scenery, provided a means of portraying the generative powers of nature. Natura was traditionally depicted as a modest goddess who did not like being gazed upon or having men tear at the fabric of her garment (the physical universe) (Economou 1972, 76–77). In the masques, on the other hand, nature becomes the object of a gaze that verges on the pornographic. This new focus upon the visual was related to the emphasis placed in the Renaissance upon the sense of sight.

SIGHT, BEAUTY, HARMONY, AND NATURE

The modern idea of nature's landscape is fundamentally visual. This, I would argue, is partially an outcome of the emphasis placed upon vision in Renaissance cosmology. The texts of *The Masque of Blackness* and *The Masque of Beauty* help elucidate the significance of this emphasis upon the visual in relation to older ideas of nature. Sight, light, and vision play key roles in the representation of natural beauty in the masques, where the principal female figures represent the "elements" of beauty.

In *The Masque of Blackness,* the "glorious *Sunne*" of King James is described as being "the best judge, and most formal cause, of all dames' beauties" (Jonson 1969, 52 [*Blackness* lines 116–17]). Sensible beauty, according to the Neoplatonic doctrine of the time, is the beauty which is perceived by the sense of sight, and which finds formal or essential cause in the colors given by the light of the sun (Gordon 1943, 129–30). Previously, romantic love was symbolized by a blinded cupid, but in seventeenth-century Europe the bandage was literally removed from Cupid's eyes so that love would no longer be entirely blind. Whereas the blind Cupid represented earthly, sensual love, the new Cupid represents Renaissance Platonism's ideal that love is the desire to enjoy beauty, and beauty can only be apprehended by sight (ibid., 130). The harmony traditionally represented by sound is subsumed by a visual concept of harmony. The result is that the women of James's court "strike a music of like hearts" and act as the feminine "souls" of the men: "So they do move each heart and eye, With the world's soul, true harmony" (Jonson 1969, 72–73 [*Beauty* lines 280–312]). This passage alludes to a prevailing Renaissance idea that provides a key to understanding the subsequent power of the concept of nature as landscape scenery: the idea that there is a parallel link between geometry, as apprehended by sight, and harmony, as apprehended in music.

HARMONY AND NATURAL LOVE

Sight is a focused sensory modality acting at a distance which can be directed (and "fixed") toward specific objects across space. It is a sense identified with such attributes as being "visionary," having "foresight" or "insight," and "seeing the light." Musical sound, on the other hand, envelops one and can give, via its mysterious harmonies, an almost tangible feeling of a harmonious oneness with the world that is not unlike that of love. Linking the visual rationality of geometry and the enveloping feeling of musical harmony within the structure of landscape scenery thus creates a very powerful effect. It provides the means of creating the illusion of an ideal landscape body geographical whose ambience or atmosphere determines the character of the body politic. The masque, with its scenes structured according to the hidden geometries of perspective and its all-pervasive music and dance, mixes, and confuses, differing sensory modalities of perception in a way that must have created an overwhelming effect upon the emotions. The masque, however, was more than a form of entertainment; it was the means of expressing, through its scenery, the conviction that the ideal society could be generated through the creation of ideal environs for that society. In the masques of *Blackness* and *Beauty,* this power of landscape scenery is symbolized by the transformation from blackness to beauty which the "Negroe" princesses undergo when they alight upon Britain's shores. They, like the shipwrecked players in Shakespeare's *Tempest,* come under the spell of the harmonious atmosphere of an enchanted isle whose natural elements are orchestrated by a sciential prince (Orgel 1987).

## LANDSCAPE AND SOCIAL HARMONY

Music, according to the Neoplatonic ideas that inspired Jonson and Jones, is an expression of the life of the soul and an earthly approximation of the harmonious movement of the heavenly spheres as they revolve through the quintessential ether, propelled by celestial love. This mode of thought derived largely from the influential aristocratic Pythagorean brotherhood, founded in Italy in the late sixth century B.C.E. by Pythagoras. The brotherhood based its thinking on the idea that "all is number" and that form precedes substance, and it promoted recognized sciences such as mathematics and astronomy while indulging in a cultic interest in astrology, numerology, and mystical ideas based on cosmological theories of world harmony. Earthly music, according to these ideas, approximates celestial music, thereby helping to reestablish the ethereal, harmonious, cosmic order of a prelapsarian age to life in a fallen temporal world (Spitzer 1963, 13, 20; Kayser [1964] 1970; Economou 1972, 8).

The landscape scenery of Jonson and Jones's stage both mirrored the elevated nature of celestial geometries and environed the players with ethereal music.[9] This connection between geometry and music is exemplified by the passage in *The Masque of Blackness,* previously quoted, where the "Negroe" princesses receive a sign from the heavens via the reflection of the moon in a lake. The mirror of the lake, as described by the figure playing the moon, does not just reflect, it reverberates:

> . . . I was that bright face
> Reflected by the lake, in which thy race
> Read mystic lines; which skill Pythagoras
> First taught to men by a reverberate glass.
> (Jonson 1969, 55 [*Blackness* lines 204–7])

This notion that visual phenomena can be connected to musical vibrations was common at the time; it is also exemplified by the ethereal music that reverberates through the courtship scene from Shakespeare's *The Merchant of Venice*:

> How sweet the moonlight sleeps upon this bank! Here will we sit and let the sounds of music creep in our ears. Soft stillness and the night, become the tourches of sweet harmony. Sit, Jessica. Look how the floor of heaven is thick inlaid with patines of bright gold. There's not the smallest orb which thou behold'st, but in his motion like an angel sings, still quairing to the young-eyed cherubins. Such harmony is in immortal souls, But whilst this muddy vesture of decay doth grossly close it in, we cannot hear it. (Shakespeare 1948, 299–332 [*Merchant of Venice* 5.1.544–65])

Though humans cannot hear the ethereal music of the spheres, it provides the archetype for the natural sublunar love that harmonizes, temporizes, and makes fertile the terrestrial elements in a world otherwise enclosed in the muddy vesture of decay. These elements are, in turn, keyed to the four bodily humors, and it is their harmony that determines a person's temper—sanguine, phlegmatic, melancholic, or choleric. Neoplatonic philosophers such as Marsilio Ficino revived these ideas in the Renaissance. According to Ficino, "harmoniously formed, harmoniously moved, the sky does everything with a harmony of sound and movement, and through this sole harmony not only men, but all inferior things are prepared to receive the celestial gifts according to their capacity" (quoted in Garin [1976] 1990, 75). The harmonic balance of the elements was, according to Greek thinking, an expression of the universal laws of nature. They were not, however, merely physical laws; they also governed human social behavior. To willfully violate this balance was thus to break the law. To act in harmony with it, on the other hand, was to obey nature's law (Spitzer 1963, 64–65).

Though Renaissance poetry was full of musical echoes of Platonic thought, and though Renaissance science was moved by its harmonies, this aural cosmology was actually on the wane.[10] The idea of a celestial, ethereal space expressing a heavenly harmony was being supplanted by a visual concept of infinite space. Both ideas, however, reflected a belief in the ability of geometry to express harmony (Spitzer 1963, 43). Renaissance space ceasing to be the enclosed space of the spheres, whose rotation endlessly repeats the same harmonic cycle; it was a visual space—an infinite space—which allowed for a more linear and visual conception of movement and time (Nicolson 1965; Tuan 1982, 114–36; Olwig 1993a). The science of perspective made it possible for Renaissance artists to create landscape paintings in which the harmony and balance of nature was expressed in visual terms. One who gave vigorous expression to these ideas was the scientist and artist Leonardo da Vinci, who was among those who first developed the science of perspective drawing. He wrote:

> If you despise painting, which is the sole imitator of all viable works of nature, you certainly will be despising a subtle invention which brings philosophy and subtle speculation to bear on the nature of all forms— sea and land, plants and animals, grasses and flowers—which are enveloped in light and shade. Truly painting is a science, the true-born child of nature. For painting is born of nature; to be more correct we should call it the grandchild of nature, since all visible things were brought forth by nature and these, her children, gave birth to painting. Therefore we may justly speak of it as the grandchild of nature and as related to God. (quoted in Turner 1966, 25–26)[11]

Visual space retains many of the quintessential qualities identified with ethereal space and love. As the space of landscape scenery, it should ideally be harmonious and balanced. As the space of the map and globe, it is also coordinated with the space of the cosmos. Just as ethereal space was thought to determine the balance of the humors, visual space was linked to theories concerning the relations between position, climate, and temperament. Visual space, however, is not ethereal—it includes the actual space of terrestrial existence. Thus, the concept provides a basis for the idea that we live within an environment, or milieu, which determines the temper of our being (Spitzer 1948).

In the masques of *Blackness* and *Beauty,* the power of vision is the shaper of beauty and love (Gordon 1943, 130). This means that the ultimate shaper is the sun itself, which both warms our bodies and gives our eyes the light to see. This sun is encapsulated by the Stuart head of state, astride his throne, viewing the bodily beauties of the ladies and gentlemen of the court cavorting on stage in a harmonious landscape. It is "his attractive beams," we are told, "that lights these skies," and upon his ocean empire this beam never "sets." This light gives beauty not only to the people in the landscape scene, but to the landscape scene itself. It is this ever shining light to which the night yields, thus liberating beauty. The masques thus conclude with a song that proclaims the advent of a paradise on earth in Britain:

> Still turn, and imitate the heaven
> In motion swift and even,
> And as his planets go,
> Your brighter lights do so.
> May youth and pleasure ever flow;
> But let your state, the while

Be fixèd as the isle.
So all that see your beauty's sphere
May know th' Elysian fields are here.
(Jonson 1969, 74 [*Beauty* lines
340–46])


## GENDER, LANDSCAPE, NATURE, AND NATION

In the masques of *Blackness* and *Beauty* the landscape is transformed from a polity ruled by the law of custom to a representation of the body politic staged upon the scenery of the nation's "body geographical." Whereas the head of state, whose gaze rules from a distance, is gendered as male, the staged "bodily part" is dominated by the feminine figure of the queen. This landscape thus had a particular notion of gender and power built into it. The power of the male gaze, shoots downwards from the throne of state, thereby giving order and perspective to the scene of the body politic depicted on the stage.

One aspect of this that is puzzling is the attitude of Anne, who appears to have played an active role in the creation of an ideological construction that apparently placed her in a passive position. If one looks, however, at this construction from her perspective, it could be argued that it is the male monarch who has been made into the passive spectator to a spectacle of the queen as the embodiment of the body politic. This is a spectacle that is engineered, furthermore, by the servants of an independent minded queen, and inventor of the "anti-masque," who kept her own court and who styled herself as the mighty monarchy's glorious patroness. Anne played an active physical role as an actor, acting out carefully orchestrated roles constructed by authors she commissioned. She, it might be argued, by exposing herself to the gaze of the monarchy's subjects, followed the precedent of the popular Queen Elizabeth, whose carefully orchestrated progresses throughout the country made her bodily presence, and power, both seen and felt (Olwig 2002). But whereas Elizabeth displayed her body in extremely heavy and constricting clothing, Anne liberated herself from this, and scandalized the straight laced, by wearing light revealing garments, of Italian inspired design, then deemed to be the appropriate dress only for ancient goddesses. The power of the male gaze, the lines of perspective shooting down from the eye, is the creature of theatrical illusion. The bodies on the stage are flesh and blood, and express a corporeal power, that may have appealed to Anne.

Landscape scenery becomes equated in these masques with the feminine qualities of nature as the source of the nation's fertility. The masques thereby generate a potent ideological cocktail that blends the normative associations of nature and the natural with gender and nation. The nation, it is suggested, is bred through the interaction of the male regent and a feminized body politic. The notion of breeding, as any animal breeder knows, raises the issue of race. The connection between landscape, nature and race is the subject of the next chapter.

# Seven

# Landscaping Racial and National Progress

The plot of *The Masque of Blackness* and its sequel, *The Masque of Beauty*, centers on a group of "negroe" princesses from Africa who come to Britain in order to be blanched white by the mild sun of its ruler.[1] As a consequence of this pilgrimage to Britain's white-cliffed shores, they are able to receive "their true beauty" (Jonson 1969, 63 [*Beauty* line 47]). The word *black* then meant ugly, whereas *fair* meant beautiful and light colored. "Fair" conduct was the opposite of "foul" behavior (Jonson 1969, 52 n.; OED: fair I: 6, 10). Beauty and fairness were thus identified with all the virtues of a good society ruled by love. These masques were produced at *White*hall for a pale blond queen. Whitehall was the court of a land called "Albion the fair" by its poets, not only because it was the land of Albion the fair, the son of Neptune, but also because, as Jonson wrote, it lifts its "snowy cliff" into the "temperate air"—according to Jonson, "Albion" also means "white land" (Jonson 1969, 54 [*Blackness* lines 180–81, n. 511]).[2] The landscape of Britain in the masques of *Blackness* and *Beauty* is the symbolic expression of the mild, sunny rule of its new Stuart dynasty of British kings. The born-again Britain promised by the Stuarts was to be composed of a fair, unified people.

The notion that the king was "the Husband" and the geographical body of the state his "lawfull Wife" (James I [1616] 1918e, 272) was related to the idea that the wise ruler rendered his land fertile. The idea of fertility and breeding was, in turn, closely linked to the idea of race. The British landscape of the Stuart dynasty would, the masques suggested, breed a fair race of Britons. It was the progress of this new breed of men, under the mild sunny guidance of the Stuarts, that would bring about the progress of the state as expressed in Inigo Jones's landscape scenery. This kind of thinking lies perilously close to one of the most dangerous dimensions of the nationalism which later evolved in Europe, that of "blood and soil"—the idea that the race of a nation was an expression of its soil or

148

landscape, and that the progress of the nation was the outcome of the evolution of the landscape and the improvement of the race.[3] This chapter seeks to show that this idea was part of the design of the nation-state from its Renaissance beginnings.

The story of the transformations of the contested meanings of landscape and nature is likewise the story of the ways in which ideas of race and national development were made to seem natural by being incorporated into the idea of landscape as nature. In the process of these transformations, the scenic conception of landscape as nature moved from the arena of art and theater out into the garden before leaping the garden fence. In this way, it eventually permeated the perception of the entire countryside, which henceforth came to be judged by the aesthetic tenets of the picturesque scene. Sexuality, race, nation, and nature were thus blended in various degrees in an intellectual tradition which influenced the theories of men like Montesquieu, Edmund Burke, and, eventually, the founders of German national ideology. At a time when Germany was seeking to emulate Britain's growth into the world's leading military and industrial power, the idea that a nation was bred through a developing intercourse with its landscape held enormous appeal. It was this thinking, in its most extreme form, which helped give rise to the English and German ideologies of Anglo-Saxon and Teutonic superiority, and hence the theories of the existence of an Aryan race, which, in America, gave rise to claims of superiority by WASPs (White, Anglo-Saxon Protestants).[4]

The emergence of a concern with race at the time of the Stuarts was closely tied to James's desire to create a single British people out of the differing countries occupying the British Isles. One of James's biggest headaches, in this respect, was the Celtic peoples of Ireland and the Scottish Highlands and islands. It was in the context of the imperial relations between the "British" court and its ethnic subjects that the subject of race began to take on importance.

NATURE, CONQUEST, AND RACE

The Irish rebellion against English rule led by Hugh O'Neill, the earl of Tyrone, was finally crushed, after years of struggle, on March 30, 1603, six days after the death of Elizabeth. When James I became king of England, not only did he effectively unite the kingdoms of England and Scotland, but he also became the ruler of a conquered Ireland. To James the progress of civilization was coequal with the realization of his dream of a British Empire encompassing the body geographical of Britain and the British Isles. In 1603, he appointed John Davies, a brilliant jurist, poet, and antiquarian (an associate of Robert Cotton and William Camden), to the position of solicitor general of Ireland, and, in 1606, to that of attorney general of Ireland. Davies, as seen in chapter 2, was a defender of English customary and common law. The story was quite different, however, when it came to Irish customary law, particularly as it applied to Irish forms of communal, or clan, land ownership. How, one might ask, could a person who passionately defended English customary law not feel compelled to defend the same principles as they applied to Ireland? The answer lies in the fact that as a jurist, Davies had been trained in two different legal traditions; one, common law, derived from English customary law, and the other, natural law, from a continental tradition inspired by Roman statutory civil law. The second tradition was applied in international contexts, such as that arising from the conquest of Ireland, where English customary law, by nature, would not be applicable. According to this idea, the law governing relations between nations should necessarily be a "natural" law of universal application (Pawlisch 1985, 3–33, 161–75). When a civilization willingly submitted to Rome, Roman precedent mandated that its customs be respected. This was not the case in a situation when a barbarian nation refused to submit and had to be conquered militarily. In this situation the natural force of might made right. The monarch as conqueror had a natural right to substitute his law for that of the conquered territories of the Irish clans, which were then called "countries."

Common law and natural law coexisted within the English judicial context in which Davies had learned his legal trade. The natural law tradition placed the estate of the monarch, as the subvicar of God, below Astraea, the goddess of justice, and hence above the law deriving from human custom but below the law of God (Kantorowicz 1957, 143–44). Even the most rigorous defenders of Parliament rarely conceived of the "ancient constitution" as justifying a republic. The king together with Parliament formed a bodily whole that it would be unnatural to dismember. There was thus no necessary contradiction between Davies' passionate defense of English customary law as it applied to the prerogatives of the English Parliament and his poetic paeans to the nature of royal justice. In his series of twenty-six fifteen-line poems, *Hymnes to Astraea,* he thus wrote of Queen Elizabeth as the "Exil'd" goddess of justice "come again" in "our *State's* faire Spring." The first letters of each line, when read downward, spell out ELISABETH REGINA. The poems were accompanied by an engraving which shows the queen as the glorious image of Natura with a crown of stars about her head (Yates 1975, 66–69).

The civil, or natural, law tradition not only gave legal power to the conqueror but also justified ignoring the property rights and legal traditions of conquered peoples, especially if they could be defined as un-Christian, uncivilized, or subhuman by virtue of race (Pawlisch 1985, 9). Davies' ability to use the force of natural law to undermine native Irish law and property rights, and thereby pave the way for the massive colonization of northern Ireland (and his own personal enrichment), was thus tied to a denigration of the Irish and their native custom, culture, and religion.

The belief that humankind belonged to a state midway between the angels and the animals in the Great Chain of Being guaranteed a certain equality before the principles of natural law (Lovejoy 1973). This equality could be denied, however, if it could be shown that a given people had not achieved a fully human status on this scale. The most thorough way of justifying a legal double standard, such as that promulgated in Ireland, was to deny the humanity of the colonized people. A precedent was set when King James branded the native Celtic peoples of the Scottish isles as animals in order in justify his policy of displacing them with English-speaking "Saxon" colonists from the lowlands of Scotland. James thus instructed his young son in *Basilicon Doron*:

> As for the Hie-landes, I shortly comprehend them all in two sortes of people: the one, that dwelleth in our maine land, that are barbarous for the most part, and yet mixed with some shewe of civilitie: the other, that dwelleth in the Isles, and are alluterlie barbares, without any sorte or shew of civilitie. For the first sorte, put straightlie to execution the Lawes made alreadie by mee against their Over-lordes, and the chiefes of their clannes, and it will be no difficultie to danton them. As for the other sorte, think no other of them all, then as of Wolves and Wilde Boares: And therefore followe foorth the course that I have begunne, in planting Colonies among them of aunswerable In-landes subjectes, that within shorte time maye roote them out and plant civilitie in their roomes. (James I [1599] 1969, 42)

The peoples of the Highlands and islands were all far enough beyond the pale for James that he did not recognize the authority of their native custom and felt that he had the right and obligation to supplant them with colonists. The Highlanders were deemed tame enough, however, to become fully human subjects under the civilizing law of the king.

James believed that, by virtue of the special status of his noble estate, he should be able to civilize and tame the Highlanders. The masques of *Blackness* and *Beauty* pictured how this process of ennoblement would be accomplished through the effect of the king's noble body and blood upon the nature of the landscape of his body politic. The identification of landscape with the ennobled blood of a unified body politic, it will be seen, helps explain the origins of key aspects of modern blood-and-soil racism.

NOBILITY AND RACE

The Latin root for noble, *nobilis,* means well known and is related to the fame achieved by people for their notable deeds. The equivalent Germanic word is *Adel.* It derives from the Nordic word *ætt,* meaning lineage. To be *ættborinn,* or lineage-born (freeborn), in the Nordic countries was to have *odel* status (to use the modern Norwegian spelling). This meant that one had rights in the land of the odel farm (inherited family farm). The status of being odel eventually became, in many areas, the privilege of an exclusive landed minority which formed a nobility or *Adel.*[5] Nobility thus came to be determined both by one's rights in land and by the *nature* of one's blood and breeding, or one's *kind*—a synonym for nature related to words like *kith* and *kin.* In Latin, one's kind would be one's *gens*—the root of words like *genesis* and *genetics* (OED: noble, nature, kin, kind, -gen). The word *Adel,* like the English word *noble,* came to connote innate quality, substance, and lineage (Gurevich 1977, 6–7; Hastrup 1985, 202). The status of being Adel brings with it the attribute of being *edel*—a German word with connotations of being refined, generous, fine, genuine, and of great value (a "precious" stone is edel) (Collins-Klett 1983: Adel, edel). Nobility belonged to those who did not work the sun-drenched fields and whose skin color would have been fairer than that of the "nut-brown" farm worker. The linking of nobility and moral fairness with fairness of complexion formed a potent synergy—a synergy that was at the heart of the masques of *Blackness* and *Beauty.*

James had the pick of the eligible princesses of Europe when he married. Choosing a princess involved many practical considerations. One of the attractions of marrying Anne was that it would strengthen Scottish claims to the Orkneys (Donaldson 1984, 23–24, 33–34). The Protestant Anne was also a good match because she was the daughter and sister of kings and because, to judge from her portraits, she had exceedingly fair hair and skin (Willson 1956, 91; Williams 1970, 11, 181). It is notable that the marriage arrangement was not sealed until James received a miniature portrait of the teenage Danish princess sent to him by the girl's shrewd mother, Queen Sophie of Denmark.

This portrait, which is thought to have clinched the wedding arrangement, may have moved James because of his belief that "vertue followeth oftest Noble bloud," or "Noble races" (James I [1599] 1969, 56–57, 83). James had a very literal conception of good breeding. In *Basilicon Doron* he thus advised his son to pick his first wife carefully, according to the same principles one would use when breeding animals:

> Marriage is one of the greatest actiones that a man doeth in all his time, especiallie in taking of his first Wife; And if hee Marie first basely beneath his ranke, he will ever be the lesse accounted of thereafter: And lastly, remember to choose your Wife as I advised you to choose your servantes, that shee be of a whole and cleane race, not subject to the hereditarie sickness, either of the soule or the bodie: For if a man will bee carefull to breede Horses and Dogges of good kindes; Howe much more carefull should he be for the breed of his own loynes? (ibid., 95)

In the "Queen's" masques of *Blackness* and *Beauty*, James does not just improve the breed of his own line—he also symbolically acts to develop and ennoble a new British race. James is thus portrayed as the enlightening sun/monarch who shines down upon the fair British landscape scene and can "wash" an Ethiop white (Jonson 1969, 64 [*Beauty* line 67]). In the masque's representation of the theater of state, fairness becomes a characteristic deriving from the climate, soil, and environment of the landscape scene under the headship of the monarch.

## The Geography of Race

The chorographic works of William Camden provided a foundation for the idea that the physical landscape of Stuart Britain had created a fair British people. According to Camden, the people of northwestern Europe had a "natural inclination by heavenly influence" that made them "answerable to the disposition of Aries, Leo, and Sagittary; and Jupiter, with Mars," and it was this that "maketh them impatient of servituede, lovers of liberty, martial and couragious." The Anglo-Saxons, according to Camden, were "by God's wonderful Providence transplanted hither out of Germany." They were composed of "valiant Angles, Jutes, and Saxons, then inhabiting Jutland, Holsten, and the sea coasts, along to the river Rhene." These peoples made themselves "absolute lords" of all the "better soyl" as far as the Orkneys, as was shown by the spread of the English language and the fact that the Celtic peoples at his time still called the English "Saxons" (Camden [1605] 1674, 11).

It was common at this time for the nobility of Europe to justify their superior status by tracing it to their right of conquest as descendants of the fair, northwestern European conquerors of Rome and its dark-skinned minions (Gossett 1963, 88; Poliakov 1974, 11–53). Camden, however, took a different tack. In Camden's version the superior nature of the British is derived not from the bloodlines of their conquerors, but from the geography of Britain itself. The fierce Anglo-Saxon conquerors were, according to Camden, conquered themselves by the mild environment of Britain. In the end, "this warlike, victorious, stiff, stout, and vigorous Nation, after it had, as it were, taken root here about one hundred and sixty years, and spread his branches far and wide" was "mellowed and mollified by the mildness of the soyl and sweet air" (Camden [1605] 1674, 11, 15). It was the mild climate that made the British people noble and fair, like the figure of "Britaine" in the frontispiece of Michael Drayton's *Poly-Olbion* (Drayton [1612–22] 1961). This figure resembles earlier depictions of Elizabeth as the goddess Astraea standing astride the map of Britain, but here she is not the queen—she is Britain herself, a map of which she wears as her cloak (Helgerson 1986, 59–64). One after another, as noted in the previous chapter, she marries the various male conquerors surrounding her figure, beginning with the Trojan Brute. She ultimately gives birth to a single British race and people.

## Neoplatonic Racism

Superficially, the masques of *Blackness* and *Beauty* might seem to be narrating a modern racist tale. Actually, however, their message differs from modern racism in an important respect. The blackness of the princesses is not a permanent racial trait, but is something they can change merely by changing their geographical location. In the masques, it requires considerably less than one hundred and sixty years for the mild British sun to blanch the black African princesses white. This transformation occurs as soon as they set foot upon British soil. For Jonson, color is only skin deep. It masks the true beauty that the princesses (one of whom is the queen) have always possessed. Jonson is thus by no means entirely negative in his characterization of the black figures in the masques. The princesses have an inner brightness and life which becomes apparent once they lose "their blackness" and one can see "their true beauty" (Jonson 1969, 63 [*Beauty* line 47]). The masque is not so much about race as about the ability of a just and fair state to bring out the love and harmony which is the foundation of true beauty. Herein lies the core issue of the masque. The blond queen put herself in a position that caused a stir when she made her court stage debut painted black because the masque was not about the permanence of racial inferiority, but the possibility of change under a wise monarch. Anne also made a bold statement on the subject when she invited the Native American princess Pocahontas to court in 1617 and honored the "red" woman by giving her the queen's seat at a masque—where seats were a mark of status and in short supply (Williams 1970, 182). If color were only skin deep, Anne could bring out Pocahontas's true civilized beauty by bringing her into the ideal realm of a court masque. Unfortunately, Pocahontas died of illness before she could escape from the inclement off-stage miseries of the real British climate.

Fig. 7.1. A Daughter of Niger, from the 1605 *Masque of Blackness*, in which Queen Anne of Denmark played a key role in both the production and the performance. Photo: Photographic Survey, Courtauld Institute of Art. Reproduced with the permission of The Devonshire Collection, Chatsworth. Reproduced by permission of the Duke of Devonshire and the Chatsworth Settlement Trustees.

The masques used arcane solar symbolism to express the role of the king as the natural embodiment of the state. Off stage, however, the mild, beclouded sun of Britain took no notice of the king when it decided if it would shine. Everyone would have been aware that the geographical body of the landscape functioned largely according to its own laws. This kind of observation allows for a shift from the ideological premise of the masques, that it is the smiling sun of the monarch that makes people fair, to the idea that the landscape itself makes fair only the people who are born there. This shift, as will be seen, is exactly what occurred in the course of the eighteenth century when the country came to be identified primarily with the natural laws embodied in the landscape scenery of Britain, rather than with the body of English customary law.

## LANDSCAPING THE LAW

The idea that the geography of the landscape body played an important role in determining the nature and progress of the body politic was given monumental form in Montesquieu's *Spirit of the Laws,* published in 1748. Montesquieu had visited Britain from 1729 to 1731 and was deeply impressed. He absorbed the parliamentary ideology of the British country elite and then returned home in order to give it a rigorous, rational form which, in turn, appealed enormously to the British. Montesquieu was a trained jurist, and he was deeply imbued with the theories of natural law going back to Aristotle. Aristotle had theorized that Greece lay in an ideal position midway between the warm, dry climate to the south and east and the cold, wet climate to the north and west. According to Aristotle:

> The peoples of cold countries generally, and particularly those of Europe, are full of spirit, but deficient in skill and intelligence, and this is why they continue to remain comparatively free, but attain no political development and show no capacity for governing others. The peoples of Asia are endowed with skill and intelligence, but are deficient in spirit; and this is why they continue to be peoples of subjects and slaves. The Greek stock, intermediate in geographical position, unites the qualities of both sets of peoples. It possesses both spirit and intelligence: the one quality makes it continue free; the other enables it to attain the highest political development, and to show a capacity for governing every other people—if only it could once achieve political unity. (Aristotle 1962, 296 [*Politics* 7.7.2–3])

The Aristotelian theories lent themselves to prevailing Renaissance ideas, developed from astrology, which linked the balance of the four elements to the balance of the bodily humors, and hence the human temperament, as discussed in chapter 6. These ideas were given added impetus by the history of the Gothic invasions of Rome, which Renaissance northwestern Europeans chose to view as a manifestation of the free northern spirit triumphing over southern servitude, thereby restoring the just balance of civilization. The outpouring of peoples from these northern climes also led to the idea, as propagated by the sixth-century historian of the Goths, Jordanes, that the Northwest was the fertile manufactory of nations (Montesquieu [1748] 1989, 283). This fertility was seen to be a consequence of the cold and humid climate, which led to a large production of the humor called phlegm.

Montesquieu followed in this tradition, but he gave these ideas the patina of Enlightenment natural science. He based theories of the morality, vigor, confidence, and courage of northerners on physiological grounds by applying "experimental" methods to the study of the reaction of skin to cold (Montesquieu [1748] 1989, 231–34). On the basis of an experiment with a frozen sheep's tongue, he argued that "Cold air contracts the extremities of the body's surface fibers; this increases their spring and favors the return of blood from the extremities of the heart. It shortens these same fibers, therefore, it increases their strength in this way too. Hot air, by contrast, relaxes these extremities of the fibers and lengthens them; therefore, it decreases their strength and their spring" (ibid., 231). Montesquieu's experiment would hardly be considered a triumph of modern science today, but it did give contemporary legitimacy to his ideas (Courtney 1963, 1–26; MacDougall 1982, 81).

Though Montesquieu's theory might seem to point in the direction of a strict environmental determinism in which climate directly determines the nature of a people, it actually allowed room for a form of dialectical interaction between society and the environment. The Scandinavians were thus seen to have created a milder climate by making clearings in the forest. This milder climate, in turn, enabled them to progress to a higher stage of society because the people became milder and more willing to submit to the strictures of laws arrived at by their representative councils, which met in the forest clearings (Olwig 1984, 17–18, 21). Montesquieu's ideas thus allowed for an initial phase in which the character of society was determined by nature, as well as a civilized phase in which change took place through a process of cultural evolution that allowed a people to modify the effect of climate.[6]

Montesquieu's theory, however, lent itself to racist beliefs based on the idea that some nations were so well adapted to particular climates that they did not modify their environment and develop. The heat of India thus had the consequence that people there were "by nature without courage" (Montesquieu [1748] 1989, 234), and blacks were by nature disposed to being enslaved: "Those concerned are black from head to toe, and they have such flat noses that it is almost impossible to feel sorry for them. One cannot get into one's mind that God, who is a very wise being, should have put a soul, above all a good soul, in a body that was entirely black. It is impossible for us to assume that these people are men because if we assumed they were men one would begin to believe that we ourselves were not Christians" (ibid., 250).

The theory of climatic determinism carried an inherent dialectical logic. If the people of the Northwest were naturally freedom loving, those of the South were naturally slaves, and, by extension, naturally the slaves of the people of the Northwest. Thus, although Montesquieu believed that "as all men are born equal, one must say that slavery is against nature," in the end, he concluded that slavery was only truly unnatural in Europe. "In certain countries," slavery "may be founded on a natural reason"; these countries "must be distinguished from those in which even natural reasons reject it, as in the countries of Europe" (ibid., 252). The reason that Europeans rejected it was because of the influence of the Scandinavians, who have "the great prerogative that should put the nations inhabiting it above all the peoples of the world: it is that they have been the source of European liberty, that is, of almost all of it that there is today among men." Scandinavia, he wrote, is "the manufactory of the instruments that break the chains forged in the south. It is there that are formed the valiant nations who go out of their own countries to destroy tyrants and slaves and to teach men that, as nature has made them equal, reason can make them dependent only for the sake of their happiness" (ibid., 283).

Montesquieu provided a natural argument for the idea held by many English parliamentarians that the Anglo-Saxons of Jutland, together with the Danes, had played an important role in transmitting the representative system of government and law to England (MacDougall 1982, 53–70). According to Montesquieu's theory, the lawmaking body of Parliament was itself the creature of natural law. Such an idea was obviously subversive of the legitimacy of absolute monarchy as a form of nonparliamentary rule (Courtney 1963, 18). It was also, however, subtly subversive of the ideals of the countrymen who had revolted against the absolutist ambitions of the Stuart court a century earlier: following Montesquieu's line of argument, the law was the creation not of custom, but of nature's physical landscape. This, in turn, meant that one way of improving the state of the body politic was to improve the landscape scene, as the Scandinavians had done by cutting clearings in their forests. Montesquieu was highly appreciative of the environmental transformations undertaken by the English country gentlemen of his day in order to improve the aesthetic appearance and productivity of their estates. He was, in fact, so enamored of William Kent's gardens, with their tree-framed clearings, that he laid out part of his ground of La Brède in France in the English style (ibid., 4).

Montesquieu became the most prominent source of ideas concerning the natural origins of parliamentarianism in Germanic and Scandinavian lands (ibid., 21). His natural theory of law suited the post–Glorious Revolution ideological climate of England, a nation that had put the egalitarian and democratic political visions of the civil war era behind it. Government was now firmly in the hands of an oligarchy of country gentry who were also landscape improvers.

## "NATURAL" LANDSCAPE AESTHETICS

### Burke's Natural Laws of Aesthetics

Edmund Burke is thought to be the most important British disciple of Montesquieu, whom Burke described as "the greatest genius which has enlightened this age" (quoted in Courtney 1963, ix). Burke tends to be known either as an archetypal Whig political thinker or as a pioneer theoretician in the realm of aesthetics and landscape taste. Rarely do students of one aspect of his work refer to the other—but this is unfortunate, because the two realms of Burke's discourse, as inherited from Montesquieu, illuminate each other.[7] By giving the British constitution a "scientific" basis in physical nature, Montesquieu provided Burke with a means of visualizing that constitution in terms of landscape aesthetics in his *Philosophical Enquiry into the Origin of Our Ideas of the Sublime and the Beautiful* (1757). It was here that he developed the theory that beauty was naturally embodied in the environment itself and had political and social implications (Burke 1759).[8]

Burke, like Ben Jonson, identified "beauty" with "love." Beauty and love are in turn, believed Burke, related to Whiggish, parliamentarian ideals of a good society. On the one hand, beauty has the force of "the common law of nature," which is "attended with a very high pleasure" that carries men "to the sex in general." This type of beauty resembles the attraction of Venus impudica, discussed in the previous chapter. On the other hand, beauty also draws us to particular members of that sex and is identified with "sentiments of tenderness and affection" and hence with the "social quality" which is necessary to "the generation of mankind" (ibid., 64). This type of beauty resembles Venus legitima, or her superior, Astraea. For Burke, however, nature and beauty are not the Platonic abstractions found in the masques of Jonson and Jones; beauty comes from the physical object itself. It is a direct expression of the physical smoothness characteristic of the contemporary Whig garden lawn and the fine ladies one might encounter walking in such a garden. This beauty is characterized by: "smooth slopes of earth in gardens; smooth streams in the landscape; . . . in fine women, smooth skins" (ibid., 213, 216).

Whereas Jonson was careful to identify his heroines with an ideal, ethereal beauty, Burke saw beauty as the expression of the sensory properties of particular physical shapes and textures. These give rise to feelings as a result of "the mechanical structure of our bodies, or from the natural frame and constitution of our minds" (ibid., 71). In the end, beauty is the barely sublimated expression of the female form's animal attraction: "Observe that part of a beautiful woman where she is perhaps the most beautiful, about the neck and breasts; the smoothness; the softness; the easy and insensible swell; the variety of the surface, which is never for the smallest space the same; the deceitful maze, through which the unsteady eye slides giddily, without knowing where to fix, or whither it is carried" (ibid., 216). The beauty of the smooth female form and its scenic landscape equivalents is related both to the physical procreation of the race and to the feelings of tenderness and love necessary for the survival of the family and society.

"Beauty" is contrasted to another aesthetic category, the regally elevated and masculine state of the "sublime." Whereas the smoothness of beauty is destroyed by "any raggedness, any sudden projection, any sharp angle," the sublime is "rugged and negligent." In contrast to the serpentine line of beauty, the sublime, as a rule of law, "loves the right line" (ibid., 213, 237). The sublime is identified with the mind-boggling force that is possessed not only by vast and enormous phenomena experienced in nature, but also by the Leviathan and other monstrous creatures.[9] The experience, at an appropriate distance, of the power of that which is "vast," "eternal," and "astonishing" produces "a sort of swelling and triumph" which gives rise to the passionate experience of sublime freedom. This is because the mind always claims to itself "some part of the dignity and importance of the things which it contemplates" (ibid., 84).

Much as the spatial structure of the masque theater can be seen to represent the body politic of the state, Burke's landscape aesthetics replicates the structure of the ancient balanced constitution. It includes both a leveling representative body, symbolized by the smooth feminine lawn, and the sublime majesty of the state rising above it. There is an interesting aesthetic parallel between Burke's notion of the sublime in relation to the urge to self-preservation and Hobbes's figure of state power as the enormous force necessary to control that urge. The frontispiece to Hobbes's *Leviathan* shows a monstrous figure rising out of the regal mountains that tower above the landscape. The frontispiece includes a quotation from what Burke saw as one of the most "sublime" books in the Bible, the book of Job. The biblical description of Leviathan, as noted in chapter 4, continues: "Upon earth there is not his like, who is made without fear. He beholdeth all high *things:* he *is* a king over all the children of pride" (Job 41.33–34 AV). The state, as conceived of by the conservative Burke, must be all powerful in order to be a match for the forces of disorder that can unleash a revolution and destroy the social continuity. In Burke's concept of the sublime, this "state," I would argue, is sublimated as a force of "nature."

There is an intrinsic connection in Burke's theory between nature, sexuality, aesthetics, and politics. Burke's beautiful smooth lawn is identified with the "sentiments of tenderness and affection" which generate family and community love and feelings of social solidarity. It is not simply a symbol—its physical smoothness is the cause of these feelings. The power of the aesthetics of smoothness is explained by invariant scientific laws and is explicitly dissociated from feelings rooted in custom (Boulton 1958, lxiv). The feeling of the sublime also has a natural cause, but its effect is quite different from that of the beautiful. The sublime is a concept taken from classical rhetoric and architecture which meant elevated. In Burke's usage, however, the sublime does not belong to the realm of human discourse but is expressed by the physical elevation of the scenery itself.

## Rugged Individual Nature

The idea that wild, rugged scenery was itself the source of sublime aesthetic expression had an obvious appeal in Scotland, where such scenery was in ample supply. One of the first of the early aestheticians to pick up on Burke's concept of the sublime was a Scot named Hugh Blair. He elaborated on the concept in a series of lectures held in Edinburgh beginning in 1759 and published in 1783 as *Lecture on Rhetoric and Belles Lettres* (Boulton 1958, lxxxiv–lxxxviii). The impact of these lectures was greatly enhanced because they were published as an essay introducing two volumes of sublime "ancient" epic poetry by the mythic Scottish bard Ossian that effectively proved Blair's theories. James Macpherson, a protégé of Blair's, claimed to have collected the poems (as "fragments") in the Highlands and translated them into English—an English as foggy as the climate and as misty as his sources (which he never was able to produce) (Blair [1765] 1803; Macpherson [1765] 1803).[10] Blair and Macpherson skillfully wedded the environmentalism of Montesquieu with the idea of the sublime as propounded by Burke. According to Blair, it was the sublime natural environment of the Highlands which gave rise to a poetry in which "the events recorded are all serious and grave; the scenery throughout, wild and romantic. The extended heaths by the seashore; the mountains shaded with mist; the torrent rushing through a solitary valley; the scattered oaks; and the tombs of warriors overgrown with moss; all produce a solemn attention in the mind." It is "no wonder," Blair exclaims, "we should so often hear and acknowledge in his [Ossian's] strains the powerful and ever-pleasing voice of nature" (Blair [1765] 1803, 72, 73).

By making the ultimate author of this epic poetry the natural geography of northern Britain, the two British loyalists, Blair and Macpherson, created the basis for a Scottish cult of "natural" scenery. This cult worked to erase the memory of Bonnie Prince Charlie and the clansmen who had supported his cause in the recent uprising against Britain. This was a time when estate owners were busily evicting, with British blessing, these same clansmen from the land. Eviction, in turn, facilitated the estate owners' improvement of the landscape scene through the creation of exclusive hunting parks for men of wealth from lowland Britain, with forests and sheep walks (Olwig 1984, 23–39).

The poetry of Ossian was collected, according to Macpherson, amongst the folk of the Highlands, who had preserved it as part of their heritage. This poetry, however, was promoted by Blair not as an expression of custom, but as the voice of the elevated, aesthetic laws of a sublime nature. Blair's idea of the sublime was taken largely from Burke, but it also owed something to Blair's intellectual mentor, Adam Smith. Prior to publishing his theories concerning the economic laws governing the wealth of nations in 1776, Smith had been a professor of belles lettres in Edinburgh. It was here that he developed his theories concerning the origins of language as a poetic expression emerging from nature. Smith helped pioneer an approach to knowledge which became known as "conjectural history," "hypothetical history," or "deductive history." "Whatever the phrase used," Robert A. Nisbet has argued, "the method was the same: to cut through the morass of customs, superstitions, traditions, and prescriptive laws, which to most of the rationalists of the age seemed to be the very stuff of the historic social order, to the underlying forces of the natural order. What was wanted was a conception of man's advancement through the ages in the terms of what was fundamental and natural to man, rather than in the terms of ordinary or conventional history" (Nisbet 1969, 140). The aesthetics of Smith, Blair, and Ossian gives the semblance of a nostalgic return to nature, but this was not the nature of native custom and tradition. The "voice of nature" we hear in Ossian is that of a raw and wild nature which speaks, unmediated by culture, through the mouths of the rugged individualists with whom Macpherson populated ancient Scotland (Olwig 1984). The voice of nature crying in the wildness of Scotland was a voice prophesying the progress to be gained by an emerging industrial

Fig. 7.2. *The Old Blind Scottish Bard Sings his Swan Song to the Accompaniment of His Harp,* by Nicolai Abraham Abildgaard (ca. 1785). This Danish painting of Ossian exemplifies the power the legendary bard exerted upon the artistic imagination throughout Europe. Statens Museum for Kunst, Copenhagen, Denmark (KMS395). Photo: DOWIC Fotografi.

society if it returned to what was imagined to be an original, wild, natural state, untrammeled by the restrictions imposed by custom.

The pastoral and agrarian landscape ideals allowed for a merging of the cultural and the natural, but the wilderness ideal created the basis for a clear-cut dichotomization of culture and nature (ibid., 23–39).[11] The next step in the evolution of the aesthetics of a wild, natural landscape would be to make the landscape of places like Scotland an object of pilgrimages undertaken with the goal of absorbing the pure aesthetic impulses generated by such scenery. This was accomplished by the promoters of picturesque travel.

## Picturesque Landscape

In his essays "On Picturesque Beauty," "On Picturesque Travel," and "On Sketching Landscape" (1792), William Gilpin drew explicitly upon Burke's aesthetics, counterposing Burke's identification of beauty with smoothness to the rough surfaces which characterized his conception of the picturesque (Gilpin 1792, "On Picturesque Beauty," 5). Rough, wild environments now came to be generally seen not only as natural, but as more natural than the smooth humanized pastoral environments which had hitherto symbolized the natural (Olwig 1984; Cronon 1995; Olwig 1995b). This was even more the case if they were grand and sublime, which transcends the simplicity of nature in its most usual forms. Picturesque travel leapt the garden fence not just visually. This form of travel required the landscape connoisseur to leave the garden and apply the techniques of landscape appreciation to a rough "scenery of nature" which "exclude[d] the appendages of tillage, and in general the works of men" (Gilpin 1792, iii). Picturesque taste accepted human elements in the landscape painting only if they were from an appropriately ancient classical or, better yet, Gothic past. The "relics of ancient architecture; the ruined tower, the Gothic arch" are thus "consecrated by time; and almost deserve the veneration we pay to the works of nature itself" (Gilpin 1792, "On Picturesque Travel," 46). Best of all, however, is when a grand sublime and rough and picturesque scene "strikes us beyond the power of thought . . . and every mental operation is suspended" so that we "*feel* rather than *survey* it" (ibid., 49, emphasis in original).

During the course of the seventeenth and eighteenth centuries, a scenic concept of landscape as nature gradually moved first from the realm of perspective drawing and the theater to the realm of landscape garden design, and finally progressively farther out into the wilder world beyond the boundary of the garden. The aesthetics of the picturesque involved a change in scenic ideal from that of classical Arcadia to a more contemporary rustic, rural ideal in which the rough material substance of the scene was considered to be the origin of the aesthetic effect. Picturesque travel and the growing taste for the sublime allowed for, and even encouraged, the appreciation of wild scenes in which the values expressed by these scenes were thought to spring directly from the physical properties of the land viewed as picture.

## The Landscaping of Landschaft

The aesthetic ideals of sublime and picturesque landscape scenery spread to continental Europe on the heels of a vogue for the British landscape garden park (Neumeyer 1947). The powerful potentates of the continent's absolutist states could bring this aesthetic/social ideal to a climax unthinkable even on the vast estates of Britain. In 1764, for example, after a study tour to England, Prince Leopold II (Friedrich Franz), of the Holy Roman Empire, went so far as to create not only a huge English-style garden at Wörlitz, but also to shape his entire principality of Anhalt-Dessau according to the principles of enlightenment, progress, and improvement which these gardens were seen to embody (Brandt 1987, 134–40; Petersen 1994, 27–33). Although this region was the Saxon home area of the ancient *Sachsenspiegel,* the ideas of law and *Land* mirrored in the natural landscape garden of this powerful prince were very different from those reflected in Saxon customary law.

In Germany, as in Britain, landscape gardens provided a didactic vehicle for the education and enlightenment of the citizenry. The philosopher Immanuel Kant gave these aesthetics added prestige when he discoursed on the elevated qualities of the sublime, an idea which he identified with Burke (Kant 1924; Boulton 1958, cxxv–cxxvii). It was, however, the poetry of Ossian, and with it Blair's aesthetics, which took the artists and writers of Europe by storm. From Friedrich Klopstock in Germany to the artists who served Napoleon in France, the "discovery" of Ossian set in motion a discovery of the European sublime by the predecessors of romanticism (Olwig 1984, 23–24; Boime 1990, 35–96, 447–52). Wealthy travelers from all over Europe soon staked out a touristic route that wound through Europe from the dunes and heaths of the Netherlands to the highlands of Switzerland. For the traveler in search of the picturesque and sublime, however, it was not the freedom-loving Landschaft polities of these places that was of interest, but the wild, breathtaking scenes of the *Landschaftsbild* (landscape picture).

The Landschaftsbild was not just something to survey; it was also something that overwhelmed one with the harmonic voice, or *Stimme,* which gave the landscape its ambiance, or *Stimmung* (Spitzer 1948, 294;

1963, 3). In the political concept of Landschaft, the people voiced their votes, *Stimmen*, and thereby created a state of justice and peace (*Landfrieden*) in the land. Stimmung, however, was the expression not of the voice of the people but of the natural harmony, or disharmony, of the *Umwelt*, or environment.[12] It was this idea of Umwelt, meaning milieu or environment, that, in the hands of natural philosophers, would unite with the idea of Landschaftsbild to lay an important groundwork, however unwittingly, for modern blood-and-soil nationalism.

## THE LANDSCAPE OF GERMAN ROMANTICISM AND NATURAL PHILOSOPHY

There were some Germans, such as the philosopher Johann Gottfried Herder or the poet Friederich Schiller, who saw virtue in preserving the identity of Germany's many Länder and Landschaften, perhaps within a federative state (Dopsch 1937, 5–25). This feeling is captured in the romanticization of the freedom-loving Switzerland, with its *Lands*, or cantons, in Schiller's *Wilhelm Tell*.[13] Tell focuses on Switzerland, but Schiller drew his inspiration from Länder and Landschaften in places as far distant as Friesland and the legendary home of the Swiss, Sweden (Schiller [1804] 1894, xvi, xxii).[14] This celebration of Germanic political diversity was brought into question, however, by Napoleon's conquest of the territorially divided Germany. Conquest caused many Germans to feel the need for a unified German national identity and state to counter the power of France (Boime 1990, 315–55). A vision of Germany was needed which somehow would allow for the transferal of identity from the various lands to a larger nation-state, while maintaining the semblance of diversity within unity. This motivation gave impetus to the idea that the Germans were originally one *Volk* and that they would once again be reunited within the territory of the state (Nitschke 1968; Zeitler 1992).

The Heidelberg school of romanticism, identified with Herder, cultivated cultural diversity. The Jena circle of romantic thinkers, on the other hand, was characterized by a universal romanticism that sought a holistic conception of art, science, and natural law. For some representatives of this school, such as the Danish-German geologist and natural philosopher Henrik Steffens, this holism led to the idea that the Prussian state and the German people formed a necessary unity (Steffens 1840–45, 6:127). As a respected geologist with close ties to A. G. Werner's world-renowned school of mining in Freiburg, Steffens had the scientific authority, and knowledge, which most of the philosophers of this school lacked (Steffens [1840–44] 1874; Snelders 1970; Mitchell 1984; Ziolkowski 1990, 18–63).[15] Steffens is a useful figure to focus upon because he brings together key intellectual currents that would eventually help generate a German concept of landscape uniting blood, soil, ethnicity, and race. Steffens, though he became an ardent German patriot, was not, to my knowledge, a racist. Like the brothers Grimm, he was a liberal and progressive thinker; but because the ideas that Steffens and the Grimms promulgated were easily integrated into the landscape politics of nationalism, they could also take on a reactionary color.

## Henrik Steffens and the Natural State of Progress

Steffens studied botany at the University of Copenhagen under Linnaeus's leading Danish student, Martin Vahl, before going on to study geology at the University of Kiel, Holstein, where he received a doctorate in 1797 (Steffens 1840–45, 1:267–75). He spent the years 1798 to 1802 living in Germany, dividing his time between three places: Freiburg, where he studied geology; Dresden, where he sought out the company of artists; and Jena, the locus of German "universal romanticism," where he developed his passion for natural philosophy with thinkers like Friedrich Schelling and the brothers August Wilhelm Schlegel and Friedrich Schlegel (ibid., 4:219–25).

In Freiburg, Steffens studied mineralogy under the so-called Linnaeus of geology, Abraham Gottlob Werner. Geology enjoyed enormous interest at this time, and Freiburg was a mecca for the intelligentsia. People ranging from poets such as Johann Wolfgang von Goethe and Novalis to the geographer Alexander von Humboldt went to study with Werner (ibid., 4:184–85; Snelders 1970, 194; Ziolkowski 1990, 18–63). Steffens, characteristically, dedicated his 1801 monograph, *Beiträge zur innern Naturgeschichte der Erde*, which is still considered to be a geological classic, to Goethe (Steffens [1801] 1973). Geology played a role in cosmological speculation similar to that of physics today. Werner's theories, which were called Neptunist, presupposed an ancient cataclysmic flood of biblical dimensions. These theories emphasized the role of water in shaping the earth, through both erosion and sedimentary deposits. The fossils found in sedimentary layers were particularly fascinating to Werner and his students, and they appear to have given rise in Steffens's mind to the idea of a biological and historical human evolution in which rocks and soil, plants, and human settlements formed a layered historical continuum (Steffens 1840–45, 4:199–201, 257).[16]

Steffens's devotion to Werner did not, however, prevent him from also studying with Werner's scientific opponent, glaciologist Jean de Charpentier, who belonged to the Vulcanist school because he emphasized the element of fire in the creation of the earth. Steffens was quite open to the

Fig. 7.3. *A Danish Coast: Motif from Kitnæs on the Isefjord* by J. Th. Lundbye (1843).
This Danish romantic painting illustrates the notion of landscape as a layered surface
upon which national culture is overlaid. Statens Museum for Kunst, Copenhagen,
Denmark (KMS412). Photo: DOWIC Fotografi.

"revolutionary" ideas of his time, which were breaking the classical
static, schematic, and classificatory approach to science and replacing it
with the idea of a process of continuous change (Foucault 1973; K. R. Olwig 1980). This generation, Steffens felt, saw itself as having made a
"revolutionary" and "natural" break with the past, and they saw their
place, Germany, as the locus of all the transformational changes, be they
in painting, poetry, philosophy, science, or politics (Steffens 1840–45,
4:105–6). The artist, according to Jena romantics like Schelling, provided
a better means of access to this revolutionary nature than the natural scientist, who tended to be absorbed with static laws rather than the generative processes which produce change (ibid., 6:40–41, 71–73; Wägenbaur 1994, 41).

Steffens took these ideas and applied them to a theory of nature as a picture. In his hands, the scene ceased to be a static stage upon which the human drama is played. Instead, the character of a particular people is
molded through a process of development through stages, each with its
own natural scenery. Much as the lines of perspective point out into infinity in space, this temporal process pointed toward an infinite potentiality

for progress. Steffens believed this process of development to be fundamentally a product of nature:

> It is weak language to say that through the influence of physical conditions human actions assume their character. Man is *wholly* a product from the hands of nature. Only in his being this wholly—not partly, but wholly—do we confess that in him nature centers all her mysteries. And so it became plain to me that natural science is bringing a new element into history, which is to become the basis of all knowledge of our race. History and nature must be in perfect concord, for they are really one. (Steffens [1840–44] 1874, 100, emphasis in original)

By focusing on the land as earth and soil, rather than as a culturally defined territory or country (*Land*), Steffens was able to envision a process of social growth that transcended and incorporated the boundaries which united a divided Germany (Boime 1990, 580).

Steffens developed a pictorial conception of natural national development which appears to have inspired, and been inspired by, his contact with the Dresden school of painters. In early nineteenth-century Dresden, landscape painting was being revolutionized by the work of Caspar David Friedrich and the aesthetic theories of Carl Gustav Carus (ibid., 428–32). The role that the idea of the picture played in providing an underlying unity for Steffens's conception of human development is illuminated by a statement Steffens made in an influential series of lectures given in Copenhagen in 1803. These lectures were instrumental in launching a Nordic nationalist movement in the arts and philosophy inspired by romanticism called "national romanticism" (Olwig 1995a). It was here that Steffens explicated his complex, pictorial conception of history as a process of development:

> Just as the individual human's existence is a string of incidents which have as an internal unifying principle the inner being of the individual himself, in the same way the history of nations consists of a string of changing events, *which* involves not only that of the single individual, but all of mankind. . . . In this eternal reciprocal interaction, in which the internal creative principle is unknown to us, the whole of mankind has a compelling effect upon the single nation and the nation has a compelling effect upon each single individual. But the single individual himself with a freedom in his breast which can be surveyed and suppressed—even to an unrecognizable minimum—but never entirely wiped out, has a reciprocal return effect of greater or lesser power upon his nation—and from his nation upon all of humanity. Through this interaction of the whole upon the individual, and the individual upon the whole, is generated an identical picture-history which presupposes the entirety of nature as the foundation for all final existence, and all of humanity as the expression

of this interaction itself. The expression of the coexistence of all these individuals' interactions in history and nature is *space*—eternity's continually *recumbent* picture. But the whole *is* only an eternal chain of changing events. Yes it *is* this constant alternating exchange, this eternal
succession of transformations itself. The constant type of these changes
is *time*—eternity's constantly moving, flowing, and changing picture.
(Steffens 1905, 91, emphasis in original)

The metaphor of the picture linked Steffens's argument to a larger German cosmology in which the three ideas of "picturing," creation, and development were conflated into one. The German word for picture, *Bild*,
and the verb *bilden* (meaning to create and, by extension, to educate and
develop), had been identified with each other at least since the Reformation, and this identification culminated with the romantics (Markus 1993,
14–15). This was an era when the Germans were seeking a form of moral
rearmament through a development of the nation-state via education and
arts that were grounded in the native soil and geology.[17] Much as the English ideal of education required a person to be able to interpret the world
as landscape scenery, *Bildung* (education) required an ability to think of
the world as a Bild. Caspar David Friedrich's famous painting of the
heroic individual figure who has climbed to the top of a rocky mountain
pinnacle to stare into the infinite through a sea of clouds is a Bild, but it
also represents Bildung. Development and growth start with the German
bedrock made visible here, which provides the sublime setting for the
spectator's visionary experience of an infinite national potentiality
(Mitchell 1984; Boime 1990, 580; Mitchell 1993, 77–78).

The art theorist Carl Gustav Carus, who belonged to the same intellectual circles as Friedrich and Steffens, developed an influential theory concerning the origins of landscape art as an expression of cultural and social
development, published in his influential *Neun Briefe über die Land-
schaftsmalerei* (1815–34). According to the art historian E. H. Gombrich,
Carus described the history of art as "a movement from touch to vision":

> Wanting to plead for the recognition of landscape painting as the great
> art of the future, he based his advocacy on the laws of historical in-
> evitability: 'The development of the senses in any organism begins with
> feeling, with touch. The more subtle senses of hearing and seeing emerge
> only when the organism perfects itself. In almost the same manner,
> mankind began with sculpture. What man formed had to be massive,
> solid, tangible. This is the reason why painting . . . always belongs to a
> later phase. . . . Landscape art . . . pre-supposes a higher degree of devel-
> opment. (Gombrich [1959] 1969, 19–20)

Carus's ideas, in Gombrich's opinion, prefigured a questionable form of modern thinking in which art is the measure of a society's stage of development. "By inculcating the habit of talking in terms of collectives, of 'mankind,' 'races,' or 'ages,'" this mode of thought, wrote Gombrich, "weakens resistance to totalitarian habits of mind" (ibid.). The nation-state becomes the totality that precedes the parts. This totality, in the hands of Steffens and Carus, then becomes the natural, national stage upon which the drama of individual and national development, from one stage of Bildung to the next, takes form.[18] This mode of thought thereby creates a form of "myth," in the sense defined by Roland Barthes, which "transforms history into nature" (Barthes [1957] 1972, 129). It is this mythic Bildung which, to use Michel Foucault's concepts, enables the development of a "total history" that links together the events occurring in "a well-defined spatio-temporal area" so that history itself may be articulated into "great units—stages or phases—which contain within themselves their own principle of cohesion"—the "'face' of a [historical] period" (Foucault 1972, 9–10).

## Nation-State Fairytales

Steffens's work brings together three topics that fascinated the universalistic German thinkers of his time: scientific natural law (especially in relation to geology), aesthetics, and human law (Ziolkowski 1990). Among those Steffens influenced were the Grimm brothers. The example of Jacob and Wilhelm Grimm illustrates how this confluence of interests could eventually lead to an unintended blood-and-soil racism. The Grimms worked closely together throughout their lives. They began their careers as students of ancient Germanic law and later developed pioneering interests in folklore and philology, but they maintained a lifelong interest in ancient law (Grimm 1854; Peppard 1971). The Grimms developed their interest in law during their youthful studies with a prominent specialist in Roman law, Friedrich Karl von Savigny, who emphasized the importance of the study of ancient German custom and language as a basis for legal understanding (Harrison 1992, 166–67). Roman law provided the point of departure, and the implicit standard, for the study of the German legal tradition. This point of departure led to a search for an original, universal body of Germanic law which could measure up to the regularity of Roman law. The Grimms' later interest in finding the universal laws governing an original, more unified Germanic language as part of the larger body of a prototypical Indo-European/Germanic language represents the same basic approach. As a result of this approach, the standard German dictionary, which the Grimms initiated, treats all the Germanic tongues (including English) as variants of what was at one time a single language (Grimm and Grimm 1855).

In their studies of folklore and language the Grimms gave priority to the oral traditions of particular localities (Grimm 1848; Foucault 1973, 286). In his early work on Germanic folklore, Wilhelm Grimm focused upon Scandinavia, which was the Germanic culture that was farthest to the northwest, and thus farthest from the influence of Rome. Grimm happened to have Steffens as a neighbor. As a native speaker of both Norwegian and Danish, Steffens was of great help to Grimm in this work. Steffens also was able to help provide a natural philosophy which enabled Grimm to root the development of differing folk cultures to differing natural landscapes (Steffens 1840–45, 6:109–10; Peppard 1971, 34; Boime 1990, 548–52; Harrison 1992, 164–77). This correlation between culture and landscape implied that Germanic folklore was ultimately the natural expression of the Nordic environment.

In and of themselves, each of the Grimms' different contributions to the development of the human sciences has been invaluable. Linked together, however, they can form an explosive mixture in which folk culture, the Teutonic or Aryan race, and the Indo-Germanic/Aryan language are seen to grow from the native soil (Poliakov 1974, 188–214, 255–325; MacDougall 1982, 73–103). In the final analysis, this pan-Germanic ideology implicates the idea of a greater Germany which absorbs neighboring territories, homogenizes German society into an abstract *Volk-Gemeinschaft,* is bound to the soil, and ultimately thinks with a single mind (Nitschke 1968; Poliakov 1974, 71–105). It was this kind of thinking that helped generate a concept of landscape in which, to use Oswald Spengler's words, as translated by Carl Sauer, "cultures grow with original vigor out of the lap of a maternal natural landscape, to which each is bound in the whole course of its existence" (quoted in English in Sauer [1925] 1969, 325).[19] Though it would be unfair to reduce the scholarly contribution of the Grimms to the status of a prelude to blood-and-soil nationalism, in the end we find Jacob Grimm polemicizing, on the basis of a specious blend of folk-cultural, linguistic, and geographic arguments, for the incorporation of all of Danish Jutland into Germany (Peppard 1971, 223, 231–32; Ødegaard 1992).

## The Landscaping of Jutland

In his *Geschichte der deutschen Sprache* of 1848, Jacob Grimm argued that Danish "Goths" from Zealand and Funen had at one time suppressed the ethnically German Jutes. This prompted Grimm to ask why Denmark shouldn't be divided between the Germans to the south and the "Gothic" Swedes to the northwest, since it was the "folk right" of peoples to be thus joined together. As he put it: "Why, when the great [Germanic] union is established, shouldn't the contested [Jutland] peninsula be joined completely to the continent, as history, nature, and situation command? Why shouldn't the Jutes return to their ancient attachment to the Angles and the Saxons, and the Danes to the Goths? As soon as Germany has reorganized itself, it will be impossible for Denmark to continue as it has up til now" (Grimm 1848, vi, 738, 837; see also Peppard 1971, 23, 231–32; Ødegaard 1992, 143).

For Grimm, history (and language), nature, and geographical situation formed a unity which commanded attachment to greater Germany. The Jutland dialect, like the German (and English) language, places the definite article *the* before the word it modifies.[20] The standard Danish of Copenhagen and the islands, however, like the other Scandinavian languages, appends the definite article to the end of the word. Ergo, Grimm's lingoracial argument concludes, the peninsular Jutlanders form a Teutonic race attached by bonds of natural landscape to continental Germany. The people of the islands that constitute the remainder of Denmark, on the other hand, must belong to the Gothic race of the adjacent Scandinavian peninsula.

In 1864 Otto von Bismarck's troops roundly defeated the Danes and conquered Jutland. Denmark was allowed to retain the ancient Danish landskab of Northern Jutland, but all of Schleswig-Holstein was incorporated into Germany—including the culturally Danish remnant of the ancient Danish landskab of Sønderjylland, which formed the northern third of Schleswig. Dithmarschen and North Friesland were swallowed up within the nationalist political landscape of the new German nation-state, thereby losing their ancient customary rights as Landschaft polities. The memory of the ancient Landschaft polities of Germany was allowed to live on, however, in picture postcards—with Gothic letterings—of fairy-tale lands in which custom became fossilized as a national heritage of local tradition, and custom became costume. With custom thus immobilized as tradition, it became the perfect backdrop for visions of national progress and modernization (Herf 1984; Olwig 2002).

## WESTERN PROGRESS AS A LANDSCAPE PICTURE BOOK

Steffens exerted considerable influence on geographers like the Swiss-American Arnold Guyot, who, as the next chapter shows, played a central role in transferring German concepts of place as territory to America. In the preface to his influential book *The Earth and Man: Lectures on Comparative Physical Geography, in its Relation to the History of Mankind* from 1849, Guyot wrote:

> There are, however, three names so closely connected with the history of
> the science to which this volume is devoted, and with the past studies of
> the author, that he feels bound to mention them here. Humboldt, Ritter
> and Steffens are the three great minds who have breathed a new life into
> the science of the physical and moral world. The scientific life of the au-
> thor opened under the full radiance of the light they spread around them,
> and it is with a sentiment of filial piety that he delights to recall this con-
> nection, and to render to them his public homage. (1849, vii)

Guyot's work sums up elements of the ideas of a highly influential generation of German geographical thinkers ranging from Steffens to Alexander von Humboldt, author of *Cosmos: A Sketch of a Physical Description
of the Universe* (1849–58), and Karl Ritter, author of the nineteen-volume
work *Die Erdkunde* (1817–18, 1822–59). The subtitle to Ritter's book is
indicative of his approach: *The Science of the Earth in Relation to Nature
and the History of Mankind; or, General Comparative Geography as the
Solid Foundation of the Study of, and Instruction in, Physical and Historical Science* (James 1972, 126–30). Ritter saw mankind as developing
through cyclical stages analogous to the cyclical movement of the heavenly bodies. The "sunrise" of civilization thus took place in the east, in
Asia (where medieval geographers had located—or *oriented*—paradise),
and the progress of civilization thenceforth followed the sun west from its
"noon" in Africa to its afternoon fullness in western Europe.

　　In *The Earth and Man,* Guyot followed Steffens and Ritter in providing a "natural" explanation for the "geographical march of history" as a
vast "theater" spectacle in which empires rise and fall, beginning in the
East and moving toward the West. Guyot presents a series of landscape
tableaux showing how civilizations are periodically rejuvenated through
implantation in the fresh soil of their wilder (north)western neighbors
(Guyot 1849, 249–57, 276). Guyot writes of the German triumph over
Rome:

> The Germans have preserved their native energy, and are still free. Rome
> is declining, and, little by little, the sources of life in that immense body
> are drying up. The weaker it grows, the more the men of the North press
> upon the mighty colossus, whose head is still of iron, though its feet are
> of clay. It falls for its own happiness and that of humanity; for a new
> sap—the fresh vitality of the Northmen—is to circulate throughout it;
> and soon it shall be born again, full of strength and life. (ibid., 257)

The fall of Rome leads to the translation of civilization to the north and
west:

> Civilization passes to the other side of the Alps, where it establishes its
> centre. A still virgin country, a people full of youth and life, receive it; it

grows under the influence of the Christian principle of unity and brotherhood. A common faith unites all the members of that society of the
middle ages, so strangely broken up; those nations, so different, so hos-
tile to each other in appearance, nevertheless look upon each other as
brothers, and form together the great family of Christianity. (ibid., 289)

For Guyot, the march of progress is through the "continents of the North
considered as the theater of history" (ibid., 249; Livingstone 1994). The
theater of future history is, following this logic, now located in North
America. Guyot's influential vision of the march of progress to North
America also helps explain how continental discourses concerning nation,
nature, landscape, and the body politic were transferred to America.

# Eight

# The "Country" of the United States contra the "Landscape" of America's New World

The ideas of landscape, country, and nature that had initially developed within a European context provided an important basis for the creation of an American national identity. This identity was wedded, on the one hand, to the idea of the nation as a political landscape making up a country of countries and, on the other, to the idea of a manifest destiny tied to the landscape of the American continent's geographical body. In the first sense the United States was a political community encompassing smaller political communities ranging downward from the states to the counties, townships, and so on. In the latter sense, the nation was defined in terms of its geographical territory as "America."

Continental bodies are delineated by humans, not nature, and for this reason their exact boundaries are rarely absolutely clear. The boundary of Asia (east) and Europe (west) has thus long been a matter of dispute. It helps, however, when defining one's continent, to have a relatively clear natural boundary, as between Europe and Africa. The people of the United States have thus tended to define their continent in terms of its eastern coast, where the country formed, and the west coast, toward which it expanded, following the sun and "manifest destiny." The people of the U.S. thus call themselves Americans, though they in fact share the continent with the people of Canada and Mexico, who also have the right to call themselves Americans. Since it has become common usage to identify the people of the United States as Americans, I do so here, even if they are not, in fact, co-extensive with the continent.

The English concepts of country and landscape were reconceived in America through the thought and practice of the people who made the continent their home. This chapter explores the works of a number of key American writers and activists. It begins with a critical examination of the

176

subtexts of works by Henry David Thoreau and Ralph Waldo Emerson. It then focuses on the idea of the natural park as a symbol of place identity and proceeds to examine the works of three practitioners who helped shape American landscape attitudes and practice: Frederick Law Olmsted, John Muir, and Aldo Leopold. The American perception of landscape and nature is a vast topic that has been treated by innumerable writers.[1] This book, though informed by those works, has a narrower focus: tracing the transformations of particular narratives as they were translocated from Europe to the United States of America. In so doing, this chapter raises fundamental questions about the very narratives that are supposed define America as a unique New World separate from the Old World of Europe. It does this by showing that we are actually dealing with the reconfiguration of older narratives that had earlier been used to define Britain in much the same way.

## A COUNTRY OF COUNTRIES

The federated structure of the United States means that there is a constant tension between the national state and the political communities united within it. There is, on the one hand, the American nation-state, which has been defined in terms of a continental manifest destiny that would create a single American people. And, on the other, there is a federation of states, each with its own body of law, which themselves are made up of countless legal and informal communities ranging from the county and township to the neighborhood. The federal system reflects the countryman ideology which flourished in the seventeenth century, when many refugees from Stuart Britain fled to a new England in America and re-created the English township or village centered on a common green. The United States can thus be said to have a dual identity both as the national state of America and as a federated country of countries or land of lands, in the Landschaft tradition of the Netherlands and Switzerland. This duality is even visible on the map. The organic forms of the eastern states follow the contours of the different ethnic and religious communities which first settled the continent, whereas settlement in the west was plotted into the quadrants mapped upon the territory of the Louisiana Purchase (Tuan 1996, 87 88). This duality is also reflected in the conception and use of public parks. At one end of the spectrum we have the country parks, village greens, and commons of the East Coast, particularly New England, which are jealously guarded as symbols of local community. At the other end we have the national parks, which tend to be defined in terms of the purple mountain majesties of a "virgin" continent.

A key symbol of the identity of the United States as a "country" is the

New England village. Donald Meinig, a prominent geographer of American place identity, has described its importance:

> As the author of a recent guidebook confidently stated: "To the entire world, a steepled church, set in its frame of white wooden houses around a manicured common, remains a scene which says 'New England.'" Our interest is not simply in the fact that such a scene "says" New England, but more especially in what New England "says" to us through the medium of its villages. . . . Drawing simply upon one's experience as an American (which is, after all, an appropriate way to judge a national symbol) it seems clear that such scenes carry connotations of continuity (of not just something important in our past, but a visible bond between past and present), of stability, quiet prosperity, cohesion and intimacy. Taken as a whole, the image of the New England village is widely assumed to symbolize for many people the best we have known of an intimate, family-centered, Godfearing, morally conscious, industrious, thrifty, democratic *community*. (Meinig 1979, 165, emphasis in original)

This is a conception of United (States) place identity that contrasts remarkably with the idea of America as a state defined by the eastern and western boundaries of a vast continent which stretches across wide open spaces, "from sea to shining sea."[2] The people of the United States tend to identify themselves as being from a particular state, but as Americans they take their name from a continent which itself is named for an Italian ex-

Fig. 8.1. Village green, Sterling, Massachusetts. Photo: author.

plorer. In this respect, Americans resemble their British forebears, who took their name from the Roman appellation for their island realm, Britannia (Smith 1986, 109).

The United States of America became the first Western nation-state whose citizens were defined almost solely in terms of birthplace (the territory of America) rather than natural rights of lineage. America, like Britain, was a nation-state that unified its diverse peoples within the bounds of a geographical body and its landscape. America, again like Britain, faced the problem of incorporating conquered national territories within its prospective bounds. Just as the Tudors and early Stuarts claimed that their natural destiny was to control Britain long before this was a political reality, the United States also claimed a manifest destiny to large stretches of America long before it had effectively taken control from its indigenous inhabitants.

## JEFFERSONIAN LANDSCAPE

An early architect of the American landscape ideal was Thomas Jefferson, who was also the architect of its political constitution. Jefferson had made a meticulous study of the landscape gardens of England, and he lavished attention upon the Palladian architecture and landscape of his estate at Monticello. Inspired by the proponents of picturesque taste, he leapt the garden fence in search of an authentically natural landscape, designed under the authority of a godlike Nature. "Nature" was the preeminent word in Jefferson's discourse (Miller 1988, 1–20). Rather than move tons of earth to create an appropriately arcadian scene, as landscape architects in England had done, Jefferson incorporated the existent natural landscape seen from Monticello into his garden. The ha-ha became superfluous when all of America was a landscape garden. Rather than build a sham bridge, as had Henry Hoare at Stourhead, Jefferson purchased the Natural Bridge of Virginia—"that most sublime of Nature's works"—and gave it to the nation (quoted in ibid., 130). He thereby set a precedent that would reach full flower with the establishment of the national parks, which were essentially landscape gardens designed by God, or "Nature," and enframed by the state.

Jefferson's idea of landscape, like that of the improving landlords of Britain, was deeply inspired by the works of Virgil (Marx 1964, 73–144). His ideal encompassed a natural temporal progression from the pastoral state described in the *Eclogues,* which he preserved in his park at Monticello, to a land subdivided into fields and worked by an improving farmer as described in the *Georgics.* A child of the Enlightenment, Jefferson thought of nature, first and foremost, as the celestial nature of geometri-

Fig. 8.2. Natural Bridge of Virginia. Photo: author.

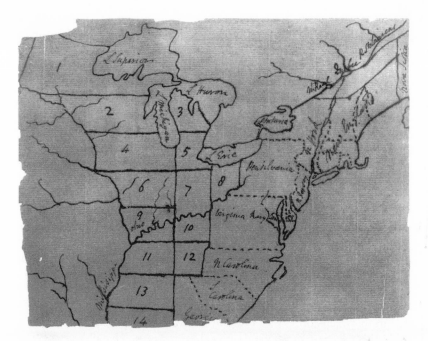

Fig. 8.3. Jefferson-Hartley Map of the Western Territory, 1784. Jefferson provided information on the states to be established in the Western Territory to David Hartley, a British official who had helped draw up the peace treaty between the two nations. Hartley's sketch illustrates the geometric order that Jefferson wished to impose on the land. Reproduced by permission of the William L. Clements Library, University of Michigan, Ann Arbor.

cal reason. He loved geography, and his proudest accomplishment in his geographical study of Virginia was his map (Miller 1988, 18, 120). Later, when, as president, he arranged for the purchase of the Northwest Territory, he had the pleasure of projecting upon it the geometrical structure of a map, thereby predetermining the structure of its colonization and cultivation (Cosgrove 1984, 161–88; Miller 1988, 138–39). It was upon the undifferentiated geometric space of the map that the national landscape was to be carved out by the plows of improving farmers. This "natural" geometric order was veritably inscribed upon the surface of the country through the efforts of the United States land survey of the 1780s. These efforts eventually resulted in the division of the states into twenty-six-square-mile townships which were systematically subdivided down to the level of the smallest unit—"the forty-acre farm" (Tuan 1996, 87–88).

The Jeffersonian landscape gave material form to the pictorial conception of development promoted by philosophers like Jefferson's contemporary Henrik Steffens. Steffens's description of "the single individual himself, with a freedom in his breast" can be read as a description of the free individual American yeoman on his own square farm. The Jeffersonian conceptualization of America as landscape begged for landscape painting. The "cult of landscape," with Frederic Edwin Church's painting *The Natural Bridge of Virginia* as its foremost example, soon became a national passion. The visual image of landscape played an extraordinary role in the development of the American national identity (Novak 1980).

A consequence of the burgeoning American interest in landscape scenery was that when explorers discovered vast areas in the west that resembled grand landscape parks, these areas became symbols of American national identity. Their enclosure as the world's first natural parks set a pattern that has since become paradigmatic for the national parks of the world. The ultimate expression of the American concept of nature, nation, and landscape was achieved when Jefferson's visage (along with that of other founding fathers) was carved into the side of a mountain in Mount Rushmore National Memorial.

The idea of America as the landscape of the nation masks vital contradictions between *country* as a legally defined community and *nation* as a single state defined by its geographical boundaries. This chapter is concerned with the role of these tensions in the development of a complex American sense of place which has its roots in the tension between the idea of England as country and the envisioning of Britain as landscape scenery.

THE LANDSCAPE TEXT

Whereas it is possible to "read" the landscapes of the great gardens of Britain as texts inscribed in the land by their architects, it is much more difficult to read the landscape scene in America, where it seems to have been shaped by God himself. America, however, has a great heritage of nature writers who have interpreted its landscape scenery and given it meaning in their texts. The landscape scenes which Americans have preserved as nature in parks are a reflection of this textual tradition. Two of the most influential early thinkers on American landscape and nature were Henry David Thoreau and Ralph Waldo Emerson. They, in turn, helped inspire three of the most important landscape practitioners, Frederick Law Olmsted, John Muir, and Aldo Leopold. A close reading of their works, and the landscape practice which they inspired, provides a useful key to understanding the tensions between the United States conceived of, on the one hand, as a "country of countries," and, on the other, as the unified nation-state of America.

## The Reconception of the British Landscape Scene in America

Henry David Thoreau, whose *Walden* and "Walking" are often read as testaments to the American wilderness preservation movement, spent most of his life in Concord, Massachusetts, a civilized locus of early American culture. Complete with a village green, Concord is a classic New England embodiment of Old Whig political and judicial values. Though Thoreau remained in Concord for most of his life, his heart was not in concordance with the place. His dissonant, dissident spirit was elsewhere.

I quote at length below from Thoreau's "Walking" because of the way it illustrates the continuity between seemingly new American ideas and the older narratives treated in the foregoing chapters. The difference between the nature of America and that of Britain, according to Thoreau, was that Britain was an old nation that had used up much of its natural potentiality and therefore had a "tame and civilized literature" similar to that of the even older civilizations of Greece and Rome. America, by contrast, was a young nation in an appropriately young and wild environment. Whereas Ben Jonson declaims (as quoted by Thoreau) *"How near to good is what is fair!"* Thoreau himself exclaims "How near to good is what is *wild!*" (Thoreau [1862] 1991, 97, emphasis in original). The British still remember their natural potentiality, and therefore there is still "plenty of genial love of Nature" in English poetry, "but not so much of Nature herself" (ibid., 103–5). "Nature herself" has left Britain, according to Thoreau, and has once again moved west to a new and more virgin territory. There is nothing virginal, however, about Thoreau's ideas; they have much in common with those which William Camden, Ben Jonson, and Inigo Jones had used several centuries earlier to "reinvent" Britain.

In Thoreau's vision, the "happy isle" of classical myth is not Britain, as it was for Jonson—it is America. Even the goddess of natural justice, Astraea, who once left Rome for Britain, takes a small bow, as will be seen, on the landscape scene of Thoreau's America. The state of America, however, is without a monarch; only the landscape scene itself is majestic. Like Inigo Jones's landscape scenery, Thoreau's ideal American landscape belongs to the realm of visionary illusion and utopia, and it is also an ideal that subsequent generations would help to materialize.

## Walking West with Thoreau

"In wildness is the preservation of the world" may well be the most famous maxim of American wilderness preservationists (Nash 1976, 84–95; Cronon 1995, 69). The full wording of Thoreau's famous sentence (which is rarely quoted) is: "THE WEST OF WHICH I SPEAK is but another name for the Wild; and what I have been preparing to say is, that in Wildness is the preservation of the World" (Thoreau [1862] 1991, 94–95, emphasis in original). Thoreau's "Wild WEST" is the same mythic "west" of national and imperial destiny with which the British and Germans had once associated themselves. Where the westward British Isles had taken the mantle once worn by Rome, westward America is now taking the mantle from Britain. Because inbreeding within the nobility had weakened its fiber, Thoreau argues, Britain is approaching the end of its day as the dominant power on the scene of history. England has become the seat of "a civilization destined to have a speedy limit" (ibid., 110). The Renaissance architects of Britain compared its "body geographical" to the western, blessèd isles of ancient myth. Now Thoreau is inspired to compare the westward continent of America with "the island of Atlantis, and the islands and gardens of the Hesperides." These isles form "a sort of terrestrial paradise" because, in Thoreau's mind, they "appear to have been the Great West of the ancients, enveloped in mystery and poetry" (ibid., 88). Whereas Britain had been separated from older civilizations by the narrow English Channel, the happy American continent is separated from the senescent continent of Europe by the vast expanse of the Atlantic Ocean. Those who cross the "Lethean stream" of the Atlantic, as Thoreau calls it, cross into an American version of the Elysian fields where a new American man is reborn to the destiny of a new and more glorious western empire:

> To Americans I hardly need to say,—
> *"Westward the star of empire takes its way."*
> As a true patriot, I should be ashamed to think that Adam in paradise was more favorably situated on the whole than the backwoodsman in this country. (Thoreau [1862] 1991, 93, emphasis in original)

Thoreau's idea of the West came, at least in part, from the influential ideas of the Swiss-American geographer Arnold Guyot. Thoreau did not subscribe to all that Guyot had written, but he was "ready to follow" him when he wrote (as quoted by Thoreau):

> "As the plant is made for the animal, as the vegetable world is made for the animal world, America is made for the man of the Old World. . . . The man of the Old World sets out upon his way. Leaving the highlands of Asia, he descends from station to station towards Europe. Each of his steps is marked by a new civilization superior to the preceding, by a greater power of development. Arrived at the Atlantic, he pauses on the shore of this unknown ocean, the bounds of which he knows not, and turns upon his footprints for an instant." When the man of the Old

World has exhausted the rich soil of Europe, and reinvigorated himself, he "then recommences his adventurous career westward as in the earliest ages." (ibid., 89–90, ellipsis in original)

The cyclical structure of the geohistorical march of history means that civilization moves forward through a constant process of returning, in the end, to its origins. If we think of time in a linear sense, this creates the apparent paradox that we move forward by moving backward. This process seems less paradoxical, however, if it is thought of as a spiral or a dialectic. We return to an earlier state, but on a higher level. The importance attached to the return to primitive origins does not, therefore, necessarily imply a nostalgic desire to return to a permanent state of "nature." Nature can be thought of as a cyclical process of growth, and the return to origins can mean an opportunity to start all over again and, it is hoped, do it better next time. The Wild West thus represented a new beginning rather than an end in itself. It was the source of natural potentiality for development, not something to preserve from development.

The sunset inspired Thoreau's desire to go west: "He [the sun] is the Great Western Pioneer whom the nations follow" (ibid., 88). West is the "way the nation is moving, and I may say that mankind progress from east to west."[3] We go eastward "to realize history," but we go "westward as into the future with a spirit of enterprise and adventure" (ibid., 86–87). The simple enterprising pioneer, in Thoreau's mind, recalls the men of "the heroic age of myth" (ibid., 94). Thoreau, who did his work as a surveyor for this sort of man, tells of a survey that ran in "a single straight line one hundred and thirty-two rods long, through a swamp." Such a survey would enable the pioneer to drain the wetland and use the muck to fertilize his crops.[4] By thus working the "virgin soil," "the farmer displaces the Indian even because he redeems the meadow, and so makes himself stronger and in some respects more natural" (ibid., 101–2).

## The Wild in the West

Thoreau's West is not just a cardinal direction in a cosmological theory of progress; it also has a living, organic nature. It is a wild place that, because it has never been cultivated, contains a reservoir of nutrients for the growth of a future empire. Just as trees send forth root fibers in search of the "wild" from which they draw their nourishment, so too, Thoreau tells us, did the shepherd founders of the Roman Empire, Romulus and Remus, draw their nourishment from the wild—a wolf. This is "not a meaningless fable," Thoreau assures us, because "the founders of every state which has risen to eminence have drawn their nourishment and vigor from a similar wild source" ([1862] 1991, 95). A few pages later, he adds: "The civilized nations—Greece, Rome, England—have been sustained by the primitive forests that anciently rotted where they stand. They survive as long as the soil is not exhausted. Alas for human culture! little is to be expected of a nation, when the vegetable mould is exhausted" (ibid., 101).

"Climate," according to Thoreau, "react[s] on man." "Will not man," he asks, "grow to greater perfection intellectually as well physically under these influences? . . . I trust that we shall be more imaginative, that our thoughts will be clearer, fresher, and more ethereal as our sky,—our understanding more comprehensive and broader, like our plains,—our intellect generally on a grander scale, like our thunder and lightning, our rivers and mountains and forests" (ibid., 91–93). The Americans are the legitimate inheritors of the civilization of the northwestern Europeans, who also drew their sustenance from the forests: "it was because the children of the [Roman] Empire were not suckled by the wolf that they were conquered and displaced by the children of the northern forests who were" (ibid., 95).

Thoreau and Guyot portray the narrative of man's progress across the scene of history as a series of new beginnings, as man moves west from the bounds of one continent to the next. At each stopping point the stages of history repeat themselves, from the wild to the pastoral and so on. The "theater" of history is a living metaphor in which the landscape scene frames and unifies each stage. This landscape imagery defined the "fields of vision," to use Stephen Daniels's phrase, that shaped national identity in the United States, much as it had in Britain (Boime 1991; Cronon 1992; Daniels 1993a).

### Wild Western Natural Landscape

When Thoreau states that "in Wildness is the preservation of the World," he is arguing for the use of the "raw material of life" that is stored in wild western nature. Thoreau's "nature" finds its origins in the heritage of the goddess Natura. The Greeks, according to Thoreau, called the world "cosmos, Beauty, or Order," and he equates this world with both "landscape" and a sublime feminine "Nature," which is "a personality so vast and universal that we have never seen one of her features" ([1862] 1991, 115).

Natura is related to Astraea, the stellar goddess of natural justice, and Thoreau also saw nature as something that descended from the heavens and was best seen from the sublime elevation of a tree top: "WE HUG THE EARTH,—how rarely we mount! Methinks we might elevate ourselves a little more" (ibid., 118). When he follows his own advice and climbs a tall white pine, Thoreau is presented with a view of the horizon and "the earth and the heavens" which he had never seen before. On the top, he finds a fertile flower "looking heavenward." Since it is "court-week," Thoreau symbolically takes this wild treetop flower and presents it both to "stranger jurymen" and to the citizens of the township. They react with wonder, "as at a star dropped down" (ibid., 103–5, 119).[5]

Thoreau's symbolic act of presenting a flower and fallen star to citizens and jurymen of a New England "shire town" during court-week expresses his ambivalence toward the common law justice meted out by such courts.[6] Thoreau had limited respect for American legislative bodies, and though he admitted that the Constitution, "with all its faults," was essentially "good," he still believed that the "fountain-head[s]," of truth were in nature and "love" ([1849] 1983, 409–12; see also editor's introduction, ibid., 32). "The man who takes the liberty to live," he tells us, "is superior to all the laws, by virtue of his relation to the law-maker" ([1862] 1991, 114). Thoreau's loyalty was primarily to the law of nature, not the common law of the New England county.

Thoreau's ambivalence toward the common law justice of the original eastern American colonies was largely due to his opposition to slavery. Daniel Webster, a senator from the Commonwealth of Massachusetts in the 1830s and 1840s, had gained respect for his defense of the constitution. But for Thoreau this defense proved the insufficiency of the common law tradition because it forced Webster to sanction slavery. Webster stated, as quoted by Thoreau: "Because it was a part of the original compact,—let it stand." Webster continued: "The manner in which the governments of those States where slavery exists are to regulate it, is for their own consideration, under their responsibility to their constituents, to the general laws of propriety, humanity, and justice, and to God" (quoted in Thoreau [1849] 1983, 411). Thoreau could not accept that the law condoned slavery, and he believed that the problem lay in the fact that "the lawyer's truth is not Truth, but consistency." American statesmen and legislators, Thoreau argues, stand "completely within the institution" of law which they represent; because "they speak of moving society, but have no resting-place without it," they cannot legislate "for all time" (ibid., 410–11). Thoreau looked to the West for a natural and timeless justice because it was here, in wild nature, that society could begin anew, unencumbered by the precedence of custom embodied in the common law of the eastern states. In this land of natural men who live in the present and future rather than the past, "no fugitive slave laws are passed" ([1862] 1991, 119–20).

The problem with Thoreau's vision of the West as the natural, wild source of national renewal is that the very process of using that resource destroys its raw life-giving power. The West is always beyond the horizon, and Thoreau envisioned a time when America, like Britain before it, would be left behind by the westward course of history. The "Elysian fields" of America, which are separated from Europe by the "Lethean stream" of the Atlantic, offer mankind a new chance. But, Thoreau warns, "if we do not succeed this time, there is perhaps one more chance for the race left before it arrives on the banks of the Styx; and that is the Lethe of the Pacific, which is three times as wide" (ibid., 87).

The teleology of Thoreau's moving world picture is so ordered that even as the nation is busy being born in the West, it is also busy dying in the East. Eventually this process will force civilization to jump across the Pacific. His idea of the West, Thoreau realized with acute prescience, belongs to the realm of myth:

> The West is preparing to add its fables to those of the East. The valleys of the Ganges, the Nile, and the Rhine having yielded their crop, it remains to be seen what the valleys of the Amazon, the Plate, the Orinoco, the St. Lawrence, and the Mississippi will produce. Perchance, when, in the course of ages, American liberty has become a fiction of the past—as it is to some extent a fiction of the present,—the poets of the world will be inspired by American mythology. (ibid., 105)

Thoreau, however, did have a truly visionary solution to the problem of the transient glory of America: to preserve the elixir of wildness by emparking some of it as a place where the nation could re-create its natural potentiality.

## Natural Recreation

Thoreau's maxim "In Wildness is the preservation of the World" appears in an essay called "Walking." It is about walking as a form of wandering pilgrimage, following the sun into western nature. It is about how to "recreate," in a very literal sense. "When I would recreate myself," he tells us, "I seek the darkest wood, the thickest and most interminable . . . swamp." He enters this swamp as "a sacred place,—a sanctum sanctorum" because it is here that he finds "the strength, the marrow of Nature," the wildwood which "covers the virgin-mould," a soil which is as good for "men" as for "trees" (Thoreau [1862] 1991, 100). The sexual connotations in Thoreau's description of man's penetration of the West were by no means exclusive to him. According to Annette Kolodny's study of sexual metaphor in America, it was common for the founding fathers to see their mission as carving a nation out of a land that they saw to be: "Like a faire virgin, longing to be sped, / And meete her lover in a Nuptiall bed"(quoted in Kolodny 1975, 12; see also Merchant 1995). Recreation involves the regeneration of the creative forces of nature within one's body. Thoreau is able to recreate in this way by walking because in his vicinity:

> The landscape is not owned, and the walker enjoys comparative freedom. But possibly the day will come when it will be partitioned off into so-called pleasure-grounds, in which a few will take a narrow and exclusive pleasure only,—when fences shall be multiplied, and man-traps and other engines invented to confine men to the *public* road, and walking over the surface of God's earth shall be construed to mean trespassing on some gentleman's grounds. To enjoy a thing exclusively is commonly to exclude yourself from the true enjoyment of it. Let us improve our opportunities, then, before the evil days come. ([1862] 1991, 84–85, emphasis in original)

Thoreau sees himself walking in a "cometary orbit," moving in "wildness and freedom" from East to West and back, through a vast, natural, open and free pleasure-ground park, with "fair landscapes" owned by God (ibid., 86). This Wild West landscape is a "common country of all the inhabitants of the globe" (ibid., 90). It is in such a landscape park that the re-creative powers of nature can be preserved.

At the conclusion of "Walking," the image of America as a free and open park returns in a sunset vision of a cranberry meadow at "Spaulding's farm." It is as if "some ancient and altogether admirable and shining family had settled there in that part of the land called Concord, unknown to me,—to whom the sun was servant." In Spaulding's cranberry meadow Thoreau finds this mystical family's "park, their pleasure-ground" in which the owners recline on sunbeams, like players in a masque. Their coat of arms is lichen, they have no politics, they do not labor, and all that one can hear is "the finest imaginable sweet musical hum." If it were not for being able to cohabit with this family of the sun, Thoreau felt that he would have to leave Concord ([1862] 1991, 116–17). The essay closes with a sunset vision of America as "Elysium," and it is into this Elysium that Thoreau saunters off into the sunset (ibid., 122).

EMERSON'S NATURAL LANDSCAPE

Thoreau's neighbor and friend Ralph Waldo Emerson taught his readers to look at nature as if in a poem or painting. The sun, by illuminating and warming this landscape scene, gives it a natural unity much like that in Thoreau's sunset vision of Spaulding's farm. Emerson writes: "The charming landscape which I saw this morning, is indubitably made up of some twenty or thirty farms. Miller owns this field, Locke that, and Manning the woodland beyond. But none of them owns the landscape. There is a property in the horizon which no man has but he whose eye can integrate all the parts, that is, the poet. This is the best part of these men's farms, yet to this their warranty-deeds give no title" ([1836] 1991, 7).

The important thing for Thoreau was the experience of nature gained by wandering through the landscape. Emerson, however, places more emphasis upon the use of the eye. This organ provides the key to the experience of a totalizing and global vision of nature. "The eye," he instructs the reader, "is the best of artists." Sight enables the perception of nature as a landscape scene in which "perspective is produced" by "the mutual action of its structure and the laws of light." It is this visual perspective "which integrates every mass of objects, of what character so ever, into a well colored and shaded globe, so that where the particular objects are mean and unaffecting, the landscape which they compose, is round and symmetrical" (ibid., 13).

Emerson's landscape vision of nature, like Thoreau's conception of the natural potentiality of the Wild West, was fundamentally directed toward the realization of human development. Much as the eye is for Emerson "the best composer," light is "the first of painters" because it creates a sense of infinitude like that of space and time (ibid., 13). Man looks into this infinite nature in order to find a reflection of his own infinite possibilities. "In the tranquil landscape, and especially in the distant line of the horizon," Emerson tells us, "man beholds somewhat as beautiful as his own nature" (ibid., 8–9). This landscape vision, like the scenery in a masque perceived from the monarch's throne, provides a reflection of nature's laws of development in a world envisioned as a scene of action for man. "The least change in our point of view gives the whole world a pictorial air" in which people become "apparent, not substantial beings." Such changes of view suggest "the difference between the observer and the spectacle,—between man and nature. Hence arises a pleasure mixed with awe; I may say, a low degree of the sublime is felt from the fact, probably, that man is hereby apprized, that, whilst the world is a spectacle, something in himself is stable" (ibid., 44). It is this stability which enables the artistic imagination, according to Emerson, to delineate, "as on air," the features of the landscape—"the sun, the mountain, the camp, the city"— as if they were "afloat before the eye." In this way he "unfixes the land and the sea, makes them revolve around the axis of his primary thought, and disposes them anew," thereby conforming "things to his thought" and impressing "his being thereon" (ibid., 44–45).

Emerson's landscape is familiar to the modern sensibility as a scene of nature. It is still, however, as for Thoreau, a nature imbued with earlier ideas of Natura and Astraea. Natura is identifiable, if only subliminally, with the passions of love. "The presence of nature," we are told, causes "a wild delight" to run through man (ibid., 7). But Emerson's Natura is a chaste goddess who will allow men to look but not to tear at her garment. She "never wears a mean [shabby] appearance," Emerson assures the reader, and the wisest man cannot "extort her secret, and lose his curiosity" (ibid., 6). The Stuart monarchs sought to cast themselves in the role of Natura as God's subvicars, applying the laws of nature to the landscape under their domain; but Emerson has changed this role. Rather than the divinely ordained monarch assuming the position of Natura and Astraea, now Emerson's transcendent individual seeks to do this.[7] Taking the traditional posture of Natura or Astraea with feet on the ground and head amongst the ethereal spheres, Emerson expounds upon the sublime, majestic vision of the individual eye: "Standing on the bare ground,—my head bathed by the blithe air, and uplifted into infinite space,—all mean egotism vanishes. I become a transparent eye-ball; I am nothing: I see all; the currents of the Universal Being circulate through me; I am part or particle of God" (ibid., 8).

By inhaling the ethereal "upper air," Emerson teaches, we are admitted "to behold the absolute natures of justice and truth" (ibid., 55). This justice does not, however, belong to a sciential body royal, but to the body of science: "The axioms of physics translate the laws of ethics" (ibid., 29). Any distrust of the "permanence" of these laws would paralyze the faculties of man because "the wheels and springs of man are all set to the hypothesis of the permanence of nature" (ibid., 42). These laws are for people to put to use because man, who "has access to the entire mind of the Creator, is himself the creator in the finite" (ibid., 55–56).

For all his praise of an ethereal nature, Emerson's vision of nature is surprisingly man centered. "The world exists for you," an unnamed poet who is quoted approvingly by Emerson tells the reader. This anonymous poet confidently prophesies "the kingdom of man over nature" (ibid., 66–67). "Nature is thoroughly mediate," Emerson himself argues; "it is made to serve." Man, in Emerson's view, is never weary of working up this nature: "one after another, his victorious thought comes up with and reduces all things, until the world becomes, at last, only a realized will,—the double of man." Nature offers nothing less than "all its kingdoms to man as the raw material which he may mould into what is useful" (ibid., 35). Whereas James I sat on his throne of state, from which he commanded a view of the landscape scenery of his kingdom spread out before him at a court masque, now it is man who occupies this position, commanding a view of his kingdom of nature. Whereas James was positioned as the author of the laws that gave structure and form to the landscape scene, now it is man who surveys a spectacle that is his double. The purple mountain majesties, following this metaphor, must thus be a reflection of the majesty of such men.

In Emerson's vision of America, the landscape belonged to the individual transcendent man. For Emerson this landscape belonged primarily to the surveying eye, whereas for Thoreau, the professional surveyor, it belonged primarily to the treading foot. The America envisioned by both men was an outgrowth of several centuries of European thought and practice concerning landscape. The countryside of the United States was not owned, however, by country gentry, as it was in Europe, but, as a scenic vision, by each and every individual. This vision, like that of Jefferson, begged to be given physical pictorial form. Just as Jefferson's vision helped stimulate a national genre of painting, Emerson and Thoreau's helped propel a movement to materialize this landscape ideal in the form of national parks for the individual members of the American nation.

EMPARKING NATURE

Emerson and Thoreau are regarded as among the most important prophets of the American park movement (Nash 1976, 84–95, 122–40). American parks were developed as places where free access would allow members of the nation to recreate, both physically and spiritually, by walking or hiking through the landscape. The great scenic beauty of these landscapes, however, would also provide the sublime visual experiences that the transcendent Emersonian eyeball craved. As spaces where people could walk and reflect upon the natural, these parks were little different from the "natural" landscape gardens of Britain. The difference was that they were not seen as the creation of a landscape architect who sought to mirror the nature of the supreme architect; rather, they were seen as having been authored by the supreme architect himself. As always, however, that architect on high could use a little help from his subvicars on earth. In America the first and foremost of those architects was Frederick Law Olmsted (Spirn 1995). Olmsted realized, in practice, the landscape visions of men like Thoreau and Emerson. In Olmsted's work, the apparent contradictions between the conception of nature as a source of national development and the need to preserve that source were played out in the American environment itself.

*Olmsted's Landscape Practice*

In 1865 Frederick Law Olmsted presented a pathbreaking report to the California Park Commission for Yosemite Valley in which he outlined his vision for an American national park. He was the first chairman of the California Yosemite Park Commission, which managed the valley until 1906, when the federal government took control of it again (Spirn 1995,

92–95). Olmsted's report never gained a wide audience. It gives, however, a good idea of the kind of arguments which Olmsted presented to his many influential friends and acquaintances as he worked to establish a park idea that he felt was "the destiny of the New World" (Olmsted [1865] 1990, 506). According to a biographer, "In this document, Olmsted elaborated, for the first time in America, the policy underlying the reservation by government to the public of a particular, and defined, scenic area; and he gave it general application. In short he formulated the philosophic base for the establishment of state and national parks" (Roper 1973, 285). Yosemite Valley is where the national park idea was pioneered.[8] The archetypal natural park, it broke ground for the establishment of the system of American parks that has inspired park development worldwide. Olmsted's Yosemite report provides insight into an important strand in American thinking about natural landscape parks, which reflects something of the heritage of Emerson and Thoreau. It also, however, differs in key respects from that tradition; it introduced ideas that were subsequently elaborated by John Muir and became the foundation of the American cult of the wilderness.

Olmsted moved in the same general circles as Thoreau and Emerson. During his formative period as a gentleman farmer on Staten Island (1848–1850), he was the neighbor and friend of Judge William Emerson, the brother of Ralph Waldo (ibid., 65). Intellectual and social circles were small. A few years earlier, in 1843, Thoreau had been on Staten Island as the tutor for the judge's children, and some years later, in 1855, Olmsted would be involved in the editing and publishing of Thoreau's book *Cape Cod* (McLaughlin et al. 1977a, 17). In the course of his activities in the New York literary scene, Olmsted met Ralph Waldo Emerson and became an enthusiastic exponent of his vision of nature (Roper 1973, 64). There are certain common elements in the approaches of these three men to the idea of the country as landscape scenery. For all of them, the landscape of the country expresses ideas of law and community that were the inheritance of the conflicts between court and countrymen in seventeenth-century England. In the case of Olmsted, this idea of landscape meant combining Emerson's identification of natural morality and landscape with the architectural practice of actually creating landscape park scenery. Olmsted began with the landscape surrounding his Staten Island farm, but by 1857 he was designing and supervising the construction of New York's Central Park. He was joined shortly thereafter by the British landscape architect Calvert Vaux. The concept of landscape that Olmsted put into practice was not limited to the law and custom of a specific community but expanded to encompass the entire realm of a nascent continental nation-state.

Olmsted, like Thoreau and Emerson, was deeply disturbed by slavery. He was actively involved in the issue of emancipation, first as a reporter and then as author of the book *A Journey in the Seaboard Slave States* (1856), which earned wide acclaim. He then became general secretary of the Sanitary Commission, which helped survey and coordinate the care of the wounded during the Civil War. Slavery and the war experience required Olmsted, like Thoreau, to think in terms of a larger and more "natural" conception of law and justice than that of the local community or the rights of the individual states. Olmsted argued in his book on the South, *The Cotton Kingdom* (1861), that the South could not be allowed to secede from the Union because there was no natural boundary to divide the American people. The natural geographic unity of the American continent and its landscape scenery mandated a natural union of the country that could not be broken by any of its member states.[9] Olmsted thought that the United States, even more than Britain, was united by the physical geography of the continent:

> The Mountain ranges, the valleys, and the great waters of America, all trend north and south, not east and west. An arbitrary political line may divide the north part from the south part, but there is no such line in nature: there can be none, socially. While water runs downhill, the currents and counter currents of trade, of love, of consanguinity, and fellowship, will flow north and south. The unavoidable comminglings of the people in a land like this, upon the conditions which the slavery of a portion of the population impose, make it necessary to peace that we should all live under the same laws and respect the same flag. No government could long control its own people, no government could long exist, that would allow its citizens to be subject to such indignities under a foreign government as those to which the citizens of the United States heretofore have been required to submit under their own, for the sake of the tranquillity of the South. Nor could the South, with its present purposes, live on terms of peace with any foreign nation, between whose people and its own there was no division, except such an one as might be maintained by means of forts, frontier-guards and custom-houses, edicts, passports and spies. Scotland, Wales, and Ireland are each much better adapted for an independent government, and under an independent government would be far more likely to live at peace with England, than the South to remain peaceably separated from the North of this country. It is said that the South can never be subjugated. It must be, or we must. It must be, or not only our American republic is a failure, but our English justice and our English law and our English freedom are failures. (Olmsted [1861] 1953, 3)

Olmsted was a vehement defender of the causes of federalism and nationalism over those of sectionalism and states' rights. He actively worked to establish organizations and found publications (such as *The Nation*) which supported the national cause (Roper 1973, 294; Censer 1986a, 40–41; 1986b, 505–6; Ranney et al. 1990, 3). The development of the civilization of the western United States was, for Olmsted, a key to the establishment of the greater continental union of the nation as ordained by nature. He therefore saw his 1863 move west, to take over the management of a large mining complex in Mariposa County, California, as part of a larger civilizing mission (McLaughlin et al. 1977a, 29; Censer 1986b, 688; Ranney et al. 1990, 3).

## Yosemite: An Anglo-American Landscape Park

Olmsted's proposal for Yosemite Park must be seen against the background of his political, legal, and landscape/geographical ideas. Olmsted's idea for Yosemite was as American as the landscape parks of England were British. In his report on Yosemite, written at the close of the Civil War, "sixteen years since the Yosemite was first seen by a white man," it is clear that Olmsted envisioned the park as a monument reaffirming America's national identity ([1865] 1990, 504, 507). He presents Yosemite as being on a par with the Statue of Liberty and Central Park or the dome of the Capitol and one of the paintings it housed, Emanuel Leutze's *Westward the Course of Empire Takes Its Way* (ibid., 488–89). Yosemite was, to Olmsted, a "wild park" that represented "the greatest glory of nature"; it was "peculiar to this ground," which "consists wholly in its natural scenery" (ibid., 506). Olmsted believed that the main difference between Yosemite and an English landscape garden was that Yosemite appeared to have been landscaped by the hand of nature.

If we are to understand the meaning of Yosemite as the world's first national nature park, we must think as much about the meaning of *landscape* and *park* as about the meaning of *nature*. According to Olmsted's conception of a park, the pastoral lawns of Yosemite were, in a sense, the natural extension of the grounds he designed for the Capitol in Washington, the nation's estate house on its elevated hill.

## The English Olmsted

Olmsted became deeply impressed by English landscaping during a visit to his ancestral homeland. His impressions were published in his 1852 *Walks and Talks of an American Farmer in England*. Though one might suppose that Yosemite is the quintessentially American landscape scene, it is clear that what impressed Olmsted was its similarity to English landscape scenery. The vegetation of Yosemite reminded him, in appearance, to that found in both New England and England itself ([1865] 1990, 506). For

Fig. 8.4. Landscape Garden at Blenheim, designed by Lancelot (Capability) Brown. This was the image of nature which explorers found "replicated" on a grand scale in the American West, as at Yellowstone. Photo: author.

Fig. 8.5. Yellowstone National Park looked like a British landscape park, but it was on a grander scale and appeared to have been designed by God or Nature. It was, in fact, a Native American cultural landscape. Photo courtesy of Thomas Vale.

Fig. 8.6. Yosemite National Park. Photo: author.

Olmsted, the spiritual headwaters of Yosemite's Merced River, with its "most placid pools . . . with the most tranquil meadows, the most playful streams, and every variety of soft and peaceful pastoral beauty," are in England (ibid., 500). It is a stream such "as Shakespeare delighted in, and brings pleasing reminiscences to the traveler of the Avon or the upper Thames" (ibid., 490). When Olmsted wrote this, he was not simply indulging in a poetic flight of fancy. The heritage of the English countryside was of great importance to him as an "American Whig."

Olmsted was born and raised in New England. One of his ancestors, the Puritan and landed gentleman James Olmsted, left England for New England in 1632 because of dissatisfaction with the Stuart regime. In 1634, the family settled in Connecticut, where Frederick Law Olmsted was born in 1822. Olmsted revered his English heritage. He took pains to visit Olmsted Hall, his family's ancient, unpretentious country estate in Essex, during his visit to England in 1850. It was during this period of his life that he settled in New York; there, as an "improving" gentleman farmer on Staten Island, he sought to realize the ideal of the "simple country life" represented by Olmsted Hall (Roper 1973, 56–65, 74–75; McLaughlin et al. 1977b, 350–54). The importance of Olmsted's English experience for his sense of America as place is reflected in a posthumously published manuscript, "Notes on the Pioneer Condition," written during the same period as his 1865 report on Yosemite. New England appears here as the inheritor of the English ideals of country and common law, and for this reason, Old England has a place of honor in his affections. The New England to which Olmsted's Puritan forefathers had fled became the preserve of this country heritage:

> By lineage, I am an Englishman and proud of it. The English queen . . . is entitled not to my obedience as a subject, but [to my affectionate and loyal reverence] as representative of historical English law and of English valor and of English reverence. . . . No Englishman loves England as I do. I mean exactly what I say, no Englishman loves or can love old England or what is characteristic of England as I do. . . . I love the land of England. I love the landscape of England, better than that of the land where I first saw light, more than any Englishman born does. . . . But I believe the American idea of government is juster, wiser, better, more respectable, and it favors more than the government of England goodness & happiness with the people, that it favors justice, gentleness, fair dealing, peace and all Christian virtue more. (Olmsted 1990, 745–46)

During his visit to England, Olmsted was impressed by the ways in which old English values were inscribed in the landscape scene and by how that landscape, when shaped into parks, served the recreational needs of the nation. He was dismayed, however, by the way these parks were monopolized by the upper classes. In his Yosemite report, he notes the existence in England of "more than one thousand private parks and notable grounds devoted to luxury and recreation." These parks were so valuable that the cost of their annual maintenance was "greater than that of the national schools." He criticizes, however, the fact that the enjoyment of the "choicest natural scenes in the country" is the monopoly of "a very few, very rich people" (Olmsted [1865] 1990, 504). After comparing the recreational value of this scenery to the collective value of the waters of a river, and favorably comparing democratic America to aristocratic Britain, he concludes that, "It was in accordance with these views of the destiny of the New World and the duty of the republican government that Congress enacted that the Yosemite should be held, guarded and managed for the free use of the whole body of the people forever, and that the care of it . . . should be a duty of dignity and be committed only to a sovereign State" (ibid., 506). Olmsted stresses that "the establishment by government of great public grounds for the free enjoyment of the people . . . is a political duty." He also notes that "rigidly enforced" laws are necessary "to prevent an unjust use by individuals, of that which is not individual but public property." It was therefore important for Olmsted to establish the principle of justice by which the state, in trust for the whole nation, could retain dominion over Yosemite in order to prevent people from establishing "customary" rights to the land (ibid., 505, 508, 511).

Some aspects of Olmsted's rhetoric recall the arguments of the English critics of enclosure. He appeals to the imagery of Oliver Goldsmith's popular *Deserted Village* (1770) in opposing the idea that anyone should be able to appropriate Yosemite "wholly to his individual pleasure," whereby it would become "a rich man's park" (ibid., 508). Yosemite is a resource which, in his opinion, belongs "to the whole community, not only of California but of the United States" (ibid., 501). Olmsted also points to the example of "certain cantons of the Republic of Switzerland, a commonwealth of the most industrious and frugal people of Europe" (ibid.). Olmsted's ideal, however, is not the commons of England or Switzerland, but the landscape garden and the aesthetics of picturesque travel. What matters in Switzerland is not the cooperative management of common resources, but the presence of grand scenery which has laid the basis for a lucrative tourist industry. Like the British country gentlemen who created their parks by incorporating common lands and displacing local communities in the process, Olmsted sees no problem in evicting native inhabitants, or even pioneer homesteaders, from a park.[10] The difference between the British park and the American park is that the American park does not belong to an individual but to a "sovereign State," which manages it for the nation as a whole (ibid., 505, 506, 508). The justification for this control is not the law of custom, but the law of nature.

## Nature's Law

Olmsted was quite aware of the monumental legal importance of his national park idea. It involved, as he puts it, "considerations of a political duty of grave importance to which seldom if ever before has proper respect been paid by any Government in the world" ([1865] 1990, 502). The justification for the state's taking on the ownership of a park for the nation is, quite literally, the law of nature. "It is a scientific fact," he argues, "that the occasional contemplation of natural scenes of an impressive character, particularly if this contemplation occurs in connection with relief from ordinary cares, change of air and change of habits, is favorable to the health and vigor of men and especially to the health and vigor of their intellect beyond any other conditions which can be offered them, that it not only gives pleasure for the time being but increases the subsequent capacity for happiness and the means of securing happiness." Deprivation from "such means of recreation" has dire effects, such as "mental disability, sometimes taking the severe forms of softening of the brain, paralysis, palsy, monomania, or insanity, but more frequently of mental and nervous excitability, moroseness, melancholy, or irascibility, incapacitating the subject for the proper exercise of the intellectual and moral forces" (ibid.). According to Olmsted, it should be obvious from such "scientific" evidence that "it is the main duty of government, if it is not the sole duty of government, to provide means of protection for all its citizens in the pursuit of happiness" by creating public parks in places like Yosemite where there is impressive "natural" scenery.

To Olmsted, the importance of preserving natural park scenery was not just that it counteracted the softening of the brain, but that it promoted the development of civilization—an idea that resembles the "picturing" conception of development identified with the Germanic concepts of bilden and Bildung. The scientific and artistic study of landscape scenery thus "tends more than any other human pursuit to the benefit of the commonwealth and the advancement of civilization" (ibid., 510). British landscape gardens were, therefore, both a sign and a source of the heights of civilization enjoyed by the few who had access to them (ibid., 502–5). To reach his goal of a democratic America whose level of civilization would equal that of aristocratic Britain, it was necessary, in Olmsted's opinion, to create parks that would be accessible to everyone: "it is the folly of laws which have permitted and favored the monopoly by privileged classes of many of the means supplied in nature for the gratification, exercise and ed-

ucation of the esthetic faculties that has caused the appearance of dullness
and weakness and disease of these faculties in the mass of the subjects of
kings. And it is against a limitation of the means of such education to the
rich that the wise legislation of free governments must be directed" (ibid.,
505).

### Recreating the Nation

Thoreau and Olmsted both had a grand vision of a nation re-creating its
moral and physical fiber through physical and aesthetic recreation in the
natural landscape scenery of America. For Thoreau this landscape provided a fountainhead of natural law that was superior to the common law
of New England. *The United States* was more than a collection of separate
states, each with its sovereign common law. It was the United States *of
America,* a natural continent belonging to the whole people. It was a place
where they could move freely in search of freedom and recreation.

One problem with the idea that the geographical landscape of a continent, or a group of islands, can unify its settlers as a nation is that this idea
ignores the presence of other nations (e.g. the Spanish), as well as indigenous peoples who might not care to become part of the nation. Much as
gaining the acceptance of the idea of Britain required considerable effort
on the part of such architects of state as Inigo Jones, the idea of an America nation, which had no real historical precedent, had to be fostered
against the claims of other conceptions of country. In Olmsted's day the
idea of the U.S. as a unified American state competed with the desire on
the part of southern and western sectionalists to divide it up.

Just as Ireland, Scotland, and Wales were not tabulae rasae waiting for
settlement, neither was the American West. The conquest of the West, like
that of Ireland, was more than the conquest of space; it was also the conquest of peoples and the place of their polities. The idea of the "manifest
destiny" of the westward course of empire rested on a concept of territory
justified by the natural law of conquest. As in the case of Ireland, the right
of the conqueror over the conquered was bolstered if the conquered were
portrayed as inferior beings. For Olmsted, the mark of a civilized American was the ability to comprehend the meaning of the American landscape
scene: "The power of scenery to affect men is in a large way, proportion-
ate to the degree of their civilization and to the degree in which their taste
has been cultivated" ([1865] 1990, 503). The power of Yosemite's landscape scenery was lost upon the Yosemite Indians because "among a thousand savages there will be a much smaller number who will show the least
sign of being so affected than among a thousand persons taken from a civilized community" (ibid.). Olmsted made no secret of his dislike of the In-

dians, who ranked even lower than the Irish in his conception of the stages of civilization. In Olmsted's opinion, "The fighting Indian met with on the frontier is the antitype and the natural enemy of the civilized man. . . . According to the civilized standard he is a lazy, ravenous, brutal, filthy, improvident, lying, treacherous, bloodthirsty, scoundrel" (ibid., 685). Olmsted decried the Native Americans' burning of the "forests and herbage" of Yosemite; a more unbiased analysis, however, would have concluded that the open pastoral landscape scene which Olmsted so admired was, in fact, the outcome of Indian burning (ibid., 507).[11] But to recognize that the landscape scenery of Yosemite was, in fact, a result of Native American customs and culture would have destroyed Olmsted's conception of Yosemite as a park intended for the recreation of a united post–Civil War America based upon Anglo-American landscape values.

Olmsted, an "American Whig," designed the prototypical "natural" landscape of the country of America, much as Inigo Jones and William Kent, a British Whig, designed the prototypical "natural" landscape of Britain. Not only did Olmsted play a direct role in planning and shaping such quintessentially American landscapes as Yosemite, Niagara Falls, and Capitol Hill, but he also created the prototypes for urban parks, suburban housing estates, and the Elysian fields of many an American cemetery (Roper 1973; Spirn 1995). Both in Britain and in America the ideal park landscape linked the scenic appearance of country with nature and was seen as the cradle of the nation. Superficially, this landscape ideal seems to represent a longing to return to a natural country existence of the past—but the pastoral, Elysian nature celebrated in these parks is not that of the historical past and customs of actual rural communities. It is rather that of an ideal golden age that obliterates the memory of such communities. The creators of these landscapes thought that they would pave the way for the re-creation of a new form of country that would develop, "naturally," stage by stage, into a new nation-state with a higher level of civilization.[12]

The park movement long thrived on the idea that it was possible to link park preservation for the masses with the progress of the nation. This idea embodies a contradiction, however, and Yosemite is one of the places where the consequences of this contradiction were made most manifest. According to the dialectics of Thoreau's logic, progress depended upon the presence of the "wild." But once progress had transformed the wild, then progress would cease and civilization would again move west, following the sun. The solution to this paradox, for Thoreau, was to empark wild nature for the continued re-creation of the nation's primal energies. The problem with this solution, however, is that as the nation grows, the use of the parks will also, inevitably, destroy the wild character that is the source of their power. If the Americans, like Romulus and Remus, are to suckle wolves (metaphorically speaking), there cannot be so many Americans that they scare the wolves away. This means, ultimately, that the only way of preserving the wild elixir of the American nation is to preserve the wild *from* the American people, not to empark it *for* the American people. Not only does this idea conflict with Olmsted's conception of Yosemite as a park for the recreation of the American national community, but it also leads to a wilder ideal of nature that excludes the bulk of Americans. John Muir was the great prophet of this more radical natural ideal and thus became the father of the American wilderness preservation movement. It is ironic that Muir found his ideal of sublime wild nature in the same Yosemite in which Olmsted found his ideal of a beautiful English pastoral landscape park for the people.

## JOHN MUIR'S SUBLIME YOSEMITE

John Muir traveled to Yosemite in 1868, just five years after Olmsted had gone to the area. Muir, an immigrant from Ossian's stormy Scotland, later reported that he went in search of "any place that is wild" (Muir [1914] 1988, 1). The experience of the wild had become, for him, a religious experience, and he heard a "sublime psalm" in the "pure wildness" of a cataract (ibid., 15). It is this quasi-religious view of nature which has fueled the purist fervor of the American wilderness preservation movement (Cronon 1995). Muir, however, initially went to what would become his temple of nature to operate a sawmill at the base of Yosemite falls, producing lumber for tourist development (Muir [1914] 1988, 193, 196, 209).

The fundamentalist fervor of Muir's conception of nature as wild landscape scenery contained the seeds of a confrontation with Olmsted's conception of natural parks as places for ordinary people's recreation. Wild nature, Muir believed, was not amenable to recreation nor was it a source of national developemental strength. When the city fathers of San Francisco elected to build a dam in the Hetch Hetchy Valley, a neighboring valley to Yosemite, Muir condemned them as "temple destroyers, devotees of ravaging commercialism, [who] seem to have a perfect contempt for Nature, and, instead of lifting their eyes to the God of the mountains, lift them to the Almighty Dollar" (ibid., 196–97; Nash 1976, 161–81).

On the mantelpiece of his Yosemite home, Muir displayed portraits of two easterners from Concord, Massachusetts: Ralph Waldo Emerson and Henry David Thoreau (Emerson [1836] 1991, vii; Nash 1976, 122–40). He carried a copy of Emerson's 1836 essay "Nature" with him on his wanderings, much as Emerson, when he visited Yosemite (and Muir) in 1871, carried a German dictionary and a work by Johann Wolfgang von Goethe (Sanborn 1989, 140–47). For all their talk of a transcendental, sublime experience of nature, Thoreau and Muir invariably used literary texts or artistic images to mediate their perceptions of nature. The image of nature in America was shaped by visual images of landscape (Novak 1980; Cronon 1992; Daniels 1993a, 146–99), particularly in the case of Yosemite, which was not only picturesque but sublimely photogenic (Demars 1991, 9–26). Pictures, however, are notorious for their deceptive polyvalence (Barthes [1957] 1972, 109–59), and this makes it useful to return to the texts which inspired them. Thus, to comprehend what Muir saw in the nature of Yosemite when he, with Emerson's essay in hand, gazed out at the commanding view of the valley, it is as useful to open the pages of Emerson's "Nature" as it is to visit the park.

An educated reader like Olmsted would have recognized in the texts of Emerson and Thoreau numerous references to the landscape scene as the embodiment of a long history of abstract ideas of nature. Muir, who was not an educated man, read in a much more literal way. For Muir, the landscape scenery of Yosemite was, itself, the transcendent nature of which Thoreau and Emerson wrote: Yosemite was a place where "no holier temple has ever been consecrated by the heart of man" (Muir [1914] 1988, 197). Here, he found a 2,500-foot-high "grand Sierra Cathedral," built by "nature," where one could worship (ibid., 10). One has the feeling that Muir, a reclusive bachelor who was fond of sleeping alone on the cliffs of Yosemite, meant it literally when he described the "mountain mansion [where] Nature had gathered her choicest treasures, to draw her lovers into close and confiding communion with her" (ibid., 5).

The difference between the meaning of nature's landscape for Olmsted and for Muir is reflected in their taste for the scenery of Yosemite. In Olmsted's ideal landscape, the beautiful was set against a sublime backdrop. The sublime landscape itself clearly had little appeal for Olmsted, who believed that nature's landscape ought to provide a recreation ground for the national collectivity. For Olmsted, it was "conceivable that any one or all of the cliffs of the Yo Semite might be changed in form and color, without lessening the enjoyment which is now obtained from the scenery." The cascades were "scarcely to be named among the elements of the scenery" ([1865] 1990, 500), and he actually preferred the park when the cascades were dry!

Muir, unlike Olmsted, was emphatically a cliff and cascade man; he climbed the valley's walls alone and preferred the sublime view from the top down. The social elite who joined the Sierra Club, which Muir founded and led, looked down on the "weaker brethren" of the hoi polloi flocked below. The differing points of view between these two groups have made of the park contested territory. As a club member wrote in 1919: "to a Sierran bound for the high mountains the human noise and dust of Yosemite [Valley] seem desecration of primitive nature" (quoted in Demars 1991, 109). As far as Muir was concerned, Yosemite was so sacred that it warranted military protection. "The effectiveness of the War Department in enforcing the laws of Congress," Muir wrote in 1895, "has been illustrated in the management of Yosemite National Park." Because of the army's efforts, "the sheep having been rigidly excluded, a luxuriant cover has sprung up on the desolate forest floor, fires have been choked before they could do any damage, and hopeful bloom and beauty have taken the place of ashes and dust." Muir concluded that "one soldier in the woods, armed with authority and a gun, would be more effective in forest preservation than millions of forbidding notices" (quoted in Runte 1990, 61–62). In this conception of a natural park, nature must be wild, and hence contain as few people, or signs of people, as possible. As a result, it can only be enjoyed by a chosen few. The need to use force to protect nature from the common people advocated by Muir gives the park the same exclusive status as that of the British landscape parks of Muir's day with their armed wardens and man traps (Graham 1973).

Despite Muir's apparent wilderness purism, it might nevertheless be argued that his work contains the same spiraling dialectic between natural landscape preservation and the development of nature's potentiality as is found in Thoreau's and Emerson's work. This helps explain the apparent contradictions between Muir the sawmill operator and Muir the preservationist. Muir's dialectic, however, has a different form from that of Thoreau and Emerson. Muir's vision of nature as a park is rooted not in the pastoral commons ideal represented by the valley floor but in the wild nature of the surrounding cliffs and mountains, which provide the proper sublime setting in which a rugged individualist can test his manhood. Muir remained proud of his friendship with Theodore Roosevelt, and he curried the support of railroad moguls for the Sierra Club. For the modern industrialist, nature was not a tended commons, but raw material to be controlled both for the creation of wealth and for the recreation of those who created that wealth. This dialectic is most clearly present in the personage of Theodore Roosevelt, who was at one and the same time an outdoorsman, a big-game hunter, a builder of dams, a conservationist, a Rough Rider, and an architect of American imperial policy. This was hardly contradictory behavior according to the ideology of people of Roosevelt's time and class, who saw recreation in the wilderness as a means of re-creating the rugged individualistic spirit identified with their White Anglo-Saxon Protestant forebears (Slotkin 1992, 29–62). Once properly hardened and shaped by confrontation with western wilderness, the young scion of East Coast wealth would then be ready to make his contribution to "progress."

## AMERICAN EMPARKMENT

Muir, who saw the Yosemite area as "a grand landscape garden," followed in the footsteps of those, like William Gilpin, who had moved out beyond the garden's walls in search of more authentically sublime and picturesque scenes ([1914] 1988, 194).[13] Just as British landscapers saw the natural-style garden as a means of establishing the idea of country as a geographically unified nation transcending the barriers of custom and law, Olmsted saw the American natural park as a means of creating a sense of national unity in a federation rent by sectional strife and civil war. Just as landscape scenery was used to create a natural, British, Elysian environment which obliterated the memory of past cultural differentiation, the framing of the American national park as nature was used to obliterate the memory of earlier cultures and their marks on the land.

The emparkment of Yosemite meant the disenfranchisement and eviction of the native tribal communities that had originally shaped that environment. The fateful refusal of Olmsted, Muir, and their successors to recognize the importance of Native American practices of environmental management through burning reflects their amnesiac attitude toward the Yosemite park landscape—complete with Lethean stream. Not only was the cultural landscape of the Native Americans to be forgotten, so too was the initial settlement by whites of European background. The need for this landscape scene to be *natural*, not *cultural*, meant that all trace of the white settlers' structures had to be removed (and replaced by an ugly but culturally neutral park compound). Between 1959 and 1963 the park service razed the old village, and an extensive project is now underway to erase all archaeological and biological traces of its existence. Just as the medieval church at Stowe was left standing when the village was obliterated, all that remains of the village at Yosemite is the church, built in 1879, whose structure and soil were apparently too sanctified to be removed, even in the name of nature (Olwig 1995b, 387–90).

When land was emparked by the British estates, and the native population was removed, the management of the parks was placed in the hands of a large staff of gardeners who managed the land according to the prescripts of the landscape architect. In the United States, by contrast, the landscapes in the parks were seen to be the creation of Nature or even of the Great Architect himself. Such a view overlooked the fact that, even us-

Fig. 8.7. The 1879 church is all that survives from Yosemite village, which was razed between 1959 and 1963. Photo: author.

ing primitive tools such as fire, humans had had an all-pervasive impact upon the land. Once humans were removed from a park, the original landscape scene would change more or less dramatically.

Because of the refusal to recognize the importance of the Native Americans' use of fire in creating the open, park-like landscape scenery of Yosemite, the landscape became more and more overgrown and it became more difficult to see the park's natural wonders. Furthermore, the park became a fire hazard. Lafayette Bunell, a visitor to the area in the 1850s, when European Americans first discovered Yosemite and expelled the Indians, described the valley as having "presented the appearance of a well kept park" (Runte 1990, 28–82, quotation on 37).[14] Bunell remembered that "there was no undergrowth of young trees to obstruct clear open views in any part of the valley from one side of the Merced River across to the base of the opposite wall." In 1894, Bunell observed, the extent of "clear open meadow land . . . was at least four times as large" in the 1850s (quoted in Sanborn 1989, 37). When a Native American, Totuya, who had been forced to leave Yosemite by Major James D. Savage's troops as a child in 1851, returned for the first time in 1929, she immediately remarked upon the deterioration of the valley. The granddaughter of Chief Tenaya, she was now the sole survivor of the band of Ahwahneeche Indians who had dwelled in the valley. The result of the white man's neglect was an environment which led Totuya to shake her head and exclaim: "Too dirty; too much bushy" (quoted in Sanborn 1989, 237–43, quotation on 238).[15] The same transformation occurred in Yosemite's eastern counterpart, Shenandoah. Today, the landscape scene has grown into a vast, dense, uniform forest where the only variation to relieve the eye is to be found on the borders of the park, where scattered farms have survived, and in the places where the park managers have actively sought to "restore" the meadowlands that existed before the creation of the park, in the interest of biodiversity.

Yosemite is not unusual—many American natural parks have been created on the site of cultural landscapes. From the visitors' center at Cape Cod National Seashore, one gazes out through huge picture windows at a site that was once a golf course. The park on St. John, in the Virgin Islands of the United States, which was created at the instigation of the Rockefellers and forms the background for one of their resorts, is a wilderness that was created on the site of former sugar plantations and the small farms of freed slaves (Olwig and Olwig 1979; K. F. Olwig 1985). Perhaps the most dramatic obliteration of a cultural landscape occurred when a large swath of the Appalachians was emparked as Shenandoah National Park. Shenandoah National Park was for the East Coast and the city of Washington, D.C., what Yosemite was for the West Coast and San Francisco. The park was a cause célèbre for the elites of Washington, with George Freeman Pollock and the Potomac Appalachian Trail Club playing analogous roles to those of Muir and the Sierra Club. The "restoration" of the park's nature in the 1920s and 1930s involved

Fig. 8.8. View of a former golf course, now a scenic natural landscape, from the visitor's center at Cape Cod National Seashore. Photo: author.

Fig. 8.9. Scene from Skyline Drive, Shenandoah National Park. Photo: author.

209

uprooting and removing several thousand inhabitants (four hundred and fifty families) whose ancestors had settled in the area in the eighteenth century (Pollock 1960; Reeder and Reeder 1978, 69–87; Heatwole 1992, 27–44). Winding through the park, the 470-mile-long mountaintop Skyline Drive, stretching from the Great Smoky Mountains to the Shenandoahs, provides a modern American equivalent of the scenic paths that wind through British landscape parks. The road, like the paths in Britain, links a progression of scenic spots from which the visitor can stop to survey a countryside framed by nature (Pollock 1960, 211–33; Heatwole 1992, 27–43; Wilson 1992, 33–37). There is even a countryseat of sorts in the park, Pollock's resort, Skyland, where those who can afford it can still recreate in genteel surroundings. The emparkment of Shenandoah has been so successful that the area is now regarded as a wilderness, and moves are being taken to severely restrict the recreative use for which the park was originally intended.

ALDO LEOPOLD: MASQUING NATURE

The paradox of the American natural parks is not only that they are expected to preserve the landscapes both *for* and *from* the nation, but also that they must preserve the landscapes as wild *nature* even though, in fact, the parks must be actively managed to preserve their aesthetic and scientific values. These paradoxes led the pioneering wilderness preservationist Aldo Leopold to rediscover the links between the scenery managed in parks and that found in the theater (Nash 1976, 182–99). To him, wilderness preservation for recreation had much in common with the creation of an opera stage set—an idea that harks back to the origins of the scenic concept of landscape in the masque (a forerunner of opera). The parallel to a stage set lay, in part, in the fact that preservation had to be done behind the scenes, at times (such as winter) when the public would not be aware that the supposedly primeval, natural landscape of the park was, in fact, carefully managed. The parallel, however, also went deeper than this. Leopold, like Ben Jonson and Inigo Jones before him, looked upon landscape scenery as a means of re-creating a vision of the national state based upon a conception of an earlier ideal condition. Leopold's landscape stage, again like that of Jonson and Jones, was that of a total theater, in which the spectator also becomes a participant. Recreation and theater are both, according to Leopold, "reviving, in a play, a drama formerly inherent in daily life"; both are, he concludes, "in the last analysis, esthetic exercises." The goal of recreation, in the final analysis, was to further "the development of the perceptive faculty in Americans" (Leopold [1949] 1966, 283, 291; see also Graber 1976, 84).

Leopold shared Thoreau's conception of wilderness as the source of vitality to which spent civilizations continually must return: "It is only the scholar who appreciates that all history consists of successive excursions from a single starting-point, to which man returns again and again to organize yet another search for a durable scale of values. It is only the scholar who understands why the raw wilderness gives definition and meaning to the human enterprise" (Leopold [1949] 1966, 279). This was an idea which Leopold would have been familiar with not only from Thoreau, but also from the "frontier thesis" of his contemporary Frederick Jackson Turner. This influential historian saw the frontier experience of the pioneers as the source of national rebirth, regeneration, and rejuvenation (Smith 1970, 250–60). The restoration of wilderness was necessary in order to allow man to continue to revive, as in a play, "a drama which supposedly had once been inherent in daily life." This is the drama of the individual hunter whose "sound instinct" has led us to preserve because it helps to perpetuate, in the form of sport, "the more virile and primitive skills in pioneering travel and subsistence," (Leopold [1949] 1966, 283).

Leopold's comparison of landscape preservation and restoration to theater scenery made explicit some assumptions that had long been taken for granted within the national park movement. Writing in 1921, Stephen T. Mather, the first director of the National Park Service, proclaimed that "our parks are not only show places and vacation lands, but also vast school-rooms of Americanism where people are studying, enjoying, and learning to love more deeply this land in which they live" (quoted in Demars 1991, 94–95). It was from nature that Americans would learn "the scheme of creation and the handiwork of the Great Architect as from no other source" (ibid., 95). This designing of America, one nation under God, was seen by Mather to be largely the work of the pioneers who conquered the West. In this scheme of things, it was the parks that preserved the memory of an era in American history when the "exemplary virtues of rugged individualism and free enterprise were the foremost commandments of Manifest Destiny," as William C. Everhart, a park service official, put it as recently as 1972 (Everhart 1972, 6).

## LANDSCAPE SCENERY AND COUNTRY

Thoreau, Emerson, Olmsted, and Muir each contributed to the development of the sense of America, stretching from sea to shining sea, as the place of an American nation. A key element in this national identification with landscape scenery is the uniquely American institution of the natural national park. The American identification with the landscape of its body geographical is deeply split, and the National Park Service, as the guardian of the nation's nature, is in the difficuldifficult position of having to protect nature both for and from the people of the American nation (Chase 1986; Runte 1990). Do the parks preserve a natural commons for the country, conceived as a legal and social community, or a landscape whose natural laws we must obey? Is the nature in parks ultimately the creation of communities of people working together to beautify the fruited plains of their country, or is it the untrammeled wilderness of the sublime majesty of the purple mountains with their commanding view from on high?[16] These issues plague the park movement, and reflect, more generally, conflicting American attitudes toward landscape and country. Though these natural, national parks are an American institution, these conflicts involving differing ideas of nature, nation, and landscape reflect a long European discourse and history. If these issues are to be adequately confronted, it is necessary, I would argue, to abandon ideas of a uniquely American New World arising from nature; it is the product of a very old cultural history.

# Conclusion

## Landscape, Place, and the Body Politic

Some time after finishing the manuscript for this book, I chanced to pick up a book by Yi-Fu Tuan, *Topophilia,* that I had read years ago. I opened it and stumbled upon a passage that I had underlined heavily. It became clear to me that the passage so neatly summarized the point of departure for my own book that it probably *was* its point of departure. I therefore decided to ask Yi-Fu Tuan if he would write the foreword for *Landscape, Nature, and the Body Politic.* I saw this as a way of engaging him in a kind of peripatetic conversation, moving backward and forward between foreword and afterword.

The passage by Tuan that I chanced upon reads:

> Scenery and landscape are now nearly synonymous. The slight differences in meaning they retain reflect their dissimilar origin. Scenery has traditionally been associated with the world of illusion which is the theater. The expression "behind the scenes" reveals the unreality of scenes. We are not bidden to look "behind the landscape," although a landscaped garden can be as contrived as a stage scene, and as little enmeshed with the life of the owner as the stage paraphernalia with the life of the actor. The difference is that landscape, in its original sense, referred to the real world, not to the world of art and make-believe. In its native Dutch, "landschap" designated such commonplaces as "a collection of farms or fenced fields, sometimes a small domain or administrative unit." Only when it was transplanted to England toward the end of the sixteenth century did the word shed its earthbound roots and acquire the precious meaning of art. Landscape came to mean a prospect seen from a specific standpoint. Then it was the artistic representation of that prospect. Landscape was also the background of an official portrait; the "scene" of a "pose." As such it became fully integrated with the world of make-believe. (Tuan 1974b, 133)

I now see that I have essentially sought to answer two clusters of questions raised in my mind by this passage. First: What is so special about the "commonplaces" designated by the word *landschap?*[1] If these places were so common, why was landschap significant enough to be "transplanted to England"? And why was *landschap* important enough to be used as the label for an entire artistic genre? Second: What was being transformed into make-believe, and what was being *made believe,* when the meaning of landscape changed from common*places* to scenic *spaces*? Why are we not "bidden to look 'behind the landscape'"? What is it that is being covered up, or masked, by the landscape? And how and why was this illusory make-believe world, created through the transformation of landscape as place into landscape as a prospect seen from a specific standpoint?

All together, these questions make up a detective story in which the (dead?) body is that of the body politic. Now is the time to gather in the drawing room and review the plot as well as the unusual suspects. After addressing the two sets of questions, I conclude by broaching the subtext of a larger metadiscourse concerning the relationships between place, space, body, and polity in the making of the political landscape.

## LANDSCAPE AS COMMON PLACE

The first chapter explored the meaning of *landscape* (landschap in Dutch, and Landschaft in German) in the sense of polity and place, and hence *country.* Landscape, we saw, wasn't just any place, but a place that found itself at the center of Renaissance struggles to represent the nature of the polity. These struggles played an important role in defining the parameters of the modern political landscape. At its core, the landscape/country polity had a representative political body, a body of living bodies. This body gave a common legal form to the customs of the landscape polity. The polity of the landscape/country was thus built on law, not blood. A most vital function of this law, in fact, was to mediate between the differing blood relations inhabiting the landscape and thereby to preserve the peace (Fenger 1992, 1993).

Custom, upon which the common law of the land was based, was inscribed in the land through physical practice. The landscape/country as a physical place was thus the manifestation of the polity's local custom and common law. At the core of this landscape/country was the meeting place of its representative legal body. In ancient times, this was the place (*Platz*), or stead (*Stätte*), where the *Ding,* or *Thing,* was held (*thingstead* in English, *tingsted* in Danish) (Collins-Klett 1983: Thingplatz, Stätte). It was here where *things* were ordered and put into place. The things at issue at the *thing* were legal matters, in accordance with the earliest meaning of the word (MWC10: thing). Later, during the Middle Ages, the representative legal body met at the village green, urban square, or marketplace (*Platz*) (Olwig forthcoming), where members of the polity who were held in good stead stood during public meetings. A person's place in society was thus manifested by his or her place in the physical place at the symbolic heart of the landscape/country—itself a place. The landscape/country was thus a nested world of places which, although they had a physical expression, primarily represented the social place of people in a polity. This nesting of landscape identities jibes with Tuan's observations about place: "Place supports the human need to belong to a meaningful and reasonably stable world, and it does so at different levels of consciousness, from an almost organic sense of identity that is an effect of habituation to a particular routine and locale, to a more conscious awareness of the values of middle-scale places such as neighborhood, city, and landscape" (Tuan 1992, 44).

"The facts of landscape," the geographer Carl Sauer noted, are "place facts" (Sauer [1925] 1969, 321). But what are "place facts"? How do we give *place* a more precise definition? Since we have begun with Tuan's conceptual framework, it is appropriate to continue. Tuan defines place in contrast to location in space:

> As location, place is one unit among other units to which it is linked by a circulation net; the analysis of location is subsumed under the geographer's concept and analysis of space. Place, however, has more substance than the word location suggests: it is a unique entity, a "special ensemble" . . . ; it has a history and meaning. Place incarnates the experiences and aspirations of a people. Place is not only a fact to be explained in the broader frame of space, but it is also a reality to be clarified and understood from the perspectives of the people who have given it meaning. (Tuan 1974a, 213)

The word *Landschaft* fits this meaning of place well. The ensemble of customs defining the Landschaft was considered to be unique to each place, incarnating the experiences and aspirations of its people, giving it history and meaning. Most memorable, perhaps, is Eiderstedt, where the inhabitants saw their laws as the very incarnation of justice. Another word for customs is *mores*, from the Latin root of *morality,* a notion of virtuous behavior that goes deeper than law in terms of its appeal to community solidarity and "moral economy," to use E. P. Thompson's phrase (Thompson 1993). These customs do not simply represent an abstract identification with place; they are an expression of a body of custom developed, through time, on the basis of individual and social practice. These practices, via the use of the body, were woven into the very fabric and texture of the land, giving it a meaning that spoke to (and with) the body as well as the mind. This fabric could be unraveled and interpreted, in the manner of a legal text. Given the political and social importance of landscape/country in the Renaissance, and given the way it embodied place identity, it is quite understandable that it formed the subject of a major new artistic genre, concerned with the representation of landscape as place. Yet, when "transplanted to England" landscape was eventually transformed into mere country scenery.

One reason the word for landscape was initially transplanted to England was that it fitted into a semantic space familiar from the parallel concept of country, as well as from other parallel words in the Romance languages. This is because many of the English, in those cosmopolitan times, were familiar with the languages and political life of the continent. England still largely felt itself to be part of Europe. For some, like King James I, this familiarity was literally a question of family. English was, likewise, kin to a larger family of labile continental languages which the nation-state had yet to formalize as rigidly bounded languages with a clear distinction between native and foreign. Both "land" and "scape," in various permutations, had a long history in English, so the transplantation of landscape to English was easy. The transplantation, however, was more than a question of language. The landscape paintings from familiar places like the Netherlands spoke a more universal artistic language of place identity that could be understood without a dictionary. Yet, landscape was eventually emptied of its place-bound meaning and came to refer to the make-believe space of scenery.

## MAKE-BELIEVE LANDSCAPE

How was the political landscape of place transformed into the space of scenery—"a prospect seen from a specific standpoint"?[2] The process of make-believe started with the development of methods of perspective drawing that created the illusion of bodily physical space. This process was related to the rediscovery of Ptolemy's geography, which was founded upon cartography. The techniques of cartography and surveying helped provide the methods for creating not only maps, but also the illusion of perspective. Chorography, a division of Ptolemy's geography, called for the artistic representation of *choros*, a word that could mean place, land, landscape territory, or country. The related word *chora*, familiar from Platonic philosophy, gave this concept feminine and bodily associations. Italian Renaissance painters obliged with paintings of an idealized natural countryside that expressed classical Roman and Neoplatonic ideals of natural law. Single point perspective was used to generate a timeless and universal geometric spatial framework within which an ideal subject was located. Place, as subject, thereby became subsumed, as location, within the coordinates of space. In this respect, Ptolemaic geography and the methods of perspective drawing contributed to that long process of "the gradual and forceful encroachment of space upon place" chronicled by the philosopher Edward Casey (1997, 333; see also Olwig 2001). Whenever this artistic approach supplanted the multi-perspective, multi-layered approach of the Netherlanders, the result, likewise, was the transmutation of the artistic representation of landscape as place to landscape as a scene in space.

The process by which space appropriated place is graphically documented in George Kernodle's classic studies of the evolution of the Renaissance theater. First, we see how medieval morality plays were performed by the townsfolk from stages erected in the marketplace, about which "the large democratic audience formed a circle" (Kernodle 1944, 179). Then we see how Italian Renaissance (court) architects created theaters in which the stage no longer was in the marketplace but became a mirror image of such a place with the help of the techniques of perspective: "Within a two-sided or four-sided frame the architect filled out a complete picture, not with a scenic symbol, but with the imitation of an actual place, usually a public square of a city. Symbols and emblems gave way to the technique of 'cheating the eye'—one book on perspective is called just that: *Lo Inganno de gl'occhi* " (ibid., 174). The whole theater, in this way, reflected a place, but now it was indoors, and the performances were under the command of the local prince or oligarchy. Kernodle comments upon the oddity, still apparent in some theaters to this day, that even though this space was indoors, it was made to look as though it were outdoors. Ceilings were decorated to look like the sky, and overhanging roof-like structures were carefully built over the boxes, to protect them from a nonexistent rain and sun (ibid., 23). The central public place had thus become incorporated into the geometric space of perspective scenery and under the control of a ruling hierarchy. This theater established a new dramatic principle based on two conventions: "the illusion of reality and the unity of place," which required "that everything seen on the stage at one time be planned as it would appear from one definite eyepoint" (ibid., 201). This illusion involved centering the lines of perspective on a position that was occupied by persons of privilege: "An exact relation, unknown before, was established between audience, actor, and setting when the eyepoint from which the stage picture was viewed was fixed at one definite point (the duke's box)" (ibid., 178). The timeless geometric laws governing the unity of time and place that were created within the space of this theater formed a dramatic contrast to custom's place-generated laws, with their emphasis upon transformation through time based upon historical precedent.

Italian Renaissance civic life focused on the town, as the center of a small polity, and the theaters reflected this narrowness of focus with their permanent stage scenes set in town squares. These scenes, however, also could include glimpses, through gateways, into the country beyond the town. In principle, the space of the theater could encompass a much larger area than that of a town plaza, as long as it preserved the rule that the entire scene be viewable from a single point. As an Italian critic put it in 1570, "the place for tragedy is restricted not only to one city or town or landscape [*campagna*] or similar place, but also to the view that can be seen by the eyes of one person" (quoted in Kernodle 1944, 201). In this way the place and polity of the larger surrounding landscape was encompassed in the focused space of the ruling elite's theater. Such scenes, as Tuan points out, "may be of a place but the scene itself is not a place. It lacks stability: it is in the nature of a scene to shift with every change of perspective. A scene is defined by its perspective whereas this is not true of place: it is in the nature of place to appear to have a stable existence independent of the perceiver" (Tuan 1974a, 236).

## Landscape and the Body Politic

The Italianate-style theater eventually spread, in various permutations, throughout Europe. The significance of the large sums spent on such theaters becomes clearer if one considers "the key question that became crucial beginning in the sixteenth century," posed by Otto Brunner and quoted at the outset of this book: "who represented the *Land*, the prince or the Estates? If the prince, then the *Landschaft* would become a privileged corporation; if the *Landschaft*, then it would become lord of the *Land*" (Brunner [1965] 1992, 341). There was a tensive relation between the representative body of the estates of the Landschaft and the state under the lord. The representative body of the Landschaft was a body of actual bodies, and the precedent of customary law rooted in bodily practice constituted its power. During a referendum, in fact, all the human bodies of the Landschaft might be assembled in the marketplace. The lord, on the other hand, followed the tradition of the Christian church in defining his state in terms of a mystic body that incorporated its member parts. The theater made it possible for the lord to make believe that the polity of the Landschaft was embodied, or incorporated, within the illusory bodily space of his state as body politic, and controlled by his vision as head of state.

One answer, then, to the question of what was being made-believe when the meaning of landscape changed from commonplaces to scenic spaces is that the illusion of a unified scenic space facilitated the "mindscaping" of imagined "natural" state communities fusing nations within a single body politic (Anderson 1991). The scenic illusion of landscape made it easier to believe that different historically constituted polities and places could be unified within the space of a body politic as embodied by a geographical body. When thus *incorporated* into a state, the polity would transmogrify into a natural national body, bound by mystical bonds of soil and blood. This notion of embodiment, as we saw, was inspired by the communion process by which Christians were incorporated as a church community through the "mystical" bond of Christ's body and blood. Through such imagined bonds of blood, a community of diverse peoples, embodied by the isles of Britain, was envisioned as a unified British nation-state. It is no accident that Hobbes's image of Leviathan, a body incorporating the bodies of the body politic, holds both the sword of state and the staff of the church: this state represented a unity of church, state, people, and territory. The myriad of immigrants to the United States from different places in the world were likewise envisioned as bound together, between sea and shining sea, as one "American" nation, under God and Nature.

Much as Britain was divided into countries, what we now know as the German nation-state was divided into a myriad of Landschaft polities. Here, the Landschaftsbild helped unite the German Reich as a single people bound by blood to their maternal soil. Whereas the Landschaft, as place and polity, was built on a law opposed to the bonds of blood that threatened to destroy the peace of the land, the nation-state sought to reconstitute blood-like ties at a higher level of abstraction and spatial scale. Congruent with the construction of the German nation-state, once independent-minded Landschaft polities were reduced to picture postcards of a national heritage. Custom became fossilized as an unchanging local tradition borne by suitably Aryan Teutons clothed in folk costume. The particular dramas each nation stages upon its landscape vary, but the underlying ideological subtext, framed by the structure of the landscape scene, remains remarkably similar. I refer, at the outset of this book, to Ernest Gellner's statement that nationalist ideology suffers from "pervasive false consciousness." It claims to defend folk culture while, in fact, forging a high culture. He later elaborates on this point, writing: "It preaches and defends continuity, but owes everything to a decisive and unutterably profound break in human history. It preaches and defends cultural diversity, when in fact it imposes homogeneity both inside and, to a lesser degree, between political units. Its self-image and its true nature are inversely related, with an ironic neatness seldom equaled even by other successful ideologies (Gellner 1983, 124–25). I would argue that the transmutation of landscape from an historically constituted place to a scenic space played a key role in this process of inversion.

## The Theater of State

The theater of the state provided the framework within which the body politic was staged against a backdrop of landscape scenery. The theater of state began as an actual theater. The theatrical element, however, became more and more metaphorical as landscape scenery was first transported into the garden, then became a landscape park, and was finally taken out of the garden and into a "picturesque" world perceived, from a particular viewpoint, as landscape scenery. Finally the metaphor hardened and reified to the point that in Germany, those thought to be without bonds of blood to the landscape, like the Jews and gypsies, were eventually removed from the scene by violence. This way of thinking is, unfortunately, becoming more common again in Europe.

What was becoming make-believe through the use of scenic illusion was in large measure the imagined community of the modern nation-state. This was literally done with mirrors, and the deliberate purpose was to deceive the eye and "masque" a state (Leviathan). We are not bidden to look behind the landscape, because, as Tuan hints, the scenic landscape masks the landscape of common historical places, the political landscape. The historically constituted landscape/country as place has been "done in" and spirited away behind the curtains. The *space* of scenery has thus appropriated the *place* of a people. A visual image of place as thing, of landscape as scene, has thus appropriated the socially defined place of people in the political landscape.

The Landschaft or country polity was what might be called a "bodies politic," where the representative body was a body of bodies. Now these bodies have been snatched up by the larger body politic of an abstract state, as embodied in its natural body geographical, and have been subsumed under its natural laws. The living land of people has become the deadened land of rock and soil, the stage upon which the drama of history is played. Some postmodernists see the landscape as even deader—as a subjectless structure of visual representation that has been reduced to pure textuality. It has thus become, according to Daniels and Cosgrove, "a flickering text displayed on the word-processor screen whose meaning can be created, extended, altered, elaborated and finally obliterated by the merest touch of a button" (1988, 8). The question, then, is who obliterated the landscape as place? The provocative answer to the question of whodunit is that somebody, or somebodies, actually does appear to have done it.

The tendency in much modern scholarship is to give some abstraction, like "capitalism" or "the state," the active role in creating history. We have also learned to look with askance at conspiracy theories of history, and rightly so. But a careful unpacking of Jonson and Jones's *Masque of Blackness* nevertheless shows that many of the ideas we now take for granted concerning race, gender, revolution, progress, nationalism, land, countryside, and landscape, were carefully and consciously *invented,* to use Inigo Jones's term for his imaginative constructions. They were invented by creative intellects ranging from William Camden and Ben Jonson to Inigo Jones and Francis Bacon. I find the idea that flesh and blood people, rather than abstractions, make history to be somehow comforting. People make the abstractions that then take on a life of their own, seeming to make history for us. But perhaps by recognizing these abstractions for what they are, maybe then we can remake history. People like Jones and Bacon were not simply "persona" acting lines given to them by history, or the state, they halped make history by helping to create the image of the British nation-state as a body politic in a body geographic, controlled by a centralized state organization. This was the central point of central point perspective, which gave the appearance of substance to a particular perspective on the political landscape. This single point perspective provided a vital counterpoint to the multiple perspectives of a representative body such as Parliament— which Bacon and James sought to do in. Parliament, however, responded by decapitating the head of state, in the person of James's son, King Charles I. This left the body politic headless, but did it kill it? The answer is "not really." The figure of Hobbes's Leviathan rose from the ashes of revolution and has stalked the political landscape, in various guises, ever since.

As Tuan makes clear in the foreword, the landscape of place and that of scenic space ultimately complement one another, even if they live in a state of mutual tension. For this reason the landscape visions of Jones were resurrected by the rival Whig countrymen, even as the Stuart dynasty fled the scene.

## THE TENSIVE RELATIONSHIP BETWEEN LANDSCAPE AS PLACE AND LANDSCAPE AS SCENIC SPACE

Yi-Fu Tuan describes the relationship between the sense of landscape and country as place and polity (he uses the word "domain") and that of landscape as scenery as being "tensive." As a result of the tension created by "combining two dissimilar entities, 'domain' and 'scenery,'" landscape generates meaning via "diaphor," a form of metaphor that "strives for the creation of meaning through juxtaposition and synthesis." Landscape thus encompasses meanings that belong to two different discourses: that of politics and economics and that of aesthetics (Tuan 1978, 366).

If one looks closely at the definition of *landscape* in a recent edition of the Merriam-Webster dictionary (MWC10), one sees that landscape's definition is not monolithic but "diaphoric," in that it contains meanings that can take on a tensive relation to each other. The dictionary gives the origin of *landscape* as the Dutch word *landschap,* from *land* plus *-schap*

(-ship), and gives the date of first recorded use in modern English as 1598. It defines the word as follows:

> land•scape . . . 1a: a picture representing a view of natural scenery; b: the art of depicting such scenery. 2a: the landforms of a region in the aggregate; b: a portion of territory that can be viewed at one time from one place; c: a particular area of activity: SCENE (political [landscape]); 3 obs[olete]: VISTA, PROSPECT. (MWC10)

We see that alongside meanings of landscape as a form of scenery, the definition includes such nonpictorial meanings as "the landforms of a region in the aggregate." The scenic and regional definitions exist in a tensive relation because, unlike a region, a scenic view has no boundary: the lines of perspective draw the eye out into infinity. Landscape is also defined in terms similar to that of the bounded region as "a particular area of activity," exemplified by the "political landscape." This area of activity is a "scene" in the sense of being "the place of an occurrence or action" rather than an open spatial vista (MWC10: scene).[3]

As useful as dictionaries are, they are also a product of the same process of nation-state building that helped construct landscape as scenery, and this explains how they come to contain conflicting diaphoric meanings. As Pierre Bourdieu writes:

> Thus, only when the making of the "nation," an entirely abstract group based on law, creates new usages and functions does it become indispensable to forge a *standard* language, impersonal and anonymous like the official uses it has to serve, and by the same token to undertake the work of normalizing the products of the linguistic habitus. The dictionary is the exemplary result of this labour of codification and normalization. It assembles, by scholarly recording, the totality of the *linguistic resources* accumulated in the course of time and, in particular, all the possible uses of the same word (or all the possible expressions of the same sense), juxtaposing uses that are socially at odds, and even mutually exclusive (to the point of marking those which exceed the bounds of acceptability with a sign of exclusion such as *Obs., Coll.* or *Sl.*). It thereby gives a fairly exact image of language as Saussure understands it, "the sum of individual treasuries of language," which is predisposed to fulfil the functions of a "universal" code. (Bourdieu 1991, 48, emphasis in original)

The definition of landscape found in such standard dictionaries involves a juxtaposition of meanings that can be mutually exclusive, as when some definitions presuppose an infinite scenic space and others the enclosed area of a region.[4] These contradictory definitions suggest that the authors of the dictionary have had difficulty making the diaphoric character of landscape compatible with a linear conception of etymological development because the differing meanings of landscape do not fit into a coherent semantic narrative.[5] The point, however, is that these meanings nevertheless reflect an historically evolving, and contested, discursive territory concerned with the nature of the polity and its laws. It is this discursive territory that has been the subject of this book.

## Space, Place, and the Just Landscape

The tensive relation between landscape and country as polity and place and landscape as scenery (scenic space) is arguably related to a similar tension, explored by Tuan, between place and space: "The ideas 'space' and 'place' require each other for definition. From the security and stability of place we are aware of the openness, freedom, and threat of space, and vice versa" (Tuan 1977, 6). In the preceding chapters, I have propounded the idea that at the heart of landscape and country as polity and place is the notion of custom and customary law, and at the heart of the Italian Renaissance attempt to frame landscape within scenic space was the ideal of natural law. Custom and customary law are based on historical precedent and are constantly undergoing a process of revision, whereas the justice of natural law is as timeless as a right angle or the *reg*ular straight line of a ruler (Benveniste 1973, 311–12). The former ideal lends itself to governance by a representative body because the fundamental purpose of such a body is to lay down common principles of law based upon the customs and practice of the populace. The latter ideal is more appropriate to the rule of an elevated regent seeking to bring uniform justice to a broad variety of polities. It was an ideal of law eminently suited to the ancient Greek and Roman empires, as well as to the Roman Catholic Church, which transmitted it to most of Europe.

The weakness of customary law is that it can lend itself to the fragmentation of polity and place, in which the people of differing places jealously guard minute differences of law and custom. Such a condition easily breeds strife, and it can hinder the growth of cosmopolitan culture because it makes it difficult for outsiders to negotiate the myriad differences among places (Tuan 1996). An example is the case of the Frisian landscapes, whose inhabitants could barely communicate with each other because of the variety of languages and eventually welcomed the mediation of higher political authority in order to reduce strife. The same occurred in Iceland (Hastrup 1985; 1990). The problem is intensified when custom is frozen as a potentially reactionary, national heritage of local "tradition" (Lowenthal 1996). The counterreaction to such provincialism can be to idealize universalistic ideals of justice, such as that identified with the *Pax Romana*. This legal ideal, however, has led to authoritarian despotism and the abuse of power. The strengths and weaknesses of the two ideals are apparent in Thoreau's ambivalence toward the justice represented by the meeting of the Concord court. For many, the Concord court represents the quintessence of New England democracy, but for Thoreau, it was associated with the tacit acceptance of Southern slavery on the basis of precedence and custom.

Thoreau, like Olmsted, sought a more transcendent ideal for the American political landscape linked to vistas opened by westward expansion beyond the bounds of the settled and custom-bound East. The linking of American national identity to the pioneer experience of carving out a nation from a supposedly virgin landscape held great promise for those who, like the historian Frederick Jackson Turner, wished to see the American frontier as a place creating a single democratized people out of an amalgam of ethnicities (Slotkin 1992, 29–62). Sectional differences have indeed become much less pronounced since the Civil War, suggesting that westward expansion might have helped reduce regional tensions. This development does not mean, however, that the frontier succeeded either in melting Americans into one ethnicity or in incorporating Native Americans into the larger culture. The metaphor of America as a "melting pot" has been replaced by that of a "salad bowl" containing a variety of culturally diverse communities (Tuan 1993, 199–209; 1996, 73–132).

The acceptance of cultural diversity might lead to an acceptance of landscape diversity in which it would be possible to celebrate the cultural dimensions of the American national parks. Rather than symbols of the supposedly "virgin" wilderness conquered by European settlers manifesting a national destiny, they could become great village greens of an ethnically complex and socially varied community identity. As individuals in a society we require common landscapes to share, not so much to teach us the laws of nature as to teach us the human laws according to which communities and countries have long shared and nurtured natural and human resources. This ideal was present, I have argued, in Olmsted's vision of the American national park. Yet, as wonderful as these parks are, we have also seen that establishing them meant expelling the native inhabitants from their ancestral lands, in the case of both the western Indians and the eastern Appalachian pioneer settlers. Under such conditions these parks appear to replicate the social injustices of the imperial mindset linked to British landscape garden parks (Olwig 1995b).[6] It must also be recognized that the "nature" perceived in these parks was initially a Native American cultural landscape. A village green, commons, or park is not simply a space shared in harmony; it is a contested place where differences must be worked out in the common interest. Communality, however, cannot be taken as a given. Those who are left out of a community, be they slaves or

Native Americans, require the protection of more transcendent ideas of law and justice.

Just as place and space require each other for definition, the same might be said of the ideals of natural and customary law and their associated landscape ideals. The earliest written laws of Scandinavia, including the famous Jutland law, were not just the reflection of custom, they appear to have been highly influenced by the canon law of the Roman Catholic Church. Without the prelates to write these laws down and give them a more general form, they would have been lost to posterity. Likewise, though the proponents of English common law stubbornly clung to the origin of this law in local custom, it is possible that it too was influenced by the generalizing tendency of Roman law. It is arguable that the greatest defender of common law, Chief Justice Sir Edward Coke, was prompted to formalize this law and make it more viable as a result of the threat posed when Sir Francis Bacon, chancellor at King James I's court, propounded legal ideals in the Roman tradition (Helgerson 1992, 65–104; Blomley 1994). The English common law tradition, which has spread to most of the English speaking world, may owe its viability to the way it redefines custom, which has its origins in specific times and places, into general principles that are common to a much larger community in law.

## LANDSCAPE AND PROFESSIONAL PRACTICE

Landscape is an important concept within a number of fields of social endeavor, particularly environmental studies (e.g., landscape geography and landscape ecology), areal planning, and environmental design (e.g., landscape architecture) (Jones 1991). In some fields of interest, such as landscape geography and landscape ecology, the interplay between society and nature has long been a primary concern (Olwig 1996b). This book does not question the importance of understanding this interplay—quite the opposite. It does, however, raise questions concerning just what is meant by nature and, hence, natural environment.

If we think of the *land* in landscape as primarily a physical quality (rocks and soil), and *nature* as primarily concerned with the unchanging laws of nature, then we are likely to conceive of landscape as a stage floor with soil and vegetation at the bottom and culture layered on top. We then run the risk of encouraging the rising tide of blood-and-soil nationalism because this model, however we might wish to qualify it, parallels the structure of nationalistic discourse (Olwig 1995a). The subtext of this discourse is a teleological narrative of nature in which the progress of culture follows a predetermined path through the body politic's stages of development. This idea then leads to the restrictive belief that only "native" people or species belong naturally to a particular area of land.

The contemporary fervor for biological authenticity and species purity comes perilously close to blood-and-soil ideology and to the racist discourse of eugenics and racial hygiene (Gröning and Wolschke-Bulmahn 1985; Gröning and Wolschke-Bulmahn 1987; Tokar 1988; Groening and Wolschke-Bulmahn 1989; 1992). The transition from scientific to nationalistic discourse occurs when the *land* in landscape is reified as a thing, material nature, the ecological niche of particular species. If, however, we think of *land* as polity and place, and *nature* as a complex, historically constituted concept imbued with social values, then landscape ceases to be a vehicle for environmental determinism and nature fanaticism identified with race and gender (Olwig 1976; Cronon 1995; Olwig 1995b).

Landscape is the expression of the practices of habitation through which the habitus of place is generated and laid down as custom and law upon the physical fabric of the land (Bourdieu 1977; Certeau 1984; Olwig 1996c). A landscape is thus a historical document containing evidence of a long process of interaction between society and its material environs. Physical science in general, and physical geography in particular, can provide assistance in interpreting this document without reducing society to a natural phenomenon (e.g., Jones 1977). As the geographer Robert Sack has argued: "A focus on place or landscape leads to an understanding of the connections while avoiding the problems of reduction. Even though place is all around us and we use it to tie the realms [of meaning, the social, and the natural] together in our daily lives it is not easy to analyze these processes. One has to be not only open-minded, but also versed in each realm" (Sack 1997, 116; see also Olwig 1984).

Landscape is a central term not only in environmental studies but also in the field of areal planning and environmental design. As architects and planners, we must learn to deal constructively with differing conceptualizations of law, both in society and in aesthetics. This book has sought to show how closely the discourses of law and polity, on the one hand, and aesthetics, on the other, have been linked throughout history, though they have often run in separate channels. Architects who think only in terms of the power of scenic space, ignoring the exigencies of community and place, run the risk of producing landscapes of social inequality like those of the great eighteenth-century British estates. It was at this time that the land in landscape was reduced to the status of a stage floor upon which to envision progressive scenes of (nation-state/imperial) improvement for a country now reified as *countryside*. It is also possible, however, for architects to shape environments that foster the desire to maintain the continuities that maintain a collective sense of commonwealth, rooted in custom but open to change—a sense of place (Hiss 1990).

As reflective scholars, and as active participants in the governing of our polities, we must be cognizant of the fact that our world is made up of front lawns and backyards, and that our living room is located between them, to use the analogy from Yi-Fu Tuan's foreword. We require the sense of closeness and place engendered by landscape as local polity, but we also need to counterbalance its confining centripetal force by movement through space. Thus, alongside the habitude of place we also need the perspectives fostered by the pilgrim's circuitous progress through a visionary landscape, beating the bounds of the cosmos.

Notes
Bibliography
Index

# Notes

In citing works in the notes, works frequently cited have been identified by the following abbreviations:

AV      Authorized (King James) Version of the Bible.

MWC10    *Collegiate Dictionary, Tenth Edition.* Springfield, Mass.: Merriam-Webster, 1993.

ODS      *Ordbog over Det Danske Sprog.* Copenhagen: Gyldendal, 1931.

OED      *The Compact Edition of the Oxford English Dictionary.* Oxford: Oxford University Press, 1971.

WC7      *Webster's Seventh New Collegiate Dictionary.* Springfield, Mass.: Merriam, 1961.

WU3      *Webster's Third New International Dictionary.* Springfield, Mass.: G. and C. Merriam, 1968.

## INTRODUCTION: NATURE, COUNTRY, AND LANDSCAPE

1. These words, inspired by the view from Pike's Peak, Colorado, are from Katherine Lee Bates's 1893 text for "America, the Beautiful," a song which has been promoted as an alternative national anthem to the warlike and unsingable "Star-Spangled Banner" (Bates [1895] 1974 ).

2. These words are from Samuel Francis Smith's 1831 text to "America." It has, perhaps coincidentally, the same melody as the British anthem "God Save the Queen" (Smith [1831] 1974).

3. Cosgrove's position has had great importance for the British-oriented "new cultural geographers." See, for example, Duncan 1990; Barnes and Duncan 1992; Seymour 2000. My own early work on landscape focused on the concept of nature (Olwig 1984). Most writers tend to focus on either landscape or nature, but not both. The important work of Denis Cosgrove and Steven Daniels on landscape has made me aware of the value of coupling theorizing on the concept of landscape with that on nature (Olwig 1996a). Cosgrove's work, however, has also made me conscious of the questionableness of reducing landscape to scenery. Cosgrove himself has recently modified his position so that he now takes greater cognizance of non-scenic conceptions of landscape (Cosgrove 1998).

4. Daniels and Cosgrove introduce the essays collected in *The Iconography of*

231

*Landscape* with this definition: "A landscape is a cultural image, a pictorial way of representing or symbolising surroundings" (1988, 1; for a critique see Ingold 1993, 154).

5. This assumption that the subject matter was "natural scenery," however, does seem to be justified by standard English dictionary definitions of landscape, such as "a picture representing a view of natural inland scenery" (MWC10: landscape; see also OED: landscape). Not all dictionaries give this as the etymologically primary definition; see, for example, Klein 1967: landscape; WU3: landscape).

6. The word *landscape* originated from the Germanic family of languages, to which the English language belongs. The Dutch spell the word *landschap*, the Danes *landskab*, the Swedes *landskap*, and the Germans *Landschaft*. When I am not referring to the use of the term in a particular continental European context, I have chosen to use the German spelling because German is spoken by the greatest number of people in continental Europe. The equivalent Anglo-Saxon word *landscipe* (meaning a district, region, tract of land or country, or simply land) appears to have become obsolete at the time the word *landscape*, as we now spell it, (re)entered the English language in the Renaissance (Onions 1966: landscape; Bosworth and Toller [1898–1921] 1966–72: landsceap, landscipe; Klein 1967: landscape; OED: landscape). Though the word might have become obsolete, it would not have been entirely unfamiliar to the English ear because the continental Germanic usage of variants of the root *Land* and the suffix *-scape* would have been similar at that time. In *paysage*, the suffix *-age* is appended to *pays* in much the way as *-schaft* is appended to *Land* in German, or *-ship* to *town* in English. *Pays* carried essentially the same connotations of areal community and people as *country* and *land*. The equivalent Italian terms, *paése* and *paesàggio*, carry the same meaning (Gamillscheg 1969: pays, paysage; Battisti and Alessio 1975: paése, paesàggio; Robert 1980: pays, paysage). John Florio, Queen Anne of Denmark's tutor in Italian, thus gave the following definition of *paése* in his famed 1611 Italian-English dictionary, *Queen Anna's New World of Words:* "the countrie. Also a countrie, a Land, a region, a province" (Florio 1611: Paése).

7. The conflict that emerged from the Stuart desire for the absolute power of continental European monarchs is linked to the conflict that emerged later in the century, known as the conflict between court and country, which is still the object of controversy amongst historians (Zagorin 1969).

8. I first worked with this approach in Olwig 1974 and elaborated upon it in a number of subsequent publications (Olwig 1981; 1984). I drew ideas particularly from the work of Yi-Fu Tuan and David Lowenthal (Lowenthal 1961; Tuan [1961] 1972; Lowenthal and Prince [1965] 1972; Tuan 1974b). Outside of geography, this work has been influenced by the literary scholars John Barrell and Raymond Williams (Barrell 1972; Williams 1973). For other relevant approaches to landscape in relation to text, see Cosgrove and Daniels 1988; Duncan 1990; Pred 1990; Barnes and Duncan 1992; Duncan and Ley 1993; Spirn 1998.

9. A person who acts upon the stage of this theater of state may, in Hobbes's words, "*represent*" either "himself," or "an other." When representing an other, "he that owneth his words and actions, is the Author: in which case the Actor

acteth by Authority" (Hobbes [1651] 1991, 112, emphasis in original).

10. The application of "duplicitous" to landscape is inspired by a seminal essay by Stephen Daniels (1989) which is not, however, about either masques or nationalism.

CHAPTER 1. THE POLITICAL LANDSCAPE AS POLITY AND PLACE

1. The stage for *The Masque of Blackness* was quite impressive. It involved complex machinery, a "greate stage . . . xl foote square and iiij or foote in heighte with wheeles to go on" (forty feet square and four feet high), and elaborate stage sets representing one of the earliest English scenic uses of perspective illusion— decades before it was to be introduced on the English theater stage. The cost of this extravaganza was rumored to have been upwards of three thousand pounds, enough to build a fair-sized country house (Summerson 1966, 22; Orgel and Strong 1973, 89).

2. Christian IV is the subject of the Danish royal anthem by Johannes Ewald, composed in 1779. He has become a legend, among other things, because of the many glorious buildings that he built during his reign, his active role as a warrior king, and his colorful lifestyle, which included a love of the theater and masques. Evidence about the early career of Jones, the son of an anonymous cloth worker, is scanty. It is almost entirely derived from publications by John Webb, a relation by marriage who was Jones's pupil and successor. According to Webb, Jones first spent a number of years in Italy before Christian IV "engross'd Him to himself, sending for Him out of Italy." One estimate is that Jones was in Italy from 1597 until 1603, when he left for Denmark. He was back in England in time to do the 1605 masque for the queen. Christian is known to have exchanged the services of favored artists with his beloved sister, so this could explain why Jones appears to have entered the service of the English court under the wing of Anne (Summerson 1966, 15–19, 21).

3. Anne first appeared on the English stage in the 1604 production of Samuel Daniel's *The Vision of the Twelve Goddesses,* which was performed by the queen and her ladies in the Great Hall at Hampton Court. Anne played the central figure of Pallas, "the glorious patroness of this mighty Monarchy" (Rygg 1996, 79–80).

4. Graham Parry notes that Inigo Jones's "first employment was with Queen Anne, whose avant-garde taste in the arts ought to be better recognized than it is. She initiated the masques that were the most distinctive expression of Court culture under the Stuarts, commissioning the first of them, *The Masque of Blackness,* in 1605, presumably after lengthy discussion with Inigo Jones over what could be achieved in the way of spectacle." He further notes the literary importance of other leading ladies of the court (who played active roles in the masques). In this connection he gives credit to Anne for the highly significant innovation of incorporating an "anti-masque" within the masque (Parry 1981, 49, 47–49). Jonson was jealous of his reputation and he did not give unwarranted share to the glory of his inventions. For this reason, it is significant that he gave Anne some of the credit for what posterity considers to be one of the

major contributions to the masque, the "anti-masque." He thus writes in the introduction to his third masque for Anne, *The Masque of Queens*, "And because her majesty (best knowing that a principal part of life in these spectacles lay in their variety) had commanded me to think on some dance or show that might precede hers and have the place of a foil or false masque" (Jonson 1969, 122–23, lines 8–19). On Anne's importance for the visual arts, see Strong 1986, 187.

5. Seven members of the earl of Leicester's troupe, including George Bryan, Thomas Pope, and William Kempe, who later became players in Shakespeare's Lord Chamberlain's Men, had been the guests of Anne's father, King Frederik II, at Kronborg Castle, Elsinore, in 1586. They came up to Denmark from Utrecht where the earl was commanding the English army. Pope and Kempe in 1599 became shareholders, with Shakespeare, in the Globe Theater (Neiiendam 1988, 89–93; Risum 1992, 47).

6. Frances Yates writes in *Theater of the World:* "When Fludd and Jones returned to England in 1605 they found it a changed country. James I had succeeded Elizabeth in 1603; the old Elizabethan strictness and economy had passed away; the Stuart monarchs were willing and eager to spend lavishly on architecture and the arts. . . . This change of temper was, of course, the making of Inigo Jones, and this made his whole career possible" (1969, 85). The difference described between the reign of Elizabeth and that of James I is likely to have had much to do with Anne, since she was Jones's mentor. This could explain the apparent anomaly, pointed out by Leah Marcus, that "contemporaries noted that James seemed not to relish plays in performance as Queen Elizabeth had. Nevertheless, he called for many more at court: twenty-three during the winter season of 1609–10 and never fewer than eleven, except in the year of Prince Henry's death" (1986, 25, 28).

7. After James's equally stormy return voyage, "evidence" of witchcraft was found in both Denmark and Scotland, and after a number of witches had been subjected to the requisite torture they admitted to having caused the storms which had bedeviled the journey. James took an active role in the Scottish witch trials and saw to it that witches were both burned at the stake and exposed in his book *Daemonologie* (Akrigg 1962, 13; Williams 1970, 38–39; Mebane 1989, 106–8).

8. All translations, including this one, are by the author unless otherwise noted.

9. The primary source of this legend is the historical writings of the English cleric the Venerable Bede (672–735). Modern scholars are divided with regard to the location of the Anglo-Saxons' homeland, but credence is still given to the location identified by Bede (Trap 1963, 10:5–6).

10. Most of the landscape polities that Trap lists are within the ancient territory of North Friesland, which is located on islands off the coast and in the marshlands bordering the north coast of the Eider and extending up the western coast to the present Danish-German border. They are, as spelled in Danish, the islands of Sild, Før, and Pelvorm, and the coastal territories of Eidersted and Bredsted. This district had a population at that time of 66,000, of whom 30,000

still spoke Frisian. It is estimated that there are today 60,000 residents of Schleswig who are of Frisian origin. Six to eight thousand of them understand one or more of the fifteen North Frisian dialects. The Frisian population is concentrated south of the present Danish border (Hellesen and Tuxen 1988, 245). The district is still called North Friesland on modern maps. The northernmost province of the Netherlands is also called Friesland.

11. When quoting from Danish sources, I use the Danish spelling of place names.

12. My thanks to Annelise Ballegaard Petersen for helping me with this translation. The English version of this tricky text is my responsibility.

13. Trap writes that the Frisians joined the Angles, the Saxons, and the Jutes in the fifth-century conquest of Britain led by Horsa and Hengist, who are named in *Beowulf* as the leaders of the Frisians (1864, 123). After being defeated by King Godfred of Jutland, Friesland lost its sovereignty and was incorporated into the Jutland kingdom in 811. The Frisians retained their native laws, however.

14. A gradual formalization of the territorial identity of the Landschaften of North Friesland and similar territories (such as adjacent Saxon Dithmarschen) appears to have occurred in the course of the fifteenth and sixteenth centuries (Bader 1957; Sante 1964, 303–9, 431–32, 637–39, 719–23, 732–36, 751–52; Bader 1978, 177–82; Köbler 1988, 114–15, 158, 373).

15. For a comparison of the history of the struggle for political freedom in Switzerland and in the marshlands of the Wadden Sea, see Hermann 1952. On the many European variations on the Tell theme, see Dundes 1991.

16. Trap also lists Bredsted as both a landscape and an *amt*. Though it is on the west coast, it had an unusually large number of manors (Trap 1864, 67; Hellesen and Tuxen 1988, 249).

17. For a useful theoretical overview of the literature on the cultures along the North Sea coastal marshes, see Knottnerus 1996, 58–63.

18. The history of this area goes against the grain of modernization theories like that of Ernest Gellner, which see modernization as a consequence of the rise of a central, homogenizing, bureaucratic nation-state; rationalism; capitalism; and industrialism (Gellner 1983). England and, to a lesser extent, Sweden are also examples of highly successful industrializing nations in which the absolute power of the central state was counterbalanced by representative institutions (Rokkan 1975, 587–89). For an incisive critique of modernization theory based on the evidence from this North Sea region, see Schilling 1992.

19. On this form of "platial" imagination, see Casey 1996; Olwig 2002.

20. Lands such as Jutland or Zealand (Sjælland) themselves incorporate older lands, just as they are now incorporated in the land of Denmark. This process of incorporation by which smaller legal areas of possible tribal or clan origin "melt together" with larger ones was widespread (Benediktsson et al. 1981, 228, 236; see also Fenger 1992, 143). Eiderstedt was thus the product of a union (in 1456) with two other "lands" now spelled: Everschop and Utholm (which had united in 1370). Each of these "lands" (as they called themselves) retained its legal and political autonomy (Trap 1864, 267; see also Köbler 1988, 127–28). During the Middle Ages these lands apparently formed a loose federation, North Friesland,

which was ruled by a common council (Trap 1864, 124–25). Switzerland and the Netherlands have retained a variant of this political structure.

21. For a useful, parallel discussion, of the meaning of *Land* as a judicial community based on Austrian material, see Brunner [1965] 1992, 139–99.

22. Brunner ([1965] 1992, 152–65) presents a useful discussion of this issue. He concludes: "[T]he *Land* was not simply a region of territorial supremacy, a complex of territories and rights that was joined together in the hands of a lord. . . . Rather, the various forms that the *Land* assumed . . . all had one thing in common: each was a judicial district in which territorial law applied. Its judicial community, the people of the land, constituted the territorial community (*Landesgemeinde, Landschaft*)."

23. This law became a foundation of subsequent Danish justice, though it was superseded (except in the Duchies) by the codified body of law promulgated by the absolute monarchy in the seventeenth century (Kroman 1945; Benediktsson et al. 1981, 228–33).

24. I am indebted to Chris Sanders at The Arnemagnæanske Commission's Dictionary, Copenhagen, for his help in tracking the older Nordic meaning of this term. The word *beskaffenhed* (*Beschaffenheit* in German) has the root *skab* (or *schaft* in German), meaning shape. *Shape* can mean to create by shaping, but it can also be used to refer to the shape or form of that which has been shaped. The *Beschaffenheit* of something is thus literally the shape something is in. The term *Landschaft*, in this sense, refers to the shape the land is in with respect to its customs, the material forms generated by those customs, and the shape of the bodies that generate and formalize those customs as law.

25. The oldest Danish application of the word *landskab* to Jutland in the lexicographic records for the forthcoming Old Danish Dictionary is from two manuscript versions of the Jutland law from 1490 and 1497 in which *land* is replaced by *landskab* (personal correspondence with Merete K. Jørgensen). Similar ancient districts such as Gothland in Sweden have been commonly termed landskap since at least the eighteenth century. Landskapet Åland is a modern landscape territory that is quite comparable in status to the Frisian territories of the past. It is culturally Swedish territory now under the Finnish state and, like the Frisian Landschaften, has considerable legal and political autonomy.

26. The cognate word in modern Danish is *fællesskab*. Its derivation gives an idea of how the English word might have evolved. The prefix *fælles-* can be translated as "common, joint, communal, public collective and general." It derives from the Old Norse *fé* (modern Danish *fæ*) meaning grazing animals such as cattle or sheep, but which became generalized to mean property or money, because grazing animals were used as a unit of payment in ancient Norse society. It is retained in modern English in the word *fee*. The "les" in *fælles* (and here the "low" in fellow) derives from the word *lag*, which means lay, and which is used here to mean lay together. When you lay your sheep together you have a *fælles* herd. You also, thereby, become a *félagi* in Old Norse, or fellow. Fellows do not, of course, simply pool their sheep and graze them on the common (*fælled—fæ land* in modern Danish). They do so according to certain agreed-upon bylaws, or

rules of order, and the suffix *-lagi* therefore also implies an order of the sort implied by the word *lay* in modern English terms such as layout, or lay of the land. It is from this sense of the word that the modern English word *law* appears to derive (*lov* in modern Danish). The law, of course, is something that we "lay down," and a bylaw, one may assume, is the law laid down by a *by* (deriving from *bygd*), meaning dwelling area (*-by* is familiar as a suffix in many English place names, e.g., Grimsby) (MWC10: bylaw). When the ending *-skab* is added to *fælles* we get the word *fællesskab*, which means community. In this context, however, *-skab* means the condition or quality of being, or the nature or character of being *fælles* or having fellowship. But *fællesskab* literally means something like "the nature of sharing sheep in a customary lawful body" (ODS: fællesskab).

27. On the importance of the symbolism of the meadow and stream for the generation of the modern concept of the park, see Olwig 1995b.

28. See the references for Mecklenburg and Austria/Voralberg (Sante 1964, 541, 751); see also Bloch [1940] 1961, 371. The standard German dictionary lists 1121 as the earliest use of the term Landschaft to refer to inhabitants of a district, and 1179 as the first use to refer to the (presumably noble) representatives in the Landtag, or Parliament. The first references to the Landschaft as being divided into estates date from the Renaissance (1420 and 1555). The use of the term for the estates excluding the nobles persisted into the late nineteenth century (Grimm and Grimm 1855: Landschaft, 5, 6; ODS: Landskab, 4). The *Oxford English Dictionary* defines *estate* as "An order or class regarded as part of the body politic, and as such participating in the government either directly or through its representatives" (OED: estate). In Dithmarschen and North Friesland the farmers were the predominant estate (Köbler 1988, 114–15, 127–28, 373–74).

29. Thus, according to the jurist K. C. Dowdall, "A *Landschaft,* which in Germany might be called a *Staat,* or in Italy a *stato,* is called by Sully [writing ca. 1628] a *gouvernement*" (Dowdall 1923, 118–19; see also Jellinek 1922, 129–35). When some version of the Latin estate/state is used we also find, as in the case of other legal bodies such as Landschaft, township, and county/country, that the term can be applied to the territory thus governed. In sixteenth-century Netherlands, which was governed by assemblies of the estates, the territories of the federation came to be known as states, or as "free states," as well as by the Germanic term *land* (as in Nether*lands*). It is thought that it was through the English involvement in the Dutch war of liberation that the term *state* came to be known and applied in a political sense in England and, eventually, in the United States (Clark 1946, 213–17).

30. The *Sachsenspiegel* also included a second section on feudal legal relations, the Lehnsrecht.

31. Since literacy was largely the monopoly of the clergy at this time, the written version of the ancient Scandinavian laws was inevitably influenced by Roman Catholic canon law (Skautrup 1941).

32. F. L. Carsten's *Princes and Parliaments in Germany* argues cogently that the estates of the German principalities saw themselves as representing "the country" much in the same sense as did the English Parliament. He feels that the

history of the German estates is "a very much neglected subject" and chides German historians for neglecting, or even denigrating, this German heritage of political liberty in order to "side with the princes, who tried to suppress" the estates in the creation of absolute monarchies (1959, v, vii, 434). Carsten's book has helped stimulate a debate on this subject that has revived awareness of the political and social meaning of Landschaft. Some of the most useful reviews of and contributions to this debate are to be found in Blickle 1973; Wallthor and Quirin 1975; Witt 1975; Oestreich 1980; and Krüger 1984. For an English-language historical study which discusses the empowerment of the Landschaft in the duchy of Württemberg during the sixteenth century, see Sabean 1984, 13.

33. Henrik had particularly close ties to the prelate and cartography publisher George Braun, and supplied Braun with important contributions (including Jordan's map) to his *Civitates orbis terrarum*, first published in 1572. Braun, who was apparently of Dutch background, was a protégé of the great Antwerp humanist and cartographer Abraham Ortelius, but he was educated in Germany and was based in Cologne (Jørgensen 1981, 7–18). Braun also published a Rantzau family tree for Henrik which shows the tree growing out of a map of the Duchies and Denmark. The map is festooned with pictures and text depicting the illustrious deeds of the Rantzaus, including a picture of the prostrate representatives of the Dithmarschen Landschaft begging for mercy from their conqueror (ibid., 16–17). It also, however, contains illustrations of more peaceful contributions of the Rantzaus, such as the building of bridges and the planting of experimental orchards.

34. The Rantzaus' support of the unity of Schleswig-Holstein under the hegemony of the Ritterschaft was not simply an academic or a military matter. The resultant control the nobles exerted over the legal system in the areas under the Ritterschaft meant that the peasantry was reduced to a state of virtual serfdom. The Ritterschaft in general, and Henrik in particular, became fabulously wealthy (Bech 1979, 11:622–27; Gregersen 1981, 256–84). The Landschaften of southwest Jutland, despite conquest, were nevertheless not brought under manorial control or the laws of the Ritterschaft.

35. As the author of the *Tetrabiblos*, Ptolemy was the master of an astrological "science" which the geographer of ideas Clarence Glacken has described as "an incredible melange" producing "an important and depressing literature" (Glacken 1967, 111–15).

36. On Ptolemy's influence see Wright 1965, 10, 19, 34, 48, 78.

37. Gadol follows Edgerton in emphasizing the direct influence of Ptolemy, whereas Kemp is more inclined to focus upon the techniques of surveying more generally, especially where the pioneering work of Brunelleschi (discussed later in this chapter) is concerned. Kemp notes, however, the rising influence of Ptolemy at this time (Edgerton 1975; Kemp 1990, 344–45). It was one thing, of course, to make specific use of the difficult techniques of Ptolemy, but it was another to adopt a cosmology colored by Ptolemy, while making more general use of available techniques of surveying. On this subject more generally, see Cosgrove 1988, 1990.

38. The word *room* (*Raum* in German) is thought to derive from a word

meaning open land, related to the Latin roots *rur-* (as in rural) and *rus-* (as in rus-tic) (MWC10: room) and to the Nordic-Germanic word for clearing, *ryding* (Falk and Torp [1903–6] 1996: Rum).

39. On the relation between *choros* as place, country, and polity, see Derrida 1995 and Olwig 2001. See also Cornford 1937 and Casey 1997.

40. This arrangement mirrored, not incidentally, a scene of architectural design based upon paradigmatic archetypal geometrical forms (*archetype, paradigm,* and *mirror* are synonyms) (Damisch [1987] 1994; MWC10: arche-type). I would like to thank Gunnar Olsson for reminding me of the importance of this demonstration, and for referring me to Damisch's ideas concerning the role of the mirror in Renaissance perspective theory. See also Olsson 2001.

41. Albrecht Dürer himself stressed the importance of cartography and chorography for painters. He wrote: "There is no art, by which Measurement is more, and more variously, needed than the Art of Painting, which not only requires Geometry and Arithmetic, the foundations of all Measurement, but, much more than any other art, depends upon Perspective, Catoptrica, Geodaesia, Chorographia" (quoted in Benesch 1965, 8). Benesch notes the parallels between the landscapes of Altdorfer and "the maps of the new cosmography," and he sees strong parallels between developments in astronomy and in the visual arts (Benesch 1965, 58–59, 143–65; see also Rees 1980, 68).

42. The earliest recorded use of the term Landschaft to designate the back-ground for a painting dates to 1490 (Gibson 1989, introduction); the French equivalent, *paysage,* dates from 1549, well after the origins of Italianate per-spective painting, but at the time of the emerging tensions between Landschaft and lord, Protestant and Roman Catholic.

43. The emphasis on perspectival style does not mean that the Italians did not paint representations of the country (paése), such as Ambrogio Lorenzetti's 1338 fresco of republican Sienna in the Sienna City Hall, that are comparable to the Landschaft paintings of the north (Welti 1983).

44. The word *Dutch* generally meant German or Germanic at this time (OED: Dutch).

45. Otto Brunner held the dictum "the estates are the country"; but more recent historians, such as G. Benecke, have argued that the identity of the coun-try was actually contested between the estates and the lords in the sixteenth cen-tury, and that in some places, such as in Heinrich Julius's home area, the lords succeeded in co-opting this identity from the estates. Benecke writes:

> In the sixteenth century the Dukes obtained regular grants from their assembled Estates. These grants the Dukes accepted not in the name of the assemblies or col-lectively in the name of the Estates, neither in the name of the *Landtag* nor in the name of the *Landstände*. Instead, the Dukes accepted grants in the name of a le-gal fiction, the *Landschaft* or country, or in a variety of shifting terms. It seems that by allowing no comprehensive nomenclature to become established by cus-tom and thereby to develop the backbone of an institution, the Dukes legally re-tained their prerogative powers fully intact. . . . Grants had been accepted in the name of the *Landschaft* by the Dukes, but who could claim at law to be the *Land-schaft?* Not the Estates alone. A mere counting of subjects' heads or of taxpayers'

heads could quickly show that they were just the privileged few. The Estates in assemblies may have granted the money but the Dukes accepted it from the *Landschaft*. (Benecke 1974, 109–13)

46. Royal Danish spectacles characteristically involved a succession of huge floats, or "inventions," which were intended to make a symbolic statement concerning the position and power of the king. Thus, whole pieces of country scenery, complete with hunters or shepherds, might be paraded by to show the ability of the king to shape the world about him (Neiiendam 1988, 81–116). The tradition of memorializing such events with theatrical performances was also known in Britain. The last production of a masque commissioned by Queen Elizabeth, a wedding gift to James VI in 1589, is listed as "a maske sent to Scotland" (Rygg 1996, 69–70). A classic study of this era's theater and street spectacle, and its importance as a means of representing princely authority over place, is Kernodle 1944, esp. 52–108.

47. In a speech to the English Parliament in 1609, James noted that "our Common Law hath not a setled Text in all Cases, being chiefly grounded either vpon old Customes, or else vpon the Reports and Cases of Iudges, which ye call Responsa Prudentum. The like whereof is in all other Lawes: for they are much ruled by Presidents (saue onely in Denmarke and Norway, where the letter of the Law resolues all doubts without any trouble to the Iudge) (James I [1616] 1918d, 312).

CHAPTER 2. COUNTRY AND LANDSCAPE

1. Some useful works on the subject of the relation between English and American ideologies about "country" are Robbins 1961; Bailyn 1967; Pocock 1980.

2. The word *country*, which entered English about 1270 (OED: country), has its etymological origin in the late Latin *contrata*, meaning "landscape, country, literally, that which is situated opposite the beholder" (WU3: country). Etymologically primary meanings of country are "land," "district," and "region" (ibid). The word *region* appears to have its etymological origins in a notion of oppositeness (Benveniste 1973, 311–12), and it is interesting to note the German equivalent, *Gegend*, in the sense "tract of country," also is rooted in a word meaning counter (Langenscheidt 1967: Gegend). The use of the mirror metaphor, or the mirror itself, as a means of representing the land, landscape, or country, is interesting in this context because what is opposite oneself comes to include oneself, or one's eye, when seen in a mirror. What is counterposed to one is thus, nevertheless, linked to one as a counterpart or complement. You see yourself, together with your surroundings, when you look in a mirror.

3. Perhaps it is because of the similarity between *county* and *country* that the two words could be used synonymously, as in a 1330 reference to "the cuntre of Dorseth" (Zagorin 1969: 33; OED: country 2). The term *county* was applied to the ancient English territories labeled variously as "shire" (as in Worcestershire) or "land" (as in Westmorland) or "folk" (as in Suffolk) without ever completely replacing the earlier terms. *County* literally means the territory of a count, but

the English counties were not governed by counts and they were not the invention of a centralized Norman state—they were ancient pre-Norman legal territories (Milsom 1981, 13–15). The English can still be heard to use "county" where this American, at least, would expect to hear "country," as in a recent BBC TV reference (shown on Danish TV on 3 June 1997) to the young Princess Diana as "simply a county girl."

4. It should be noted that the *Oxford English Dictionary* gives 1660 as the earliest date for use of the word *representation* to refer to royal representation at Parliament, and 1729 as the earliest reference to parliamentary representatives (OED: representation 7, 8). This statement by James I suggests that the word was current in the parliamentary context well before these dates.

5. Drummond had studied law in Bourges and was familiar, no doubt, with the legal thinking behind the parliamentarians' concept of commonwealth and representative councils (MacDonald 1971, 84–90). One of the principal sources of biographical knowledge about Jonson is Drummond's record of their conversations when Jonson walked to Scotland in 1619; see Drummond [1619] 1985.

6. This idea of country was thus in keeping with the root *contrata*. James is here implicitly opposing the regional body of the state to its capital, as the seat of rule (the word *region* comes from the Latin *regere* meaning "to rule").

7. The *Oxford English Dictionary* lists regular references to this use of county up until 1549; the last reference is from 1700.

8. The designation *Fylke*, which is etymologically related to *folk*, was used in ancient Norway to refer to jurisdictions equivalent to the county and the Landschaft (as, for example, the roughly equivalent territorial entities know as *landskap* across the border in Sweden). The term *Fylke* has been revived in modern Norwegian, where it is now used to designate the state administrative units termed *amt* during the period of Danish rule.

9. Alan G. R. Smith has argued that Zagorin has exaggerated the nature of this dichotomy. According to Smith, "virtually all members of the gentry class—the backbone of the political nation—had a divided loyalty; to the royal Court to which they owed such status symbols as their appointment as JPs [justices of the peace] in the localities and to which they looked for future profit in either money or position, and to their own 'countries', the county societies in which they lived and worked and which they could not afford to offend too much if they were to retain their local influence. As Professor Stone so aptly put it, 'the conflict between loyalty to the particularistic locality and loyalty to the nation was fought out within the mind of each individual gentleman'" (1984, 278).

10. The Oxford legal historian W. S. Holdsworth describes the importance of Coke in the following terms: "If the Stuart kings and the prerogative lawyers had prevailed, it would have been a tradition very different from that which we know to-day. Because Parliament, in alliance with the common lawyers, gained the victory, it was shaped by the man who embodied the ideals of both—Edward Coke. . . . The result was that, when the Parliamentary party triumphed after 1641, lawyers and politicians alike accepted his statements as not only authoritative, but almost infallible" (Holdsworth 1928, 14–15; see also Hill 1965, 225–65).

11. The original is from *Irish Reports,* London edition of 1674. This quotation should not be taken to mean that Davies was ignorant of continental civil law in the tradition of Roman natural law. Nor should it be taken to mean that he was unwilling to apply arguments from the Roman tradition in situations where he found them appropriate—for example, with regard to the rights of the English king over the conquered "countries" of Ireland. He showed little sympathy for the customary law of the Irish (Brooks and Sharpe 1976; Eccleshall 1978, 123–25; Pawlisch 1985, 3–33, 161–75).

12. Milsom gives the following explanation for this flexibility: "The starting-point is in customs, not the customs of individuals but the customs of courts governing communities. Those courts, in England essentially community meetings, had to make all kinds of decisions. What shall we do now? What do we usually do? Factually the human and sometimes supernatural pressures to do the same thing again may be strong. But if the body is sovereign in the matter and its decisions final, legal analysis can get no more out of this kind of customary law than those two questions. What matters is the present decision, the choice made now. . . . It is the past that must give way, and then the present will have refined or modified the custom. Explicit legislation may indeed be embodied in a particular decision; and early records show this sometimes happening at all levels in England, even the king's courts being first seen as applying customs of the community of the realm" (1981, 1–2).

13. Parliament, however, could also be legitimated as a body which included the monarch and which derived its legitimacy from its ability to formulate, on behalf of the body politic, eternal principles of natural law (Eccleshall 1978, 97–125). Jurists like Hotman were not consistently pro-Germanic and pro–customary law or anti-Roman and anti–natural law. It was only in a later era, when the "country" became polarized against the "court," that relatively more consistent positions began to emerge and people like Edward Coke and Robert Molesworth began to interpret their predecessors in terms of this polarity (Molesworth 1738; Giesey and Salmon 1972).

14. Pocock writes: "The concept of the immemorial encouraged the fabrication of myths about immensely remote times, and the fact that the appeal to early national history took the form of partisan controversy between sovereign and constitution enhanced this tendency" (1957, 19).

15. I have treated this nondichotomous concept of nature at length in Olwig 1984. For a pertinent anthropological treatment of the relationship between nature and the idea of communality, see Pálsson 1996. On dualistic versus monistic concepts of nature more generally, see Descola and Pálsson 1996.

16. Coke's expression is very much in agreement with the derivation of the concept of law from the Old English *lagu,* which was akin to *licgan,* meaning "to lie."

17. Rogation week is a fortnight before Whitsunday, the seventh Sunday after Easter (Bushaway 1982, 81). This method of binding memory was not peculiar to England; Marc Bloch, writing of customary law in Europe more generally, tells us that: "Since memory was obviously likely to be the more enduring the longer its possessors were destined to remain on this earth, the contracting parties often

brought children with them. Did they fear the heedlessness of childhood? Various methods could be used to overcome it: a box on the ear, a trifling gift, or even an enforced bath" (Bloch [1940] 1961, 114).

18. According to Victor Turner, the setting chosen for such ritual functions is "a place that is not a place, and a time that is not a time." The symbolic activities engaged in within this setting "operate culturally as mnemonics . . . not about pragmatic technique, but about cosmologies, values, and cultural axioms, whereby a society's deep knowledge is transmitted from one generation to another" (Turner 1974, 239).

19. The court was held on special holy days, particularly Yule and Midsummer, which were believed to create a special sacred time and place, divorced from normal space and time, in which justice could prevail (Eliade 1971, 49–92). Ritual combat was used as a method of legal adjudication in ancient North European society (Baker 1979, 11) .

CHAPTER 3. "MASQUING" THE BODY POLITIC OF BRITAIN

1. The first masque performed in connection with the new reign was Samuel Daniel's *The Vision of the Twelve Goddesses,* which was performed on Twelfth Night, 1604, by Queen Anne and her ladies in the Great Hall at Hampton Court. In this masque, a central perspective stage was not used. Rather, according to Tudor custom, the scenery was scattered about the hall. The plot concerns the visit of twelve Greek goddesses to the "Western Mount of *mighty Brittany,* the land of civil music and of rest." Anne played the central figure of Pallas, "the glorious patroness of this mighty Monarchy" (quoted in Rygg 1996, 79–80, emphasis in original). *The Masque of Blackness* marked the move of the masque to a Whitehall setting, complete with central-perspective stage scenery by Jones and a unified story line by Jonson. On the relation between street theater the evolution of the theater stage, see Kernodle 1944.

2. When James took the throne, the idea of Britain became foundational to his idea of the state, and it became fashionable to credit him with reviving the name. This is seen, for example, in the title to John Speed's *The Historie of Great Britaine under the Conquests of the Romans, Saxons, Danes and Normans: . . . and Issues of the English Monarchs, from Julius Cæsar, to our most gracious Soveraigne King James,* and from his dedication to James as the "inlarger and Uniter of the British Empire; Restorer of the British name" (Speed 1623).

3. In his conversations with William Drummond, Jonson reported that: "[Jonson] himself was posthumous born a month after his father's decease; brought up poorly, put to school by a friend (his master Camden)" (Drummond [1619] 1985, 600, lines 194–96). Camden was usher and then headmaster of Westminster School. He was the son of a painter and possibly lost his father at an early age, which allowed him to be admitted to school as an orphan. This might have disposed him to take Jonson under his wing, since Jonson was the fatherless, adopted son of a bricklayer (Gough 1806, ix–x).

4. Ortelius, the editor and publisher of *Theatrum orbis terrarum* ([1570] 1595), fled from Antwerp to allied Protestant England in 1576 at the time of the

worst Spanish atrocities in the Lowlands (Kunst 1994, 31–36). The idea of the world as theater was common throughout Europe at this time (Yates 1969). It also clearly played a role in the way northern European landscape painters such as Pieter Brueghel, another Ortelius protégé, sought to give visual representation to the idea of landscape as a territory expressing the customs of a people. Ortelius, who was proud of his cultural heritage, also published pictorial works celebrating the ancient customs of his forebearers as described by Tacitus (Ortelio 1596; MacDougall 1982, 48). Maps had a special meaning in the lowlands of Europe because they provided both a tool and a means of visualizing the communities that formed on lowlands wrested from the sea by draining and diking. These maps served the interests of self-governing, representative, local polder and drainage boards called *waterschappen* or, on a larger scale, *hoogehemraadschappen* (Kain and Baigent 1992, 7, 11–39).

5. Dating the origin of Western Nationalism is a subject of controversy. Most authorities tend to locate it a cantury or two later than the period of James I, though some have noted the apparent anomaly of English nationalism in this period (Smith 1986, 109, 139–40, 228 n. 14; Anderson 1991, 4; Helgerson 1992).

6. Jonson also made use of this marriage motif for the union of Great Britain with and under its monarch in the 1606 masque *Hymenaei* (Parry 1981, 16, 175–76). The idea of England as a jewel might have come from a famous passage in Shakespeare's drama *Richard II* (ca. 1594):

> This other Eden, demi-Paradise,
> This fortress built by Nature for herself
> Against infection and the hand of war,
> This happy breed of men, this little world,
> This precious stone set in the silver sea,
> Which serves it in the office of a wall
> Or as a moat defensive to a house
> Against the envy of less happier lands—
> This blessed plot, this earth, this realm, this England,
> . . . . . . . . . . . . . . . . . . . .
> . . . bound in with the triumphant sea,
> Whose rocky shore beats back the envious siege
> Of watery Neptune.
> (Shakespeare 1948, 201 [*Richard II* 2.1.42–62];
> see also note for lines 40–56)

7. These ideas were clearly "in the air" at this time. James may well have derived some inspiration from the Shakespearian figure of "Gaunt's" famous lines, cited above, about England from Shakespeare's *Richard II,* which were much admired at the time and quoted in *England's Parnassus* (1600).

8. This idea of the marriage of monarch and state was well established in the tradition that conceived of the state as the secular parallel to the church as mystical body of Christ. The mid-fourteenth-century Neapolitan jurist Lucas de Penna thus used the marriage metaphor to compare the relationship of Christ to his church with that of the prince to his state: "And just as men are joined togeth-

er spiritually in the spiritual body, the head of which is Christ . . . , so are men joined together morally and politically in the *respublica,* which is a body the head of which is the Prince" (quoted in Kantorowicz 1957, 216). The idea of the state as a body politic with the king as head was established by the era of Henry VIII, who used it to refer to "This Realm of England" (OED: body).

9. The islands, as noted in chapter 1, were pawned to Scotland as a form of security for the dowry of King Christian I of Denmark's daughter Margrethe, who married James III of Scotland in 1469 (Bech 1963, 516; Donaldson 1984, 13).

10. The idea of Britain as a world empire had already developed under Elizabeth. George Peele, in *Polyhymnia* (1590) thus writes: "Elizabeth, great Empress of the world, / Britannia's Atlas, star of England's globe" (quoted in Bennett 1956, 125).

11. James I believed that he had a divine right to rule over his imperial British theater of power. In a 1605 speech to Parliament he made the implications of this divine claim clear: "That since Kings are in the word of GOD it selfe called Gods, as being his Lieutenants and Vice-gerents on earth, and so adorned and furnished with some sparkles of the Diunitie; to compare some of the workes of GOD the great KING, towards the whole and generall world, to some of his workes towards mee, and this little world of my Dominions, compassed and seuered by the Sea from the rest of the earth" (James I [1616] 1918a, 281).

12. James I's book *The Trew Laws of Free Monarchies* describes the mutual duties and allegiance "betwixt a free and absolute *Monarche,* and his people." James makes clear here that, as king of Scotland, he built his law first upon divine guidance, then from the "fundamental Laws of our owne Kingdome," and finally from "the law of Nature." In James's opinion, "by the law of Nature the King becomes a naturall Father to all his Lieges at his Coronation" (James I [1616] 1918f, 54–55). This position gave him the right, for example, to suspend "vpon causes onely knowen to him" generall laws "made publikely in Parliament" (ibid., 63). James later explained, in a speech to the English Parliament, what he meant by fundamental laws. They are "onely those Lawes whereby confusion is auoyded, and their Kings descent mainteined, and the heritage of the succession and Monarchie, which hath bene a Kingdome, to which I am in descent, three hundreth yeeres before Christ: Not meaning it as you doe, of their Common Law, for they [the Scots] haue none, but that which is called IVS REGIS" (James I [1616] 1918c, 300). It should be noted, however, that Scottish legal authorities would dispute this, arguing that Scotland did have a common law tradition, though it might diverge in some respects from that of England.

13. Bacon's blending of judicial and scientific concepts of law is manifest in his discourse, as when he writes in "Preparative towards a Natural and Experimental History": "I mean (according to the practice in civil causes) in this great Plea or Suit granted by the divine favor and providence (whereby the human race seeks to recover its right over nature) to examine nature herself and the arts upon interrogatories" (Bacon 1860, 263, quoted in Merchant 1995, 493 n. 10). Michel Foucault has pointed out that Bacon transferred the methodology of the inquisition and the judicial investigation to the empirical sciences (Foucault 1979, 226).

14. The polity had been primed for this form of emperor worship by the earlier deification of Queen Elizabeth (Yates 1975, 29–87). King James shone not only as a sun god, but as an example for the people to follow. As James advised his son, a king must "shine as far before your people in all vertue and honestie, as in greatnesse of ranke, that the use thereof in al your actions, may turne (with time) in a natural habitude unto you, that as by their hearing of your Lawes, so by their sight of your person, both their eies and their eares, maie lead and allure them to the love of vertue and hatred of vice" (James I [1599] 1969, 120). The idealization of the virtue embodied in the king and aristocracy was a moral act through which earthly creatures were to be transformed into beings worthy of the roles as demigods which they were expected to fill (Orgel 1969, 2; Mebane 1989, 156–73).

15. Kirsten Rygg argues that the echo "is clearly coming *from* Elysium; the voice is a voice from the heavenly spheres and speaks of a divine presence, called forth in the end by the dancing of the world's soul" (1996, 310, emphasis in original). This would make sense given the theme of reflection found in the reference in *The Masque of Blackness* to the Pythagorean message of the moon (which Rygg does not discuss) seen in the water of the Nile.

16. This justification for a British Atlantic empire was argued, for example, by the Elizabethan mathematician, magician, and imperial ideologist John Dee (Boon 1987, 3).

17. James wrote: "For when the Bastard of *Normandie* came into *England,* beeing come of the *Norman* blood, and their old Lawes, which to this day they are ruled by, are written in his language, and not in theirs: And yet his successours haue with great happinesse enioyed the Crowne to this day; Wherof the like was also done by all them that conquested them before" (James I [1616] 1918f, 62–63, emphasis in original). The opponents of absolutism, as James notes, argued that "the Lawes and state of our countrey were established before the admitting of a king" but James dismisses them as "seditious writers" (ibid., 62). The opponents of absolutism also argued for the basic continuity of English law, tracing the "ancient constitution" back to pre-Norman societies (like that of the Anglo-Saxons), which were thought to have a parliamentary tradition, with elected monarchs (Pocock 1957; Hill 1958, 50–122; MacDougall 1982, 31–86). This is the established view in England today (Baker 1979, 1–10). The right of conquest did not apply, however, to Scotland, which had not been conquered.

18. Camden recognized that the idea that the Trojan Brute, or Brutus, had settled Britain was so entrenched that "to slight it, would be a war against Time, and combating a received and common opinion." It is for this reason that he has "frequently exerted my utmost to support it." He goes on, nevertheless, to add: "My regard to truth obliges me, however, to premise, that I see men of distinguished judgment and eminent learning endeavouring by various methods to discredit this story, and as often as I undertake its defence I feel the force of their arguments." There follows a page of counterarguments that completely discredit the Trojan thesis (Camden [1607] 1806, li–liv).

19. The fact that relatively little was actually known about pre-Anglo-Saxon

Britain, and that Monmouth's historiographic methods contradicted the scholarly standards being developed by the humanists, created problems for Camden and his contemporary English antiquarians. Camden went along with the Trojan myth while plunging into the more accessible history of the Romans and the Germanic Anglo-Saxons. This interest in the Germanic heritage of Britain, in turn, helped pave the way for the interest, later in the seventeenth century, of the parliamentarian countrymen in the political heritage of the "Gothic" Anglo-Saxons (Douglas 1939, 60–92; Kliger 1952; MacDougall 1982, 31–70; Kunst 1994, 95–99). James clearly knew what he was doing in 1614, when he ordered the disbandment of the Society of Antiquaries (which Camden had helped found), overriding its members' protests that it was not engaged in political speculation (MacDougall 1982, 42).

20. Vitruvius and Palladio were both, according to Kristin Rygg, influenced by Pythagorean mysticism in their use of geometrical and numerical proportions (Rygg 1996, 185–89).

21. For the 1608 *Haddington Masque,* which Ben Jonson wrote for a noble wedding, Jones designed:

> [A] huge revolving globe, with golden band placed around it to represent the ecliptic (the line followed by the planets). Twelve masquers were placed on this construction to represent the twelve signs of the zodiac, and were presented one by one, commencing in the conventional way with Aries and ending with Pisces. The symbolism of each sign is interpreted in relation to marriage. The summer solstice (the entry of Cancer) is construed in terms of reversal, the wife yielding to the authority of her husband. The winter solstice (Capricorn) is related to the sun, i.e. male passion, renewing his fires. (Wiles 1993, 50)

22. For a description of how a gentleman of the time might have understood the revolution of the celestial spheres and Plato's revolutionary cosmology, see Peacham 1962, 70–71.

23. This Virgin goddess was identified with the astrological sign of Virgo, which dominates the month named for Augustus. This was the time of harvest, so she also carries a sheaf of wheat, which helps link her to fertility goddesses such as Ceres, but also to the figure of Natura (Economou 1972, 85; Yates 1975, 30–33).

CHAPTER 4. LANDSCAPING THE BODY POLITIC
OF THE BRITISH STATE

1. The word *state* was synonymous with *throne,* the monarch's seat. A primary meaning of *seat* is "a special chair (as a throne) of one in eminence; also: the status of which such chair is an emblem" (WU3: seat, 1a). The status, or standing, attributed to this elevated seat was emphasized by the fact that most guests at a court masque had to stand up, and the best standing position was closest to the monarch. The words *estate* and *state* likewise suggested position, status, or station in a hierarchy which involved a form of graduated relation between a number of parts (Dowdall 1923, 102). The word *stage* has an etymology similar to words like *status, station,* and *state;* it still carried such mean-

ings during the Stuart era, whereas the application of the word *stage* to the platform upon which players perform was of relatively recent date (1551) (OED:
stage 2, 5). On the construction of the masque theater and its political implications, see Orgel and Strong 1973, 1–14; Orgel 1975.

2. Jones would have learned this idea from the theater designers of Renaissance Italy, particularly Palladio. He later rebuilt a theater (the Cockpit
Theater at Whitehall) along Italian lines for James's son King Charles I (Parry
1981, 160–61).

3. The frontispiece to the *Basilicon Doron* (The kingly gift) includes the figure of a prince looking into a mirror. The opening dedicatory sonnet begins with
the lines: "Lo heere (my Sonne) a mirrour vieue and faire, Which sheweth the
shaddow of a worthy King." Premonitions of death are supposed to have
prompted James I to write this book in 1598 as a private political testament for
the edification of the infant "Henrie my Dearest sonne and natural svccessour"
(whom the king was to outlive). Various unauthorized editions of the book were
circulated despite the king's apparent prohibition, so a revised authorized version was published in 1599 (James I [1599] 1969, introductory note). It became a best-seller both in England and abroad during the Renaissance, and it was
quickly translated into a variety of languages including Latin, French, Welsh,
and Swedish.

4. On the influence of Pythagorean mysticism upon the masque, see Rygg
1996. Pythagoras is discussed further in chapter 6.

5. On the role of the principles of perspective in allowing the simultaneous,
rather than successive, perception of figure and ground in a unified space, see
Kernodle 1944; Spitzer 1963, 43.

6. My thanks to historian and pastor Torben Damsholt, Vartov Church,
Copenhagen, for help with this translation from the Latin (Vulgate) Bible,
Job 41.24. It is interesting to note that the King James version of the Bible is
worded slightly different from Hobbes's Latin Bible. It does not include the word
*power,* or *potestas* in the Latin. *Potestas* was used in the English of Hobbes's day
to refer to forms of power that were quite relevant to Hobbes's conception of the
state (OED: potestas, potestate).

7. The emerging importance of the landscape scene as a metaphor for the
body politic is also evident in the work of Niccolò Machiavelli, one of the first
and most influential Renaissance writers on the state. In the dedication to *The
Prince,* Machiavelli is careful to position the estate of the prince in relation to
himself, and to the prince's subjects, in the cartographic space of a landscape. It
is this spatialized political landscape that the author presumes to survey from his
humble position:

> Nor, I hope, will it be considered impudent that a man of low and mean station
> presumes to discuss and arrange the governments of princes. For just as those who
> draw maps place themselves low down on the plains to consider the nature of the
> mountains and high place, and place themselves in the mountains and high place
> to consider the plains, so in the same way it is necessary to be a prince in order to
> understand clearly the nature of the people and to be of the people to understand
> the nature of princes. (Machiavelli [1513] 1995, 37)

8. Hobbes, as noted in the introduction to this book, discusses the persona in terms of stages and masks (the word *person* coming from the Latin for mask); see Hobbes [1651] 1991, 112–13.

9. My thanks to the anthropologist Judith Ennew, Cambridge, for reminding me of Elizabeth's peripatetic movements.

10. According to the literary scholar David Wiles: "While the Jacobean play offered a mimesis of social reality, the Jacobean masque offered a Neoplatonic vision of the ideal. While common players performed plays, masques were for the elite. Through music, dance and tricks played with light and stage machinery, the Jacobean masque suggested the existence of a transcendent reality" (Wiles 1993, 43).

11. In the Machiavellian concept of the state as theater, there is a clear line of demarcation between the actual behind-the-scenes machinations of the prince and the mask which the state presents to the public. (Jonson, himself, was known to play upon this kind of duality between the ideal and the pragmatic in his work and was sometimes known as "Monsieur Machiavelli" [Boughner 1968, 73–88].)

12. The use of the word *stage* to refer to segments in a journey, such as a progress, was peculiarly English and first developed around 1600 (OED: stage 4).

13. The author of the 1618 "Maxims of State" (one of the earliest formulations of the idea of the territorial state, long presumed to be by Walter Raleigh) gave expression to this idea in the following words: "State is the frame or set order of a commonwealth, or of the governor that rule the same, especially of the Chief and Sovereign Governor that commandeth the rest. State or sovereignty consisteth of five points: 1. The making or annulling of laws. 2. Creating and disposing of magistrates. 3. Power over life and death 4. Making of war or peace. 5. Highest or last appeal. Where these five are either in one or more there is the State" (quoted in Dowdall 1923, 121). The idea of the "frame" at this time was closely related to the Neoplatonic-Platonic ideal of the grid underlying the surface design of the map, the perspective drawing, or the architecture of the theater of state as envisioned by Jones (Yates 1969, 27–28, 80–91, 169–85). On Raleigh's Neoplatonism, see Mebane 1989, 79–83. Although it is no longer certain that Raleigh was the author of this work, it reflects the kind of thinking he espoused (Pocock 1975, 355–56).

14. On the connection between Jones's architecture and stagecraft, see Yates 1969, 80–91, 169–85.

15. For Jonson, the importance of the masque lay in the ability of the text to express abstract ideas in poetic form—the true soul of the masque. The invention was the creation of the poet; it was the idea for the whole dramatic fable, which is the "device" or narrative that carries its "argument." This division of labor was clear in *The Masque of Blackness*, where he wrote "Invented by Ben Jonson" on the title page (Jonson 1969, 48). Jones, on the other hand, is only mentioned in passing: "So much for the bodily part, which was of Master Inigo Jones his design and act" (Jonson 1969, 50). Later, no doubt reluctantly, Jonson listed Jones as co-inventor of their masques. The final dramatic blow-up between the two occurred when Jonson infuriated Jones by listing himself first on the title

page as the inventor of the 1631 masque *Love's Triumph through Callipolis* (Gordon 1949, 153).

16. Jonson was disturbed by the way the apparent realism of the illusions created by the surveyor-architect upstaged the abstract mental principles, or "soul," of the masque (Gordon 1949). The mystification generated by masque scenery plays upon the confusion between the concrete form of a symbol and the content of its abstract message. For Jonson, the body of the masque belonged to the world of the senses—it was the outward celebration or show. His statement that for Jones, "painting and carpentry are the soul of masque" was a bitter reversal of his own real position (Gordon 1949, 159–160; Jonson 1985, 463 n. 722). The problem of confusing the sign for the thing signified appears to have been endemic to the Neoplatonism of the Renaissance. According to Ernst H. Gombrich: "Where every natural object can be conceived as a sign or symbol, every symbol, in its turn, will be thought of as existing 'by nature' rather than by convention. . . . The very confusion of Neoplatonic thought helped to weld form and content, symbolic significance and aesthetic effect, together" (Gombrich 1948, 181).

17. This passage occurs in the opening scene of a welcome "entertainment" performed before the king and queen during a visit to the fantasy castle of Bolsover, the home of the earl of Newcastle, on July 10, 1634. In this sketch Jones is portrayed as a "mechanic surveyor" who choreographs a dance performed by a group of "mechanics" (craftsmen in the building trade), with a blacksmith named Smith beating out the rhythm. At the end of the dance Iniquo exclaims: "Well done, my musical, arithmetical, geometrical gamesters; or rather my true mathematical boys! It is carried in number, weight, and measure, as if the airs were all harmony, and the figures a well-timed proportion!" (Jonson [1634] 1873, 664).

18. The king, surveying the scene from his elevated throne of state, bears a certain resemblance to prison personnel surveying the prisoners in Jeremy Bentham's nineteenth-century panopticon, as described by Michel Foucault. Foucault traces the development of state surveillance back to the Renaissance (Foucault 1979, 195–228). Bentham was a jurist who, like James I and Francis Bacon, was an advocate of statutory law (Baker 1979, 186–87).

19. The poem reads, in part:

> . . . O showes! Shows! Mighty shows!
> The eloquence of masques! What need of prose,
> Or verse, or sense, to express immortal you?
> You are the spectacles of state! Tis true
> Court hieroglyphics, and all arts afford
> In the mere perspective of an inch-board [painted scenery].
> You ask no more than certain politic eyes,
> Eyes that can pierce into the mysteries
> Of many colours, read them, and reveal
> Mythology there painted on slit deal.
> Oh, to make boards to speak! There is a task!
> Painting and carpentry are the soul of masque
> Pack with your peddling poetry to the stage:
> This is the money-get, mechanic age!

To plant the music where no ear can reach,
Attire the persons as no thought can teach
Sense what they are: which, by a specious, fine
Term of the architects, is called *design*!
But in the practised truth destruction is
Of any art beside that he calls his.
 ("An Expostulation with Inigo Jones" [1631]
  in Jonson 1985, 462–65).

20. Shakespeare's plays were performed at the Globe Theater, and the famous phrase about the world's being a stage may have been inspired by the Globe's motto, "Totus mundus agit histrionem" (The whole world plays the actor) (Shakespeare 1948, 493, 509–10, [*As You Like It* 2.7.138–66]; Yates 1969; Tuan 1982, 86–113).

21. The transition from the symbolism of punishment by violating the body as a spectacle to punishment by putting the accused under surveillance, as institutionalized in the prison, is described and analyzed in Foucault 1979. The theatrical qualities of Charles's execution (see Orgel 1975) combine, I would suggest, both forms of symbolism at an important juncture in the evolution of the mentality of surveillance.

22. As the literary critic David Wiles puts it: "When Elizabeth and James laid claim to the emblems of the Moon and the Sun, they took control of a discourse that could easily threaten them. For every Ulysses [a figure in Shakespeare's *Troilus and Cressida*] championing the established political order, there was a Richard Harvey looking to the skies for the possibility of subversion" (Wiles 1993, 134). This sort of cosmic revolutionary threat is suggested in a short treatise from 1648 on "the birth, increase and decay of monarchies," in which it is written that "it is impossible for the greatest Princes, or Statesmen to prevent the change and revolutions of Common-weales and Monarchies, by their wisdom, policy, valour, and the powere of their men of warre, if the day of their ruine, appointed by the secret counsell of God, be come" (quoted in Rachum 1995, 199).

23. Much of the scholarly debate concerning the seventeenth-century origins of the modern concept of revolution has revolved around the question of whether revolution meant a cyclical return to the past or a progressive lineal break with the past. This, to my mind, is something of a moot point because the concept of revolution can mean the return to a new and fresh beginning (Lovejoy and Boas 1935, 5; Nisbet 1969, 44–61). Plato's cosmology thus allowed both for progressive development within our age and the possibility of a cataclysmic break which ushers in a new age under a different form of governance. The modern revolutionary theory of Marx and Engels similarly involves a return to a state of communism that is the primitive state of man, even though the utopian communist society envisioned for the future represents a radical break with the past and with history (Marx [1848] 1969; Hyams 1974, 43–64).

CHAPTER 5. LANDSCAPING BRITAIN'S COUNTRY AND NATURE

1. The worthies included in the temple were, as listed by Clarke "Pope, Gresham, Inigo Jones, Milton, Shakespeare, Locke, Newton, Bacon, Coke,

Alfred, Edward Prince of Wales, Queen Elizabeth, William III, Raleigh, Drake, Hampden, and Barnard" (Clarke 1973, 571).

2. It has been suggested that the idea of dedicating a location to British worthies derived from a royal masque, *Coelum Britannicum,* with text by Thomas Carew and scenery by Inigo Jones (Woodbridge 1974, 133). It was first performed at Jones's Whitehall Banqueting House on Shrove Tuesday night, February 18, 1634, and was "danced" by a cast including the king, eleven Lords (a-leaping) and ten pages. It included a magnificent scene celebrating the "genius" of Britain, who unites England, Scotland, and Ireland. This genius calls upon the wild mountainous landscape scenery of the place:

> . . . from your womb,
> Which is the cradle and the tomb
> Of British worthies, fair sons, send
> A troop of heroes, that may lend
> Their hand to ease this loaden grove
> And gather the ripe fruits of love.

At this point the worthies emerged from a cave and the wild scenery was replaced by a scene of a garden filled with architecture reminiscent of that in Stowe's Elysian fields (masque reproduced in Orgel and Strong 1973, 567–89, quotation on 578). This particular garden was in the formal style of the time, but Jones also created pastoral landscape scenes which clearly resemble the informal style of gardening pioneered by Kent.

3. For a comparison of Dryden's translation with a more literal translation, see chapter 6.

4. The juxtaposition of temples appears to have been inspired by a passage by Addison (Clarke 1973). On Addison's Whig interpretation of landscape as scenery, see Bermingham 1994, 84–85.

5. Compare Dryden's version with a modern and more literal translation of the ancient text which reads: "Happy was he whose wit availed to grasp the origin of things" (Virgil 1946, 115 [*Georgics* 2.585–86]).

6. The following passage from a topographical poem by Gilbert West describes the view from Queens Theater, with her statue erected on four columns, as well as the King's Pillar and statue:

> Beyond, a sylvan Theatre displays
> Its circling Bosom to the noon-tide Rays.
> In shade, o're shade, the sloping ranks ascend . . .
>
> .   .   .   .   .   .   .   .   .   .   .   .   .   .   .   .
> And see! Where, elevated far above,
> A Column [the King's Pillar] overlooks yon nodding Grove;
> On which, the Scene of Glory to compleat,
> Deck'd with the Ensigns of Imperial State,
> Stands the great Father, George, whose equal Sway,
> With Joy Britannia's happy Realms obey.
> Thence round, he views the cultivated Plain,
> That smiling speaks the Blessings of his Reign.
> Thus, o'er their Planets radiant Suns preside,

By Heav'n's fixt Laws their various Courses guide;
And shedding round Benevolence divine,
Bless'd by depending Worlds, indulgent shine.
(West [1732] 1990, 46–47, lines 256–58, 279–90)

7. This reification of the meaning of land eventually made it necessary to create such neologisms as *seascape,* which dates from the late eighteenth century, and *townscape,* which dates from the late nineteenth century (OED: seascape, townscape).

8. For pertinent discussions of differing conceptions of space, see Tuan 1977 and Sack 1980.

9. The word *moral* derives from the Latin *morals,* from *mor-* (as in *mores*), meaning custom (MWC10: moral).

10. Civic humanism was an idea that found support in the influential ideas of Machiavelli who, though he is most famous for his work on the position of "the prince," also gave representative institutions an important role in his ideas concerning the state. This complex of ideas gave rise to what the historian J. G. A. Pocock has termed a "Machiavellian moment" in British history that found expression in the ideology of "civic humanism" (Pocock 1975, 401–61). Civic humanism required the participation of the educated citizen of standing in the governing of the country. Another source of these ideas was the ancient Arcadian historian Polybius (ibid., 593). On Polybius's importance to Camden as "the great master of history" and to other writers of "civil" history, see Trevor-Roper 1971, 21.

11. The garden historian Kenneth Woodbridge writes of Walpole: "Walpole's greatest disservice to the history of gardening was his prejudice. By opposing the English style to the French, exaggerating the artificiality of the one and the naturalness of the other, he inhibited a true appreciation of either. What countryman of Le Nôtre could tolerate the arrogant assertion 'We have discovered the point of perfection. We have given the true model of gardening to the world'?" (Woodbridge 1974, 126).

CHAPTER 6. GENDERING THE NATION'S NATURAL LANDSCAPE

1. The scanty apparel worn by the masquers struck some members of the court audience as being "too light and Curtizan-like for such great ones" (quoted in Orgel and Strong 1973, 89). Many of the opponents of the court were scandalized.

2. The lone riverine male that I can discern on the map is the Thames, who must be male because he is made to marry the female Isis.

3. One meaning of nature is, of course, "man's original or natural condition" (WC7: nature 7a).

4. On the relation between ideas of paradise and ideas of nature, see Merchant 1995 and Olwig 1995b.

5. On the meanings of choros and chora, see Cornford 1937, 177–210; Liddell 1940, 2016–17: choros, chora.

6. On this distinction between a vertical and horizontal cosmology, see Tuan

1974b, 129–49.

7. The classic study of this cosmology is Eliade 1971.

8. Serenitas is dressed "in a garment of bright sky color, a long tress, and waved with a veil of diver colors, such as the golden sky sometimes shows; upon her head a clear and fair sun shining, with rays of gold striking down to the feet of the figure." She holds "a crystal cut with several angles and shadowed with divers colors, as caused by refraction," whereas Germinatio is clad "in green, with a zone of gold about her waist, crowned with myrtle, her hair likewise flowing, but not of so bright a color; in her hand a branch of myrtle. Her socks of green and gold" (Jonson 1969, 67 [*Beauty* lines 163–72]).

9. The importance of harmony explains why the nymph who dominates the masque is Harmonia, who is "a personage whose dressing had something of all the others, and had her robe painted full of figures. Her head was compassed with a crown of gold, having in it seven jewels equally set [the seven planets and their spheres enumerated by Pythagoras]. In her hand a lyre whereon she rested" (Jonson 1969, 69, n. 513 [*Beauty* lines 195–98]).

10. The harmonic element in Renaissance science is most notable in Johannes Kepler's revolutionary *Harmonice Mundi* from 1618, which combined geometric and harmonic conceptualizations (Koestler 1964).

11. According to Leonardo this sense of vision is active, not passive—it appeals to an uneasy soul. One could stay in place, but then, "your soul could not enjoy the pleasures that come to it through the eyes, the windows of its habitation." Vision is "the very quintessence, the spirit of the elements, which finding itself imprisoned within the soul is ever longing to return from the human body to its giver, and you must know that this same longing is that quintessence, inseparable from nature, and that man is the image of the world" (quoted in Turner 1966, 25–26, 37). This visual, embodied space suffuses the landscape scenery that Jones constructed to represent the reign of rational, sciential law proclaimed by the Stuart monarchs.

CHAPTER 7. LANDSCAPING RACIAL AND NATIONAL PROGRESS

1. Jonson concludes the introduction to the masque with the words "Hence, because it was her majesty's will to have them blackamores at first, the invention was derived by me, and presented thus" (Jonson 1969, 48). The idea of a "black masque" may have come to Anne from reports of a masque performed at her brother Christian's coronation in 1596. It involved a scene with *blaamænd*, literally "blue men," which is to say actors costumed as naked Africans. They were played by members of her brother-in law Julius of Braunschweig-Wülfenbüttel's English troupe that, in turn, had ties to the Admiral's Men, who played at the Rose Theater in London. The players at the Rose later became associated with the troupe called the Queen's Men (Neiiendam 1988, 96–99; Risum 1992, 49).

2. Jonson appears to have gotten this idea about the white land from William Camden's *Britannia*. Jonson gives the source as Orpheus's *Argonautica*, but the editor of the masques could not trace this reference and attributes it rather to Camden (Jonson 1969, 54 [*Blackness* lines 180–81, n. 511]). Camden is the

likely source not only because of Jonson's personal ties to him, but because such key elements in *The Masque of Blackness* as the idea of Albion as the son of Neptune, the reference to the white cliffs, and a discussion of the meaning of *tania* (land) are all found in Camden's work within a few pages of each other, under the heading "Name of Britain" ([1607] 1806, 1:lxv–lxix). Camden gives credence to the idea that the land of Albion was named for Albion son of Neptune and that Albion derives from the Greek word for white, "for it is encompassed with white rocks, which Cicero calls *mirificæ moles,* 'amazing masses,' whence, on the coins of Antoninus Pius and Severus, Britain is represented as a woman sitting on rocks, and British poets themselves call her *Inis Wen* (S) q.d. *White Island* (T)" (ibid., 1:lxv–lxvi).

3. An important analysis of the relationship between racism and the origins of the nation-state is to be found in Segal and Handler 1992.

4. Teutonism refers to the idea of a supposed single national origin of the Germanic tribes of northern Europe. Teutonism was by no means limited to Germany; it is found, for example, in the French identification with the Germanic Franks (as opposed to the Celtic Gauls). Arianism was the outgrowth of linguistic speculation that saw the Indo-European language as an indicator of race.

5. The noble status of the odel was not the case everywhere; in Norway, to this day, an odel farmer is not a nobleman, but a yeoman with an ancestral farm.

6. There was nothing new about the idea that human activity could modify the climate; it can be traced back at least as far as the Greek historian Polybius (ca. 205–ca. 125 B.C.E.), whose works were very influential in the seventeenth and eighteenth centuries (Glacken 1967, 96).

7. Burke's aesthetics and politics are examined in Mitchell 1986, 116–49; see also Wood 1964.

8. Because of his opposition to John Locke and others who propounded theories of innate natural rights, Burke is often described as being opposed to natural law. Burke's political ideas, however, were thoroughly rooted in the tradition of natural law. The confusion concerning this issue derives from the fact that the traditional religious ideas of natural law were being conflated at this time with the laws of natural science by thinkers like Locke and Thomas Hobbes. Burke, on the other hand, was inclined to give weight to the relative importance of inherited tradition rather than to absolute scientific principles (Stanlis [1958] 1965).

9. On Leviathan, see Burke 1759, part 2, section 5 ("Power"); on other monsters, see ibid., 58–61, 305–6.

10. Macpherson appears to have combined "fragments" of actual Scottish folklore, collected on field trips to the Highlands, within an epic framework constructed according to the ideas of Blair. This has created considerable confusion because defenders of the genuineness of the Ossian corpus can legitimately point to clear parallels in Scottish folklore, whereas critics tend to focus on the suspect character of the epic framework, with all too obvious parallels, for example, to the works of Homer. It does not help that both pro- and anti-Celtic feelings sometimes makes these waters even murkier (Olwig 1984, 23).

11. On the contemporary implications of the dichotomy of culture and nature

for social science, see Pálsson 1996.

12. The Danish-German poet Jens Baggesen was perhaps the first to coin (ca. 1800) what has become the modern German word for environment, *Umwelt* (*omverden* in Danish). The first recorded English use of the term *environment* comes from a passage by Thomas Carlyle (1795–1881) in which Carlyle discusses Goethe's commentary on the fact that Ossian had found the perfect locale for English melancholy (Spitzer 1948, 236–45).

13. *Wilhelm Tell* is full of references to the ancestral customs of the Swiss lands; at the famous meeting at Rütli Mead, for example, the representative of a land proclaims: "'Tis well. Let our old customs here prevail; Though night be dark, the light of justice shines" (Schiller 1972, 49, 2.2).

14. Though Schiller made free use of myth and imagination, he also undertook in-depth historical research, as exemplified by his history of the revolt of the United Netherlands (Schiller [1788] 1889; [1788] 1922). Schiller's Swiss express a love of freedom, which he believed had been preserved not only in Switzerland, under the protection of difficult mountainous terrain, but also in Frisia, by the marshes; he admired the Frisians for preserving the ancestral customs which guaranteed their *Landesfreiheit,* "the liberty of the country" (Schiller [1788] 1889, 22; [1788] 1922, 21).

15. Two of Steffens's weightier contributions to historical geology are Steffens [1801] 1973 and Steffens 1810. The importance of Steffens's geology is indicated by the fact that the latter work was recently (1973) republished in facsimile in a series of geological classics published by Meridian in Amsterdam.

16. For a highly relevant overview of the geographical ideas of this era, see Livingstone 1992, 216–59.

17. The art historian Timothy Mitchell suggests that the German *Kulturlandschaft* paintings from this time should be termed *Bildunglandschaft* because of the emphasis upon the historical process of development (Mitchell 1993, 143).

18. W. J. T. Mitchell has described the conception of landscape developing at this time as "imperial" because it legitimizes "the claim that not merely landscape *painting,* but the visual perception of landscape is a revolutionary historical discovery of the European Renaissance that marks, in Ruskin's words, 'the simple fact that we are, in some strange way, different from all the great races that existed before us.'" This form of argument exemplifies what Mitchell has termed "the 'natural history' of modernity," or "the teleology of modernism," or, alternatively, "the teleology of landscape"—that is, the idea that phylogenesis recapitulates ontogenesis in the stratified development of a mature civilization. This development can be measured by a society's ability to comprehend its world as a horizontal landscape scene, controlled by abstract laws (Mitchell 1995, 104; see also Mitchell 1994).

19. The quotation is from Spengler, *Der Untergang des Abendlandes: Umrisse einer Morphologie der Weltgeschichte* (The Decline of the West) (Munich, 1920), 1:28. It reads, in the original, "Kulturen, die mit urweltlicher Kraft aus dem Schosse einer mütterlichen Landschaft, an die jede von ihnen im ganzen Verlauf ihres Daseins streng gebunden ist, aufblühen." For the role of German geo-

graphical science in generating this concept of landscape, see Sandner 1994.

20. A Jutlander would thus say, "*Æ* Jyde" (the Jute), whereas it would be "Jyd*en*" (Jute the) in standard Danish.

## CHAPTER 8. THE "COUNTRY" OF THE UNITED STATES CONTRA THE "LANDSCAPE" OF AMERICA'S NEW WORLD

1. Some relevant studies are Lowenthal 1964; Smith 1970; Graber 1976; Nash 1976; Cronon 1983; Cosgrove 1984; Boime 1991; Daniels 1993a; and Tuan 1996.

2. The quoted passages are from two popular American national songs (Smith [1831] 1974; and Bates [1895] 1974).

3. This tenet about westward progress was proved, according to Thoreau, by Australia's lack of progress: "Within a few years we have witnessed the phenomenon of a southeastward migration, in the settlement of Australia; but this effects us as a retrograde movement, and, judging from the moral and physical character of the first generation of Australians has not yet proved a successful experiment" ([1862] 1991, 86–87).

4. Thoreau uses imagery taken from a well-known passage in Virgil's *Georgics* to argue that the pioneer's heroism lies not in his use of "the sword and lance" but in "the buschwhack, the turf-cutter, the spade, and the bog-hoe, rusted with the blood of many a meadow" (ibid., 102). Compare with Virgil: "Now hear what weapons hardy rustics need, Ere they can plough or sow the crop to come: Firstly a ploughshare and the curvèd plough" (1946, 70–71 [*Georgics* 1.193–95]).

5. Thoreau continues the theme of justice in the following paragraph, by praising he who looks not to the past for precedence but to the present and future as "an expression of the health and soundness of Nature." Where such thinking prevails, "no fugitive slave laws are passed. Who has not betrayed his master many times since last he heard that note?" ([1862] 1991, 120). The counterposing of natural, timeless justice to the tyranny of custom and the past is a familiar theme in discussions of natural justice as personified by Astraea.

6. The term "shire town" is taken from Thoreau's description of Concord in "Civil DisobedianceDisobedience" ([1849] 1983, 405).

7. The idea of Nature as the vicar of God seems to occur several times in Emerson's text. In a passage which distinguishes natura naturata from natura naturans, he writes: "Nature, in its ministry to man, is not only the material but also the process and result." Later, he writes: "That essence [Spirit] refuses to be recorded in propositions, but when man has worshipped him intellectually, the noblest ministry of nature is to stand as the apparition of God" ([1836] 1991, 11, 54).

8. Yellowstone, established in 1872, is technically the first national park. Because there was no state to administer Yellowstone at the time, it was born a national park, and it set a precedent for the nationalization of Yosemite. Yosemite was placed under the control of the state of California in 1864, but it was the first park set aside by act of Congress. A national park was created for

the area surrounding Yosemite Valley in 1890. The National Park Service first assumed control of the valley in 1906.

9. See also McLaughlin et al. 1977a, 24; and Censer 1986b, 516–19.

10. Olmsted's parks, like those of the English aristocrats, were to be kept clear of the native population as well as homesteaders claiming land on the basis of "customary" law (Olmsted [1865] 1990, 508).

11. On the role of fire in maintaining such environments, see Stewart 1956 and Vankat 1977.

12. Olmsted began his career as a country gentleman farmer. He believed he had a mission to improve agricultural practices in America and often used methods first developed in Britain. He eventually became a landscape architect who, like Kent, worked on the estates of others. This career began on the vast Mariposa mining estate in California and drew to a close when the sixty-seven-year-old architect planned the grounds of George W. Vanderbilt's Biltmore estate in Asheville, North Carolina, which combined landscape aesthetics with improved techniques of forestry (Spirn 1995, 92–95, 99–102). It is significant that the man recruited to head the forestry project at Biltmore, Gifford Pinchot, later became one of the chief architects of Theodore Roosevelt's conservation crusade, which wedded conservation to a vision of progress (McLaughlin et al. 1977a, 44). It was during this time that the American government began to undertake vast conservation projects which combined huge dams for irrigation and power with landscape restoration projects for forestry and recreation (Hays 1959).

13. In this quotation, Muir was writing of Yosemite Valley's smaller twin, the Hetch Hetchy Valley.

14. Bunell was the diarist for the military expedition of Major James D. Savage, whose mission was to further mining interests by evicting the Ahwahneeche Indians from Yosemite.

15. On St. John, in the Virgin Islands of the United States, there is another national park which has grown unkempt. The "native born" St. Johnians have a phrase which suggests an environmental aesthetic similar to that of Totuya: "man die, bush grow a he door mout" (K. F. Olwig 1980, 22–31).

16. See Tuan 1996, 76–99.

CONCLUSION

1. I explore the rhetorical connection between *common* and *place* in Olwig 2001.

2. Tuan may have inadvertently reversed the process when he wrote: "Landscape came to mean a prospect seen from a specific standpoint. Then it was the artistic representation of that prospect." I believe the reverse order to be true, and standard dictionaries also place artistic representation prior to the sense of landscape as a "portion of territory that can be viewed at one time from one place" (MWC10: landscape).

3. The character of political landscape is exemplified in a passage by the American jurist Lawrence H. Tribe about a deceased justice of the Supreme

Court: "To describe William J. Brennan Jr. as one of the greatest justices of all time is to put things too abstractly. Before Brennan, the Bill of Rights protected people mostly from the federal government but scarcely from states and cities. . . . Through his 1,360 opinions, Justice Brennan changed all that, building an edifice of common sense and uncommon wisdom that transformed the landscape of America" (Tribe 1997, 19).

4. These definitions also appear to be historically or socially at odds, as when the dictionary makes landscape a "view of natural inland scenery" at a time when such paintings were rarely of "nature" (which the language was yet to define as scenery) and not necessarily "inland," but frequently of country life in coastal places.

5. This may explain why some dictionaries, like the *Oxford English Dictionary,* overlook the early primacy of landscape's meaning as region or country in both the Dutch and English (Klein 1967: landscape; WU3: landscape). This lacuna facilitates the linear presentation of landscape as a scenic concept derived from painting. Yet other senses have survived alongside that of the scenic.

6. On landscape and the "imperial" mindset, see Mitchell 1994 and Olwig 2001.

# Bibliography

Addison, Mr. [Joseph]. [1697] 1806. "An Essay on the Georgics." In *The Works of Virgil, translated into English Verse by Mr. Dryden,* edited by John Carey, 83–95. London: Vernor et al.

Akrigg, G. P. V. 1962. *Jacobean Pageant: or The Court of King James I.* London: Hamish Hamilton.

Alberti, Leon Battista. [1435–36] 1956. *On Painting.* London: Routledge and Kegan Paul.

Alpers, Svetlana. 1983. *The Art of Describing: Dutch Art in the Seventeenth Century.* Chicago: University of Chicago Press.

Ancher, Peder Kofod. 1809. "Bevis at vore gamle Love ikke er tagne af Saxenspiegel." In *Samlede Juridiske Skrifter,* edited by R. Nyerup and J. F. W. Schlegel, 110–89, 190–96 (editors' commentary). Copenhagen: Soldin.

Anderson, Benedict. 1991. *Imagined Communities: Reflections on the Origin and Spread of Nationalism.* Revised ed. London: Verso.

Anderson, Perry. 1974. *Lineages of the Absolutist State.* London: New Left Review Books.

Anonymous. [1738] 1990. "Lord Cobhams Gardens 1738." In *Descriptions of Lord Cobham's Gardens at Stowe (1700–1750),* edited by G. B. Clarke, 66–76. Buckinghamshire: Buckinghamshire Record Society.

Anonymous. [1743] 1990. "To the author of the poem on Lord C-B-M's Gardens." In *Descriptions of Lord Cobham's Gardens at Stowe (1700–1750),* edited by G. B. Clarke, 111. Buckinghamshire: Buckinghamshire Record Society.

Appleton, Jay. 1975. *The Experience of Landscape.* London: Wiley.

Aristotle. 1934. *The Nicomachean Ethics.* Cambridge, Mass.: Harvard University Press.

Aristotle. 1962. *The Politics of Aristotle.* New York: Oxford University Press.

Aubin, Robert Arnold. 1936. *Topographical Poetry in XVIII Century England.* New York: Modern Language Association of America.

Auden, W. H. 1967. *The Enchafèd Flood: Three Critical Essays on the Romantic Spirit.* New York: Vintage.

Bacon, Francis. [1627] 1915. *New Atlantis.* Oxford: Clarendon Press.

Bacon, Francis. 1860. "Preparative Towards a Natural and Experimental History, Such as May Serve for the Foundation of a True Philosophy." In *The Works of Francis Bacon,* edited by James Spedding, 249–71. London: Longman.

Bader, Karl Siegfried. 1957. *Das mittelalterliche Dorf als Friedens- und Rechts-bereich.* Weimar: Böhlau.

Bader, Karl Siegfried. 1978. *Der deutsche Südwesten in seiner territorial-staatlichen Entwicklung.* 2d ed. Sigmaringen: Jan Thorbecke.

Bailyn, Bernard. 1967. *The Ideological Origins of the American Revolution.* Cambridge, Mass.: Harvard University Press.

Baker, J. H. 1979. *An Introduction to English Legal History.* 2d ed. London: Butterworths.

Bakhtin, Mikhail. 1984. *Rabelais and His World.* Bloomington: Indiana University Press.

Barber, C. L. 1959. *Shakepeare's Festive Comedy.* Princeton, N.J.: Princeton University Press.

Barkan, Leonard. 1975. *Nature's Work of Art: The Human Body as Image of the World.* New Haven: Yale University Press.

Barnes, Trevor J., and James S. Duncan, eds. 1992. *Writing Worlds: Discourse, Text and Metaphor in the Representation of Landscape.* London: Routledge.

Barrell, John. 1972. *The Idea of Landscape and the Sense of Place.* Cambridge: Cambridge University Press.

Barrell, John. 1986. *The Political Theory of Painting from Reynolds to Hazlitt: "The Body of the Public."* New Haven: Yale University Press.

Barrell, John. 1992. *The Birth of Pandora.* London: Macmillan.

Barthes, Roland. [1957] 1972. *Mythologies.* New York: Hill and Wang.

Bataille, Georges. [1957] 1987. *Eroticism.* London: Marion Boyars.

Bates, Katharine Lee. [1895] 1974. "America, the Beautiful." In *The Good Times Songbook,* edited by James Leisy, 24–26. Nashville: Abingdon Press.

Battisti, Carlo, and Giovanni Alessio. 1975. *Dizionario etimologico italiano.* Florence: Instituto di Glottologia, G. Barbèra.

Bech, Svend Cedergreen. 1963. *Danmarks Historie: Reformation og Rennæssance, 1533–1596.* Copenhagen: Politiken.

Bech, Svend Cedergreen. 1979. *Dansk Biografisk Leksikon.* 16 vols. Copenhagen: Gyldendal.

Bender, Barbara. 1993. "Landscape—Meaning and Action." In *Landscape: Politics and Perspectives,* edited by Barbara Bender, 1–17. Oxford: Berg.

Benecke, G. 1974. *Society and Politics in Germany, 1500–1750.* London: Routledge and Kegan Paul.

Benediktsson, Jakob et al. 1981. *Kulturhistorisk Leksikon for Nordisk Middelalder fra Vikingtid til Reformationstid.* 10 vols. Copenhagen: Rosenkilde og Bagger.

Benesch, Otto. 1965. *The Art of the Renaissance in Northern Europe.* London: Phaidon.

Bennett, J. A. 1982. *The Mathematical Science of Christopher Wren.* Cambridge: Cambridge University Press.

Bennett, Josephine Waters. 1956. "Britain among the Fortunate Isles." *Studies in Philology* 53 (1): 114–40.

Benveniste, Emile. 1973. *Indo-European Language and Society.* London: Faber and Faber.

Berger, John. 1972. *Ways of Seeing.* Harmondsworth: Penguin.

Bermingham, Ann. 1987. *Landscape and Ideology: The English Rustic Tradition.* London: Thames and Hudson.

Bermingham, Ann. 1994. "System, Order, and Abstraction: The Politics of English Landscape Drawing around 1795." In *Landscape and Power,* edited by W. J. T. Mitchell, 77–101. Chicago: University of Chicago Press.

Bevington, Michael. 1997. *Stowe Church.* Stowe: Capability Books.

Blair, Hugh. [1765] 1803. "A Critical dissertation on the Poems of Ossian the son of Fingal." In *The Poems of Ossian, the Son of Fingal,* edited by James Macpherson, 48–155. Edinburgh: Denham and Dick.

Blickle, Peter. 1973. *Landschaften im Alten Reich: Die statliche Funktion des gemeinenen Mannes in Oberdeutschland.* Munich: C. H. Beck.

Bloch, Marc. [1940] 1961. *Feudal Society.* Chicago: University of Chicago Press.

Boime, Albert. 1990. *Art in an Age of Bonapartism, 1800–1815.* Chicago: University of Chicago Press.

Boime, Albert. 1991. *The Magisterial Gaze.* Washington, D.C.: Smithsonian Institution Press.

Blomley, Nicholas K. 1994. *Law, Space, and the Geographies of Power.* New York: Guilford Press.

Boon, George C. 1987. "Camden and the *Britannia.*" *Archaeologia Cambrensis* 136:1–19.

Boserup, Esther. 1965. *The Conditions of Agricultural Growth: The Economics of Agrarian Change under Population Pressure.* Chicago: Aldine.

Bosworth, Joseph, and T. Northcote Toller. [1898–1921] 1966–72. *An Anglo-Saxon Dictionary.* London: Oxford University Press.

Boughner, Daniel C. 1968. *The Devil's Disciple: Ben Jonson's Debt to Machiavelli.* New York: Philosophical Library.

Boulton, J. T. 1958. Editor's introduction to *Edmund Burke: The Sublime and Beautiful.* London: Routledge and Kegan Paul.

Bourassa, Steven C. 1991. *The Aesthetics of Landscape.* London: Belhaven Press.

Bourdieu, Pierre. 1977. *Outline of a Theory of Practice.* Cambridge: Cambridge University Press.

Bourdieu, Pierre. 1991. *Language and Symbolic Power.* Cambridge: Polity Press.

Boyse, Samuel. [1742] 1990. "The Triumphs of Nature: A Poem, on the magnificent Gardens at Stowe in Buckinghamshire, the Seat of the Rt. Hon. Lord Cobham." In *Descriptions of Lord Cobham's Gardens at Stowe (1700–1750),* edited by G. B. Clarke, 94–110. Buckinghamshire: Buckinghamshire Record Society.

Bramsen, Bo. 1965. *Gamle Danmarkskort: En Historisk Oversigt med Bibliografiske Noter for Perioden, 1570–1770.* Copenhagen: Grønholt Pedersen.

Brandt, Jesper. 1987. "Afgrunden mellem landskabsøkologi og landskabsplanlægning." In *Sådan ligger landet,* edited by Annelise Bramsnæs et al., 127–40. Copenhagen: Dansk Byplanlaboratorium.

Bridenbaugh, Carl, and Roberta Bridenbaugh. 1972. *No Peace beyond the Line: The English in the Caribbean, 1624–1690.* New York: Oxford University Press.

Brooks, Christopher, and Kevin Sharpe. 1976. "History, English Law and the Renaissance." *Past and Present* 72:133–42.

Brunner, Otto. [1965] 1992. *Land and Lordship: Structures of Governance in Medieval Austria.* 5th ed. Philadelphia: University of Pennsylvania Press.

Bunce, Michael. 1994. *The Countryside Ideal: Anglo-American Images of Landscape.* London: Routledge.

Burd, Henry A. 1915. "The Golden Age Idea in Eighteenth Century Poetry." *Sewanee Review* 23 (2): 172–85.

Burke, Edmund. 1759. *A Philosophical Enquiry into the Origin of Our Ideas of the Sublime and the Beautiful.* 2d ed. London: J. Dodsley.

Bushaway, Bob. 1982. *By Rite: Custom, Ceremony, and Community in England, 1700–1880.* London: Junction Books.

Butlin, Robin A. 1978. "Regions in England and Wales c. 1600–1914." In *An Historical Geography of England and Wales,* edited by R. A. Butlin and R. A. Dodgshon, 223–54. 2d edited by London: Academic Press.

Butlin, Robin A. 1982. *The Transformation of Rural England c. 1580–1800: A Study in Historical Geography.* Oxford: Oxford University Press.

Butterfield, Herbert. [1931] 1973. *The Whig Interpretation of History.* Harmondsworth: Penguin.

Cafritz, Robert C. 1988. "Netherlandish Reflections of the Venetian Landscape Tradition." In *Places of Delight: The Pastoral Landscape,* edited by Robert Cafritz, Lawrence Gowing, and David Rosand, 112–30. London: Weidenfeld and Nicolson.

Camden, William. [1605] 1674. *Remains Concerning Britain.* London: Charles Harper.

Camden, William. [1607] 1806. *Britannia.* 2d ed. 4 vols. Translated and enlarged by Richard Gough. London: John Stockdale.

Carsten, F. L. 1959. *Princes and Parliaments in Germany: From the Fifteenth to the Eighteenth Century.* Oxford: Oxford University Press.

Casey, Edward S. 1996. "How to Get from Space to Place in a Fairly Short Stretch of Time." In *Senses of Place,* edited by Keith H. Basso and Steven Field, 13–52. Sante Fe: School of American Research Press.

Casey, Edward S. 1997. *The Fate of Place: A Philosophical History.* Berkeley: University of California Press.

Censer, Jane Turner. 1986a. Introduction to *The Papers of Frederick Law Olmsted: Defending the Union, The Civil War and the U.S. Sanitary Commission, 1861–1863.* Baltimore: Johns Hopkins University Press.

Censer, Jane Turner, ed. 1986b. *The Papers of Frederick Law Olmsted: Defending the Union, The Civil War and the U.S. Sanitary Commission 1861–1863.* 4 vols. Baltimore: Johns Hopkins University Press.

Certeau, Michel de. 1984. *The Practice of Everyday Life.* Berkeley: University of California Press.

Chambers, E. K. 1951. *The Elizabethan Stage.* Oxford: Clarendon Press.

Chase, Alston. 1986. *Playing God in Yellowstone: The Destruction of America's First National Park.* Boston: Atlantic Monthly Press.

Clark, G. N. 1946. "The Birth of the Dutch Republic." *Proceedings of the British Academy,* 189–217.

Clark, Kenneth. 1949. *Landscape into Art.* London: John Murray.

Clarke, George B. 1973. "Grecian Taste and Gothic Virtue: Lord Cobham's Gardening Programme and Its Iconography." *Apollo* 97 (May–June): 566–71.

Clarke, George B. 1990. Introduction and notes to *Descriptions of Lord Cobham's Gardens at Stowe (1700–1750)*. Buckinghamshire: Buckinghamshire Record Society.

Cohen, I. Bernard. 1976. "The Eighteenth-Century Origins of the Concept of Scientific Revolution." *Journal of the History of Ideas* 37 (2): 257–334.

Colley, Linda. 1992. *Britons: Forging the Nation, 1707–1837*. New Haven: Yale University Press.

*Collins Dictionary of British History*. 1997. Glasgow: Harper Collins.

Collins-Klett. 1983. *The Collins-Klett German English Dictionary*. London: Collins-Klett.

Congreve, William. [1728] 1990. "Of Improving the Present Time." In *Descriptions of Lord Cobham's Gardens at Stowe (1700–1750)*, edited by G. B. Clarke, 24–27. Buckinghamshire: Buckinghamshire Record Society.

Copley, Gordon J. 1977. Preface and introduction to *Camden's Britannia*. London: Hutchinson.

Cormack, Lesley B. 1994. "The Fashioning of an Empire: Geography and the State in Elizabethan England." In *Geography and Empire*, edited by Neil Smith and Anne Godlewska, 15–30. Oxford: Blackwell.

Cormack, Lesley B. 1997. *Charting an Empire: Geography at the English Universities, 1580–1620*. Chicago: University of Chicago Press.

Cornford, Francis Macdonald. 1937. *Plato's Cosmology: The Timaeus of Plato Translated with a Running Commentary*. London: Routledge and Kegan Paul.

Cosgrove, Denis. 1984. *Social Formation and Symbolic Landscape*. London: Croom Helm.

Cosgrove, Denis. 1985. "Prospect, Perspective and the Evolution of the Landscape Idea." *Transactions of the Institute of British Geographers*, n.s., 10:45–62.

Cosgrove, Denis. 1988. "The Geometry of Landscape: Practical and Speculative Arts in Sixteenth-Century Venetian Land Territories." In *The Iconography of Landscape*, edited by Denis Cosgrove and Stephen Daniels, 254–76. Cambridge: Cambridge University Press.

Cosgrove, Denis. 1990. "Platonism and Practicality: Hydrology, Engineering and Landscape in Sixteenth-Century Venice." In *Water, Engineering and Landscape: Water Control and Landscape Transformation in the Modern Period*, edited by Denis Cosgrove and Geoff Petts, 35–53. London: Belhaven.

Cosgrove, Denis. 1993. *The Palladian Landscape: Geographical Change and Its Cultural Representations in Sixteenth-Century Italy*. University Park: Pennsylvania State University Press.

Cosgrove, Denis. 1998. "Cultural Landscapes." In *A European Geography*, edited by Tim Unwin, 65–81. London: Longman.

Cosgrove, Denis, and Stephen Daniels, eds. 1988. *The Iconography of Landscape*. Cambridge: Cambridge University Press.

Courtney, C. P. 1963. *Montesquieu and Burke*. Oxford: Basil Blackwell.

Cronon, William. 1983. *Changes in the Land: Indians, Colonists, and the Ecology of New England*. New York: Hill and Wang.

Cronon, William. 1992. "Telling Tales on Canvas: Landscapes of Frontier Change." In *Discovered Lands, Invented Pasts,* edited by Jules David Prown, 37–87. New Haven: Yale University Press.

Cronon, William. 1995. "The Trouble with Wilderness; or, Getting Back to the Wrong Nature." In *Uncommon Ground: Towards Reinventing Nature,* edited by William Cronon, 69–90. New York: W. W. Norton.

Cronon, William, ed. 1995b. *Uncommon Ground: Towards Reinventing Nature.* New York: W. W. Norton.

Damisch, Hubert. [1987] 1994. *The Origin of Perspective.* Cambridge: Mass.: MIT Press.

Daniels, Stephen. 1988. "The Political Iconography of Woodland in Later Georgian England." *The Iconography of Landscape,* edited by Denis Cosgrove and Stephen Daniels, 43–82. Cambridge: Cambridge University Press.

Daniels, Stephen. 1989. "Marxism, Culture and the Duplicity of Landscape." In *New Models in Geography,* edited by Richard Peet and Nigel Thrift, 196–200. London: Unwin and Hyman.

Daniels, Stephen. 1993a. *Fields of Vision: Landscape Imagery and National Identity in England and the United States.* Cambridge: Polity Press.

Daniels, Stephen. 1993b. "Re-visioning Britain: Mapping and Landscape Painting, 1750–1820." In *Glorious Nature: British Landscape Painting, 1750–1850,* edited by Katharine Baetjer, 61–72. New York: Hudson Hills Press.

Daniels, Stephen. 1999. *Humphry Repton: Landscape Gardening and the Geography of Georgian England.* New Haven: Yale University Press.

Daniels, Stephen, and Denis Cosgrove. 1988. "Introduction: Iconography and Landscape." In *The Iconography of Landscape,* edited by Denis Cosgrove and Stephen Daniels, 1–10. Cambridge: Cambridge University Press.

Daniels, Stephen, and Susan Seymour. 1978. "Landscape Design and the Idea of Improvement, 1730–1900." In *An Historical Geography of England and Wales,* edited by R. A. Butlin and R. A. Dodgshon, 487–520. London: Academic Press.

Defoe, Daniel, and Samuel Richardson. [1742] 1990. Excerpts from "A Tour thro' the Whole Island of Great Britain." In *Descriptions of Lord Cobham's Gardens at Stowe (1700–1750),* edited by G. B. Clarke, 78–93. Buckinghamshire: Buckinghamshire Record Society.

Demars, Stanford E. 1991. *The Tourist in Yosemite, 1855–1985.* Salt Lake City: University of Utah Press.

Derrida, Jacques. 1995. "Khora." In *On the Name,* edited by Thomas Dutoit, 88–127. Stanford: Stanford University Press.

Descola, Philippe, and Gísli Pálsson, eds. 1996. *Nature and Society: Anthropological Perspectives.* London: Routledge

Donaldson, Gordon. 1984. "Problems of Sovereignty and Law in Orkney and Shetland." In *Miscellany Two,* edited by David Sellar, 13–40. Edinburgh: The Stair Society.

Donaldson, Gordon, and Robert S. Morpeth. 1977. *A Dictionary of Scottish History.* Edinburgh: John Donald.

Dopsch, Alfons. 1937. *The Economic and Social Foundations of European Civilization.* New York: Harcourt, Brace.

Douglas, David C. 1939. *English Scholars.* London: Jonathan Cape.

Dowdall, K. C. 1923. "The Word 'State.'" *Law Quarterly Review* 39 (153): 98–125.

Drayton, Michael. [1612–22] 1961. *Poly-Olbion: Or A Chorographicall Description of Tracts, Rivers, Mountains, Forests, and other Parts of this renowned Isle of Great Britaine.* Oxford: Basil Blackwell.

Drummond, William. [1619] 1985. "Conversations with William Drummond of Hawthornden." In *Ben Jonson,* edited by Ian Donaldson, 595–611. Oxford: Oxford University Press.

Drummond, William. [1638] 1976. "Irene: A Remonstrance for Concord, Amitie and Love, Amongst his Majesties Subjects." In *William Drummond of Hawthornden: Poems and Prose,* edited by Robert H. MacDonald, 179–90. Edinburgh: Scottish Academic Press.

Dryden, John. [1697] 1806. *The Works of Virgil, translated into English Verse by Mr. Dryden.* London: Vernor et al.

Duerr, Hans Peter. 1985. *Dreamtime: Concerning the Boundary between Wilderness and Civilization.* Oxford: Basil Blackwell.

Duncan, James S. 1990. *The City as Text: The Politics of Landscape Interpretation in the Kandyan Kingdom.* Cambridge: Cambridge University Press.

Duncan, James, and David Ley, eds. 1993. *Place/Culture/Representation.* London: Routledge.

Dundes, Alan. 1991. "The Apple-Shot: Interpreting the Legend of William Tell." *Western Folklore* 50:327–60.

Eccleshall, Robert. 1978. *Order and Reason in Politics.* Oxford: Oxford University Press.

Eckhardt, Karl August. 1955. *Sachsenspiegel Landrecht.* Göttingen: Musterschmidt.

Eco, Umberto. 1983. *The Name of the Rose.* London: Picador.

Economou, George D. 1972. *The Goddess Natura in Medieval Literature.* Cambridge, Mass.: Harvard University Press.

Edgerton, Samuel. 1975. *The Renaissance Rediscovery of Linear Perspective.* New York: Basic Books.

Eliade, Mircea. 1971. *The Myth of the Eternal Return: or, Cosmos and History.* Princeton, N.J.: Princeton University Press.

Emerson, Ralph Waldo. [1836] 1991. "Nature." In *Nature/Walking,* edited by John Elder, 1–67. Boston: Beacon Press.

Empedocles. 1981. *The Extant Fragments.* Edited by M. R. Wright. New Haven: Yale University Press.

Everett, Nigel. 1994. *The Tory View of Landscape.* New Haven: Yale University Press.

Everhart, William C. 1972. *The National Park Service.* New York: Praeger.

Everitt, Alan. 1979. "Country, County and Town: Patterns of Regional Evolution in England." *Transaction of the Royal Historical Society* 29:79–108.

Evernden, Neil. 1992. *The Social Creation of Nature.* Baltimore: Johns Hopkins University Press.

Ewell, Barbara. 1978. "Drayton's Poly-Olbion: England's Body Immortalized." *Studies in Philology* 75:297–315.

Falk, Hjalmar, and Alf Torp. [1903–6] 1996. *Etymologisk ordbog over det norske og det danske sprog.* Oslo: Bjørn Ringstrøms Antikvariat.

Fenger, Ole. 1992. "Magten." In *Den nordiske verden,* edited by Kirsten Hastrup, 117–66. Copenhagen: Gyldendal.

Fenger, Ole. 1993. *Fred og Ret i Middelalderen.* Århus: Bogformidlingens Forlag.

Florio, John. 1611. *Queen Anna's New World of Words, or Dictionairie of the Italian and English tongues.* London: Edw. Blount and William Barret.

Foucault, Michel. 1972. *The Archaeology of Knowledge, and The Discourse on Language.* New York: Harper and Row.

Foucault, Michel. 1973. *The Order of Things: An Archaeology of the Human Sciences.* New York: Vintage.

Foucault, Michel. 1979. *Discipline and Punish: The Birth of the Prison.* Harmondsworth: Penguin.

Friedländer, Max J. 1949. *Landscape, Portrait, Still-Life: Their Origin and Development.* Oxford: Bruno Cassirer.

Fritzner, Johan. 1886–96. *Ordbog om Det Gamle Norske Sprog.* Kristiania: Ny Norske Forlagsforening.

Frye, Northrop. 1965. *A Natural Perspective: The Development of Shakespearean Comedy and Romance.* New York: Columbia University Press.

Frye, Northrop. 1967. "The Argument of Comedy." In *Shakespeare: Modern Essays in Criticism,* edited by Leonard F. Dean, 79–89. Oxford: Oxford University Press.

Frye, Northrop. 1971. *Anatomy of Criticism: Four Essays.* Princeton, N.J.: Princeton University Press.

Frye, Northrop. 1980. *Creation and Recreation.* Toronto: University of Toronto Press.

Fussel, G. E. 1972. *The Classical Tradition in West European Farming.* Rutherford, N.J.: Fairleigh Dickinson University Press.

Gadol, Joan. 1969. *Leon Battista Alberti: Universal Man of the Early Renaissance.* Chicago: University of Chicago Press.

Gamillscheg, Ernst. 1969. *Etymologisches Wörterbuch der französischen Sprache.* 2d ed. Heidelberg, Winter.

Gamrath, Helge. 1993. "Town Planning in Denmark and Norway in the First Half of the Seventeenth Century." In *City and Nature: Changing Relations in Time and Space,* edited by Thomas Møller Kristen and Per Grau Møller, 117–32. Odense: Odense University Press.

Garin, E. [1976] 1990. *Astrology in the Renaissance: The Zodiac of Life.* Harmondsworth: Penguin Arkana.

Gellner, Ernest. 1983. *Nations and Nationalism.* Oxford: Blackwell.

Gibson, Walter S. 1989. *"Mirror of the Earth": The World Landscape in Sixteenth-Century Flemish Painting.* Princeton, N.J.: Princeton University Press.

Giesey, Ralph E. and J. H. M. Salmon. 1972. Editors' introduction to *Francogallia* by François Hotman. Cambridge: Cambridge University Press.

[Gilpin, William] [1748] 1976. *A Dialogue upon the Gardens of the Right Honourable The Lord Viscount Cobham at Stow in Buckinghamshire*. Los Angeles: William Andrews Clark Memorial Library.

Gilpin, William. 1792. *Three Essays: On Picturesque Beauty; on Picturesque Travel and on Sketching Landscape. To which is added a poem, on Landscape Painting*. London: R. Blamire.

Glacken, Clarence J. 1967. *Traces on the Rhodian Shore: Nature and Culture in Western Thought from Ancient Times to the End of the Eighteenth Century*. Berkeley: University of California Press.

Goldberg, Jonathan. 1983. *James I and the Politics of Literature*. Baltimore: Johns Hopkins University Press.

Goldsmith, Oliver. [1773] n.d. *The Deserted Village*. Philadelphia: Porter and Coates.

Gombrich, E. H. 1948. "*Icones Symbolicae:* The Visual Image in Neo-Platonic Thought." *Journal of the Warburg and Courtauld Institutes* 11:163–92.

Gombrich, E. H. [1959] 1969. *Art and Illusion: A Study in the Psychology of Pictorial Representation*. 3d ed. Princeton, N.J.: Princeton University Press.

Gombrich, E. H. 1972. *The Story of Art*. 12th ed. London: Phaidon.

Goody, Jack. 1975. Introduction to *Literacy in Traditional Societies,* edited by Jack Goody, 1–26. Cambridge: Cambridge University Press.

Goody, Jack. 1977. *The Domestication of the Savage Mind*. Cambridge: Cambridge University Press.

Gordon, D. J. 1943. "The Imagery of Ben Jonson's *The Masque of Blackness* and *The Masque of Beautie*." *Journal of the Warburg and Courtauld Institutes* 6:122–41.

Gordon, D. J. 1949. "Poet and Architect: The Intellectual Setting of the Quarrel Between Ben Jonson and Inigo Jones." *Journal of the Warburg and Courtauld Institutes* 12:152–78.

Gossett, Thomas F. 1963. *Race: The History of an Idea in America*. Dallas: Southern Methodist University Press.

Gotch, J. Alfred. 1968. *Inigo Jones*. New York: Benjamin Blom.

Gough, Richard. 1806. "The Life of Mr. Camden." In *Britannia by William Camden,* edited by Richard Gough, xi–xxx. London: John Stockdale.

Graber, Laura H. 1976. *Wilderness as Sacred Space*. Washington, D.C.: Association of American Geographers.

Graham, Alistair D. 1973. *The Gardeners of Eden*. London: George Allen and Unwin.

Gregersen, H. V. 1981. *Danmarks Historie: Slesvig og Holsten før 1830*. Copenhagen: Politiken.

Grimal, Pierre. 1990. *A Concise Dictionary of Classical Mythology*. Oxford: Basil Blackwell.

Grimm, Jacob. 1848. *Geschichte der deutschen Sprache*. Leipzig: Weidmannschen.

Grimm, Jacob. 1854. *Deutsche Rechtsalterthümer.* 2d ed. Göttingen: Dieterich-sche Buchhandlung.

Grimm, Jacob, and Wilhelm Grimm. 1855. *Deutsches Wörterbuch.* Leipzig: S. Hirzel.

Groening, Gert, and Joachim Wolschke-Bulmahn. 1989. "Changes in the Philos-ophy of Garden Architecture in the Twentieth Century and Their Impact upon the Social and Spatial Environment." *Journal of Garden History* 9 (2): 53–70.

Groening, Gert, and Joachim Wolschke-Bulmahn. 1992. "Some Notes on the Mania for Native Plants in Germany." *Landscape Journal* 11 (25): 116–26.

Gröning, Gert, and Joachim Wolschke-Bulmahn. 1985. "Die Landespflege als In-strument National-sozialistischer Eroberungs-politik." *Arch +*, no. 81:46–59.

Gröning, Gert, and Joachim Wolschke-Bulmahn. 1987. "Politics, Planning and the Protection of Nature: Political Abuse of Early Ecological Ideas in Germany, 1933–45." *Planning Perspectives* 2:127–48.

Gurevich, A. 1977. "Representations of Property During the High Middle Ages." *Economy and Society* 6:1–30.

Gurevich, A. J. 1985. *Categories of Medieval Culture.* London: Routledge and Kegan Paul.

Guyot, Arnold. 1849. *The Earth and Man: Lectures on Comparative Physical Geography, in its Relation to the History of Mankind.* Boston: Gould, Kendall, and Lincoln.

Hacket, John. 1693. *Scrinia Reserata: A Memorial Offer'd to the Great Deserv-ings of John Williams, D. D. . . . Containing A Series of the Most Remarkable Occurrences and Transactions of his LIFE, in Relation both to Church and State.* London: Samuel Lowndes.

Harrison, G. B. 1948. "Introductions and Appendices to Shakespeare: Major Plays and the Sonnets." In *Shakespeare: Major Plays and the Sonnets,* edited by G. B. Harrison. New York: Harcourt, Brace and World.

Harrison, Robert Pogue. 1992. *Forests: The Shadow of Civilization.* Chicago: University of Chicago Press.

Hastrup, Kirsten. 1985. *Culture and History in Medieval Iceland: An Anthropo-logical Analysis of Structure and Change.* Oxford: Clarendon Press.

Hastrup, Kirsten. 1990. *Nature and Policy in Iceland, 1400–1800: An Anthropo-logical Analysis of History and Mentality.* Oxford: Clarendon Press.

Hatto, Arthur. 1949. "'Revolution': An Enquiry into the Usefulness of an Histor-ical Term." *Mind,* n.s., 58:495–517.

Hays, Samuel P. 1959. *Conservation and the Gospel of Efficiency: The Progressive Conservation Movement, 1890–1920.* Cambridge, Mass.: Harvard University Press.

Heatwole, Henry. 1992. *Guide to Shenandoah National Park.* 4th ed. Luray, Va.: Shenandoah Natural History Association.

Hedeager, Lotte. 1993. "The Creation of Germanic Identity: A European Origin-Myth." Frontières d'empire, Actes de la Table ronde internationale de Nemours 1992. *Mémoires du Musée de préhistoire d'Ile-de-France* 5:121–31.

Helgerson, Richard. 1986. "The Land Speaks: Cartography, Chorography, and Subversion in Renaissance England." *Representations* 16:51–85.

Helgerson, Richard. 1992. *Forms of Nationhood: The Elizabethan Writing of England*. Chicago: University of Chicago Press.

Hellesen, Jette Kjærulff, and Ole Tuxen, eds. 1988. *Historisk Atlas Danmark*. Copenhagen: Gad.

Hemmingsen, Niels. [1562] 1991. *Om naturens lov, 1. del*. Copenhagen: Øresund.

Herf, Jeffrey. 1984. *Reactionary Modernism: Technology and Politics in Weimar and the Third Reich*. Cambridge: Cambridge University Press.

Hermann, Aubin Von. 1952. "Das Schicksal der schweizerischen und der friesischen Freiheit." *Jahrbuch der Gesellschaft fur bildende Kunst* 32:21–42.

Hesiod. 1987. *Hesiod's Theogony*. Cambridge, Mass.: Focus Information Group.

Hill, Christopher. 1958. *Puritanism and Revolution: Studies in Interpretation of the English Revolution of the Seventeenth Century*. London: Secker and Warburg.

Hill, Christopher. 1965. *Intellectual Origins of the English Revolution*. Oxford: Clarendon Press.

Hill, Christopher. 1975. *The World Turned Upside Down: Radical Ideas during the English Revolution*. London: Penguin.

Hilliard, Sam B. 1990. "Plantations and the Molding of the Southern Landscape." *The Making of the American Landscape*, edited by Michael P. Conzen, 104–26. Boston: Unwin Hyman.

Hiss, Tony. 1990. *The Experience of Place*. New York: Knopf.

Hobbes, Thomas. [1651] 1991. *Leviathan*. Cambridge: Cambridge University Press.

Hobsbawm, Eric. 1983. Introduction to *The Invention of Tradition*, edited by Terrence Ranger and Eric Hobsbawm, 1–14. Cambridge: Cambridge University Press.

Hoff, Annette. 1998. *Lov og Landskab*. Aarhus: Aarhus Universitetsforslag.

Holdsworth, W. S. 1928. *The Historians of Anglo-American Law*. New York: Columbia University Press.

Holmes, Clive. 1979–80. "The County Community in Stuart Historiography." *Journal of British Studies* 19:54–73.

Holt, J. C. 1982. *Robin Hood*. London: Thames and Hudson.

Hotman, François. [1573] 1972. *Francogallia*. Edited by Ralph E. Giesey and J. H. M. Salmon. Cambridge: Cambridge University Press.

Huizinga, Johan. 1955. *Homo Ludens: A Study of the Play-Element in Culture*. Boston: Beacon Press.

Humboldt, Alexander von. 1849–58. *Cosmos: A Sketch of a Physical Description of the Universe*. London: Henry G. Bohn.

Hunt, John Dixon. 1991. "The Garden as Cultural Object." In *Denatured Visions: Landscape and Culture in the Twentieth Century*, edited by Stuart Wrede et al., 19–32. New York: Museum of Modern Art.

Hunt, John Dixon. 1992. *Gardens and the Picturesque: Studies in the History of Landscape Architecture*. Cambridge, Mass.: MIT Press.

Hyams, Edward. 1974. *The Millennium Postponed: Socialism from Sir Thomas More to Mao Tse-tung*. New York: Taplinger.

Imsen, Steinar, and Günter Vogler. 1997. "Communal Autonomy and Peasant

Resistance in Northern and Central Europe." In *Resistance, Representation, and Community*, edited by Peter Blickle, 5–64. Oxford: Clarendon.

Ingold, Tim. 1993. "The Temporality of Landscape." *World Archaeology* 25 (2): 152–72.

Jackson, John Brinckerhoff. 1984. *Discovering the Vernacular Landscape*. New Haven: Yale University Press.

Jacob, Margaret C. 1976. "Millenarianism and Science in the Late Seventeenth Century." *Journal of the History of Ideas* 37 (2): 335–41.

Jacob, Margaret C., and W. A. Lockwood. 1972. "Political Millenarianism and Burnet's *Sacred Theory*." *Science Studies* 2:265–79.

James I. [1599] 1969. *Basilicon Doron*. [Edinburgh: Robert Walde-grave]; Menston, Eng.: Scholar Press Facsimile.

James I. [1616] 1918a. "A Speach in the Parliament Hovse, As Neere The Very Words as Covld Be Gathered At The Instant (1605)." In *The Political Works of James I*, edited by Charles Howard McIlwain, 281–89. Cambridge, Mass.: Harvard University Press.

James I. [1616] 1918b. "A Speach In The Starre-Chamber, The XX. of Jvne. Anno 1616." In *The Political Works of James I*, edited by Charles Howard McIlwain, 326–45. Cambridge, Mass.: Harvard University Press.

James I. [1616] 1918c. "A Speach To Both Hovses of Parliament, Delivered In The Great Chamber At White-Hall, The Last Day of March 1607." In *The Political Works of James I*, edited by Charles Howard McIlwain, 290–305. Cambridge, Mass.: Harvard University Press.

James I. [1616] 1918d. "A Speach to the Lords and Commons of the Parliament at White-Hall. On Werdnesday the XXI. of March. Anno 1609." In *The Political Works of James I*, edited by Charles Howard McIlwain, 306–25. Cambridge, Mass.: Harvard University Press.

James I. [1616] 1918e. "A Speach, As It Was Delivered In The Vpper Hovse Of The Parliament To The Lords Spiritvall And Temporall, And To The Knights, Citizens And Burgersses There Assembled, On Mvnday The XIX. Day of March 1603. Being The First Day of The First Parliament." In *The Political Works of James I*, edited by Charles Howard McIlwain, 269–80. Cambridge, Mass.: Harvard University Press.

James I. [1616] 1918f. "The Trew Law of Free Monarchies: Or The Reciprock and Mvtvall Dvetie Betweixt a Free King, and His Naturall Subjects (1598)." In *The Political Works of James I*, edited by Charles Howard McIlwain, 53–70. Cambridge, Mass.: Harvard University Press.

James, Preston E. 1972. *All Possible Worlds: A History of Geographical Ideas*. Indianapolis: Bobbs-Merrill.

Jansen, F. J. Billeskov, and P. M. Mitchell, eds. 1971. *Anthology of Danish Literature (Bilingual Edition)*. Vol. 1, *Middle Ages to Romanticism*. Carbondale: Southern Illinois University Press.

Jellinek, Georg. 1922. *Allgemeine Staatslehre*. Berlin: Julius Springer.

Jones, Michael. 1977. *Finland, Daughter of the Sea*. Folkestone, Eng.: Dawson-Archon.

Jones, Michael. 1991. "The Elusive Reality of Landscape: Concepts and Approaches in Landscape Research." *Norsk Geografisk Tidsskrift* 45:229–44.

Jonson, Ben. [1634] 1873. "Love's Welcome: The King's and Queen's Entertainment at Bolsover." In *The Works of Ben Jonson*, edited by William Gifford, 663–64. New ed. London: Routledge.

Jonson, Ben. 1969. *The Complete Masques*, edited by Stephen Orgel. New Haven: Yale University Press.

Jonson, Ben. 1985. *The Oxford Authors: Ben Jonson*, edited by Ian Donaldson. Oxford: Oxford University Press.

Jørgensen, Ove. 1981. "Otonivm i Vrbivm Praecipvarvm Mvndi Theatrvm Qvintvm Avctore Georgio Bravnio Agrippinate Odense 1593." In George Braun and Frans Hogenberg, *Civitates orbis terrarum*, vol. 5 (Cologne, 1597), section 30. Reprinted in *Faksimileudgave af beskrivelsen og kortet med oversættelse til dansk*. Odense: Odense University Press.

Kain, Roger J. P., and Elizabeth Baigent. 1992. *The Cadastral Map in the Service of the State: A History of Property Mapping*. Chicago: University of Chicago Press.

Kalkar, Otto. [1881–1918] 1976. *Ordbog over det ældre danske Sprog (1300–1700)*. 2d ed. Copenhagen: Akademisk Forlag.

Kant, Immanuel. 1924. *Kritik der Urteilskraft*. Hamburg: Felix Meiner.

Kantorowicz, Ernst H. 1955. "Mysteries of State: An Absolutist Concept and Its Late Mediaeval Origins." *The Harvard Theological Review* 48 (1): 65–91.

Kantorowicz, Ernst H. 1957. *The King's Two Bodies: A Study in Mediaeval Political Theology*. Princeton, N.J.: Princeton University Press.

Kayser, H. [1964] 1970. *Akróasis: The Theory of World Harmonics*. Boston: Plowshare Press.

Kemp, Martin. 1990. *The Science of Art: Optical Themes in Western Art from Brunelleschi to Seurat*. New Haven: Yale University Press.

Kernodle, George R. 1944. *From Art to Theatre: Form and Convention in the Renaissance*. Chicago: University of Chicago Press.

Klein, Ernest. 1967. *A Comprehensive Etymological Dictionary of the English Language*. Amsterdam: Elsevier.

Kliger, Samuel. 1945. "The 'Goths' in England: An Introduction to the Gothic Vogue in Eighteenth-Century Aesthetic Discussion." *Modern Philology* 43 (2): 107–16.

Kliger, Samuel. 1947. "The Gothic Revival and the German Translatio." *Modern Philology* (45): 73–103.

Kliger, Samuel. 1952. *The Goths in England: A Study in Seventeenth- and Eighteenth-Century Thought*. Cambridge, Mass.: Harvard University Press.

Knottnerus, Otto S. 1992. "Moral Economy behind the Dikes: Class Relations along the Frisian and German North Sea Coast during the Early Modern Age." *Tijdschrift voor sociale geschiedenis* 18 (2/3): 333–52.

Knottnerus, Otto S. 1996. "Structural Characteristics of Coastal Societies: Some Considerations on the History of the North Sea Coastal Marshes." In *The North Sea and Culture (1550–1800): Proceedings of the International Confer-*

*ence held at Leiden, 21–22 April 1995,* edited by Lex Heerma van Voss and Juliette Roding, 41–63. Hilversum, Netherlands: Verloren.

Köbler, Gerhard. 1988. *Historisches Lexikon der deutschen Länder: Die deutschen Territorien vom Mittelalter bis zur Gegenwart.* Munich: C. H. Beck.

Koestler, Arthur. 1964. *The Watershed: A Biography of Johannes Kepler.* New York: Doubleday.

Kohn, Hans. 1940. "The Genesis and Character of English Nationalism." *Journal of the History of Ideas* 1:69–94.

Kolodny, Annette. 1975. *The Lay of the Land.* Chapel Hill: University of North Carolina Press.

Koschorreck, Walter. 1970. *Die Heidelberger Bilderhandschrift des Sachsenspiegels.* Frankfurt am Main: Insel.

Kroman, Erik. 1945. *Danmarks Gamle Love.* Vol. 2. Copenhagen: Gad.

Krüger, Kersten. 1984. "Die landschaftliche Verfassung Nordelbiens in der frühen Neuzeit: Ein besonder Typ politischer Partizipation." In *Civitatum Communitas: Studien zum europischen Städtewesen,* edited by Helmut Jäger et al., 458–87. Vienna: Böhlau.

Kuhn, Thomas S. 1957. *The Copernican Revolution: Planetary Astronomy in the Development of Western Thought.* Cambridge, Mass.: Harvard University Press.

Kunst, Christiane. 1994. *Römische Tradition und englische Politik: Studien sur Geschichte der Britannienrezeption zwischen William Camden und John Speed.* Hildesheim: Georg Olms.

Ladner, Gerhart B. 1959. *The Idea of Reform: Its Impact on Christian Thought and Action in the Age of the Fathers.* Cambridge, Mass.: Harvard University Press.

Ladurie, Emmanuel Le Roy. 1980. *Carnival: A People's Uprising at Romans, 1579–1580.* London: Scholar Press.

Langenscheidt. 1967. *Handwörterbuch Englisch.* Berlin: Langenscheidt.

Leach, E. R. 1966. *Rethinking Anthropology.* London: Athlone Press.

Leopold, Aldo. [1949] 1966. *A Sand County Almanac, with Essays on Conservation from Round River.* New York: Ballantine.

Lewis, C. S. 1967. *Studies in Words.* Cambridge: Cambridge University Press.

Liddell, Henry George, and Robert Scott. 1940. *A Greek-English Lexicon,* a new edition revised by Henry Stuart Jones and Roderick McKenzie. Oxford: Clarendon Press.

Livingstone, David N. 1992. *The Geographical Tradition: Episodes in the History of a Contested Enterprise.* Oxford: Blackwell.

Livingstone, David N. 1994. "Climate's Moral Economy: Science, Race and Place in Post-Darwinian British and American Geography." In *Geography and Empire,* edited by Neil Smith and Anne Godlewska, 132–54. Oxford: Blackwell.

Loomis, Charles P. 1955. Translator's introduction to *Community and Association,* by Ferdinand Tönnies. London: Routledge and Kegan Paul.

Lovejoy, Arthur O. 1927. "'Nature' as Aesthetic Norm." *Modern Language Notes* 42 (7): 444–50.

Lovejoy, Arthur O. 1973. *The Great Chain of Being.* Cambridge, Mass.: Harvard University Press.

Lovejoy, Arthur O., and George Boas. 1935. *Primitivism and Related Ideas in Antiquity.* Baltimore: Johns Hopkins Press.

Lowenthal, David. 1961. "Geography, Experience and Imagination: Towards a Geographical Epistemology." *Annals of the Association of American Geographers* 51 (3): 241–60.

Lowenthal, David. 1964. "Is Wilderness 'Paradise Enow'? Images of Nature in America." *Columbia University Forum* 7 (2): 34–40.

Lowenthal, David. 1985. *The Past Is a Foreign Country.* Cambridge: Cambridge University Press.

Lowenthal, David. 1996. *Possessed by the Past: The Heritage Crusade and the Spoils of History.* New York: Free Press.

Lowenthal, David, and Hugh C. Prince. [1965] 1972. "English Landscape Taste." In *Man, Space, and Environment,* edited by Paul Ward English and Robert C. Mayfield, 81–112. New York: Oxford University Press.

Lukermann, Fred. [1961] 1967. "The Concept of Location in Classical Geography." In *Introduction to Geography: Selected Readings,* edited by Lawrence M. Sommers and Fred E. Dohrs, 54–74. New York: Thomas Y. Crowell.

MacDonald, Robert H. 1971. *The Library of Drummond of Hawthornden.* Edinburgh: Edinburgh University Press.

MacDougall, Hugh A. 1982. *Racial Myth in English History: Trojans, Teutons, and Anglo-Saxons.* Hanover, N.H.: University Press of New England.

Machiavelli, Niccolò. [1513] 1995. "The Prince." In *The Prince and Other Political Writings,* edited by Stephen J. Milner and Robin Kirkpatrick, 36–128. London: J. M. Dent.

McIlwain, Charles Howard. 1918. Introduction to *The Political Works of James I.* Cambridge, Mass.: Harvard University Press.

McLaughlin, Charles Capen, et al. 1977a. "His Life and Work." In *The Papers of Frederick Law Olmsted: The Formative Years, 1822–1852,* edited by Charles Capen McLaughlin et al., 3–55. Baltimore: Johns Hopkins University Press.

McLaughlin, Charles Capen, et al. 1977b. *The Papers of Frederick Law Olmsted: The Formative Years, 1822–1852.* Vol. 1. Baltimore: Johns Hopkins University Press.

Macpherson, James. [1765] 1803. *The Poems of Ossian, the Son of Fingal.* Edinburgh: Denham and Dick.

Malcolmson, Robert W. 1973. *Popular Recreations in English Society. 1700–1850.* Cambridge: Cambridge University Press.

Mander, Karel van. [1603–4] 1994. *The Lives of the Illustrious Netherlandish and German Painters (the Schilder-boeck).* Doornspijk, Netherlands: Davaco.

Manwaring, Elizabeth Wheeler. [1925] 1965. *Italian Landscape in Eighteenth-Century England: A Study Chiefly of the Influence of Claude Lorrain and Salvator Rosa on English Taste, 1700–1800.* London: Frank Cass.

Marcus, Leah S. 1986. *The Politics of Mirth: Jonson, Herrick, Milton, Marvell and the Defense of Old Holiday Pastimes.* Chicago: University of Chicago Press.

Markus, Gyorgy. 1993. "Culture: The Making and the Make-Up of a Concept (An Essay in Historical Semantics)." *Dialectical Anthropology* 18:3–29.

Marx, Karl. [1848] 1969. *Communist Manifesto, with Preface by Frederick Engels.* Chicago: Henry Regnery.

Marx, Leo. 1964. *The Machine in the Garden: Technology and the Pastoral Ideal in America.* London: Oxford University Press.

Mebane, John S. 1989. *Renaissance Magic and the Return of the Golden Age: The Occult Tradition and Marlowe, Jonson, and Shakespeare.* Lincoln: University of Nebraska Press.

Meinig, D. W. 1979. "Symbolic Landscapes: Some Idealizations of American Communities." In *The Interpretation of Ordinary Landscapes: Geographical Essays,* edited by D. W. Meinig, 164–92. New York: Oxford University Press.

Mennell, Stephen. 1985. *All Manners of Food: Eating and Taste in England and France from the Middle Ages to the Present.* Oxford: Basil Blackwell.

Mensing, Otto. 1931. *Schleswig-Holsteinisches Wörterbuch (Volksausgabe).* Neumünster: Karl Wachholtz.

Merchant, Carolyn. 1995. "Reinventing Eden: Western Culture as a Recovery Narrative." In *Uncommon Ground: Towards Reinventing Nature,* edited by William Cronon, 132–59. New York: W. W. Norton.

Miller, C. 1988. *Jefferson and Nature: An Interpretation.* Baltimore: Johns Hopkins University Press.

Milles, Jeremiah. [1735] 1990. "From An Account, of the Journey that Mr. Hardnesss and I took in July 1735." In *Descriptions of Lord Cobham's Gardens at Stowe (1700–1750),* edited by G. B. Clarke, 60–65. Buckinghamshire: Buckinghamshire Record Society.

Milsom, S. F. C. 1981. *Historical Foundations of the Common Law.* London: Butterworths.

Mitchell, Timothy. 1984. "Caspar David Friedrich's *Der Watzmann*: German Romantic Landscape Painting and Historical Geology." *The Art Bulletin* 56 (3): 452–64.

Mitchell, Timothy F. 1993. *Art and Science in German Landscape Painting, 1770–1840.* Oxford: Clarendon Press.

Mitchell, W. J. T. 1986. *Iconology: Image, Text, Ideology.* Chicago: University of Chicago Press.

Mitchell, W. J. T. 1994. "Imperial Landscape." In *Landscape and Power,* edited by W. J. T. Mitchell, 5–34. Chicago: University of Chicago Press.

Mitchell, W. J. T. 1995. "Gombrich and the Rise of Landscape." In *The Consumption of Culture, 1600–1800: Image, Object, Text,* edited by John Brewer and Ann Bermingham, 103–18. London: Routledge.

Molbech, Christian. 1813. *Historie om Ditmarskerkrigen Aar Fenten Hundrede og Ditmarskens Erobring under Kong Frederik den Anden med en historisk Udsigt over Ditmarskerfolkets Vilkaar og Skiebne i ældre Tider.* Copenhagen: Andrea Seidelin.

Molesworth, Robert. 1694. *An Account of Denmark as it was in the year 1692.* 3d ed. London: Timothy Goodwin.

Molesworth, Robert. 1738. Translator's preface to *Franco-Gallia: or, an Account of the Ancient Free State of France and Most other Parts of Europe, before the Loss of their Liberties written Originally in Latin by the Famous Civilian Francis Hotoman*, by François Hotman, i–xxxvi. London: T. Longman.

Monmouth, Geoffrey of. [ca. 1136] 1966. *The History of the Kings of Britain*. Harmondsworth: Penguin.

Montesquieu. [1748] 1989. *The Spirit of the Laws*. Cambridge: Cambridge University Press.

Muir, John. [1914] 1988. *The Yosemite*. San Francisco: Sierra Club.

Munsche, P. B. 1981. *Gentlemen and Poachers: The English Game Laws, 1671–1831*. Cambridge: Cambridge University Press.

Murphy, David T. 1999. "'A Sum of the Most Wonderful Things': *Raum*, Geopolitics and the German Tradition of Environmental Determinism, 1900–1933." *History of European Ideas* 25 (3): 121–33.

Muus, Bent. 1996. "Eftermiddagens indlæg, Professor Bent Muus, Zoologisk Museum." In *Natursyn: Miljø- og Energiministerens konference med organisationerne om natursyn*, 40–41. KolleKolle: Miljø- og Energiministeriet, Skov- og Naturstyrelsen.

Nairn, Tom. 1981. *The Break-up of Britain: Crisis and Neo-Nationalism*. 2d ed. London: Verso.

Nash, Roderick. 1976. *Wilderness and the American Mind*. 3d ed. New Haven: Yale University Press.

National Maritime Museum. n.d. *The Queen's House: A Royal Palace by the Thames*. London: Centurion Press.

Neeson, J. M. 1993. *Commoners: Common Right, Enclosure and Social Change in England, 1700–1820*. Cambridge: Cambridge University Press.

Neiiendam, Klaus. 1988. *Renaissanceteatret i Danmark*. Copenhagen: Det teatervidenskabelige Institute, Københavns Universitet.

Neumeyer, Eva Maria. 1947. "The Landscape Garden as Symbol in Rousseau, Goethe and Flaubert." *Journal of the History of Ideas* 3:187–217.

Newman, Jane O. 1990. *Pastoral Conventions: Poetry, Language, and Thought in Seventeenth-Century Nuremberg*. Baltimore: Johns Hopkins University Press.

Nichols, John. 1828. *The Progresses, Processions, and Magnificent Festivities, of King James the First, His Royal Consort Family, and Court. . . .* London: J. B. Nichols.

Nicolson, Marjorie Hope. 1965. *The Breaking of the Circle: Studies in the Effect of the "New Science" upon Seventeenth-Century Poetry*. New York: Columbia University Press.

Nisbet, Robert A. 1969. *Social Change and History: Aspects of the Western Theory of Development*. New York: Oxford University Press.

Nitschke, August. 1968. "German Politics and Medieval History." *The Journal of Contemporary History* 3 (2): 75–92.

Novak, Barbara. 1980. *Nature and Culture: American Landscape and Painting, 1825–1875*. New York: Oxford University Press.

Ødegaard, Tina Vibe. 1992. *Af En Oldgranskers Virke: Om arkæologen J. J. A. Worsaae og hans forfatterskab indtil 1850 med særligt henblik på forholdet til*

*1840'ernes politiske og nationale bevægelser.* Copenhagen: University of Copenhagen, Department of Archaeology.

Oestreich, Gerhard. 1980. *Strukturprobleme der frühen Neuzeit: Ausgewählte Aufsätz.* Berlin: Duncker und Humblot.

Ogden, Henry V. S., and Margaret S. Ogden. 1955. *English Taste in Landscape in the Seventeenth Century.* Ann Arbor: University of Michigan Press.

Olmsted, Frederick Law. [1861] 1953. *The Cotton Kingdom: A Traveller's Observations on Cotton and Slavery in the American Slave States.* London: Routledge and Kegan Paul.

Olmsted, Frederick Law. [1865] 1990. "Preliminary Report upon the Yosemite and Big Tree Grove." In *The Papers of Frederick Law Olmsted: The California Frontier, 1863–1865,* edited by Victorian Post Ranney et al., 488–516. Baltimore: Johns Hopkins University Press.

Olmsted, Frederick Law. 1990. "Notes on the Pioneer Condition (Unpublished Manuscript Written between 1863 and 1868)." In *The Papers of Frederick Law Olmsted: The California Frontier, 1863–1865,* edited by Victorian Post Ranney et al., 577–763. Baltimore: Johns Hopkins University Press.

Olsson, Gunnar. 2001. "Washed in a Washing Machine (TM)." In *Postmodern Geographical Praxis,* edited by Claudio Minca, 254–81. Oxford: Blackwell.

Olwig, Karen Fog. 1980. "National Parks, Tourism, and Local Development: A West Indian Case." *Human Organization* 39 (1): 22–31.

Olwig, Karen Fog. 1985. *Cultural Adaptation and Resistance on St. John: Three Centuries of Afro-Caribbean Life.* Gainesville: University of Florida Press.

Olwig, Karen Fog. 1993. *Global Culture, Island Identity: Continuity and Change in the Afro-Caribbean Community of Nevis.* Reading: Harwood.

Olwig, Karen Fog, and Kenneth Olwig. 1979. "Underdevelopment and the Development of 'Natural' Park Ideology." *Antipode* 2 (2): 16–25.

Olwig, Kenneth R. 1974." Place, Society and the Individual in the Authorship of St. Blicher." In *Omkring Blicher 1974,* edited by Felix Nørgaard, 69–114. Copenhagen: Gyldendal.

Olwig, Kenneth. 1976. "Menneske/natur problematikken i geografi." *Fagligt forum: kulturgeografiske hæfter,* no. 9: 5–15.

Olwig, Kenneth Robert. 1980. "Historical Geography and the Society/Nature 'Problematic': The Perspective of J. F. Schouw, G. P. Marsh and E. Reclus." *Journal of Historical Geography* 6 (1): 29–45.

Olwig, Kenneth R. 1981. "Literature and 'Reality': The Transformation of the Jutland Heath." In *Humanistic Geography and Literature,* edited by Douglas C. D. Pocock, 47–65. London: Croom Helm.

Olwig, Kenneth Robert. [1983] 1987. "Art and the Art of Communicating Geographical Knowledge: The Case of Pieter Brueghel." *Journal of Geography* 86 (2): 47–51.

Olwig, Kenneth Robert. 1984. *Nature's Ideological Landscape: A Literary and Geographic Perspective on Its Development and Preservation on Denmark's Jutland Heath.* London: George Allen and Unwin.

Olwig, Kenneth R. 1993a. "Harmony, 'Quintessence,' and Children's Acquisition of Concern for the 'Natural Environment.'" *Children's Environments* 10 (1): 60–71.

Olwig, Kenneth Robert. 1993b. "Sexual Cosmology: Nation and Landscape at the Conceptual Interstices of Nature and Culture, or: What does Landscape Really Mean?" In *Landscape: Politics and Perspectives*, edited by Barbara Bender, 307–43. Oxford: Berg.

Olwig, Kenneth Robert. 1995a. "Landscape, *Landskap*, and the Body." In *Nordic Landscopes: Cultural Studies of Place*, edited by Jan Olof Nilsson and Anders Linde-Laursen, 154–69. Copenhagen: Nordic Council of Ministers.

Olwig, Kenneth Robert. 1995b. "Reinventing Common Nature: Yosemite and Mt. Rushmore—A Meandering Tale of a Double Nature." In *Uncommon Ground: Towards Reinventing Nature*, edited by William Cronon, 379–408. New York: W. W. Norton.

Olwig, Kenneth R. 1996a. "Environmental History and the Construction of Nature." *Environment and History* 2 (1): 15–38.

Olwig, Kenneth R. 1996b. "Nature—Mapping the 'Ghostly' Traces of a Concept." In *Concepts in Human Geography*, edited by Carville Earl, Kent Mathewson, and Martin S. Kenzer, 63–96. Savage, Md.: Rowman and Littlefield.

Olwig, Kenneth Robert. 1996c. "Recovering the Substantive Nature of Landscape." *Annals of the Association of American Geographers* 86 (4): 630–53.

Olwig, Kenneth R. 1999. "The Destruction and Construction of Place: Landscape, Utopian Displacement and Topian Identity." In *Stedet som Kulturell Konstruksjon*, edited by Dagfinn Slettan, Brit Maehlum, and Ola Svein Stugu, 53–74. Trondheim: University in Trondheim.

Olwig, Kenneth R. 2001. "Landscape as a Contested Topos of Place, Community and Self." In *Textures of Place*, edited by Steven Hoelscher, Paul Adams, and Karen Till, 95–119. Minneapolis: University of Minnesota Press.

Olwig, Kenneth R. 2002. "Landscape, Place and the State of Progress." In *Progress: Geographical Essays*, edited by Robert D. Sack. Baltimore: Johns Hopkins University Press.

Onions, C. T. 1966. *The Oxford Dictionary of English Etymology.* Oxford: Oxford University Press.

Olwig, Kenneth R. Forthcoming. "The Jutland Cipher—Unlocking the Meaning and Power of a Contested Landscape Terrain." In *Nordscapes: Thinking Landscape and Regional Identity on the Northern Edge of Europe*, edited by Kenneth R. Olwig and Michael Jones. Minneapolis: University of Minnesota Press.

Orgel, Stephen. 1969. Editor's introduction to *Ben Jonson: The Complete Masques.* New Haven: Yale University Press.

Orgel, Stephen. 1975. *The Illusion of Power: Political Theater in the English Renaissance.* Berkeley: University of California Press.

Orgel, Stephen. 1987. Editor's introduction to *The Tempest.* Oxford: Clarendon Press.

Orgel, Stephen, and Roy Strong. 1973. *Inigo Jones: The Theatre of the Stuart Court.* Berkeley: University of California.

Ortelio, Avctore Abrahamo. 1596. *Aurei Sæculi Imago, sive Germanorvm Vetervm, Vita, Mores, Ritus, & Religio.* Antwerp: n.p.

Ortelius, Abraham. [1570] 1595. *Theatrum Orbis Terrarum.* Antwerp: n.p.

Pálsson, Gísli. 1996. "Human-Environmental Relations: Orientalism, Paternalism and Communalism." In *Nature and Society: Anthropological Perspectives*, edited by Gísli Pálsson and Philippe Descola, 63–81. London: Routledge.

Parry, Adam. 1957. "Landscape in Greek Poetry." *Yale Classical Studies* 15:3–29.

Parry, Graham. 1981. *The Golden Age Restor'd: The Culture of the Stuart Court, 1603–1642*. Manchester: Manchester University Press.

Parry, Graham. 1995. *The Trophies of Time: English Antiquarians of the Seventeenth Century*. Oxford: Oxford University Press.

Passmore, John. 1974. *Man's Responsibility for Nature*. New York: Charles Scribner's Sons.

Pawlisch, Hans S. 1985. *Sir John Davies and the Conquest of Ireland: A Study in Legal Imperialism*. Cambridge: Cambridge University Press.

Peacham, Henry. 1962. *The Complete Gentleman [1622] and Other Works (The Truth of Our Times [1638], and The Art of Living in London [1642])*. Ithaca, N.Y.: Cornell University Press.

Pearson, Karen Severud. 1976. Germania Illustrata: The Discovery of the German Landscape in Sixteenth-Century Geography, Cartography and Art. Working paper, University of Wisconsin–Madison, Art History.

Peppard, Murray B. 1971. *Paths Through the Forest: A Biography of the Brothers Grimm*. New York: Holt, Rinehart and Winston.

Perceval, Viscount John. [1724] 1990. "From Letter to Daniel Dering, 14 August 1724." In *Descriptions of Lord Cobham's Gardens at Stowe (1700–1750)*, edited by G. B. Clarke, 14–16. Buckinghamshire: Buckinghamshire Record Society.

Petersen, Annelise Ballegaard, ed. 1994. *Tyskland: En Kulturhistorie*. Copenhagen: Munksgaard.

Petersen, Carl S. 1929. *Illustreret Dansk Litteraturhistorie: Den Danske Litteratur fra Folkevandringstiden indtil Holberg*. Copenhagen: Gyldendal.

Piaget, Jean. 1973. *The Child and Reality*. New York: Viking.

Piggot, Stuart. 1976. *Ruins in a Landscape: Essays in Antiquarianism*. Edinburgh: University of Edinburgh.

Pirenne, Henri. 1958. *A History of Europe: From the Thirteenth Century to the Renaissance and Reformation*. Garden City, N.Y.: Doubleday Anchor.

Plato. 1961a. "Statesman." In *The Collected Dialogues of Plato*, edited by Edith Hamilton and Huntington Cairns, translated by J. B. Skemp, 1018–85. New York: Pantheon.

Plato. 1961b. "Timaeus." In *The Collected Dialogues of Plato*, edited by Edith Hamilton and Huntington Cairns, translated by Benjamin Jowett, 1151–1211. New York: Pantheon.

Pocock, J. G. A. 1957. *The Ancient Constitution and the Feudal Law*. Cambridge: Cambridge University Press.

Pocock, J. G. A. 1972. *Politics, Language and Time*. London: Methuen.

Pocock, John. 1975. *The Machiavellian Moment: Florentine Republican Thought and the Atlantic Tradition*. Princeton, N.J.: Princeton University Press.

Pocock, J. G. A. 1980. *Three British Revolutions: 1641, 1688, 1776*. Princeton, N.J.: Princeton University Press.

Poliakov, Léon. 1974. *The Aryan Myth: A History of Racist and Nationalist Ideas in Europe.* New York: New American Library.

Pollock, George Freeman. 1960. *Skyland: The Heart of the Shenandoah National Park.* N.p.: Chesapeake Book Co.

Pontoppidan, Erich. 1781. *Den Danske Atlas, eller Konge-Riget Dannemark.* Copenhagen: A. H. Godiche.

Pope, Alexander. [1704] 1963. "A Discourse on Pastoral Poetry." In *The Poems of Alexander Pope,* edited by John Butt, 119–23. London: Methuen.

Pope, Alexander. [1711] 1963. "An Essay on Criticism." In *The Poems of Alexander Pope,* edited by John Butt, 143–68. London: Methuen.

Pope, Alexander. [1731] 1988. "An Epistle to Lord Burlington." In *The Genius of the Place: The English Landscape Garden, 1620–1820,* edited by John Dixon Hunt and Peter Willis, 211–14. Cambridge, Mass.: MIT Press.

Poulsen, Bjørn. 1988. *Land-By-Markede: To økonomiske landskaber i 1400-tallets Slesvig.* Flensborg: Studieafdelingen ved Dansk Centralbibliotek for Sydslesvig.

Pred, Allan. 1990. *Lost Words and Lost Worlds: Modernity and the Language of Everyday Life in Late Nineteenth-Century Stockholm.* Cambridge: Cambridge University Press.

Ptolemy, Claudius. 1991. *The Geography.* New York: Dover.

Putnam, Michael C. J. 1970. *Virgil's Pastoral Art.* Princeton, N.J.: Princeton University Press.

Rachum, Ilan. 1995. "The Meaning of 'Revolution' in the English Revolution (1648–1660)." *Journal of the History of Ideas* 56 (2): 195–215.

Ranney, Victoria Post et al. 1990. Introduction to *The Papers of Frederick Law Olmsted: The California Frontier, 1863–1865,* edited by Victoria Post Ranney et al. Baltimore: Johns Hopkins University Press.

Reeder, Carolyn, and Jack Reeder. 1978. *Shenandoah Heritage: The Story of the People Before the Park.* Washington, D.C.: Potomac Appalachian Trail Club.

Rees, Ronald. 1980. "Historical Links between Cartography and Art." *Geographical Review* 70:61–78.

Relph, Edward. 1976. *Place and Placelessness.* London: Pion.

Risum, Janne. 1992. "De tidligste teaterformer." In *Dansk Teaterhistorie 1: Kirkens og kongens teater,* edited by Kela Kvam et al., 9–56. Copenhagen: Gyldendal.

Ritter, Carl. 1817–18, 1822–59. *Die Erdkunde, in Verhältniss zur Natur und zur Geschichte des Menschen, oder allgemeine vergleichende Geographie, als sichere Grundlage des Studiums und Unterrichts in physikalischen und historischen Wissenschaften.* Berlin: G. Reimer.

Robbins, Caroline. 1961. *The Eighteenth-Century Commonwealthman: Studies in the Transmission, Development and Circumstance of English Liberal Thought from the Restoration of Charles II until the War with the Thirteen Colonies.* Cambridge, Mass.: Harvard University Press.

Robert, Paul. 1980. *Dictionnaire alphabétique et analogique de la langue française.* Paris: Le Robert.

Rokkan, Stein. 1975. "Dimensions of State Formation and Nation-Building: A

Possible Paradigm for Research on Variations within Europe." In *The Formation of National States in Western Europe,* edited by Charles Tilly, 562–600.
Princeton, N.J.: Princeton University Press.

Roper, Laura Wood. 1973. *FLO: A Biography of Frederick Law Olmsted.* Baltimore: Johns Hopkins University Press.

Rose, Gillian. 1993. *Feminism and Geography: The Limits of Geographical
Knowledge.* Cambridge: Polity Press.

Rosenthal, Michael. 1982. *British Landscape Painting.* Oxford: Phaidon Press.

Runte, Alfred. 1990. *Yosemite: The Embattled Wilderness.* Lincoln: University of
Nebraska Press.

Rygg, Kristin. 1996. *Masqued Mysteries Unmasked: Pythagoreanism and Early
Modern North European Music Theatre.* Doctoral diss., Department of Music-
ology, The University in Trondheim.

Rying, Bent, ed. 1974. *Denmark—An Official Handbook.* Copenhagen: Ministry
of Foreign Affairs.

Sabean, David Warren. 1984. *Power in the Blood: Popular Culture and Village
Discourse in Early Modern Germany.* Cambridge: Cambridge University Press.

Sack, Robert D. 1980. *Conceptions of Space in Social Thought: A Geographical
Perspective.* London: Macmillan.

Sack, Robert David. 1997. *Homo Geographicus: A Framework for Action,
Awareness, and Moral Concern.* Baltimore: Johns Hopkins University Press.

Sanborn, Margaret. 1989. *Yosemite: Its Discovery, Its Wonders and Its People.*
Yosemite, Calif.: Yosemite Association.

Sandner, Gerhard. 1994. "In Search of Identity: German Nationalism and Geography, 1871–1910." In *Geography and National Identity,* edited by David
Hooson, 71–91. Oxford: Blackwell.

Sante, Georg Wilhelm, ed. 1964. *Geschichte der deutschen Länder, "Territorien-
Ploetz."* Würzburg: Ploetz.

Sauer, Carl O. [1925] 1969. "The Morphology of Landscape." In *Land and Life:
A Selection from the Writings of Carl Ortwin Sauer,* edited by John Leighly,
315–50. Berkeley: University of California Press.

Schama, Simon. 1987a. "Dutch Landscapes: Culture as Foreground." In *Masters
of Seventeenth-Century Dutch Landscape Painting,* edited by Peter C. Sutton,
64–83. London: Herbert Press.

Schama, Simon. 1987b. *The Embarrassment of Riches: An Interpretation of
Dutch Culture in the Golden Age.* London: Collins.

Schama, Simon. 1995. *Landscape and Memory.* London: Harper Collins.

Schiller, Johann Christophe Friedrich von. [1788] 1889. *The Revolt of the United
Netherlands.* London: George Bell and Sons.

Schiller, Johann Christophe Friedrich von. [1788] 1922. *Geschichte des Abfalls
der Vereinigten niederlande von der spanischen Regierung.* Munich: O. C.
Recht.

Schiller, Johann Christophe Friedrich von. [1804] 1894. *Wilhelm Tell.* Boston:
D.C. Heath.

Schiller, Johann Christophe Friedrich von. 1972. *Wilhelm Tell.* Chicago: University of Chicago Press.

Schilling, Heinz. 1992. "The Netherlands—The Pioneer Society of Early Modern Europe." In *Religion, Political Culture and the Emergence of Early Modern Society: Essays in German and Dutch History,* edited by Heinz Schilling, 305–52. Leiden: E. J. Brill.

Schmithüsen, Josef. 1976. *Allgemeine Geosynergetik: Grundlagen der Landschaftskunde.* Berlin: Walter de Gruyter.

Segal, Daniel, and Richard Handler. 1992. "How European Is Nationalism?" *Social Analysis,* no. 32: 1–16.

Seymour, Susanne. 2000. "Historical Geographies of Landscape." In *Modern Historical Geographies,* edited by Catherine Nash and Brian Graham, 193–217. Harlow, U.K.: Pearson Education.

Seymour, Susanne, Charles Watkins, and Stephen Daniels. 1998. "Estate and Empire: Sir George Cornwall's Management of Mocas, Herefordshire and La Taste, Grenada, 1771–1819." *Journal of Historical Geography* 24:313–51.

Shakespeare, William. 1948. *Shakespeare: Major Plays and the Sonnets.* New York: Harcourt, Brace and World.

Skautrup, Peter. 1941. *Den Jyske Lov: Text med Oversættelse, Kommentar og Ordbog.* Aarhus: Universitetsforlaget i Aarhus.

Slotkin, Richard. 1992. *Gunfighter Nation: The Myth of the Frontier in Twentieth-Century America.* New York: Atheneum.

Smith, Alan G. R. 1984. *The Emergence of a Nation State: The Commonwealth of England, 1529–1660.* London: Longman.

Smith, Anthony D. 1986. *The Ethnic Origins of Nations.* Oxford: Basil Blackwell.

Smith, Henry Nash. 1970. *Virgin Land: The American West as Symbol and Myth.* Cambridge, Mass.: Harvard University Press.

Smith, Samuel Francis. [1831] 1974. "America." In *The Good Times Songbook,* edited by James Leisy, 22–23. Nashville: Abingdon Press.

Smithers, Peter. 1968. *The Life of Joseph Addison.* 2d ed. Oxford: Clarendon Press.

Snelders, H. A. M. 1970. "Romanticism and Naturphilosophie and the Inorganic Natural Sciences, 1797–1840: An Introductory Survey." *Studies in Romanticism* 9 (3): 193–215.

Snell, Bruno. 1953. *The Discovery of the Mind.* Cambridge, Mass.: Harvard University Press.

Speed, John. 1611. *The Theatre of the Empire of Great Britaine.* London: John Sudbury and George Humble.

Speed, John. 1623. *The Historie of Great Britaine under the Conquests of the Romans, Saxons, Danes and Normans: . . . from Julius Cæsar, to our most gracious Soveraigne King James.* 2d ed. London: George Humble.

Spirn, Anne Whiston. 1995. "Constructing Nature: The Legacy of Frederick Law Olmsted." In *Uncommon Ground: Toward Reinventing Nature,* edited by William Cronon, 91–113. New York: W. W. Norton.

Spirn, Anne Whiston. 1998. *The Language of Landscape.* New Haven: Yale University Press.

Spitzer, Leo. 1948. "Milieu and Ambiance." In *Essays in Historical Semantics,* 179–316. New York: S. F. Vanni

Spitzer, Leo. 1963. *Classical and Christian Ideas of World Harmony*. Baltimore: Johns Hopkins Press.

Stanlis, Peter J. [1958] 1965. *Edmund Burke and the Natural Law*. Ann Arbor: University of Michigan Press.

Steffens, Henrik. [1801] 1973. *Beyträge zur innern Naturgeschichte der Erde*. Amsterdam: Meridian.

Steffens, Henrik. 1810. *Geognostisch-geologische Aufsätze als Vorbereitung zu einer innern Naturgeschichte der Erde*. Hamburg: B. G. Hoffmann.

Steffens, Henrik. [1840–44] 1874. *German University Life: The Story of My Career as Student and Professor*. Philadelphia: Lippincott.

Steffens, Henrik. 1840–45. *Hvad jeg oplevede*. 10 vols. Copenhagen: C. Steen.

Steffens, Henrik. 1905. *Indledning til Philosophiske Forelæsninger i København 1803*. Copenhagen: Gyldendal.

Stewart, Omer C. 1956. "Fire as the First Great Force Employed by Man." In *Man's Role in Changing the Face of the Earth*, edited by W. L. Thomas, 115–33. Chicago: University of Chicago Press.

Strauss, Gerald. 1959. *Sixteenth-Century Germany: Its Topography and Topographers*. Madison: University of Wisconsin Press.

Strong, Roy. 1977. *The Cult of Elizabeth: Elizabethan Portraiture and Pageantry*. London: Thames and Hudson.

Strong, Roy. 1979. *The Renaissance Garden in England*. London: Thames and Hudson.

Strong, Roy. 1984. *Art and Power: Renaissance Festivals, 1450–1650*. Woodbridge, Suffolk: Boydell Press.

Strong, Roy. 1986. *Henry, Prince of Wales and England's Lost Renaissance*. London: Thames and Hudson.

Sullivan, Garrett A. Jr. 1998. *The Drama of Landscape: Land, Property, and Social Relations on the Early Modern Stage*. Stanford: Stanford University Press.

Summerson, John. 1966. *Inigo Jones*. Harmondsworth: Penguin.

Sutherland, Donald. 1972. "Conquest and Law." *Studia Gratiana* 15:35–51.

Tacitus. 1942. "Germany and Its Tribes." In *The Complete Works of Tacitus*, edited by Moses Hadas, 709–32. New York: Modern Library.

Tacitus. 1948. *On Britain and Germany*. Baltimore: Penguin.

Taylor, E. G. R. 1934. *Late Tudor and Early Stuart Geography: 1538–1650*. London: Methuen.

Thomas, Keith. 1971. *Religion and the Decline of Magic: Studies in Popular Beliefs in Sixteenth and Seventeenth Century England*. London: Weidenfeld and Nicolson.

Thompson, E. P. 1975. *Whigs and Hunters: The Origin of the Black Act*. New York: Pantheon.

Thompson, E. P. 1993. *Customs in Common*. London: Penguin.

Thoreau, Henry David. [1849] 1983. "Civil Disobedience." In *Walden and Civil Disobedience*, edited by Michael Meyer, 385–431. New York: Penguin.

Thoreau, Henry David. [1862] 1991. "Walking." In *Nature/Walking*, edited by John Elder, 71–122. Boston: Beacon.

Thoren, Victor E. 1990. *The Lord of Uraniborg: A Biography of Tycho Brahe.* Cambridge: Cambridge University Press.

Tillyard, E. M. W. 1960. *The Elizabethan World Picture.* London: Chatto and Windus.

Tokar, Brian. 1988. "Social Ecology, Deep Ecology and the Future of Green Political Thought." *The Ecologist* 18 (4/5): 132–41.

Tönnies, Ferdinand. [1887] 1974. *Community and Association.* London: Routledge and Kegan Paul.

Tönnies, Ferdinand. [1887] 1979. *Gemeinschaft und Gesellschaft: Grundbegriffe der reinen Soziologie.* Darmstadt: Wissenschaftliche Buchgesellschaft.

Trap, Jens Peter. 1864. *Statistisk-topographisk Beskrivelse af Hertugdømmet Slesvig.* Copenhagen: Gad.

Trap, Jens Peter. 1963. *Danmark.* 15 vols. Copenahgen: Gad.

Trench, Charles Chenevix. 1967. *The Poacher and the Squire: A History of Poaching and Game Preservation in England.* London: Longman.

Trevelyan, George Macaulay. [1925] 1960. *England under the Stuarts.* 2d ed. Harmondsworth: Penguin.

Trevor-Roper, Hugh. 1971. *Queen Elizabeth's First Historian: William Camden and the Beginnings of English "Civil History."* London: Jonathan Cape.

Tribe, Laurence H. 1997. "Lion of Liberalism." *Time.* 4 August, 19.

Tuan, Yi-Fu. [1961] 1972. "Topophilia: Personal Encounters with the Landscape." In *Man, Space, and Environment,* edited by Paul Ward English and Robert C. Mayfield, 534–38. New York: Oxford University Press.

Tuan, Yi-Fu. 1968. *The Hydrologic Cycle and the Wisdom of God: A Theme in Geoteleology.* Toronto: University of Toronto Press.

Tuan, Yi-Fu. 1974a. "Space and Place: Humanistic Perspective." *Progress in Geography* 6:211–52.

Tuan, Yi-Fu. 1974b. *Topophilia: A Study of Environmental Perception, Attitudes, and Values.* Englewood Cliffs, N.J.: Prentice-Hall.

Tuan, Yi-Fu. 1977. *Space and Place: The Perspective of Experience.* Minneapolis: University of Minnesota Press.

Tuan, Yi-Fu. 1978. "Sign and Metaphor." *Annals of the Association of American Geographers* 68 (3): 363–72.

Tuan, Yi-Fu. 1982. *Segmented Worlds and Self: Group Life and Individual Consciousness.* Minneapolis: University of Minnesota Press.

Tuan, Yi-Fu. 1992. "Place and Culture: Analeptic for Individuality and the World's Indifference." In *Mapping American Culture,* edited by Wayne Franklin and Michael Steiner, 27–49. Iowa City: University of Iowa Press.

Tuan, Yi-Fu. 1993. *Passing Strange and Wonderful: Aesthetics, Nature, and Culture.* Washington, D.C.: Island Press.

Tuan, Yi-Fu. 1996. *Cosmos and Hearth: A Cosmopolite's Viewpoint.* Minneapolis: University of Minnesota Press.

Turner, James. 1976. *The Politics of Landscape: Rural Scenery and Society in English Poetry, 1630–1660.* Cambridge, Mass.: Harvard University Press.

Turner, Richard A. 1966. *The Vision of Landscape in Renaissance Italy.* Princeton, N.J.: Princeton University Press.

Turner, Victor. 1974. *Dramas, Fields and Metaphors: Symbolic Action in Human Society.* Ithaca, N.Y.: Cornell University Press.

Underdown, David. 1985. *Revel, Riot, and Rebellion: Popular Politics and Culture in England, 1603–1660.* Oxford: Clarendon Press.

Unwin, Tim. 2000. "A Waste of Space? Towards a Critique of the Social Production of Space . . . ." *Transactions of the Institute of British Geographers,* n.s., 25:11–29.

Vankat, John L. 1977. "Fire and Man in Sequoia National Park." *Annals of the Association of American Geographers* 67 (1): 17–27.

Vinterberg, Herman, and C. A. Bodelsen. 1966. *Dansk-Engelsk Ordbog.* 2d ed. Copenhagen: Gyldendal.

Virgil. 1946. *Eclogues and Georgics.* Revised ed. London: Dent.

Virgil. 1990. *The Aeneid, A New Prose Translation.* London: Penguin.

Wägenbaur, Thomas. 1994. "The Irony of Ecology: The Construction of Nature in German Idealism." In *The Construction of Nature,* edited by Stipe Grgas and Svend Erik Larsen, 40–71. Odense: Odense University Press.

Wallthor, Alfred Hartlieb von, and Heinz Quirin. 1975. "Landschaft" als interdisziplinäres Forschungsproblem. *Veröffentlichungen des Provinzialinstituts für westfälische Landes: Und Volksforschung des landschaftsverbandes Westfalen-Lippe,* Reihe 1, Heft 2. Münster, Westfalen: Aschendorffsche Verlagsbuchhandlung.

Walpole, Horace. [1782] 1943. *Horace Walpole: Gardenist—An Edition of Walpole's "The History of the Modern Taste in Gardening" with an Estimate of Walpole's Contribution to Landscape Architecture,* edited by Isabel Wakelin and Urban Chase. Princeton, N.J.: Princeton University Press.

Welti, Alfred. 1983. "Europas Maler entdecken ihre Umwelt: Maler erfinden die Landschaft." *Art—Das Kunstmagazin,* no. 2: 26–45.

West, Gilbert. [1732] 1990. "The Gardens of the Right Honourable Richard Lord Viscount Cobham." In *Descriptions of Lord Cobham's Gardens at Stowe (1700–1750),* edited by G. B. Clarke, 36–51. Buckinghamshire: Buckinghamshire Record Society.

Wheelock, Arthur K. Jr. 1977. *Perspective, Optics, and Delft Artists around 1650.* New York: Garland.

Whistler, Laurence, George Clarke, and Michael Gibbon. 1968. *Stowe: A Guide to the Gardens.* Buckingham: E. N. Hillier.

Wiles, David. 1981. *The Early Plays of Robin Hood.* Cambridge: D. S. Brewer.

Wiles, David. 1993. *Shakespeare's Almanac: A Midsummer Night's Dream, Marriage and the Elizabethan Calendar.* Cambridge: D. S. Brewer.

Wilkinson, L. P. 1969. *The Georgics of Virgil: A Critical Survey.* Cambridge: Cambridge University Press.

Willey, Basil. 1940. *The Eighteenth-Century Background.* London: Chatto and Windus.

Williams, Ethel Carleton. 1970. *Anne of Denmark: Wife of James VI of Scotland, James I of England.* London: Longman.

Williams, George H. 1962. *Wilderness and Paradise in Christian Thought: The Biblical Experience of the Desert in the History of Christianity.* New York: Harper and Brothers.

Williams, Raymond. 1972. "Ideas of Nature." In *Ecology, the Shaping Enquiry,* edited by J. Benthall, 146–64. London: Longman.

Williams, Raymond. 1973. *The Country and the City.* New York: Oxford University Press.

Williams, Raymond. 1976. *Keywords.* London: Fontana.

Williamson, Tom, and Liz Bellamy. 1987. *Property and Landscape: A Social History of Land Ownership and the English Countryside.* London: George Philip.

Willson, D. Harris. 1956. *King James VI and I.* London: Jonathan Cape.

Wilson, Alexander. 1992. *The Culture of Nature: North American Landscape from Disney to the Exxon Valdez.* Oxford: Blackwell.

Witt, Reimer. 1975. *Die Privilegien der Landschaft norderdithmarschen in gottorfischer Zeit 1559 bis 1773.* Neumünster: Karl Wachholtz.

Wood, Neal. 1964. "The Aesthetic Dimension of Edmund Burke's Political Thought." *Journal of British Studies* 4:41–44.

Woodbridge, Kenneth. 1970. *Landscape and Antiquity: Aspects of English Culture at Stourhead, 1718–1838.* Oxford: Clarendon Press.

Woodbridge, Kenneth. 1974. "William Kent as Landscape-Gardener: A Re-Appraisal." *Apollo,* no. 100: 126–37.

Wordsworth, William. [1810] 1968. *A Guide to the District of the Lakes in the North of England.* New York: Greenwood Press.

Wright, John Kirtland. 1965. *The Geographical Lore of the Time of the Crusades: A Study in the History of Medieval Science and Tradition in Western Europe.* New York: Dover.

Yates, Frances A. 1934. *John Florio: The Life of an Italian in Shakespeare's England.* Cambridge: Cambridge University Press.

Yates, Frances A. 1969. *Theater of the World.* London: Routledge and Kegan Paul.

Yates, Frances A. 1975. *Astraea: The Imperial Theme in the Sixteenth Century.* London: Routledge and Kegan Paul.

Zagorin, Perez. 1969. *The Court and the Country: The Beginning of the English Revolution.* London: Routledge and Kegan Paul.

Zeitler, Rudolf. 1992. "Johann Gottfried Herders och de tyska romantikernas folktanke och dess inflytande i Norden, särskilt i Norge." In *Natur och Nationalitet: Nordisk bildkonst 1800–1850 och dess europeiska bakgrund,* edited by Per Jonas Nordhagen and Jörgen Weibull, 9–109. Stockholm: Wiken.

Ziolkowski, Theodore. 1990. *German Romanticism and Its Institutions.* Princeton, N.J.: Princeton University Press.

# Index